C000274304

10010010026681

Irène Heidelberger-Leonard is an Honorary Professorial Fellow at Queen Mary, University of London and was for nearly 30 years Professor of German Literature at the Université Libre de Bruxelles. A Member of the German Academy (Deutsche Akademie für Sprache und Dichtung), she has written extensively on post-war German literature, including books on Günter Grass, Alfred Andersch, Peter Weiss, Jurek Becker, Ingeborg Bachmann, Ruth Klüger, Thomas Bernhard, and W. G. Sebald. She is the editor of the 9-volume edition of Améry's Collected Works. Her biography of Jean Améry was named as non-fiction Book of the Year by the German Cultural Foundation in 2004, won the Raymond Aron Prize for translation into French (2004) and was awarded the prestigious biennial Einhard Prize for Outstanding European Biography in 2005.

Jean Améry

The Philosopher of Auschwitz

Jean Améry and
Living with the Holocaust

Irène Heidelberger-Leonard

I.B. TAURIS

LONDON · NEW YORK

Published in 2010 by I.B.Tauris & Co Ltd
6 Salem Road, London W2 4BU
175 Fifth Avenue, New York NY 10010
www.ibtauris.com

Distributed in the United States and Canada Exclusively by Palgrave Macmillan
175 Fifth Avenue, New York NY 10010

ISBN: 978 1 84885 150 4

A full CIP record for this book is available from the British Library
A full CIP record is available from the Library of Congress

Library of Congress Catalog Card Number: available

Printed and bound in India by Thomson Press India Ltd

For Dick
For Mark and Gabrielle
For Miriam and Phiroze
For Jakob
For Anne

Contents

Chapter 7
Drama of the Mind in Three Acts – *The Autobiographical Trilogy* 133

Chapter 8
Jean Améry as a Writer of Fiction 187

Illustrations

Acknowledgements

I received valuable suggestions from Hubert Arbogast, who unfortunately did not live to see the publication of this biography.

I owe particular thanks to the Fonds National de le Recherche Scientifique (Brussels) and the Université Libre de Bruxelles, which gave me a sabbatical from my teaching duties in 2002–2003. I would like to thank the staff of the German Literary Archive, Marbach, for their support over the years. My thanks to Thomas Weck (in memoriam) for his sensitive companionship and to Michael Klett for entrusting the letters of Jean Améry to me.

For ideas and conversations, I would like to thank Jürg Altwegg (Geneva), Lothar Baier (in memoriam), Claire Billen (Brussels), Siglinde Bolbecher (Vienna), Stefan Braese (Hamburg), David Caplin (London), Jean-Michel Chaumont (Brussels), Jenefer Coates (London), André Combes (Toulouse), Hans-Martin Gauger (Freiburg), Holger Gehle (Bonn), Axel Gellhaus (Aachen), Rüdiger Görner (London), Murray G. Hall (Vienna), Hartmut von Hentig (Berlin), Michael Hofmann (Liège), Konstantin Kaiser (Vienna), Joachim Kalka (Stuttgart), Barbara Kappen (Berlin), Hanjo Kesting (Hanover), Wulf Kirsten (Weimar), Regine Krochmal (Brussels), Hanno Loewy (Frankfurt), Hubert Matt (Dornbirn), Wilhelm Mayer (Vienna), Christoph Meckel (Berlin), Robert Menasse (Vienna), Horst Meier (Hamburg), Albert Mingelgrün (Brussels), Heidy M. Müller (Brussels), Norbert Oellers (Bonn), Leonard Olschner (London), Beate Pinkernell (Berlin), Ralf Piorr (Herne), Doron Rabinovici (Vienna), Philipp Schöbi (Feldkirch), Mireille Tabah (Brussels), Gérard Tancman (Vernas), Anne-Marie Roviello (Brussels), Robert Schindel (Vienna), W.G. Sebald (in memoriam), Stephan Steiner (Vienna), Erika Tunner (Paris), Jochen Vogt (Essen), Hermann Wallmann (Münster), Bernd Witte (Düsseldorf), Harry Zimmermann (Vienna).

First and foremost, my thanks to Joachim Oxenius for the documents from the private archive of Maria Améry.

The research for this book would have been impossible without the help of Friedrich Pfäfflin (Marbach), Ingrid Kussmaul (German Literary Archive), Friedrich Wiener (Bad Ischl), Johannes Inama (Jewish Museum, Hohenems), Petra Zudrell (Dornbirn), Isolde Moser (Kötschach), Christian Moser (Vienna), Heinz Bachmann (Abingdon), Jörg Hucklenbroich (SWF), Ina Andrae (*Merkur*), Christoph Stamm (Friedrich Ebert Foundation), R.B. Kitaj (in memoriam). New perspectives were opened up to me in conversations with Lore Wald (London), Heinz Pollak (Vienna), Jacques Sonnenschein (in memoriam), Ilya Prigogine (in memoriam), Paul Kitaj (Gilbert, Arizona), Karma Kitaj (Boston), Heinz Robert Schlette (Bonn), Manfred Franke (Cologne) and Michael Krüger (Munich). Jan Philipp Reemtsma has been invaluable in promoting the entire great Améry project, especially through his support for the full edition of Améry's works.

I am deeply grateful to my unwavering colleagues and friends in reading, reflecting on and championing Jean Améry and his works – Hans Höller (Salzburg) and Gerhard Scheit (Vienna), Monique Boussart (Brussels), Ruth Klüger (Irvine), Sylvia Weiler (Brussels) and Anne Hallauer (Bonn).

I wish to express my gratitude to the following organisations whose generous financial assistance made it possible for this work to appear in an English translation: The Fondation Universitaire (Brussels), the Chancellor of the Université Libre de Bruxelles (ULB), the Faculty of Philosophie et Lettres of the ULB, the Österreichische Gesellschaft für Literatur (Vienna), the Zukunftsfonds der Republik Österreich (Vienna) and the Bundesministerium für europäische und internationale Angelegenheiten (Vienna).

I would like to thank my editor Liz Friend-Smith for seeing this project through. Above all I am immensely indebted to my translator Anthea Bell, a recent recipient of an OBE, who showed incomparable skill and sensitivity in transforming my German text into the best of English prose.

Irène Heidelberger-Leonard

CHAPTER 1

Village Idyll (1912–1924)
Bad Ischl and the Magic of the Forest

In the beginning was the name, and the name was Hans Maier, or Mayer, or Hanns Mayr, or Johann Mayer or Johannes Maier.[1] Even as a boy he was unhappy with his name; it seemed to him too 'ordinary'. But so was his childhood; that is to say ordinary in the best sense of the word – one might also say idyllic. An unpublished retrospective piece, an autobiographical sketch written in 1957, provides some information:[2] 'Writing books of memoirs,' the 45-year-old author begins, 'is the privilege of important people. I am not among them'. His reflections on his childhood are intended to suggest that the 'real' Améry is to be found in his origins. He writes triumphantly:

> The hours when the melancholy story of my life was not yet melancholy, and its sad outcome was still undecided and indeed could hardly be anticipated – those are my finest hours, and it is my right, as a failure, to remember them. Only in the past do I recognize myself again.

Hohenems: certificate of citizenship and ostensible homeland

Some details, then, about that past: 'Hans Maier' was born on 31 October 1912 in Vienna but in Vienna 'almost by chance', for on the paternal side, his family came from Hohenems in Vorarlberg. 'My grandfather was very proud of his family tree (...) which went back to the seventeenth century. I am completely indifferent to my origins',[3] he claimed in 1978 in a conversation with Ingo Hermann.

Améry may have thought so at the end of his life, but in the 1930s he was far from indifferent to acquiring confirmation of his place of origin. When it mattered, the capricious spelling of his surname was to become a question of life and death. The German scholar Petra Zudrell has recently discovered two applications by Hans Mayer for a certificate of citizenship, now both preserved in the Hohenems town archives. He made his first application in 1931: 'As I am

Zahl 379/2 – 31   12. März 1931
Paul Mayer
Heimatsrecht.   *ausgetragen*

                         An

    das Magistratische Bezirks-Amt

                         in

                    W i e n IV

        In Wien IV, Trappelgasse 7 wohnt ein gewisser Hans
Mayer, welcher nach Hohenems zuständig sein soll. Derselbe ist
angeblich ein Sohn des am 11. Juli 1883 in Wien geborenen Paul
Mayer der am 13. Juli 1917 in Innsbruck gestorben sein soll.
Zweckes Ergänzung der Heimatrolle wird ein Geburtsschein des Paul
Mayer sowie ein Trauschein benötigt. Herr Hans Mayer wurde wie-
derholt um Vorlage dieser Dokumente ersucht , ohne dass er die-
sem Ersuchen bisher nachgekommen wäte.

        Es wird gebeten zu veranlassen, dass dem gefertigten
Amte die verlangten Dokumente baldmöglichst in Vorlage gebracht
werden.

                    Der Bürgermeister:

                                        16. April 1931

                                                    IV./4

*Reply from the local district authority to Hans Mayer's application for a change
in the spelling of his name*

going away on the 30th of this month, I require a passport, but before it can be issued I urgently need a certificate of citizenship.'[4] He signs his letter 'Hanns Mayer' and comments on the spelling of his name in a postscript: 'With respect, let me point out that my surname is Mayer, and not, as incorrectly recorded in my birth certificate, Maier.' The market town of Hohenems complied with his request, and the certificate of citizenship dated 1931 was indeed made out in the name of Mayer with a 'y'.

In 1938, as a Jew, he faced a far more dramatic situation: since the other papers confirming his identity gave the name of Maier with an 'i', he had to retract the 'y' that he had gone to so much trouble to gain. Only an 'i' could save his skin.

On 4 November 1938, in the best bureaucratic style, Améry writes:

> As I require a certificate of citizenship for the purpose of my emigration from German Austria, and also for the acquisition of a passport, and as I am not in a position to travel to my birthplace, I turn to the civic authorities of that place requesting a certificate to be sent.

He is, in fact, in possession of a certificate dating from 1931, he says, but it is now invalid, 'since it spells my name, Maier, with a "y" and not, correctly, with an "i". (...) I would most respectfully request such a certificate to be sent quickly, to allow me, as a non-Aryan, the chance of emigrating as soon as possible'. He was to continue these deadly tactics of deliberate confusion until 1955.

Just under 20 years later, when Jean Améry was awarded 'honorary citizenship of the Land of Vorarlberg',[5] he did not refuse the honour, but he was in no great hurry to accept it in person. In 1977, one year before his death, he finally made a last pilgrimage to Vorarlberg, 'the land of my fathers', as he says on a card to Hans Paeschke (J.A. to H.P., 12.2.77).[6] Unlike to his own, he was never indifferent to his father's place of origin. There was, in fact, a thriving Jewish community in Hohenems in the middle of the nineteenth century; its activities culminating in the building of a synagogue in 1881. As early as 1617, Count Kaspar granted the Jews permission to stimulate the economy with goods and money. 'Despite these favourable circumstances, none of them were interested at first. Only around 1630 did Jews flee from the effects of the Thirty Years' War to the imperial county of Hohenems.'[7] Anton Legerer wrote the following in the *Jüdische Rundschau Maccabi:*

> The Jews of Hohenems were noted for being assimilated and liberally-minded citizens, and were responsible for building the first coffee-house in the area at the beginning of the last century. They wished to integrate with the cultural

as well as the political life of the town. In 1878 four Jews were elected to the Hohenems town council.[8]

The family

The Jewish Museum in Hohenems, opened in 1991,[9] thus has a genealogical table recording the year of birth of Jean Améry's great-great-grandfather, Bernhard Mayer, born on 20 May 1815.[10] His grandfather Siegfried Maier – 'bearded like Emperor Franz Joseph and an equally stately figure in other respects' – was born on 15 August 1856, also in Hohenems, where he owned a factory making lace, curtains and clothing. He married Helene Krakauer, with whom he had four sons: Julius,who died young, Hans, Karl and Paul. It was Paul's son, little Hans, who would later become Jean Améry. Paul was the eldest of the four brothers and was born on 21 July 1883, not in Hohenems but in Vienna.

Améry's grandfather was to outlive his son Paul. Unlike Améry's father, whom he mentions only as being dead, his grandfather played a strong role in his life. He is evoked as an admonitory figure of authority, intent on giving his grandson a good education. One day Siegfried was to surprise the nine-year-old by visiting him in Bad Ischl. On that occasion he heard little Hans talking to a country girl in heavy Austrian dialect. 'This,' Améry recollects in 1957, 'caused some very uncomfortable complications'. His grandfather gave the author the impression of being a distinguished gentleman who looked down on the rustic folk of Bad Ischl:

> He had a fine white beard, and always carried a cane with a goldknob. At home his study was lined with awards for distinction and letters of appreciation from first the Imperial and Royal, then the Republican authorities of Austria. He used to frown sternly when I explained, in my country accent, that it was time for me go 'hoam', and he made his dignified reproaches to my mother. She, poor woman, burst into tears, and I felt ashamed of myself.[11]

Early years in Vienna

Améry's father, Paul (1883–1917), was less successful in business than his own father, Siegfried. His profession before he went to fight in the First World War, as may be gathered from the records of the Jewish Community, was only some sort of company representative or commercial traveller. He died at the age of 34, serving as an Imperial and Royal Austrian Soldier in the Tyrolean Kaiserjäger regiment, and was buried first in Innsbruck on 1 August 1917,[12] then in a regimental grave in the Jewish section of Vienna Central Cemetery on 21 February 1918.[13] Jean Améry's cousin, Lore Wald, put it on record that he died on the Italian front of an inguinal hernia, correcting the official cause of death.[14]

Hans Mayer (Jean Améry) with his parents Paul Maier (1883–1917) and
Valerie Maier (1879–1939), 1916

Jean Améry's mother, Valerie Goldschmidt, four years older than her
husband (b. 31 August 1879), married Paul Maier, an observant Jew, on
5 July 1908 in Vienna. In 1914, the year when war broke out, they moved
from District 8 to District 4, first into Number 19 Schleifmühlgasse, then into
Number 19 Wiedner Hauptstrasse, where they obviously did not stay long: in
1915, 35-year-old Valerie Maier moved with Hans, who was then aged one-
and-a-half, for the third time, into Number 2 Proschkog-Gasse in District 6
of the city.[15] A single picture of father, mother and son has been preserved:
all three adopt a pose of determination, and the picture shows tiny Hans in a
formal sailor suit, standing on a bench between his mother, who sits very erect,
and his soldier father, straight as a ramrod in his uniform, against the background of a romantically blurred seascape.[16] All three of them are following
the photographer's instructions to look straight at the camera. Améry's later
photographs show a striking likeness to his mother, with her heavy eyelids and
melancholy expression.

Améry described his mother as

> ...half-Jewish, and on her marriage had converted from the Catholic Church
> to become a member of the Jewish Community. Her knowledge of Judaism was
> not therefore very deep. She liked to say *nebbich*, a very expressive exclamation
> of regret, and described her women friends as *meschugge* when they put on airs.
> But she invoked the names of 'Jesus-Mary-and-Joseph' even more frequently,
> and among us there was usually good reason for her to do so.[17]

Her family lived in District 4, at Number 9 Wiedner Hauptstrasse. Améry's
mother came from a 'good family', a cultured and educated background, with
'maidservants and ladies paying calls'. She found it harder and harder to maintain
this bourgeois standard of living and 'post-war comfort'. She had two brothers
and three elder sisters, Herta, Adele and Mila, two of whom had settled in Bad
Ischl and the vicinity.

In 1918, after the death of Améry's father, his mother moved first with
her son and her sister Herta, like her a 'war widow', into 'a very nice apartment in Kleine Neugasse in District 4 of Vienna', where Herta's daughter Lore,
five years younger than Hans, was born. The two children grew up together
until Lore was 17. Améry clearly remembered the day when electric light was
installed, 'something that seemed to me highly magical, and which I never
understood even later'. He also said that he still felt 'the cold, damp, misty
smell emanating from the so-called "servants' rooms" that opened into the
corridor'.[18] The most important people in Améry's life at this time were the
succession of maids:

> As a child I loved them like mothers, all of them, the Mitzis, Lintschis, Fannys,
> I slept with them when I was 15, and later, when they were not maids any more
> but waitresses in the various unsuccessful boarding houses we ran, I systemati-
> cally shielded them from my mother.

His soft spot for the opposite sex was an open secret to his friends and acquaint-
ances. As he grew up he was, in fact, entirely surrounded by women: his mother,
his aunts, his female cousins and sisters-in-law, and the ever-changing succession
of maids. Of the maids employed in the years 1918–19 he mentions Anna, who
told him 'about the sufferings of the Saviour, in gruesome detail', and Loisi, who
gave him 'a skin infection that was common at the time, known in the vernacular
as the itch'.

The food shortages of the early post-war period also linger in Améry's
mind. 'There was often no sugar, and then I was sent to a sweet-shop in
Margarethenstrasse to buy fondants, which we used to sweeten coffee.'[19]

Otherwise, there might be a shortage of potatoes, and his mother sent him to see 'a man called Pilz – a little hunchbacked fellow – and ask him for some potatoes'.[20]

Hans and Ernst Mayer: friends in life and death

Hans Mayer also started school in District 4 of Vienna on 1 September 1918, at the Phorus School. Here he met Ernst Theodor Mayer, and the two were to be bound by a lifelong friendship, expressed since 1946 in an almost unbroken correspondence. In 1964, Jean Améry concluded one of his 241 letters to Ernst Mayer with the following injunction:

> For today, my warm greetings, dear friend. As always I wait patiently – or impatiently – for a note from you, and I remain, as I have been now for 46 years (Class One at the Phorus School, Rötzer, wan gaslight, Matuschek, Fesenmeier, Fuchs Ernst, Mayer Ernst, Mayer Hanns), your old friend (...). (Jean Améry to Ernst Mayer, 24.10.64)[21]

In a much later letter he speaks of his awareness of the 'higher community of interest' between them:

> The chance fact that Herr Rötzer the teacher put the two Mayers side by side influenced the course of two lives, neither of them great, to be sure, but not worthless. There are people more stupid and less gifted than you and I, as we have always known, and as the world has been ready to confirm. (J.A. to E.M., 17.4.71)

So great was the 'community of interest' between them that Ernst Mayer took his own life two years after Jean Améry's suicide.[22]

Améry also dates his political awareness from the year 1918: 'My Austrian life was a political one. Events in public life caught my ear even as a boy.'[23] He remembers that at the age of five he was alarmed by the January strike rallies:

> A swelling chorus of voices comes from somewhere or other. It is raining. I'm frightened.
> 'Come along,' says my mother, affectionately pressing my hand.
> 'Who are those people shouting?'
> 'They're the workers,' says my mother, and I imagine the workers as a black and dangerous mass that is going to crush us.

A year later his mother sends him to a 'tobacconist's to buy cigarettes and a newspaper, the *Neues Wiener Tagblatt*. The *Tagblatt* was sold out, so instead the boy buys *Die Rote Fahne*, because its name, *The Red Flag*, seems 'attractive and

Hans Mayer outside the inn his mother used to manage, 1956

exciting. My mother laughs until she cries at my purchase. I don't understand.'
But then he does understand after all: ' "Oh, child, that's a workers' newspaper,"
says my mother.'[24]

She was a gentle woman, and his relationship with her was a loving one:
'She neither hit me nor threatened me, but loved me with a kind of abstracted
fondness.'[25] Leafing through a family album at the time of his sixtieth birthday,
he feels 'as if I were hearing the voice of my mother, who even in poverty liked
to talk about the bold lieutenants in the Third Coffee-House and the members of
the archducal family' (J.A. to E.M., 4 November 1972). He himself had not, he
admits much later, been 'a very good son' to his mother, the war widow.[26] For all
her 'fondness', his mother does not seem to have given the boy much sense of his
own worth, or at least she did not build up his self-confidence; on the contrary,
he says, she kept telling him, 'I would never amount to anything, and if she happened to be furiously jealous, like a deceived lover, she would say bluntly that
I would end up on the gallows – in which she was to prove very nearly right in
1943,' as he recollects in a late letter to Ernst Mayer. Yet, he says, she deserves to
be 'remembered with honour, if critically' (J.A. to E.M., 20 May 1976). He had
been an only son, he explains to Ingo Hermann in their last conversation:

> We need no psychological training to know that that meant a strong Oedipal
> relationship. My mother was both excessively affectionate and excessively

authoritarian, and something of that remains. A mother figure is one of the things I always look for in women.[27]

Bad Ischl

The boy was sickly. His disorder was described as 'pulmonary apicitis', and the doctor recommended country air as a matter of urgency. Perhaps Mila would be able to help; her husband Dr Stroessel ran a sanatorium in Bad Goisern. The boy's mother and his Aunt Herta decided to move to nearby Bad Ischl. How was the war widow to support her son? She signed a lease and was now landlady of the 'Gasthof zur Stadt Prag' at Number 9 Eglmoosgasse.[28] 'My mother took over the business of the inn,' Améry speculates, 'because she (...) was obliged to earn a living for herself and for me.' Apart from a knowledge of French, an ability to play the piano and 'those frivolities that were taught to the daughters of good families,' he writes, her main talent was that she was a very good cook. She thought, erroneously, that 'this would suffice for the management of a small inn'.[29] They were coming down in the world to a proletarian level, for the Gasthof zur Stadt Prag was not a flourishing concern.[30] 'Suddenly we were innkeepers

Hans Mayer, 1917

after a fashion (...) running a small and unprepossessing establishment (...) on the rising ground in Ischl that forms the foothills of the Kalvarienberg.'[31]

Améry is entered in the class register of the Bad Ischl Boys' Elementary School on 23 May 1921, with the note 'has come from Vienna to stay in the country'. His name does not reappear until 11 January 1923, and it is not clear where he spent the year in between. His reports were satisfactory, marked as 'Good' in German, mathematics, history, geography, civics and gymnastics, and 'Satisfactory' in Latin, natural history, drawing and writing.

In fact, he found school very much 'an evil that must be endured'. Only the journey there seemed attractive, 'when it was dark in winter and the world, with forest and mountain, market-place and little streets, showed the strange face of night'. The lessons themselves were largely 'unappetising'. The aesthete in him was already emerging:

> The room was overheated, stale with the vapour coming from poor people's clothes as they dried out. (...) [The] thin-haired, thin-lipped, thin-voiced teacher laboriously spoke standard High German. I was well able to understand how ridiculous it was, and the silly rough-and-tumble of break seemed to me and my friend Luk Kefer childish enough.

His whole-hearted admiration goes to Luk Kefer as a representative of the 'indigenous' countrified population of Bad Ischl. Culturally, he feels greatly superior to the teacher, for at the age of eight he had already read the complete works of Schiller. Only when the teacher recites a little poem by the dialect poet Stelzhammer, 'the poem about a little bird freezing in winter to whom no one would give any carpet slippers', is he moved to tears.

It was otherwise with the 'gigantic' and 'muscular' catechist, 'a fat man with a voice like thunder who was able to put much feeling into the stories of the wedding at Cana and the raising of poor Lazarus'. Religious instruction filled Améry with enthusiasm:

> If I just listened a little, I noticed things for myself instead of having to study, and so I shone in 'religion'. It was to him that they turned when the Catholic creed must be recited 'devoutly and with gravity', or when some rustic hobble-dehoy, no doubt understanding 'the resurrection of the flesh' as the apparition of ten kilograms of salt meat floating in the sky, stuck at these words and looked around helplessly, but without venturing to ask for elucidation.[32]

Who or what is a Jew?

Did Améry really believe in the Lord God? Probably not; he was just imitating what others do. But even at home, he said his prayers before going to sleep. He liked going to church, and enjoyed the smell of incense and the sound of the organ; they gave him a sense of security, of being at home and protected:

> The child believes in the life and suffering of the Lord no more deeply – but neither does he doubt them more fundamentally – than he knows that it is a good thing to have clean fingernails, not to use bad words, and to honour old age in the form of Aunt Rosalia's nasty old-lady smell.[33]

Yet he comments:

> I loved the house of God, although it was too closely connected for my liking with school, which I certainly did not love. I particularly liked the solemn High Mass on Easter Sunday – and yet I was vaguely aware that 'in reality' we were Jews.[34]

At the time, being Jewish – however much one tried to gloss it over, or perhaps for that very reason – already meant 'the constant awareness of being an outsider. We were different from other people, to my distress and deep uneasiness.' Furthermore, they were 'townsfolk in country surroundings, Viennese citizens among farmers and rustic tradesmen'. His mother herself embodied this discrepancy, since to judge by her 'legal and economic status she was landlady of an inn, but she was both inappropriately and undeniably a lady'. In addition, his lack of a father 'emphasized the dubious nature of my existence'. He wished that his mother would be stricter, and when playing with other boys he would invent stories of punishments at home, just so that he could keep up with the hobbledehoys at school.

The distinction between Christians and Jews was obvious to him even as a child. After all, his grandfather, a disapproving witness of this rural idyll, had already expressed his displeasure. Jews were in a better social position; they spoke properly – they said 'ja' and not 'jo'; Jews wore good clothes; they went not to the inn but to the spa assembly rooms or a café: 'In short, the visitors who stayed at our guest house during the summer were Jews.'

A divided heart

Although Améry's formal education may have left much to be desired in both quality and quantity, he had plenty of schooling of a different kind. In fact, the growing boy had been confronted, from his early childhood, with a dangerous split in his ego. From the first his childhood was divided, depending on the season of the year.

'My heart was torn', torn between the deep vowels of rural dialect and the pure vowels of educated speech. In winter Améry's mother wore dirndls,

Luk Kefer took out his stiletto blade and breathed hot brandy-laden fumes in his face. It was winter when Sepp announced his departure from the farm to train as a welder, and Moni confessed to her mother that she was expecting a child out of wedlock. But his new city comrades, acquired during their summer visits

> ...[did not bear] rural names, they spoke properly, they wore fine lederhosen and did not have grazed knees. At the same time my knowledge of rustic dialect and my familiarity with interesting localities in the Kaltenbach area made me feel both immensely superior to them – and entirely inferior in my decidedly slower powers of comprehension and my total ignorance of the city parks of Vienna. I was shaken by a storm of feeling when I met my schoolmates while in their company.

The boy dreams of a symbiosis; he wants town boy Goldstein to admire country boy Zeppezauer's boldness, he wants Zeppezauer to bow to 'Goldstein's wealth and distinction'. 'It seemed to me that each set of boys, the cultivated Jews and the rustic tearaways, ought to respect me for the skill with which I moved in the other set's world.' That skill did not come easily, 'because country Lois thought town Egon stupid, and Egon thought Lois dirty'. For Jews and non-Jews alike, 'to bridge the gap between those correct vowels and Luk Kefer' was impossible, even then.

Winter world versus summer world

So here we have the roots of incipient schizophrenia, as a result of the boy's social background. There seemed no escape from it. Hans Mayer belonged equally to both worlds, and in the same way he ultimately belonged to neither. First, however, he tried to become part of the winter world – for in winter, Bad Ischl was 'a real Upper Austrian village' – with its winter pleasures and winter friends, wild sleigh rides, mountain and forest walks, and the bawling of the unforgettable Pernecker Quadrille to the accompaniment of the piano accordion. He was a member of the German Gymnastics Society! Furthermore, there were his 'winter girlfriends'. For instance, Vroni Hiezl: a girl of 'painful beauty when she sat on the swing fitted in our bowling alley, flushed with heat, blonde strands of hair over her forehead, bending her thin, black-stockinged legs at the knees'. Or Gretl Gruber, with whom he would 'steal out into our garden after the May church service in honour of Our Lady', to play a 'heated and dangerous' game: 'Yes, we all started very young in Bad Ischl, and I wasn't going to court contempt as the exception.' Even as a grown man, he congratulates himself on the 'education in love' that he enjoyed so early. 'When I come to think of it, it gave me (...)

an erotic freedom that many a town boy acquires only with difficulty because of all kinds of scruples.'

Summer, 'with the arrival of distinguished Jewish people', was the time for 'higher love' of an elegant nature. At the age of ten Hans Mayer fell 'passionately in love' with the leading ingénue of the then well-known Bad Ischl Spa Theatre – a theatre, moreover, in which his aunt 'had a great reputation around the turn of the century under the name of Mila Theren'.[35] The lady of his heart was called Maria Hain. From the age of ten he haunted her doorway, for two years, in the hope of being able to offer her his 'Book of Songs'. He imagined Luk Kefer threatening her with his stiletto just so that he himself could rescue her. No such thing happened – Maria's fancy was caught by 'a person who rolled his eyes and spoke with a Hungarian accent' and who seemed to be on very friendly terms with her. His unsuspecting mother was worried, for the sorrows of love were draining the boy, and she took him to the doctor, but the doctor knew better than she did: 'The boy is perfectly healthy,' said this forthright man, 'the few moist patches on his lungs are calcified now.' The boy hated the doctor for that, because he didn't want to be healthy; he wanted to lie on his pillows looking pale, 'lamented by Maria, who in view of the wrong she had done me would sink beside my deathbed in tears of remorse'.

In fact, only the landscape was no source of conflict; he could be a part of it just as it was a part of him. At that stage he was anything but indifferent to his place of origin; his identification with the Kalvarienberg even went so far that in his memoir 30 years later he speaks of a 'fateful attachment' to that area of land: 30 years later Jean Améry concludes that it was an attachment to which the Nazis told him he was not entitled.[36]

The tribulations of the young grammar-school boy

A new era began. After passing his entrance examination, 'Johann Mayer' was registered at the grammar school in Gmunden as a 'private pupil'. During the week he stayed with his piano teacher, Bertha Schwarzwald, at Number 1 Marktplatz, and he spent weekends with his family circle. His mother had to pay only half the school fees for his first term. He was 'likely to do well', commented the headmaster on his report, but his scholastic achievements were only average – perhaps that was why his mother had to pay the full fee for him in his second term.

He longs to be back in Bad Ischl and his village idyll there. 'The little town and my fellow pupils were strange to me (...) for the first time in my life I was completely at a loss.' He felt like a poverty-stricken proletarian; the other pupils were better dressed, better at sports, rode bicycles, shot down the local slopes on their skis, knowledgeably exchanged views on their preferences for this or that ski-binding, had plenty of pocket-money, and spoke casually of the *consilium abeundi*,[i] 'while I myself was so dazed by all these novelties that I regularly missed hearing my own name when it was read out, for in such surroundings it seemed to me particularly feeble and unimpressive'. These boys were so much more dangerous than the kind of boy who was the son of summer guests at the inn, and whose clean lederhosen were their only sign of status. So this was how the synthesis he longed for looked: these sons of local big businessmen and industrialists united in themselves distinction, wealth and a sense of belonging to the land.

Hans had enjoyed a sheltered childhood so far. He was used to hearing his aunts and sisters-in-law, the guests at the inn and the summer visitors, saying how 'precocious and clever for his age' he was, what an 'early reader', gifted and intelligent, and now, suddenly, he was still the same Hans but he knew 'nothing about anything':

> In history lessons the man at the teacher's lectern talked about the Egyptians, who made me daydream (...) in Latin I couldn't tell the second declension from the fifth. In botany I was so intrigued by the word 'labiate', which seemed to me to have sexual connotations, that I escaped finding out who or what something labiate was. But mathematics was worst of all. Unable to make the faintest sense of the confusing signs on the board, I dozed, and was sometimes so far away that when it came to school tests I handed in totally blank sheets of paper with mingled fear and defiance.

No wonder the 'failed grammar-school boy' stayed on for only a single semester in his second year. In January 1925 Hans Mayer left the Gmunden grammar school before taking his exams and without any marks on his leaving certificate. He was 12 years and 3 months old, and nothing is known about any further schooling.[37] A life full of blank spaces; how else could a biography be written?

---

i Warning given before exclusion of a student from an educational establishment in punishment for some misdemeanour.

CHAPTER 2

Zirkusgasse (1924–1935)
The Enticements of Reason

In September 1926 mother and son returned to Vienna. Hans, now 14 years old, appears in the files of the Residents' Registration Office as 'commercial college student'. They set up home in Wollzeile in District 1 of Vienna. In 1929–30 his mother sent the teenager to his uncle, Hans May, in Berlin. His father's brother, a composer,[1] had a music-publishing firm there and could make good use of the lad as an errand boy. Améry himself, however, remembered more agreeable occupations; he tells us that he played the piano in a bar called 'Die Venusdiele', the Hall of Venus. 'A very pretty girl called Erika sang as I strummed on the keys,' he adds. 'I was very close to her.' Erika was not the only one to take his fancy; it was here that he was first to set eyes on the great Marlene Dietrich, whom he greatly admired.[2] Apart from this advantage, however, there was nothing to keep him in Berlin. He hated his work, and a little later he was hurrying back to Vienna and the Wollzeile.[3]

Leopold Langhammer, Mayer's mentor

It was here, in the Hermann Goldschmid Bookshop and Press Cuttings Agency, Vienna District 1, Number 11 Wollzeile, today the Morawa bookshop,[4] that the boy trained under Leopold Langhammer before being employed for eight years – from 1930 to 1938 – in the bookshop of the Leopoldstadt Adult Education Centre.[5] His encounter with Leopold Langhammer (1891–1975) was to have a lasting effect on his intellectual development. Not only was Langhammer, whom Améry describes 40 years later in a letter to his childhood friend Ernst Mayer as his mentor, an outstanding authority on literature and philosophy, he was also the author of 'an expressive body of poetic works'. These began with a volume of poetry, *Die Gesänge von den kleinen Leuten* [The Songs of the Little People], which appeared in 1946, and continued to the still unpublished *Buchenwald-Lied* [Buchenwald Song] (1966).[6] It was as a figure in adult education, however, that Langhammer was distinguished in the city of Vienna, and he was indeed an 'adult

Hans Mayer's mentor Leopold Langhammer, c. 1937

education teacher' by both profession and vocation.[7] As early as 1924, having taken his doctoral degree, the philosopher and literary critic was appointed director of the adult education centre known as the Wien Volksheim [Vienna People's Home], a post that he filled until the German invasion. In 1938, although an Aryan, he was interned by the Nazis in Buchenwald. In 1945, immediately after the end of the war, he was reinstated as adviser-in-chief on adult education in the city of Vienna. In this capacity he also appointed 'Hanns Mayer', who after his liberation from Bergen-Belsen briefly considered returning to Vienna, 'as adviser and lecturer'. Langhammer stated in a testimonial written in the autumn of 1945:

> The lecturer Hanns Mayer is an outstandingly valuable colleague in the rebuilding of Austrian popular education, not only because of his political dependability, but in particular for his thorough knowledge of the language, literature, and liberal arts of France.[8]

However, Hans Mayer decided against returning to Vienna. A year later, on 12 December 1946, Langhammer wrote another and slightly altered testimonial, this time in relation to opportunities for working and teaching in Belgium:

> This is to confirm that Herr Hanns Mayer was a colleague of mine and a lecturer at the Adult Education Centres of Vienna. He gave classes and lectures on literary history and philosophy. Herr Hanns Mayer, who is also active in journalism and writes for leading Belgian, Dutch, and other publications, is to be warmly recommended as a lecturer on the liberal arts and literary subjects at adult education centres and similar institutions.[9]

DR. LEOPOLD LANGHAMMER
Hauptreferent für die Wiener Volkshochschulen
im Amt für Kultur und Volksbildung
der Stadt Wien
WIEN, I., Neues Rathaus, Stiege 3
Tel. B 40-5-00, Kl. 157

Wien, den 25. Juni 194 6

WIEN, IX., Boltzmanngasse 8
Telephon: A 11-8-15

Es wird hiermit bestätigt, dass Herr
HANS MAIER
geb. 31.Oktober 1912 in Wien, dzt. wohnhaft Brüssel
in den Jahren 1931 -1936 an der Volkshochschule Wien Volksheim
Literaturwissenschaft und Philosophie studierte und hierbei namentlich
folgende Vorlesungen und Kurse gehört hat:

Geschichte der Philosophie : Dr. Leopold Langhammer

Logik:Prof. Dr. Edgar Zilsel

Deutsche Literatur: Dr. Leopold Langhammer

Weltliteratur :Prof. Dr. Fritz Lehner

Dr. Ernst Schönwiese

Neuere Philosophie:Dr. Wilhelm Löwinger,

Dr. Fritz Feigl u.a.

Herr Hans Maier hat die entsprechenden Prüfungen mit sehr gutem Erfolg
abgelegt und hat auch später in eigenen Vorträgen und Referaten an der
Volkshochschule Wien Volksheim seine ausgezeichnete Kenntnis und Beherr-
schung der Materie bewiesen. Für seine eigenen literarischen Arbeiten
wurde ihm 1936 der (Emil) Reich-Preis verliehen.

Der Hauptreferent und öffentliche
Verwalter der Wiener Volkshochschulen :

Der kommissarische Leiter

Volkshochschule Wien Volksheim

Leopold Langhammer

*Retrospective testimonial by Leopold Langhammer to Hans Mayer's study programme
at the Adult Education Centre in Vienna*

Hans Mayer, c. 1928

Red Vienna

Of course, Hans Mayer never, in fact, merited the title of 'lecturer'. He studied at grammar school, as we know, only until his twelfth year and was never 'officially registered' at Vienna University, although we do know that he attended literary and philosophical lectures there while not attached to the university and derived great benefit from them.

However, the Adult Education Centre at Number 48 Zirkusgasse was Hans Mayer's university, first as a listener, then as an active member of the staff. Langhammer introduced the youthful would-be writer Hans Mayer to the life of 'Red Vienna', and under him it saw a flowering it had never known before. The Zirkusgasse became a centre of the Austrian intelligentsia.

It was here that Mayer met not only Leopold Langhammer but also Ernst Schönwiese, editor of the journal *das silberboot* [The Silver Boat]. 'At that time (...) around 1935, you were the teacher and I the student,' says Jean Améry in 1978 (the year of his death), paying homage to the 73-year-old poet and critic:

> Did you not acquaint me with Musil when I was a very immature young man of 20, still determined to cling to a *Neue Sachlichkeit*[i] that had already outlived its usefulness? (...) Did not your classes at that secret hotbed of the intelligentsia,

---

i   The *Neue Sachlichkeit* [New Objectivity or New Realism] was not an actual movement, but a general term in the arts for a trend opposed to Expressionism.

the Adult Education Centre in Vienna, point me the way out of the Austrian and German literary ghetto in which I was absurdly at ease, transporting me across the borders into modern international literature? I first read a work by Mauriac in your *silberboot*, without the faintest premonition that this author was to be one of my favourites, just as an earlier favourite, I confess frankly but with some shame, had been Karl Heinrich Waggerl?[10] And finally, did you not help me to get a story or poem printed now and then? It meant a great deal in the Austria that we knew.[11]

First encounters: Broch, Canetti and the Austrian literary scene

Hans Mayer met Hermann Broch in person when, on 29 April 1932, Broch read from *Die Schlafwandler* [The Sleep-Walker], a work that influenced Améry not a little both in form and content, when he came to write *Lefeu oder Der Abbruch* [Lefeu or the Demolition]. On 12 November 1936, Elias Canetti paid tribute to Hermann Broch on his fiftieth birthday, and Hermann Broch supported the still unknown young writer Canetti when he read from his novel *Die Blendung* [Auto-da-fe], as yet unpublished at the time. Forty years later, in his essay 'Zentrum Zirkusgasse 1935',[12] Ernst Schönwiese remembers giving lectures on Shakespeare's tragedies at the Centre, in a crowded hall full of young people and up-and-coming writers. We are told that Robert Musil, 'an elegant, well-groomed figure', frequently appeared there, 'always with his wife, an uncommonly clever woman'. Among the many authors to be heard at the Adult Education Centre in the 1930s were Paris Gütersloh, Franz Blei, Max Brod, Theodor Csokor, Felix Braun, Benno Geiger, Theodor Kramer, Ernst Waldinger, Friedrich Torberg, Erika Mitterer, Soma Morgenstern and Heinz Politzer, who at the time was helping Max Brod to produce the first complete edition of Kafka's works. Albert Ehrenstein and Karl Otten too stopped for a while in Vienna before emigrating.[13] The Adult Education Centre thus became a forum for contemporary poets and novelists – and the self-taught Hans Mayer took what he could use from it.

Hans Mayer's personal revolution

The period 1926–1938, his years in Vienna before he emigrated to Belgium, opened up entirely new perspectives to Hans Mayer. This is the time in which he took his first steps as writer, storyteller and editor. As a child, at the time of his village idyll in the Gasthof zur Stadt Prag at the foot of the Kalvarienberg, he got on well with rustic boys and girls such as Luk Kefer and Vroni Hiezl, was fondly indulged by his mother and aunts, and waxed enthusiastic on the subject of the darkness and solitude of the woods, 'the magic of the constant and eternal symbolism of the forest'. He now felt that his encounter with his intellectual mentor Langhammer was a journey of initiation into the literary and philosophical urbanity of the cosmopolitan city of Vienna.

In his *Unmeisterliche Wanderjahre*[ii] [Years of Wandering], published in 1971, the writer, looking back as he meditates, delights in a thorough process of self-demolition. He mocks himself as a 'stolid reactionary', a 'blind and dumb *petit bourgeois*' who thought himself at home in 'mountain and valley, country lane, sunken path, forest track', indeed in all varieties of the landscape of the Austrian Alpine region. In Bad Ischl, as a member of the lower middle class who had come down in the world, he had felt excluded from the brilliance of Vienna, the city of lights. He ironically quotes Fontane's lines on Paris: 'I am, perhaps, too old / For splendours such as these, / Too German, certainly.' The impoverished young man had anxiously set the landscape of the country against the city townscape, and this is a *leitmotiv* of his youthful years, for, as the author of *Unmeisterliche Wanderjahre* reflects, 'you were as poor in spirit as in your purse'. Up to this point he had recited poems by Wilhelm von Scholz and had sworn by Will Vesper, Börries von Münchhausen and 'fat Frau Agnes Miegel' – all of them 'insidious reactionaries', as he was to see them later, but figures whom he was predisposed to like because of his sense of closeness to the land, of being rooted in the soil. But the year 1930 saw a very personal revolution take place in the mind of the bookseller's trainee, Hans Mayer, in the Zirkusgasse in Vienna.

His 'forest (...) was felled', and the woodland darkness gave way to a clearing. He learned to read the political signals:

> 1927 – and this was an experience of the utmost significance to me – saw a situation resembling civil war flare up for the first time. On 15 and 16 July 1927 the Heimwehr, that is to say the clerico-Fascist Austrian militia, came up against the Republican Defence Corps of the Austrian Social Democratic Party, the famous or notorious Austro-Marxists.

However, when the Palace of Justice went up in flames, and the Social Democratic workers clashed with the Fascist Heimwehr, the young writer was still among those frequenting coffeehouses for abstract debates 'in an atmosphere removed from reality'. He would not actually become a party member until 1934, when Dollfuss suspended the Austrian parliament and a general strike was called.

---

ii   The title translates literally as 'Unmasterly Years of Travel', but it derives, with a pun, from the title of Goethe's last novel *Wilhelm Meisters Wanderjahre*.

Approaches to the Wiener Kreis [Vienna Circle]

Adult education in Vienna had its own story.[14] Dvořak writes:

> The particular feature of Viennese adult education, and especially the work of the Volksheim, was its markedly scientific orientation. Taking a scientific approach did not necessarily mean merely condescension on the part of middle-class scholars to those in need of education, but entailed providing the tools of thought for everyday use, in line with the concept of knowledge at the time as represented, for instance, by Ernst Mach.[15]

Knowledge and education, Dvořak continues, were not regarded as ends in themselves; what always mattered was the 'practical application of knowledge once acquired, in shaping both the life of the individual and that of society as a whole. "Popularization without simplification" was a major guiding principle.'[16] Dvořak tells us how the 'concept of university lectures on a popular level' had the Ottakring Volksheim presenting what amounted to a programme of 'the radical democratization of knowledge and education'.

Every effort was made to establish a link between scientific findings and the conduct of everyday life, between knowledge and improved living conditions:

> Influential members of the Wiener Kreis, the discussion circle that formed around Moritz Schlick – for instance Hans Hahn, Ludwig Wittgenstein, Friedrich Waismann, Otto Neurath, Rudolf Carnap, Edgar Zilsel – were often as much concerned with the reorganization of scientific philosophical activity as they were with school reform and adult education.[17]

However, the Vienna Circle is generally regarded – particularly in the English-speaking world – as a group of philosophers, and the commitment of its members to the field of education is disregarded. Yet Carnap, Hahn and Neurath, in their 1929 manifesto 'A Scientific Concept of the World', laid particular emphasis on their 'efforts (...) to re-invigorate schooling and education'. They owed their anti-metaphysical stance, their materialistic understanding of history and their opposition to the rampant irrationalism of religion and politics entirely to the spirit of the Enlightenment. They were concerned 'to create tools of thought for use in ordinary life (...), for the everyday existence of all who are in some way working on the conscious organization of their lives.'[18]

They were especially anxious to convey to a wide public 'the present state of a scientific concept of the world' and to develop 'intellectual tools of modern empiricism': 'Good order and clarity are the ideals, dark distances and unfathomable depths are repudiated'. Such a remark was bound either to be vigorously rejected by Hans Mayer, still a wanderer in forests at the time, or – and this is just what happened – to inspire him to a new enthusiasm, one opposed to his previous state of mind: an enthusiasm for clarity. 'There are no "depths" in science; the surface is everywhere (...) Everything is accessible to humanity,' we read in the manifesto. 'Man is the measure of all things.'

It is here, then, under the influence of the Vienna Circle – which was anything but homogeneous – and the Logical Empiricism of the Austrian First Republic, that the roots of Améry's new perceptions are to be sought. He was particularly strongly influenced by the neo-positivist Moritz Schlick,[19] teaching in Vienna at the time, although he considered Rudolf Carnap[20] the more important philosopher.[21] He also refers to Ernst Mach and the linguistic critic and philosopher Fritz Mauthner[22] in his work.[23] Although only a few years earlier, in his back-to-the-land forest darkness, he had rejected rationality, armed with Mach, Schlick and Carnap he now rejects the irrationality of Austrian clerico-Fascism. 'One can wake from a dream and immediately fall in reverie into another (...) One can renounce one belief and adopt another,' is his retrospective criticism of himself in *Unmeisterliche Wanderjahre* (Vol. 2, p. 212).

The future writer

What Langhammer does not mention is that the 'bookseller's assistant' – for it was in this capacity that the 15-year-old made his living until 1938 – was not only getting an education but also being featured as the editor of a journal and as a writer himself. His first publication of the year 1928, *Der Schüler Hauser wird zum Herrn Direktor gerufen* [The School Student Hauser is Appointed Headmaster], is lost.[24] 'It was a story, obviously a school story, written to some extent under the influence of Hermann Hesse's *Unterm Rad* and Emil Straussen's *Freund Hein*', as we learn from a conversation with Ingo Hermann. Here he was taking up the tradition of the German school story, of which his own traumatic experience of grammar school was a part. There is also mention of poems at this time. On 23 March 1934, in the context of an 'evening of young authors', unpublished works by Mayer were read aloud at 48 Zirkusgasse.

Die Brücke

The school friendship of Hans and Ernst Mayer reached its zenith in their joint editorship of the literary journal *Die Brücke. Kritische Beiträge* [The Bridge. Critical Essays]. The first issue appeared on 12 February 1934.[25] Jean Améry wrote to Ernst Mayer on 12 February 1964:

> I think 30 years back (...) The two of us, you and I, were not 'committed' yet, but felt that events concerned us. I was sitting in Kolonitzgasse in melancholy mood,

and exactly 14 days later the first number of the duplicated *Brücke* came out. How long ago that is – and yet sometimes, particularly now, I feel as if it were only yesterday that I was leafing through the first number of that same *Brücke*, with a pride much more fervent than my feelings on the publication in 1961 of the *Geburt der Gegenwart* [*Preface to the Future*].[26]

How little Hans Mayer actually was 'committed' at this time, indeed how deeply attached he still was to his 'village idyll', is clearly illustrated by the journal's language and content. In fact, that is what makes *Die Brücke* such a valuable document; there could hardly be a more forceful illustration of the desperate conflict between Améry's two souls – his 'country soul' and his 'city soul'.

Four issues are still preserved, and although monthly publication was envisaged it is likely that no more were produced, so dire were the financial difficulties of the journal (not to mention difficulties of the political variety). It proudly emphasizes its independence in the issues published in 'Feber',[iii] April, May and October. The editors present it, in their 'manifesto', as a forum for their own literary reflections and for the first publication of works by Austrian authors:

> If an attempt is to be made in the following pages to transcend the intellectual disintegration of the present and find a new point of view, one where what was divided is reunited, and perhaps both parts are repudiated (...) then bear in mind that we are judging from the narrow viewpoint of personal knowledge, and that we derive our right to do so from the shared experience of the intellectual situation that, to the minds of later generations, will unite us all not just temporally but intellectually as well.

With their euphemistic remark about the 'intellectual disintegration' of the time which must be transcended, they refer to the apocalyptic mood of an Austria already striding towards its dissolution in the Thousand-Year Reich. The foreword paraphrases the title. A 'bridge' is to unite what was 'divided', although exactly what that may be is not clear. The editors intend to offer something like a 'literary spectacle' which, for all its subjectivity and its location outside all systems, will be 'just' and 'unbiased' in taking up the battle against 'unthinking prejudice, the crowd mentality, and philistinism of every kind'. Here at least they speak to the point.

Hans Mayer sets the tone with his first essay, 'The Present State of German Literature'. He begins with a consideration of the Jewish Nobel Prize winner Bergson – thus marking his political 'independence' in the year 1934. In the April

---

iii Austrian dialect for February.

edition, the journal prints a eulogy by the Jewish author Friedrich Bergammer on the occasion of Hugo von Hofmannsthal's sixtieth birthday; in May, Alfred Weber's glowing account of the 'Jewish prophet', Karl Kraus, appears, and Ernst Mayer reviews the second volume of Thomas Mann's biblical trilogy *Joseph und seine Brüder* [Joseph and His Brothers]. The 'line of division' mentioned in the foreword is first described – and deplored – in Hans Mayer's introductory essay: 'From the end of the Great War until March 1933, German literature was dominated (...) almost without exception by intellectual works from the big cities (...) literature written by metropolitan writers for metropolitan readers.' He further describes it as 'the literature of progress', a 'humanist literature' drawing its inspiration from the spirit of classicism, under the aegis of Goethe, Schiller and Kant. Under the new political regime, amoral literature replaces this moral kind:

> Paradoxically, the artistic tendency that had arisen from reconstruction and ethics ultimately became destructive and unethical. For when a community's idea is to analyse ideas and dismantle them into their causal driving forces, and when its ethic consists in finding every human sentiment understandable and excusable, it cannot last. The latest works before us appear to be hovering in a complete void, presenting such a dreadful aspect of total pointlessness that one might almost be tempted to fall back on an ideological lie simply to call a halt to the head-over-heels *ratio*, to preserve the possibilities of humanity at all.

This is how the 'intellectual disintegration' of his time presents itself to Hans Mayer, in the confrontation of two literary tendencies. For, to the political monopoly of literature by the metropolitan kind, sketched above, he contrasts 'rural and provincial literature', where 'the concepts of good and evil' still 'live on in simplicity and clarity'. He pleads for

> ...both varieties of literature to complement each other in concord. Now more than ever our field of vision must not be narrow, the valuable forces of German writing on both sides of the borders must be recognized and distinguished from all that is dishonourable, amateurish and worthless. Merely drawing a distinction between good and bad can be of importance. Germany's literature still has two directions, both equally valuable, both equally essential. Let it be our effort to promote that understanding.

February 1934, then, represents the interface in Hans Mayer's intellectual biography, the point at which he calls on the familiar and much-loved rural element to save its metropolitan counterpart from the perversion of National Socialism.

Ernst and Hans Mayer, editors of the literary journal Die Brücke, c. 1934

We can see how deeply immersed in his childhood village idyll Hans Mayer still was at this time, not just from his grandiloquent style but also from the mystic content:

> It must be the mission of rural literature to call on the cities, showing that there are still tender, sensitive souls in the country, that comfort may still be found in the landscape and in solitude (...) Let them be supported by a non-political conservatism. Let them remain quiet, clear, and pure, the quiet country people, for the stridency of those who would improve the world today suits them ill.

In the last issue, October, this lament was given even more insistently:

> If we spoke of a non-political vantage-point, then we did so above all because today, when we consider German literature, almost all subtlety of differentiation (...) seems to have disappeared, because the camps are clearly divided, stretched taut in a rough outline showing folklorism opposed to cosmopolitanism. Here the soil, there asphalt; here feeling, there intellect; here experience, there analysis.

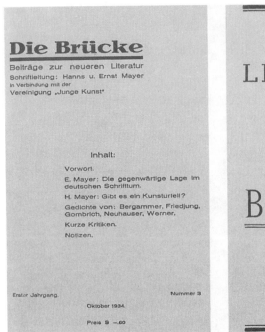

Left: October 1934; right, announcement in the October issue

Once again Hans Mayer was pleading for the fusion of city-based writing 'that draws on the sphere of ethics and humanity', and 'the writing of the countryside', accused, but falsely so, of 'viscous romanticism', 'sombre atavism' and 'silly superstition':

> We will try to show how much we need both elements in German literature today: we need to be shaken out of apathy and to reflect, we need the city and the country, myth and intellect. And we will try to show how both tendencies, although neither may wish to perceive it today, can come together in a third and more purified sphere.

No year in Hans Mayer's life was to be so polarized as 1934: on one hand the enthusiastic conservative lover of the landscape and saviour of rural literature; on the other the socialist revolutionary and reformer of the world, who has already, if tentatively, tasted the fruit of the tree of knowledge and is the political resistance fighter of the future. For we know that at the same time, to be precise between 12 and 15 February 1934, during the February Uprising, Hans Mayer flung himself whole-heartedly into the activities of the Republican Defence Corps,[27] which left 320 dead. His 'urban' actions speak a far more radical language than the emphasis on rural tradition in his prose.

The uprising has broken out (...) there will be fighting (...). The young man suddenly has a task to perform. There were pistols and ammunition in unsafe places. It was dangerous but not difficult to get hold of them and take them somewhere more secure. You do not refuse such a request, although you may feel a momentary fear in the pit of the stomach, addresses in cipher are noted down. You set off and soon you are carrying the sinister items around in a large briefcase, again and again, for there seem to be a great many guns lying about with no one making use of them.[28]

With or without smuggled weapons, the uprising fails, the revolution is dead. So much for the first Republic, the one that no one wanted.

Life under the clerico-Fascist dictatorship begins.

None other than the poet Franz Werfel basks in the reflected glory of our new Chancellor Schuschnigg, or so it is generally rumoured. Sigmund Freud lives and has his consulting rooms in Berggasse, in District 9, and will not hear of emigrating, as friends have long been recommending him to do. How was a young man, coming from the Austrian province of Vorarlberg, reared in Ischl and Gmunden, nurtured in foolish tradition and committed to a mediocre type of literature bound to the land, to 'know better'?[29] He knows a little better already because, unlike accredited intellectuals, he speaks the dialect of the workers and farmers. He knows he ought to disappear, but like Sigmund Freud he does not want to, in the subjectively real but objectively stupid belief that he belongs here, that only here will he be able to write his verse and his novellas.[30]

CHAPTER 3

Die Schiffbrüchigen [The Shipwrecked] (1935–1945)

Hans Mayer as a Writer of Fiction

1935: Préludes

For he is also writing verse and novellas, *Die Brücke* is still able to appear. In the April issue, he publishes the five-page 'study' *Nächtliches Geschehen* [Nocturnal Incident], not under his own name but as Peter Frühwirth, obviously one of the many pseudonyms given by Hans Mayer to other literary works, for instance, the poem *Beim Einbruch der Nacht* [At Nightfall] in the May issue, also incorporated like a piece of mosaic into his first novel, which he is writing in parallel. The identical lines, their authorship here attributed to the protagonist of the novel, reappear in its sixth chapter. We know that Mayer's dissatisfaction with his very ordinary name has always been a problem to him, inducing him to make many experiments with his identity up to 1955, when he finally decides on adopting the French-sounding name with an anagram of the surname, Jean Améry. At this time, no doubt the editorial team of 'Hanns and Ernst Mayer' intend to demonstrate an intellectual 'brotherhood' to the public in the spelling of their surname. However, Hans Mayer will have resorted to the pseudonym Peter Frühwirth for purely pragmatic reasons, as a useful method of concealing the fact that the journal, operating as it was on a shoestring, did not have a large body of contributors writing for it.[1]

This prose piece, *Nächtliches Geschehen*, is the psychogram of 'a man betrayed'. In this connection we may think of the late novella *Die Betrogene* [The Woman Betrayed] by Thomas Mann, or Th. M., as Mayer apostrophizes him in *Die Schiffbrüchigen* [The Shipwrecked], describing Mann as 'a sign and portent in his life' with his novels *Buddenbrooks, Königliche Hoheit, Joseph und seine Brüder,* and above all *Der Zauberberg.* Since his eighteenth year, after all, he has been 'wandering in' its 'magical mountain range' and he knows 'whole

29

paragraphs of Thomas Mann's prose by heart, so that they have long become a part of his inner world'.[2] In Améry's short study, feelings of jealousy and humiliation are described in meticulous detail: an unnamed protagonist seeks refuge at a dilapidated inn, where a pimp presses a pathetic young whore on him. But the protagonist is finally able to withstand the temptation 'to take a pointless and unworthy revenge' on the girl.

A striking feature in this sketch is the mention of a small item indicating the close autobiographical connection between this study, early as it is, and future works: Améry speaks of 'a small gold chain' belonging to Eugen Althager, the central character of the novel *Die Schiffbrüchigen*[3] – a chain that we shall meet again a little later. It is surprising to find the same 'little chain' surfacing once more after the war, in Jean Améry's 1966 essay 'On Torture', in which he describes the moment in July 1943, at the time of his second arrest in Brussels, when 'a thin gold bracelet aroused derisive attention', and a Flemish SS man '[explained] to his German comrades that this was the sign of the partisans'.[4] This coded mention suggests the origin of a primal grouping of ideas: outsider (as in *Nächtliches Geschehen*), nay-sayer (as in *Die Schiffbrüchigen*), partisan (as in 'Torture'), all of them stages in an aesthetic progression reflecting the intensification of a political commitment that has its biographical equivalent in Hans Mayer as the outsider of the 1920s, the nay-sayer of the 1930s and the partisan of the 1940s.

The first novel

The youthful work *Die Schiffbrüchigen*, written in 1934–1935 under the name of Hans Mayer, continues on a fictional level the ideas already broached in his critical writings in *Die Brücke*. It is probably Mayer's most extensive examination of the period. Until the end of his life, it remains fundamental to his view of himself as a narrative writer, so much so that, in his mind, the mere idea of its publication makes sense of his survival. This vocation as a writer of fiction seems to him so natural that he sees the journalism that occupies him for 20 years merely as the means to that end: to tell a tale.

In 1949 Mayer writes repeatedly to his future wife – Maria Améry, as she would become – telling her how much the revision and publication of the novel means to him. He has re-read it, he says, 'in a mood beyond even euphoria'. He adds that 'it strikes me as good, very good in some parts, excellent. However, I cannot, *au nom de Dieu*, be entirely deserted by all the benevolent spirits of self-criticism!'[5] A few months later he already dreams of seeing it brought out by Thomas Mann's publisher. 'Now that I have a certain connection with *Die Neue Rundschau*,' he says, he will 'submit it to Berman-Fischer.'[6] In 1950 he has another plan in mind. In a letter to his former mentor Ernst Schönweise, writer and patron of the arts, he speaks triumphantly of the 'incredible coincidence' whereby he recovered his youthful novel *Die Schiffsbrüchigen*.[7] Indeed, when he came home he thought that his novel (which, as he saw it, made him a writer) had been destroyed.

Recovering the manuscript thus seems to him like gaining a new lease of life. It had spent the years of National Socialism at 16 Berggasse, in the 'Viennese agency for manuscripts', in the building where Ernst Schönwiese had the editorial offices of *das silberboot* during 1935–6. This manuscript is still extant today, a bundle of 392 typed pages of flimsy paper with a few deletions and manuscript corrections. He wrote to Schönwiese:

> After demolishing in my mind, not without some lamentation, the mythical version of my life presenting this book as a small work of genius, I imagined for some weeks that it was no good, had never been any good – and only now have I been able to give it sober consideration, coming to the conclusion that, after a certain amount of revision, the book would still, after all, be very readable and useful.[8]

However, neither the *Neue Rundschau* nor Ernst Schönwiese's publisher seem to show any interest. 'I began my first novel, which fortunately was not published, at the age of 22 and finished it when I was 23 (The novel was at last published in 2007[9]). 'It was called, grandiloquently, *Die Schiffbrüchigen*,' he tells Ingo Hermann shortly before his death:

> I was going to send it to Thomas Mann for his opinion, for I thought it such a fine work that only he could do it justice. Thomas Mann wrote a very kind reply, making the unforgettable request: 'Please recollect that my powers are not equal to everything, and turn to someone in your own city. You might try Robert Musil, one of the finest of artists, and very knowledgeable.' Robert Musil assured me that the novel showed great talent, but also a certain immaturity. I think that Robert Musil was very kind to me, only too kind. For when I read the novel now (...) a cold shudder runs down my spine.[10]

Although in retrospect he smiles at a young man's ambitions, we know that, in fact, he never let go of them to the end of his life. Forty-five years later – even in a state of complete sobriety – he is still firmly convinced that the novel, although 'an immature, youthful work', would certainly 'have appeared in Austria or Germany in normal political circumstances. But the fact was that I was a Socialist, and as such naturally *persona non grata* in clerico-Fascist Austria.'[11] Nonetheless, Hans Mayer is invited to read an extract from the novel at the Leopoldstadt Adult Education Centre on 28 November 1935.

Hermann Hakel, 1937

In the same year his contemporary, the poet and publisher Hermann Hakel, prints a 12-page 'partial chapter' from it under the title of 'Die Entwurzelten' [The Uprooted] in his *Jahrbuch 1935* [1935 Annual]. The passage chosen describes the protagonist's visit to his home village of Kirchleiten.[12] Here the terms 'uprooted' and 'shipwrecked' are synonymous; in both cases he is dwelling on exile from a childhood paradise of mountains and forests. Ernst Schönwiese, remembering *Die Schiffbrüchigen* from Mayer's stories in the 1930s, even speaks of it as a 'psychological rural novel'.[13]

Autobiography as historical writing

In 1955, in what was probably his last attempt to find a publisher for the novel, the author provides a summary of its contents:[14]

> We are in Vienna in the spring of 1933. Unemployed Eugen Althager wakes up in his untidy room, a lumpenproletariat dwelling, and wonders how to spend the day that lies ahead of him. (...) He was born a Catholic and has been brought up as a Jew; his irregular studies, interrupted for economic reasons, were of literature and philosophy. The very first scenes appear in the light cast on them by his times. On his morning walk, Eugen Althager witnesses anti-Semitic street brawling in the university quarter.

Two other main characters are his Communist girlfriend Agathe, a 'young office worker anxious to acquire an education', who supports Eugen financially, and his friend Heinrich Hessl, 'a young doctoral student, of Catholic leanings, living in comfortable circumstances,' whose intelligence and ambition promise him a swift rise 'within the semi-Fascist elite determining the fate of Austria'.

Hans Mayer describes Eugen Althager as a 'nihilist of the interwar period', whose attitude is determined by his 'race' and his social situation. Heinrich Hessl, 'the man who, in sharp contradiction to the character of Althager, stands for work and the bourgeois desire for constructive activity (...), chooses flight forward' into the Catholic world of the mind. Agathe becomes the mistress of a wealthy man, first out of necessity – he gives her money for an abortion, after Hessl has refused her request for it – and then out of her own inclinations. The father of her child, Althager, disowns any responsibility, and although he is now entirely isolated and has no financial means without his girlfriend, he himself urges Agathe to take her new path in life.

Apart from these socio-psychological complications, *Die Schiffbrüchigen* is also a 'close-up of Austria's last dramatic crisis – the February Uprising of 1934'.[15] Deprived of his last political hopes, Althager thinks of a way out:

> The idea of suicide, lying like a shadow over the entire course of Eugen Althager's development, urgently demands resolution. But Eugen, who has never had any illusions about his powers, knows that he is not strong enough for that. So he allows (...) chance to decide his fate, and makes use of an ordinary street brawl as a means of 'indirect' suicide.

The genesis and writing of this youthful work coincide with the period of the publication of *Die Brücke*. Not, of course, that the problems studied in the critical essays are pursued in the novel, but here too the dichotomy between town and country forms the background for conflicts that we encounter nowhere else on this scale in Hans Mayer, and certainly not in Jean Améry. For instance, we see it in the tension between the bourgeoisie – especially when they have come down in the world – and the proletariat, with economic differences leading to anti-social behaviour.

Faithful to his great example, Thomas Mann – indeed, his attitude towards Mann lies somewhere between symbiosis and imitation[16] – the 22-year-old writer links the class conflict with the conflict between art and life, love and death. He writes to his friend in a much later letter that he is reading Thomas Mann again and feels

> ...uplifted, moved, enthusiastic. It is all absolutely unique, *indépassable* in beauty, charm, intellect and virtue. With genuine emotion I have been re-reading – for the first time in perhaps 30 years – the *Betrachtungen eines Unpolitischen*

[Reflections of a Non-Political Man] on the tragic confrontation with his brother Heinrich. Heinrich Mann was right – there is no doubt of that, and Thomas Mann admitted it later in the most noble way. But how lovable Thomas Mann still is, even when he is in the wrong!

Hermann Broch also makes his mark on Mayer. Broch's *Die Schlafwandler* [Sleepwalkers] and his comments on the decline in values are influential here. Philosophically, the entire drama – or perhaps one should say melodrama – of the hapless Eugen Althager is embedded in Hans Mayer's new understanding, gleaned from Fritz Mauthner's *Kritik der Sprache*, Ernst Mach's *Die Analyse der Empfindungen* and Rudolf Carnap's *Der logische Aufbau der Welt*. Politically, it arises from the author's awakening Socialist ethic after the February Uprising of 1934. The realistic style – the Améry of 1955 sees his younger self as close to the New Objectivity movement – does not disguise the fact that we are dealing here with his first *roman à thèse*; at least with his first 'novel as essay'.

Although it is written at the same time as Mayer's essays in *Die Brücke*, the novel goes much further and is more explicit and radical. The 'psychological rural novel' of Schönwiese's description has become more of a 'socio-cultural urban novel', indeed a history of Austrian mentality in the 1930s from the point of view of an unemployed and self-taught Jewish intellectual. His 'mission' of writing works in tune with the countryside that will 'cry out to the cities' is reduced to a mere trace, for he has come to recognize its irrationality, if not its absurdity. If the longing for a 'non-political idyll' is still a crucial component of the essays in literary criticism; it is portrayed guiltily in the novel as illusory, a wrong direction, so to speak, only a distraction from the necessity of adopting a stance in the coming political struggle.

We may speak of a materialistic concept of history in *Die Schiffbrüchigen*, for it is money or the lack of it that determines the conduct of the protagonists. Heinrich Hessl, Althager's friend or adversary, the yea-sayer, an insider par excellence, opts for the path of adjustment, financial gain and social success. He disowns his Jewish identity, gains his doctorate and adapts to a society that, at heart, he despises. He wants order at any price, something like 'peace with a God' in whom he does not believe. As an uncomprehending philistine, he lives out a form of 'bureaucratic metaphysics' that he abhors at the same time. Finally, Althager's girlfriend Agathe also turns traitor and surrenders, like Hessl, to the power of money. She too, first encountered by the reader as Eugen's comrade and accomplice in the struggle, exchanges the suffering of the mind and poverty for the pleasures of the body and prosperity.

There remains the nay-sayer Eugen Althager, an intellectual turned proletarian, the eternal outsider – the opposite pole to Hessl, a spirit of disorder
and hysteria. *Nomen est omen*: he is a descendant both young and old who has
come down in the world of the tribe of Eugen,[i] an old Austrian duellist avid
for death,[17] representative of a dying epoch, an emblem of the decadent and
degenerate land that is hurrying towards its downfall. Here it is impossible not
to think of Joseph Roth's *Radetzkymarsch* [The Radetsky March]. Even if Hans
Mayer does not know that novel at this time, he is writing in and continuing the
old tradition of the Austro-Hungarian empire.

Althager – an alter ego?

Undoubtedly the hero of the novel represents fictionalized biography – the parallels, although slightly shifted in time, between the story of Althager's life and the
author's are obvious: the father is a 'Jewish businessman', the mother 'a devoutly
Christian half-Jew', widowed early and left without financial resources. After a
carefree childhood and early youth, the protagonist moves to Vienna. 'That was
when Eugen became rootless' (Sch. p. 43). He finds it difficult to cope with the
city, poverty and care make inroads into his life, 'the gentleman's son' becomes
an apprentice in a bookshop, where he is ill at ease, 'dusty, crumpled and helpless' (Sch. p. 44).

> Longing had been aroused in him (...) for the forests he had lost, and in his nos-
> talgia he had sought and found comfort in books about the landscape, in poems
> of dream and loss, in songs of remote seclusion from the world and the shelter
> of the forests. The boy liked all that was dark and sombre, all that opposed
> cold reason, symbolized to him by the life of commerce that he shunned, by
> calculating-machines and card indexes. (Sch. p. 44)

Nietzsche and Wagner, Schopenhauer, Klages and Novalis stand beside
him, promising release.

Nothing comes of that promise. He flees to the capital of the Reich. Political
events in Berlin open his eyes, and once they are opened he returns to Vienna. At
this point – April 1933 – the action of the novel begins.

> Eugen Althager, (...) coldly surrounded by perceptions that only made life hard
> for him to bear, did not even have the chance of submerging himself in the trou-
> bled frenzy that had anaesthetized Germany. Not because he was any cleverer,
> not because he was any better than the thousands who sought such a way out,

---

i   The name Eugen or Eugene originally means 'well-born'.

but because, by the chance of his birth, he was condemned to see things in all
their cold clarity. As half Jewish, Eugen Althager could not let the shouting of
the German crowd drug him, for that same crowd cast him out.(Sch. p. 53)

So we are shown the precise point at which Althager turns away from the 'shelter
of the forests' and constructs a new edifice of ideas for himself: he discovers that
'Metaphysics are atavism' (Sch. p. 48). Now all he cares for is the path of reason.
'What values had reason spared?' (Sch. p. 50.) 'All that is left to him,' comments
the narrator, 'is a heroic Nihilism, endurance despite the realization that everything is pointless. A harsh life without illusions, yet one that may not fall prey to
anarchy' (Sch. pp. 52–3).

    The omniscient narrator is not so omniscient after all. He expresses devout
wishes in his protégé's name, but the protagonist sinks lower and lower. Only
after a year with nothing to cling to is the Jew able to counter the negativity of
his life with the positive nature of his death. His dying wish is fulfilled when,
as a Jew, he stands up to a Fascist member of a student society. In fact, the duel
scene of the final chapter is nothing but a staging of the struggle between two
opposing mental principles:

> I sense your hatred, bull-headed fellow from the Uckermark that you are, I
> sense your noisy anger against us all. You hate us, we are ideas to you, abstracts,
> you hate our hopeless heroism – yes, heroism. But we can hate too, that hatred
> gives us our last strength (...) I too am not alone, I too say 'we'. Our hatred is
> bloody. We: ideas, abstracts. And that is at stake now, that alone. It is not about
> me any more, it is not about Eugen Althager, it means more, much, much more!
> (Sch. p. 375)

'The time is exactly a year after the beginning of the book,' says Hans
Mayer in his 1955 summary of the contents. 'A pointless life ends in an almost
grotesquely pointless death.'

    The ending is certainly 'grotesque' and 'pointless', yet it is not without a
certain dignity, a recurrent theme in Améry's work – one already heard in this
first novel. Neither narrator nor protagonist has any illusions. The process of
Althager's decline is described, almost clinically, up to his end. But his attitude
is not necessarily entirely nihilist. Althager as a Jew and a bourgeois who has
come down in the world, excluded from society twice over, so to speak, is not,
like the other 'shipwrecked' characters of the title, just a passive representative
of a world doomed to fall; he hastens its fall by seeking his death.

    His concern with suicide is one of the themes to emerge for the first time
in *Die Schiffbrüchigen*, and another is his 'compulsive' concern with his Jewish

identity. The relationship of mind and pain, mind and body – 'the mind failed entirely in the face of this pain' (Sch. p. 199) – is also explored even at this early date. How striking that these primal themes emerge so soon in his career.

History, for Améry, is always manufactured, and that also applies to historical acts of destruction – the repression of the Socialist workers, the persecution of the Jews – individual human beings are responsible for them. Althager too, for all his social determination, is partly responsible for his own wretchedness. Historical destiny never becomes an alibi for either Mayer or Jean Améry as writers of narrative.

The relationship to 'the Other'

In fact, this first novel provides more information about Améry's idea of the world than any of his later writings. This is not only because here he gives more rein to his imagination and tells a story for the reader to follow but also because human beings engage with each other. There is something like a fictional everyday background to the novel. In this sense it is fundamentally different from the prose that was to follow, which, as we shall see later, is not only considerably more abstract but – and this is perhaps Améry's outstanding characteristic as an essayist – also entirely in the nature of monologue.

Die Schiffbrüchigen cannot be described as a novel of dialogue, but the presence of a 'you' is part of it: Althager has two friendships to support him – one is his relationship of solidarity and apparent harmony with Agathe, and the other is his elective affinity with Hessl.[18] These friendships make up his life. He loves Agathe, or maybe thinks he loves her. However, when she is pregnant with his child he abandons her to her fate. Indeed, he deliberately destroys the relationship, and with it himself. The same can be said of his friendship with Hessl, to whom, for all his own wretched and dependent situation, he is constantly intent on demonstrating his moral superiority. Althager's egomania, which does not stop short of self-destruction, is a quality which, even at this early point in time, the author seems to share with his protagonist.

The female characters described here – besides Agathe, there is the submissive prostitute and 'concubine' Mimi, and the self-confident singer Doris Hechler – are more rounded than in later works. Sexuality plays a central part. However, there is also love – love of another living being expressed in the community of their hearts, minds and bodies. Non-conformist, emancipated and progressive as Althager likes to appear, his image of women as he knows them is more like that constructed by an authoritarian chauvinist: he longs for a lover who will think as he does, but she may think only in her capacity as his pupil and audience; in no case may she be intellectually ahead of him as the man. Her business is to give her philosophizing partner home comforts and warmth, supporting him psychologically, morally and financially. As long as Agathe plays that part, Althager's world is in good order. But as soon as she needs comfort and support herself, she must turn elsewhere.

Genophobia

The body, as well as the mind, is already a subject of this first novel: the body in pain, the body in desire, but never the body in joy, let alone in procreation. Agathe's reflections on pregnancy are especially poignant:

> Agathe [had] been standing naked in front of the mirror. She had been stroking her belly gently. Something was growing in it. (...) A plant-like sensation had overcome her, strongly and dreadfully. Is it growing already? she had thought, oh, disgusting, something is developing inside me, a horrible tadpole. It will crawl out of me, screaming, it will distend my body and suck at my breasts (...). I feel a creature growing in my well-formed body as a sickness, dirt, something vile deforming me.

She comes to the conclusion, 'I am a lover (...), a woman, I am not a mother. I hate those screaming, dirty little monsters' (Sch. p. 82).

This is the way the author, at 22, imagines ideas and experiences of approaching maternity. Yet this rejection of it already points to Améry's later writing. To him, irrespective of his experience of Auschwitz, the idea of procreating was appaling; the mere thought of a pregnant woman disgusted him, let alone the sight of one, as if the most primal form of life owed its existence to something of an unappetisingly animal nature. The physicality of living creatures repels him. One wonders whether this deep dislike of all that was not of the mind, surely for aesthetic rather than for ideological reasons, is not another aspect of his drive to self-destruction.

'Art should not describe life, but create life'[19]

Of course, Hans Mayer's main fictional characters, their remarks and actions, are not to be equated with the intellectual opinions of their author, particularly as the narrator's analyses are quite often critical of the conduct of the protagonists within the world of the novel. Yet we can discern approaches to a poetology in which the axes of Améry's future coordinates are clearly perceptible. This is particularly true of the basic atmosphere dominating the book, the alienation affecting all aspects of it, subjects that 30 years later find their way into *Jenseits von Schuld und Sühne* (1966, translated into English by Sidney Rosenfeld and Stella P. Rosenfeld as *At the Mind's Limits*) under very different historical conditions, in the headings of the following chapters 'On the Necessity and Impossibility of Being a Jew' and 'How Much Home Does a Person Need?' Other thematic complexes also begin here: Althager's meditations on suicide prefigure the *Diskurs über den Freitod* (1976, translated into English by John D. Barlow as *On Suicide*), which appeared 40 years later.

However, the scene in *Die Schiffbrüchigen* in which Althager's shoulder is dislocated in a Fascist-instigated brawl will seem to today's reader of Améry eerily prophetic, as if the author were anticipating his real experience of ten years later, even before Jean Améry reflects on it in his essay 'On Torture' (Sch. p. 325). In this anticipation the visionary Hans Mayer created more art than can have been comfortable for him.

Finally, Althager's story is also a prelude to the *Years of Wandering* (1971) and like that book, a Bildungsroman[ii] turned upside down: here the hero, with his nature anaesthetized, intellectually making his way from darkness to light, travels through his 'years of wandering' for the first time.

Die Schiffbrüchigen is valuable evidence that Améry's political and philosophical positions were formed early and were not just the outcome of his concentration camp experiences. A question arises: do they also exist independently of Améry's genesis as a writer? As a document of their time, they do, in fact, offer a rare insight into the inexorable rise and fall of Red Vienna in the early 1930s. They bring the modern reader close to the 'utility value' of positivism, a movement that is dismissed today as merely an abstruse construct of ideas. Much later, Jean Améry defines positivism, in all its variants, as an 'anti-metaphysical, anti-irrational view of the world, resting on the two pillars of empirical testing (or falsification) of the truth, and logical analysis. It is (...) the philosophy of the scientific concept of the world.'[20] He describes it as a 'non-dogmatic' and 'unsystematic' form of thought which is ready 'to question its own conceptual bases at any time'. In *Die Schiffbrüchigen* it appears as 'critical rationalism' and 'linguistic criticism'. We experience it, embedded as it is in the course of the novel, as a philosophy put to practical use, *applied* philosophy, as a democratic aid to life, education and culture, and as a political counterweight to the emergent Austrian Fascism of the time.

---

ii Bildungsroman: a novel describing a young man's development to adulthood.

The cultural scope of the novel, its complex philosophical combination of politics, sociology and psychology, corresponds to the self-reflexivity and contradictory nature of the heroic anti-hero Althager, as he grapples desperately with his period. The fact that this ideological state of collapse, which is what makes the book so modern as a study of the conscious mind, is not in any way transferred to the form or the style of the novel makes *Die Schiffbrüchigen* an aesthetic work of dubious value. It is as if its traditional narrative structure and conventional dialogue fall far behind the actuality of its contents. It will be another 40 years exactly, with *Lefeu oder Der Abbruch* [Lefeu, or The Demolition], before Améry is able to make the deconstruction of his characters go hand in hand with a deconstructing idiom.

1945: To be or not to be

Hans Mayer felt this imbalance between the content and form of his novel very clearly. *Die Schiffbrüchigen* gives him no peace, even during his time in the concentration camps. Having narrowly escaped death, the survivor makes the revision of his youthful novel into a test of his right to exist. In 1945 he writes to his long-lost friend Ernst Mayer:

> So I have ventured on it: it will be a novel whose skeleton is the recent unhappy history of our time, but – in contrast to the former *Die Schiffbrüchigen* – I have approached this 'pastime', as Thomas Mann would call it, with my mind fully opened up. I connect entirely freely with this fourth dimension of our existence – and find that I have given a comprehensive autobiographical account. It is the last and utmost that I have to offer. If it turns out well, there will be meaning to my life; if it is nothing, I will know that I myself am nothing.[21]

The stakes could not have been higher. And the profit? 'The recent unhappy history of our time,' is indeed merely a skeleton in the fragments we have, it is the framework, a stage set with occasional pieces of scenery. The 'flesh' of the novel is the 'myth of love'. Here Eugen Althager is directing the action; this time, like the author, he is a reluctant journalist. There is no narrator in charge, as in the first version; he speaks for himself and often also addresses himself as 'you', just as the later Améry does in dialogue with himself.

The occasional self-criticism of his predecessor, the Althager of the first version, is interesting. He wonders why he did not treat Agathe more affectionately:

> Was it because I was younger, because Agathe loved me more than I loved her? (...) Or was it because at the time I believed I had a mission giving me the right

to counter the dawning day with extensive silent monologues about the sufferings of the world?[22]

Althager's 1945 self-portrait is also revealing:

> In the shadows under the eyes, we see the death of Agathe; the twisted mouth is
> tightened by Carnap's logical structure of the world and by the glazed carp-like
> eyes of Gestapo Secretary Walter Altenhof; morning light from the peak of the
> Glockner lies on the forehead (...) Jewish forebears reside in the nose (...).

Auschwitz – a mass fate?

Elsewhere in the novel, in connection with his new lover Odette, Althager identifies himself as 'Prisoner 172364' – the number is the same as Hans Mayer's
in Auschwitz.[23] Should there ever have been any doubt of the autobiographical
character of the new version, there can be none now. His letter to his friend
Ernst Mayer stated in advance that his literary intention was to write 'a radical
autobiography'. The 'purpose of writing', as Althager defines it, is the 'purpose
of self-constitution'.

Besides the complete manuscript of 1935, Améry's literary estate contains
five handwritten prose passages which are all closely connected with this first
novel.[24] These are Hans Mayer's fragments of his *Recherche du temps perdu*, even
if no *Temps retrouvé* can be found in his work. Hans Mayer had thought that the
original manuscript was lost. Ten years separate the first version from these new
passages, ten endless years – the years of emigration, resistance, torture, imprisonment in the concentration camps and return to exile in Brussels. The reader of
the new text is surprised – one might expect more history, but the precise opposite is the case. There is hardly anything about imprisonment in the concentration camps. It is mentioned, yes; even his arrest is described in retrospect: 'You
pick up a few pamphlets and say, "I'll take these round to Marianne now."' Hans
Mayer was, in fact, arrested over the matter of some pamphlets in Brussels on
23 July 1943, together with the resistance fighter Marianne Brandt. ' "I'll be back
in half an hour (...)"' he assures his wife, who is trying to keep him from going:

> You step out through the door, there would still be time to turn back, but you
> step out (...). Ten minutes later you are facing the muzzles of three pistols, you
> put your hands up and are led away in handcuffs. (...) The trains race through
> the countryside (...) through many years, through an entire human life. They
> stop at the muddy and lonely abodes of Death (...).[25]

A few facts are given in these fragments, and some of those are described
more fully, but he never expresses all that is outrageous in what happened to

him. The few references remain surface mentions, merely stage setting. There is not a single reflection, at least not about these events.

The driving force behind this 'autobiographical fiction', the force dominating it, is 'the myth of a great love', and his 'memorial', which he raises to the status of a literary manifesto, is to 'the life of my (dead) wife'.[26] Here again he is making a connection, by association, with Proust's *Recherche*, in particular *Albertine disparue*.

The projected titles match this approach: *Dornenkrone der Liebe* [Love's Crown of Thorns], or *Die Distelkrone* [The Crown of Thistles]. In the foreground is the despair of a man returning from the war whose wife has disappeared – because she has been unfaithful? Because she is dead? Jealousy and a sense of humiliation drive the bereaved man into madness to the point of suicide. There is not a trace of objectivity, even of commentary on the action, not to mention the lack of authorial distance from the material. There is no attempt to present a historical event in literary terms, as he was still doing with Althager. Here an ego wounded to death cries out in highly subjective pain at the loss of the beloved and its own pointless survival. These are raw fragments, the unpolished emotional hinterland, of the brief statement made 20 years later in *At the Mind's Limits*: 'Once again (...) I was back in the world (...) after the death of the only person for whose sake I had held on to life for two years' (JSS Vol. 2, p. 89; AML p. 43). The 1945 narrative fragments have long since given up holding on to life and instead call on the 'deathly powers' that will bring extinction.

Yet the frenzy of love is presented in context. Very precisely, if in a deliberately derogatory manner, almost apologetically, the man returning home traces his fatal wanderings, thus giving his ordinary tragedy the stature of an extraordinary historical situation. 'The way it was' – these are the words with which the first-person narrator, who here is identical with Althager as a protagonist, introduces 'a letter sent into the unknown', a fictional letter dated 'Brussels, September 1945'.

> You will allow me to tell you the wretched odyssey of my life since this war began. It is not important. It is a fate of the kind reported by journalists, a mass fate long known to you from the newspapers.

He speaks of 'concentration camps, standing in line, deportation', of 'death, hunger, cold' and their 'diabolical and hateful simplicity'.

> I have experienced it, in others and in myself, and it has not made me more profound or more stupid, it has not made me any cleverer or more careless, it has not made me better or worse. Only the grief of the heart is left behind, a certain sense of being distraught, a stranger to this world.

'The soul,' the letter-writer begins again, 'or the mind have nothing to do with this bloodthirsty film. Nor does art (...)'. He imparts the only thing 'worth reporting' to his friend in a confidential tone:

> I have lost Beate. (...) Beate has gone. Vanished without trace, my dear friend, struck down by bombs? Died on a sickbed? Married to another man under a false name? I do not know (...) I have tried everything, have been to all the authorities.

This is, in fact, unfiltered autobiography: Hans Mayer lived for months in uncertainty about the mysterious disappearance of his wife, whom he expected to find in Brussels when he came back. Only many months later would he hear, through third parties, of her death and the circumstances leading to it:

> You see, this is *my* experience, unlike war and deportation in which I was only a supernumerary, scarcely any different from millions of others. Beate has disappeared, I have lost her. I shall not see her again. It is as if I had never had her.

Such a reversal of priorities, giving the torments of love precedence over the torments of the tortured prisoner, may disappoint today's readers, who perhaps expect a description of imprisonment in the camps, but from the point of view of a man returning from them it is understandable. Instead of bearing witness to the 'breach with civilization that was Auschwitz', the suffering of the journalist Althager centres on what he suspects to be his beloved's breach of faith with him.

However, there is one exception: a narrative fragment of 1945 bears the chapter heading *Journey around Death. The Fortress of Derloven*.[27] This is indeed a find, for there is no mistaking its close connection with the essay 'Torture', written 20 years later. The author is trying his hand at his first account of torture, solitary confinement and finally his first suicide attempt in the Belgian 'camp', the fortress of Breendonck. He had suffered these experiences himself barely two years earlier. There is mention of a 'meeting with the Grim Reaper', with whom Eugen Althager 'conducted a conversation on almost familiar terms'. Torture is described in detail.

An experience that covers seven pages in Hans Mayer's account of the process in 1945 is later condensed into 32 lines in 1966. Twenty years later, he has lost the self-certainty of the narrator of 1945:

> It would be totally senseless to try and describe here the pain that was inflicted on me. Was it 'like a red-hot iron in my shoulders', and was another 'like a dull wooden stake that had been driven into the back of my head'? One comparison

would only stand for the other, and in the end we would be hoaxed by turn on the hopeless merry-go-round of figures of speech. The pain was what it was. Beyond that there is nothing to say.

In 1945, when Hans Mayer was still very close to the event, he did not yet have any doubts of the ability of language to communicate it; he said 'everything', yet says so much less. The narrator simulates history, and in his simulation minimizes it. Because his documentary descriptions remain on the surface of the incident, because he is faithful to reality in his presentation of the course of the action, history becomes, to him, a descriptive account of events. In the essay, 'Torture', the text itself becomes the event, his memories do not represent the reality but are its subjective interpretation, the evaluation of a past trauma from the perspective of distance. Nowhere is it made so clear as in comparison of the descriptive presentation of torture in 1945, and the analytical account of it in 1966, that the autobiographical writing of history – for that is what we have in both Mayer's fiction and Améry's essays – is not primarily concerned with whether the facts can be verified but with the reconstruction of an interpreting ego who not only describes the pain but also investigates its causes and effects.

The Auschwitz discourse then and now

For a twenty-first century reader, Althager's playing down of his imprisonment in the camps could not be more revealing, giving as it does so much information on what a Jew could and could not say or write in 1945, indeed what he could and could not think or feel. Such an attitude could hardly document the history of memory and the history of the Auschwitz discourse more precisely. It illustrates the fact that the unique nature of the murder of the Jews, which now, 50 years later, stands at the centre of our culture of remembrance, was dismissed directly after the event as 'a mass fate', and indeed *had* to be thus dismissed. It was done, so to speak, with the collusion of the prisoners who had suffered racial persecution, because they had so wholly internalized the 'shame and disgrace' of their imprisonment. It was shame and disgrace because, unlike political prisoners, they did not know how to make moral capital out of their 'merely' passive role as victims. It is not mere chance that Hans Mayer puts the very episode in which he played a comparatively heroic part under the microscope: the account of his torture in Fort Breendonck for distributing pamphlets as a resistance fighter.

Not that he makes much of his resistance work – on the contrary, to a certain extent he derides his own naivety – but nonetheless he looks closely only at this part of his sufferings. All the other stages, from Malines, Auschwitz, and Buchenwald-Dora to Bergen-Belsen, are omitted. The struggle to recognize the racial killing of the Jews, the history of the degradation of the Jewish deportees and the way in which they were disdained and stigmatized lasted for 20 years.[28]

In these times of boom we have forgotten that the climate of the immediate post-war period was actually hostile towards the story of the sufferings of the Jews, that the deportation and survival of those racially persecuted victims – unlike that of political prisoners – was, if not exactly a disgrace in the public eye, at least a taboo subject. The French parliamentary deputy Simone Veil called the cover-up of the memory of the *déportés raciaux* 'a second death'.[29] In West Germany they did not receive a hearing until the Auschwitz trials in Frankfurt, at the same time as *At the Mind's Limits* was being written.

However, we are anticipating very distant events by looking at the rewriting of *Die Schiffbrüchigen* in 1945. We must return to pre-war Vienna. The bloody repression of the Socialist workers' uprising is a torch to the young writer, impelling him into his political initiation. Hans Mayer also decides on his stance on his Jewish identity and in 1937 – that is to say, after the implementation of the Nuremberg Laws – rejoins the Jewish community which he had left in 1933.[30] 'However, the reasons were not solely philosophical,' he admits; the discovery of his 'belonging to the Jewish race' had been hastened by his marriage in the Israelite Community on 12 December 1937 to Regine Berger (born 16.5.15), real surname Baumgarten, an office worker from Graz.

Regine Mayer-Berger

Hans Mayer's last registration form for residence in Vienna before his emigration

'No one will get me away from here,'[31] he swears. At the same time he is thinking: 'Finis Austriae (...). Is it over now? He knows it. Yet he stays in Vienna – until he is hunted out like a hare.'[32] The Anschluss of Austria to the German Reich makes Hans Mayer, aged 26, break with his country. In retrospect, Jean Améry sees it thus: 'An Austrian died in December 1938. May he rest as he was, not in peace.'[33]

The last registration form – he changed his place of residence in Vienna so often that there are about 20 of them – gives his address as Phorusgasse in the Fourth District, the place where he began at the Adult Education College and worked with his friend Ernst Mayer. He is reported as living there on 31 December 1938 – but the Vienna Registration Office has no information about his next address, and there is only a question mark here. That question mark is not just a symbol standing for Hans Mayer's emigration and his time in the camps; it is no less than a symbol standing for our own world history.

CHAPTER 4

Years of Wandering (1938–1945)

The Mind Knows No Limits

Vienna before and after the Anschluss

The Austrian who is hunted like a hare in 1938 does not really die but takes his version of Austria with him wherever he goes – first in pain, then in anger, then, again and again, in pain. He misses his native land above all because he does not have and may not have access to it; the land of his childhood and youth is suddenly denied to him as if it had never been his. 'I was no longer an I and did not live within a We.'[1]

> In December 1938 a friend turns up to visit me and my young wife in my tiny furnished apartment in Vienna, a colleague of my student days who had been attracted by the smart brown and black uniforms and was now himself a uniformed 'legal administrator'. He had some friendly advice for me.[2]

The advice is short and to the point: the recent events of Kristallnacht in the neighbouring country were just the start; Mayer would be well advised to disappear at once. And he does disappear, 'travelling with the lightest of baggage'. However, the hasty journey to the Westbahnhof in Vienna was only the ultimate outcome of a process that had begun on 30 January 1933.

It saddens Mayer to realize that his career as a writer, to which he has devoted himself, is over before it has ever really begun:

> For the novice, even if he had been a genius, which I neither was nor imagined myself to be, there was no chance. He wrote for his desk drawer, or at most for a small circle of friends, he placed a story or an article now and then in local newspapers and anthologies, he tried publishing a magazine of his own which was as ambitious as it was inexpertly edited (*Die Brücke*, author's note),

he wrote a novel (*Die Schiffbrüchigen*, author's note), whose remarkable fate did not include finding its way into print.[3]

So he lives at first in hiding, even delivering and giving houseroom to pistols and ammunition belonging to the defeated Republican Defence Corps, and withdraws into 'internal emigration'. He is still 'wholly Austrian', speaking in Austrian dialect and bearing the 'superlatively ordinary Austrian name' of Mayer.

'After the summer of 1934 a form of Fascism that was moderate by comparison with Nazism prevailed in Austria. A tiny little man called Dollfuss, upon whom even death by Nazi bullets has been unable to confer historical stature, set himself up as a reasonably easygoing dictator. He was followed by a Jesuit-educated intellectual, Kurt von Schuschnigg, a man of no pronounced views. The German style of Fascism was taken up in Austria: despotism mitigated by slackness. There was an SA, known as the Heimwehr [home guard], and there was something like Dachau at Wöllersdorf in Lower Austria. (...) Our Fascists merely dabbled in bestiality.'[4] Or so it seems at the start. Hans Mayer thinks he can 'survive the winter' of Hitler, sees himself living as 'a hermit in the mountains, or a farm labourer in the Marchfeld region'.

That is to change on 11 March 1938, the day of the Anschluss. The majority of the population greet their annexation by the Reich with enthusiasm, an enthusiasm that expresses itself in violent anti-Semitic agitation.[5] On 15 March Göring is appointed to head the Austrian economy, and on 18 March Himmler is empowered to seize Jewish property. A total of 444 Jewish organizations in Vienna and 181 in the provinces have to cease their activities.[6] Jews are dismissed from their positions in theatres, community centres, public libraries, universities and schools. On 1 April and 15 May, 110 figures in public life are deported to Dachau.[7] That year, from September onwards, Eichmann decides who may emigrate and who may not. On the day when Hitler overwhelms Austria, Jean Améry remembers, 'the people (celebrated) a festival of "German-ness" that lasted for weeks.'

Now Améry too entertains thoughts of emigration. But a passport, a visa, an affidavit – where is he to get those without money, connections, a knowledge of foreign languages? A school friend appears, proud of his position of power in the Office of Genealogy, and makes him an offer: 'You are not an observant Jew (...) there is an Aryan line in your family. I could fix something there,'[8] he says enticingly. Conditions follow the offer: first, a divorce from Mayer's Jewish wife. Second, his mother must make a declaration on oath that he, Hans, is not the son of his Jewish father but 'the offspring of her adultery with an Aryan'.[9] The offer is turned down. So he must try legal methods; after days of standing in line, they too prove hopeless. How is he to get out of his 'native land, now a battlefield'? 'The title of his unpublished novel, now lost in all manuscript copies, *Die Schiffsbrüchigen* [The Shipwrecked], fitted him like a glove. All that was left to him was to act out the role of the shipwrecked.'[10]

They go away, he and his young wife, without making any preparations, without money, armed only with invalid Austrian identity cards. In the crowded train he meets a companion more knowledgeable in matters of misfortune, who advises him to go to Brüsseler Strasse in Cologne – again, *nomen est omen* – where he will find a Jewish woman called Schmengler, said to have connections with those who are crossing borders. During the journey he sees daily life under the Nazis in Germany and is surprised by its 'firm anchoring in reality', its normality; he still has the picture of Austria revelling in its good fortune before his eyes. There is no trace here of Brecht's 'pale Mother Germany' groaning under the dictator's yoke – nothing but approval. Miracles happen: a stranger finds him a way of escape and demands 400 Reichsmarks for it; the family he has left behind sends the smuggled money and the stranger keeps his promise. Despite their lack of papers and against all the rules, the couple enters Belgium at the border town of Kalterherberg – the name, 'cold shelter', is pregnant with meaning – through the agency of a people-smuggler from Cologne. So this is how emigration begins.

Antwerp (1938–1940)[11]

He finds himself in Antwerp, one of 50,000 Jews. 'I was not a writer, not an intellectual, I had no name, no origin and (...) most certainly I had no future.'[12] The local Jewish Aid Committee[13] takes on his case: 'This Jewish colony, in which there were some very rich diamond merchants, but also poverty-stricken dealers in second-hand goods, showed almost incredible and inexhaustible generosity', writes Améry in 1969.[14] He particularly admires the generous stance of the Jews from Eastern Europe who, unlike the German and Austrian Jews, show solidarity with the new emigrants. He himself is still playing the part of a writer, knowing well that it is only a role he is acting:

> He gave classes in a room made available by the Jewish Aid Committee, calling them ironically rather than boastfully a 'seminar in intellectual history'. After his lectures on German Romanticism, on Neo-Positivism, on the realistic novel, one of his audience (...) took up a collection for him; the fee came to 50 Belgian centimes. What he had to offer was (...) not in great demand.[15]

Links are made with friends both old and new who have also fled to Antwerp: for instance, Jean Améry first meets Maria Eschenauer-Leitner, who will later

Rudolph Leitner and Maria Eschenauer: wedding picture, 3 August 1936

become his second wife, in Antwerp at the beginning of 1939. At this time she is the wife of the Austrian Rudolph Leitner, whom she married in Vienna in 1936. She later becomes a friend of Hans Mayer's first wife Regine (Gina). He also meets the Viennese painter Erich Schmid, to whom the writer of fiction will set up a memorial in his essay-novel *Lefeu oder der Abbruch* in 1974[16] – a photograph taken in 1939 records their friendship. We see three flâneurs, Erich, Regine and Hans: Hans Mayer in a very elegant suit and white spats, looking more like a fashion plate than a refugee from racial persecution living in the poor quarter of Antwerp. Furthermore, there is the Viennese doctor Heinz Pollak, one of the most important figures in Hans Mayer's life to the end. It is he who, in 1939, is the first to diagnose Gina's fatal heart defect, which will kill her in April 1944, a year before her husband's return from concentration camp.

War breaks out. 'I breathe again,' admits the refugee, tired of waiting for the catastrophe, for he would like to bring down 'this Reich of hatred and violence' with his own hands, with his own 'hatred and violence'. 'Are you ready to fight? (...) No one is readier than he, and he goes from committee to committee to volunteer.'[17] He wants to join the Belgian Resistance, but Belgium is neutral.[18]

Hans and Regine Mayer in Antwerp, 1939, with Erich Schmid, left

St. Cyprien – Gurs (1940–1941)

There is worse to come: on 10 May 1940 Belgium is attacked by German troops, and all German men – who in the eyes of the Belgians are 'enemy aliens' – must gather outside Antwerp Town Hall. Hans Mayer, Erich Schmid and Heinz Pollak are interned for five days in Malines, before being arrested and deported to France. Their first stopping-off point is the temporary Camp de St. Cyprien (Pyrénées-Orientales).

His wife Regine goes underground with the help of Maria Leitner. In 1947 Maria writes an article about Regine, who by then is dead (she died in 1944), and publishes it in the Viennese *Arbeiter-Zeitung* under the title of 'Belgischer Frühling 1940' [Belgian Spring 1940].

> Ever since the night when I had to leave you, shivering with cold, in the blacked-out concourse of Brussels Station, and waved a last goodbye to you from the window (...), ever since then I have carried the memory of the war in Belgium in May 1940 around with me, hoping for the day when we would meet again.[19]

They never did. Maria Leitner thinks back to the 'carefree days' she spent with Regine, to the evenings 'that you brightened for us with your songs'. They shared their hiding place in an attic room for ten months; it was 'the time of a good

Memorial placard of the internment camp Gurs

friendship'. In November 1941 Maria managed to escape to the United States. 'I would like to ask your forgiveness for being able to save myself,' she writes in this imaginary conversation with Regine Mayer:

> [w]hile you were left to the mercies of the storm, and I will confess that I was never really glad of my escape. (...) I felt it almost wrong to be in safety. Your death, and that of many millions of innocent victims, has imposed a duty on those who were saved, one that we must make our first commandment: to fight for humanity to become human!

On the way to St. Cyprien, according to Heinz Pollak in conversation with the author, a rumour circulates that the French were going to hand over all prisoners to the Germans at once, with the exception of Jewish men. So they will have to check who is and who is not circumcised. Hans Mayer is not. In the grip of fear that the French will not believe he is Jewish, he begs his friend Pollak, who is a doctor, to 'help' him in this matter – 'perhaps circumcision could be faked'. There was nothing that Pollak could do, but these fears were to turn out unfounded; no such inspection took place, and they were not handed over to the Germans.[20] As the transport takes them further on, Hans Mayer jumps from the moving train but is arrested and handed over to the French authorities.

The next stage of the journey is Gurs, Block C, Hut 3, France's first and largest internment camp, some 80 km from the Spanish border, originally a reception camp for Spanish Republicans in flight from Franco. He is interned there on 28 July 1940.

> The 'Garde Mobile' of the glorious French Republic received those who were fighting for Spanish freedom as if they were riffraff (...). Soldiers became prisoners. (...) And so, on the small plateau of Gurs, the camp came into being. It was erected with the functionality of misery.[21]

Twenty-eight years later, Jean Améry makes a pilgrimage to the Pyrenees.

> The traces are all erased. The visitor thinks, not without horror and a deep fear of death: grass has grown over my past, real grass has grown over it, and I always thought that was just a figure of speech.[22]

In fact, 'nothing (is) more deceptive than memory that dredges up an image, once it has registered itself on the mind, from the depths, while it extinguishes others. (...) It will produce only isolated crystals of life.'[23]

One such 'crystal of life' is surely the fact that despite his wretchedness, Hans Mayer, with a fellow prisoner, succeeds in 'digging up an anthology of late nineteenth and early twentieth-century German poetry out of his head, writing it down on small scraps of paper in the darkness of night'.[24] With the Viennese philosopher Georg Grelling he sets to work on 'jointly writing a book on Neo-Positivist philosophy.'[25]

Flight to occupied Belgium

The Gurs camp, Jean Améry insists, was *not* a concentration camp along the same lines as Dachau, Buchenwald, Mauthausen and other such places.[26] 'The mind's limits' had not been reached here as they were in Auschwitz. In spite of the harsh living conditions there were many cultural activities: concerts, theatrical performances, language classes, lectures, even exhibitions.[27] 'They never practised the refinements of cruelty. We were left to starve and freeze in peace. France was still lovely under its unlovely new masters – *la douce France*, even in Gurs.'[28]

It was also 'lovely' enough for Améry to try escaping from the camp on 6 June 1941. It would be easy, his fellow prisoner Jacques Sonnenschein assured him, to break out of the camp; much more difficult were the actual logistics of the escape itself. Indeed, surviving the escape proved to be the real art of it.[29] They slunk away to the toilets in the dark and from there got out of the camp. Rain is the great enemy, as he tells in his story, for the French shut up their barns, and there is nowhere for uninvited guests to take refuge. In Bidache the authorities took pity on them; the commandant was an Austrian. In Bayonne they were imprisoned by the Germans. At the end of August they were released and went to Paris by way of Bordeaux. There the Jewish community helped them and enabled them to return to occupied Belgium, where their wives were waiting, longing to see them.

> In Brussels, hair as red as tea falling softly over her cheeks, a smile that brightens the world at even the most terrible moments of life, a slightly freckled, very white skin. That is enough to make anyone set course for the sabre-rattling new lords of Europe.[30]

This is his only description of Regine. His beloved wife, with her hair as red as tea, living at 49 rue de Livourne in Brussels, is just managing to scrape a living as a bra saleswoman. In September 1941 he holds her in his arms again; the dangerous odyssey has lasted four months. Naturally they are still in deadly danger; the occupying power is everywhere, rejoicing in spectacular victories, but when victory turns to defeat they call for collaboration against British and American imperialism. To keep from starving to death, Hans Mayer does occasional work as a furniture remover[31] and then as a German teacher at the Ecole Moyenne Juive de Bruxelles.[32]

Resistance in Brussels

Some time ago he has made contact with the Communist Resistance movement, as he had been trying to do even before he was first arrested. 'At the time when Hanns Mayer first joined us, the group had about 30 to 40 members,' according to Gundl Herrnstadt-Steinmetz.[33] It was Hans Mayer's task, she said, to edit the four-page Resistance newspaper *Die Wahrheit* [The Truth], together with Marianne Brandt, and write material to be duplicated. He now offers his services to the Austrian Freedom Front in Brussels, under the cover name of Roger Lippens.[34] Marianne Brandt, a German girl ten years his junior who had joined the group even before the occupation of Belgium, had strong literary interests, we are told; she and Hans Mayer 'always worked together as a team'.[35] The printing works, as they called the Gstettner printing machine, even stood in her apartment for some time. Jacques Sonnenschein was also involved. He remembers nocturnal ventures – for Jews were not allowed out on the streets after 8 pm – in which they tried to distribute material encouraging agitation in the right places. Suitable locations for distribution were the barracks quarters and the rue Américaine, where there was a large car repair workshop.

Entrance to Breendonck

Breendonck (1943)

On 23 July 1943, the moment comes. Just under three years after his first detention, Hans Mayer and Marianne Brandt, one of the most fearless of the women
activists – it was she who had originally put him in touch with the Austrian
Resistance group – are arrested by the Gestapo.[36] 'It was a matter of flyers,' Jean
Améry reconstructs the incident 20 years later:

> The group to which I belonged, a small German-speaking organization within
> the Belgian resistance movement, was spreading anti-Nazi propaganda among
> the members of the German occupation forces. We produced rather primitive
> agitation material, with which we imagined we could convince the German
> soldiers of the terrible madness of Hitler and his war. Today I know, or at least
> believe I know, [he mocks himself in 1965] that we were aiming our feeble mes-
> sage at deaf ears. I have much reason to assume that the soldiers in field-grey
> uniform who found our mimeographed papers in front of their barracks clicked
> their heels and passed them straight on to their superiors, who then, with the
> same official readiness, in turn notified the security agency. And so the latter
> rather quickly got on to our trail and raided us. One of the fliers that I was
> carrying at the time bore the message, as succinct as it was propagandistically
> ineffectual, 'Death to the SS bandits and Gestapo hangmen!'[37]

The tone of this retrospective account has understandably given considerable
offence to his surviving Resistance colleagues, in particular Gundl Herrnstadt-
Steinmetz, who complains, in her introduction to the volume of documents

Torture chamber in Breendonck

entitled *Österreichischer Widerstand im Exil. Belgien 1938–1945*, that Améry's account of this period is 'not precisely flattering'. But this does not prevent her from directing the reader at the same time to Améry's book *At the Mind's Limits*, describing it as 'acknowledged to be the best book about this period'.[38]

After his arrest, Hans Mayer is taken to Gestapo headquarters in the Avenue Louise, now the most elegant shopping street in the capital of the European Union, where he is interrogated. Accomplices? Addresses? He gives nothing away, neither then nor later. As a political prisoner, he is sent off that same day to Detention Cell 13 in Breendonck, where he stayed until 2 November 1943. 'There I experienced it: torture.'[39]

Torture in the novel (1945)

What exactly he 'experienced' on 23 July 1943 finds written expression twice in his works, first in the 'fictionalization' of 1945 and again in the now canonical essay 'Torture' written in 1965. In the new version of his novel *Dornenkrone der Liebe*, which he describes to Ernst Mayer as 'radical autobiography', the former concentration camp inmate has just returned to his Belgian exile. The fragment mentioned in the last chapter, 'Reise um den Tod: Die Festung Derloven' [A Journey around Death: The Fortress of Derloven], is thus his first attempt to convey the subject in 'telling the tale' of his alter ego Eugen Althager's torture in Breendonck.

It begins pleasantly, with an idyllic picture of the Flemish scenery bathed in tones of gold, blue and green: 'Between Mechelen and Antwerp, a gentle

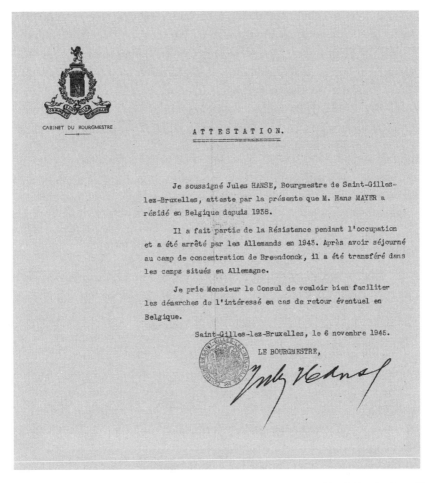

Certification of Hans Mayer's wartime activities issued by the Mayor of St. Gilles–lez–Bruxelles

CERTIFICATION

I, the undersigned Jules HANSE, Mayor of Saint-Gilles-les-Bruxelles, do hereby confirm that Monsieur Hans Mayer resided in Belgium from 1938 onwards.

He was a member of the Résistance during the occupation, and was arrested by the Germans in the year 1943. After being held in Breendonck concentration camp he was transferred to other camps in Germany.

I would like to ask the Consul, should the above-mentioned Hans Mayer return to Belgium, to assist him in all the necessary procedures.

Saint-Gilles-les-Bruxelles, 6 November 1945
The Mayor
Jules Hanse

landscape flows in calmly undulating fields and meadows. Brooks with willows growing beside them run gently through it.' He speaks of 'the faintly quivering sky' and 'the Flemish light, damp and matt silver, falling to earth'. The 'heavy Brabant farm horses' that 'stride on with high, powerful croups'[40] lead almost without transition to the 'menacing half-moon mouths, emerging from the ground' of the 'heavily barred small windows' of 'the worst camp in Europe'.[41] The tempo of the narrative accelerates to the point of paroxysm. A spectrum of the most refined forms of death is listed here:

> Derloven was a battlefield of death. Of slow and fast death, of death by starvation and cold, of the sudden apoplexy of fear, of death by the snapping of the spine and the neck, death by breaking on the wheel of torture, death by revolver shot, death by kicking with boots, and death by the comparatively humane method of shooting by firing squad carried out in due form.[42]

From the general he moves on to the particular: 'It was there (...) that in the past Eugen Althager looked death in the eye, as we say.'[43] The narrator has taken even the authentic date from his author: 'He (Althager; author's note) was tortured there that day, 23 July 1943. It was nothing out of the ordinary,' he says, adjusting the historical perspective, in case the reader has forgotten that the criteria of normality became their precise opposite between 1933 and 1945, 'insofar as we are inclined to describe the derangement of Derloven as the ordinary attitude that it undoubtedly was for its masters.'[44] Now the narrator comes to the methods of torture reserved especially for the hero of his novel. The technically perfect construction of the instrument of torture is precisely described, and so is its functioning. Passages crossed out in the manuscript reflect Hans Mayer's difficulty in phrasing this description:

> Classic torture was inflicted on Eugen Althager. He [was] bound, and a ten-inch long iron hook was attached to the steel shackle holding his hands behind his back. This hook in turn was fastened to a chain hanging from a winch in the ceiling. The chain was pulled up, and his bound hands rose behind his back, until the delinquent, to avoid the dislocation of his arms, had to exert all his muscular power (...) to support and maintain his own weight with his arms stretched behind him, as he hung about half a metre above the floor.[45]

This state of hovering lasts only a few seconds until Althager's arms – with a 'rushing' and 'cracking' sound – spring out of the joint sockets. The pain is 'murderous' and causes total 'confusion of the senses', which plunges him into 'fervent respect for his torturers', he screams for help, 'madly appealing to their sense of human kindness'.[46] His call is heard: 'one of the functionaries took a metre-long oxhide whip with a lash as thick as your arm and brought it down with all his might on the man swaying as he hung there.'[47] This 'ceremony' lasts about half an hour, and 'then Eugen Althager lost consciousness'. The prisoner is thrown into his cell, bound.

Once conscious again, he considers his situation. His guard speaks his own language. 'The two men, one standing upright, one beaten into the ground, the prisoner and his guard [spoke] the same dialect, in the same low-voiced and fearful tone.'[48] The Wehrmacht soldier leaves the cell and a moment later throws a burning cigarette in through the barred window for him. Sudden happiness overcomes Althager, inspiring his decision to take his own life, for he knows that in a second interrogation under torture he will give away anything he is asked. Next all the stages of his (unsuccessful) attempt to commit suicide are described. The piece of 'metal corroded with rust' found in his cell is too blunt for him to cut his wrists with it but sharp enough for self-mutilation. Furthermore, the friendly soldier preserves him from the worst. Althager comes to the conclusion that he was trying his 'venture with the piece of metal' only to divert danger from his girlfriend Agathe, not because he really wanted to die. Finally, he is able to divert danger from Agathe without killing himself. He produces an invented tale convincing enough to satisfy the authorities. 'The prisoner became a teller of fairy tales,' the narrator says. 'It was an absolute triumph of mind over matter.'[49]

Torture in the essay (1965)

Twenty years later, the author of the essay knows better. Without a doubt, 'matter' triumphs over the mind here. It is physical pain, it is the body, or more precisely it is the flesh in pain that extinguishes the spirit. The aesthetic imagination celebrating its triumph in the fictional Derloven is powerless in the real fortress of Breendonck; to quote Améry himself, nothing can now bridge the gap between *Death in Venice* and death in Auschwitz. The sovereign power of the torturer presupposes the negation of the tortured; the torturer literally decides on his victim's life or death. In contrast to the fictional version, Améry's essay leaves out the biographical aspect to distil a fundamental paradigm.

Only a posteriori does he realize how great the gulf is between ideas before the event and the real experience of it. At the time of his arrest on 23 July 1943 in Brussels, Hans Mayer is quite sure that 'there could be nothing new for me in this area. (...) Prison, interrogation, blows, torture; in the end, most probably death. Thus it was written and thus it would be.'[50] However, when prison, interrogation, blows and torture actually take place, the discrepancy between the idea of these events and suffering them in reality is so incommensurable that the one can hardly be reconciled with the other. In the imagination, however close it may come, the anticipated reality, for all the mind's flights of fantasy and poetic intensification, ultimately remains a 'ciphered abstraction'.

The essay 'Torture' has its own dramatic form, a dramatic form that is in a hurry and does not proceed chronologically but depends on leaps in time – first the event and then its consequences in the present. There is no landscape-painting prelude to delay events, as in 'Die Festung Derloven', no narrator – the self speaks in the essay, a self with no guarantor. The precision of the style is astonishing, particularly in translating feelings into words.[51] The writer aims for a certain procedure: first inquiry (how did I get here?) and then communication: historical and philosophical, existential. Memory is not called upon to simulate feelings here, memory forms only through the interpretation of the story. The interrogation of the victim by his torturer becomes, in the later essay, an interrogation of the victim by himself.

In the essay 'Torture', the victim Hans Mayer understands himself in general as a victim of National Socialism, not a specifically Jewish victim as in his later writings. There is a difference here, for the Jewish victim is excluded from the outset from the general human condition.[52] 'Torture,' Améry points out, was 'the essence of National Socialism,' it was not its invention, but 'its apotheosis'.[53] Only in inflicting torture does the 'Hitler vassal' achieve his full identity.

> For National Socialism (...) was the only political system of this century that (...) had not only practised the rule of the anti-man, as had other Red and White terror regimes also, but had expressly established it as a principle. (...) The Nazis tortured, as did others, because by means of torture they wanted to obtain information important for national policy. But in addition they tortured with the good conscience of depravity. (...) They placed torture in their service. But even more fervently they were its servants.[54]

The 'first blow' appears, to Améry, as the quintessence of de-individualization. He establishes an example:

> In the end, we would be faced with the equation: Body = Pain = Death, and in our case this could be reduced to the hypothesis that torture, by which we are turned into body by the other, blots out the contradiction of death and allows us to experience it personally.[55]

Extreme isolation, a lasting sense of abandonment, is the result of torture. However, Améry's conclusion is anything but hypothetical: 'Whoever was tortured, stays tortured. (...) 22 years later I am still dangling over the ground by dislocated arms (...).'[56]

Auschwitz – Dora-Mittelbau – Bergen Belsen (1944–1945)

After the torture chamber comes solitary confinement. The remark 'Subversion of the military forces' is noted on his Gestapo file. This is the offence that has brought him to Breendonck. On 2 November 1943 he is transferred to the Dossin barracks in the transit camp at Malines.[57] It is a reception camp for Belgian Jews before their deportation east. Here he will first meet the physicist Ilya Prigogine, professor of physical chemistry at the Université libre de Bruxelles, later a Nobel Prize winner. Prigogine is freed, and out of friendship he gives Hans Mayer his coat when he says goodbye. It was the natural thing to do, he jokes later in conversation, making light of his generosity, there's no need for me to mention it in my biography.[58]

For Hans Mayer, however, it all continues. In a letter of 9 December 1943, the head of Military Administration in Belgium and northern France asks the representative of the head of the Security Police and the Security Service whether 'a ban on professional work' should be issued against the 'former language teacher Hans Maier', or whether 'it can be expected that M. will remain in detention for the duration of the war'.[59] The representative, SS Obersturmführer Hartnagel, informs the 'Military Commander in Belgium and Northern France' that Hans Maier is 'a Communist functionary who until his arrest was involved in the production of illegal Communist writings. He is a Jew, and as such will be transferred from here.'[60] The political prisoner was tortured as an individual; his survival was in the hands of his torturer. The Jew is not an individual any more but is by definition marked down to be murdered. His reception form for Breendonck still bears the remark 'Religious affiliation: Evangelical.' Once

Ilya Prigogine

unmasked as a Jew, Hans Mayer is deported to Auschwitz on 15 January 1944, as Prisoner 379, on Transport No. XXIII, comprising 655 people. He arrives on 17 January.

An unpublished text, 'Zur Psychologie des deutschen Volkes' [On the Psychology of the German People], partly conceived in the camp, tells us the story:

> Auschwitz concentration camp, January 1944: on the arrival of a transport of several hundred Jews, men, women, and children, they are divided up in the usual way by SS men. First of all, men capable of working are separated from women, the children and the elderly. Then this second group is divided by taking children away from their mothers (...). One woman (...) suddenly breaks away from her companions, her hair coming down, her gestures tragic, already showing visible signs of the onset of mental disturbance, and screams for her children. (...) She reaches one of the SS men on guard. 'My child,' she says, 'haven't you seen my child anywhere?' 'You want a child?' replies the SS man with perfect composure. 'Wait a minute.' And he goes, very slowly, towards the group (...) of children. Bending down, he picks up a boy of about four by the foot. He lifts him and swings him several times through the air, shattering the child's little head against an iron pillar (...).[61]

Hans Mayer himself is assigned to a labour detachment in the Auschwitz-Monowitz camp, as Prisoner 172364.[62] Of the 655 members of this group, 417 are murdered at once.

In June 1944, six months later, he is moved to the Buna works as a clerk because of his 'abilities as a writer'. This is also the point when he becomes aware of the presence of Primo Levi. A second unpublished text, 'Arbeit macht unfrei' [Work will make you unfree], gives an account of this period of his imprisonment:

> I have been working for several weeks as a clerk, so-called, in the office of an I.G. Farben factory under construction. As before, of course, I am a perfectly ordinary concentration camp prisoner, I have to stand on the parade ground for hours, I get 200 grams of bread and two servings of watery soup a day, and am no different in outward appearance from my comrades dragging cement sacks about or loading coal. It just so happened that among about 1000 employees of the factory, there were very few able to master German orthography.[63]

Chance played into his hands, giving him this opportunity not to carry cement sacks any more, and not, like the great majority of prisoners, to be beaten for working too slowly. Out of solidarity with that abused majority he expresses indignation to his superior in the office over the murderous conditions of labour which the other prisoners continue to suffer. 'Well, Mayer,' says Master Pfeifer,

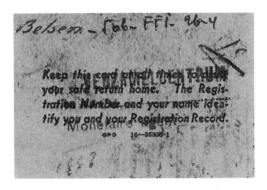

Temporary identity card, made out by the British Armed Forces

'that's not the way to look at it. You can't please everyone. But the work has to be done, Mayer, I'm expected to work myself.'[64] His protest could have cost him his life, but Master Pfeifer is kindly disposed to him.

In mid-January 1945, the Soviet army begins its offensive. Auschwitz-Monowitz is evacuated between 17 and 26 January. Hans Mayer is forced to take part in the march to Gleiwitz II on foot, and then on an open rail transport to the province of Saxony. Between 1 and 4 February 1945 he is taken to Dora-Mittelbau as Prisoner 108327. Early in April, in an evacuation-move, the inmates of this camp too are transported, again on open rail trucks, this time to Bergen-Belsen. The transport leaves Mittelbau on 5 April. Finally, Bergen-Belsen is liberated by the British on 15 April.

> A jeep drives into the underworld. A sergeant of military police with a red cap and a sandy moustache that gives him a gruff appearance announces, through a loudspeaker: From now on this camp is under the protection of His Britannic Majesty's fighting forces.[65]

Even 25 years later, he is overcome by gratitude at the thought of it. He has spent 642 days in German concentration camps; so much for the facts.

Wherever Hans Mayer / Jean Améry remembers his personal sufferings, in both the novel of 1945 and the essays written 20 years later, a clear hierarchy of horror crystallizes. Torture leaves an indelible signature on the individual's identity, and the experience of the camps takes on the appearance of a 'mass fate'. He is already calling it that in the 'Brief ins Ungewisse' [Letter into the Unknown], which is a kind of preface to the fragment of a novel 'Reise um den Tod' [Journey around Death].

> Please allow me to tell you the wretched odyssey of my poor life from the beginning of this war. (...) It is a mass fate, long known to you from newspapers, (...). A standard fate (...) suitable for a novel of political propaganda, marked by those

rough, surreal feelings that we call elemental, and even the fact that I experienced them cannot induce me to take an interest in them.[66]

The intellectual Althager is far above 'novels of propaganda' expressing 'rough, elemental feelings'. He sees his attitude better expressed in the phrase 'culture is differentiation', and his experience of Auschwitz could not change that, for after all '[it] affected E.A. only as a contemporary; it did not go very deep into his own intellectual destiny'.[67] There are undoubtedly several reasons for Améry's wish to distance himself from summary descriptions of mountains of corpses, and certainly, as previously mentioned, the historical climate of the immediate post-war period plays an important part here. No one wanted to know about the liberated Jewish inmates of the concentration camps; they should be glad to have survived, the Germans had enough worries of their own. For all its ambivalence, this defensive German attitude – although giving extreme offence to the victims – did to some extent, if inadvertently, meet the survivors' needs. For they too now had to try building a new future – although they would have liked the *opportunity* of communicating rather than having silence imposed on them. As Ruth Klüger in *weiter leben* [Still Alive] said:

> We all joined in the suppression of the past, even if former prisoners connived in it less than those who had remained free, while the former perpetrators suppressed it most of all. The ground was too hot for all of us, and we almost all moved on to new things (...).[68]

But besides the suppression of the past forced by necessity, there is an injury of an entirely different kind to explain Améry's apparent banalization, for at heart this offhand gesture is nothing but a stifled protest against a never-ending chain of injustices. In 'The Fortress of Derloven' we learn more about the real nature of this disparaging approach.

> Eugen Althager thought seldom and only unwillingly of his experiences in wartime and the camp. Not so much because they had been painful – his principal state of mind was painful – but because that part of his life was not his own any more. His knowledge of that time had been stolen from him by cinema newsreels showing horrors to a large and horrified audience before showing an enjoyable feature film, by newspaper articles, by countless books about hell, the hell of Belsen, the hell of Mauthausen, Buchenwald, Gross-Rosen, Auschwitz, Ebensee, the hell of Derloven.[69]

He is arraigning all that usurps the experience of Auschwitz. Films, the popular press, banal books, and the mass media in general, avid for sensation, have 'stolen' Althager's personal property from him. With their vociferous falsifications, those who were not in the camps and those who may even have been the perpetrators of horrors there have cheated him of that part of his life.

Jean Améry / Primo Levi – an excursus

What is true of Althager is, mutatis mutandis, also true of Hans Mayer / Jean Améry. It was not just the coarsening effect of 'reports', written by sensation-mongers with no real authority, that deprived him of what was his own. More important is the 'theft' from him committed by a very sophisticated initiate, a man who also knew all about it and who got his word in first with his own account. I am speaking of Améry's fellow prisoner Primo Levi and his ground-breaking work *If This Is a Man*, published in Italy as early as 1947 and in Germany in 1961, which set the tone for discussion of Auschwitz five years before Jean Améry was to attract attention with his own account in *At the Mind's Limits*. The tense relationship between the two 'professional Auschwitz inmates', as Jean Améry ironically describes the public perception of his role,[70] can be traced back not the least to these circumstances. Primo Levi, to some extent, had 'stolen the show' from him. Perhaps, without his predecessor, Jean Améry's 'Auschwitz diaries' would have been different. In 1966, when in *At the Mind's Limits* Améry reflects on this time in his very different style of thinking and writing, he is building, whether consciously or unconsciously, on Levi's memoirs to the same extent as he uses them as a launching pad, continuing analytically from the inimitable concrete basis created by Levi.

However, the shadows lying over this relationship were to grow longer and longer, even after the death of both men. Primo Levi reacts to Améry's volume of essays with total incomprehension. Améry, for his part, angry with Levi's 'narrow-mindedness', pays him back in the same coin in his letter to a third party, their joint friend Hety Schmitt-Maas, who herself has spoken enthusiastically to Améry of her first meeting with the man from Turin. She praises Levi's cheerfulness, his 'wonderful sense of humour', his easy command of himself, his relaxed attitude. 'Perhaps I am mistaken, but Levi seemed to me entirely free of resentment (...) standing above such things.'[71] She was bound to provoke Améry with this catalogue of qualities – 'free of resentment'! – all characteristics that Améry cannot or will not show. Yet with the best of intentions, she had wanted to forge a link between her 'two new friends'. Instead, she found herself confronted with two rivals competing for her approval.

Améry's reply to Schmitt-Maas opens with notable self-control: 'I was greatly moved to hear that, as I gather from your letter to Langbein' – the resistance fighter and former Auschwitz inmate Hermann Langbein was the third in the trio[72] – 'you have seen Primo Levi. I myself do not know him as the post-Auschwitz Levi, who must be quite a different man from the one I met in the hut at Monowitz. We exchanged letters only once. As chance would also have it,' says Améry, referring as casually as possible to the wound dealt him by his colleague; 'I received from quite a different quarter a document in which he [Primo Levi; author's note] spoke of my book *At the Mind's Limits* without any understanding at all, and showed himself disposed to drown everything in ontological jargon. Unlike Levi,' he says, preparing to retaliate, 'I am not a man to forgive, and have no sympathy for the gentlemen who belonged to the "management staff" of IG Auschwitz. But enough of that.'[73]

In Jean Améry's eyes, then, Primo Levi was a 'man who forgave', an attitude that Améry thinks he deduces not only from Levi's book but also from the fact that he was in correspondence with one Dr F. Meyer, who had belonged to the 'management staff of IG Auschwitz' at the time of his arrest in 1944 and who remained in Primo Levi's memory as a 'humane' man. This 'gentleman' (Dr Meyer) now writes a letter to Jean Améry after reading his book *At the Mind's Limits*, and it reaches Améry at the same time as Hety Schmitt-Maas's account of her first meeting with Levi. He chooses more moderate language in writing to this 'hostile' outsider but in no way retracts his denunciation of Primo Levi:

> I can understand that Primo Levi's book, which I too greatly admire, spoke more eloquently to you than mine. Levi's greater readiness to be reconciled may well arise from the fact that he is an Italian, and Italians of certain classes were not affected by imprisonment and all that went with it, while my own cultural background is German. To put it in plain and even crude terms: an inn which we do not want to visit is of no interest to us if it refuses us entry, but when it is our own regular inn and the landlord throws us out, we cannot feel the same lack of concern.[74]

Levi too feels that he has been misunderstood. In an interview, he vigorously rejects Améry's comment that he shows 'readiness to be reconciled':

> I have been trying for 40 years to understand the Germans. To understand how all this could come about is one of my purposes in life (...). Forgiveness is not a word to be associated with me. (...) General forgiveness, which is expected of me, is not in my nature. Who are the Germans? I am not a religious believer; absolution has no precise significance. No one, not even a priest, has the power to justify and forgive anything. (...) A man who commits a crime must pay for it, or at least must show genuine remorse. But not with words. Words of remorse are not enough. I will forgive a man whose actions have shown that he is now someone different. And has not left it too late.[75]

Levi's earlier public argument with Améry is more amicable only on the surface:

[Jean Améry; author's note] was (...) sent to Monowitz-Auschwitz, the same Lager in which I too would be imprisoned a few months later. Even though we never saw each other again, we exchanged several letters, having recognized, or, more accurately, come to know each other through our respective books. Our memories of down there coincide reasonably well on the plane of material details, but they diverge on one strange fact: I, who have always maintained that I preserve of Auschwitz a total, indelible memory, have forgotten his appearance; he declares that he remembers me, even though he confused me with Carlo Levi, who at that time was already well known in France as a political exile and painter. Indeed, he says that for a few weeks we lived in the same hut, and that he did not forget me because the Italians were so few as to constitute a rarity; furthermore, since in the Lager, during the last two months, I basically exercised my profession, that of chemist, and that this was an even greater rarity.[76]

Levi's biographical knowledge of Jean Améry is scanty, not to say defective; he obviously knows nothing of Améry the self-taught man, whose education was acquired in a highly idiosyncratic way. To Levi, he is something of a parvenu German intellectual who 'obtained his degree in literature and philosophy in Vienna'.[77] In the opening words of Levi's essay 'The Intellectual in Auschwitz', published just before his death, one senses an ambivalence between virtual proximity and factual distance: 'To argue with a dead man is embarrassing and not very loyal. It is all the more so when the absent one is a potential friend and a most valuable interlocutor.' Améry *could* have been a potential friend, he *could* have been a valuable interlocutor, but he was not. He never became such a friend and interlocutor, and there are reasons for it.

The concordance of their lives arises primarily from persecution and resistance, deportation and forced labour, and not least from 'the cruellest irony', writes W.G. Sebald, from 'the burden of survival', which perhaps caused them to choose the same end.[78] They would have had little in common in their theories and practice of life, Sebald continues, not even their Jewish identity, which for Levi at least consisted of a framework of family traditions, whereas for Améry it was nothing but pure abstraction. What makes them appear comparable seems here to arise from the 'distortions' of their time.[79]

However, there were some very real differences; one was an Italian and a natural scientist, and came from the secure, prosperous Jewish upper middle class with its built-in intellectual options. The other was an Austrian German of the lower middle class on his way down to membership of the proletariat, with

gaps in his education, fatherless, without money or a country to call his own –
even his Jewish identity had to be worked out *ex negativo* – and made his way
from nothing, through confused social notions of belonging to the Alpenland
rural tradition, and on to 'French *clarté*'. Not only were Améry's origins inse-
cure from the start, his 'future', by comparison with Levi's, was more extreme
in three important points: through his betrayal by his own countrymen, which
ruled out any immediate return to Vienna after the war; through his exile in
Belgium; and, even more importantly, through his torture. For Levi, on the
other hand, it was perfectly natural to return to his mother tongue and his
family in Turin.

   Yet they were close enough to inflict deliberate injuries on each other, injuries that Levi seeks to clothe in intellectual argument. Primo Levi's 'contrasting'
analysis of the camp, by a man whose kindliness is able to win over others as well
as Hety Schmitt-Maas, is astonishing in its unconcealed aggression. He presents
his essay as a discussion and criticism of Améry's own, which he describes as
'bitter' and 'icy' (Italian: *gelido*).[80]

   He is referring to Améry's legendary essay 'At the Mind's Limits', written
in 1966, the essay that was to make him a much-courted German writer over-
night. It is also the only essay by Améry that, after his summary 'treatment'
of the subject of the camps in his fictional text 'The Fortress of Derloven', sets
out, looking back over 20 years, to study the power of the mind to resist in the
extreme situation of Auschwitz, a subject that has concerned him ever since he
wrote *Die Schiffbrüchigen*.

Friends strange to each other

'Did intellectual background and an intellectual basic disposition help a camp
prisoner in the decisive moments? Did they make survival easier for him?'[81] Jean
Améry comes to the clear conclusion not only that the intellectual was much
worse qualified to deal with the physical slave labour demanded of him but
also that on the very grounds of his analytical intellect he was doomed to self-
destruction. In Auschwitz 'the intellect very abruptly lost its basic quality: its
transcendence'.[82] He uses a line by Hölderlin as demonstration. At the sight of
a flag waving, he murmurs, like an incantation, 'The walls stand speechless and
cold, the flags clank in the wind.' But the sound of the words is no longer what
it was, it remains silent: 'The poem no longer transcended reality. There it was
and all that remained was objective statement; there it was, and the Kapo roars
"left", and the soup was watery, and the flags are clanking in the wind.' Not only
did German culture belong to the enemy, which was bad enough, but also 'where
the subject, faced directly with death through hunger or exhaustion, is not only

de-intellectualized, but [also] in the true sense of the word dehumanized,'[83] the mind must fail as it faces reality.

With Levi it is the reverse. In his memory, he gives himself up to delight when he succeeds in reciting lines from the 'Canto of Ulysses' in Dante's *Divine Comedy* to his French friend Jean, known as Pikolo:

> Here, listen Pikolo, open your ears and your mind, you have to understand, for my sake: 'Think of your breed; for brutish ignorance / Your mettle was not made; you were made men, / To follow after knowledge and excellence.' As if I also was hearing it for the first time: like the blast of a trumpet, like the voice of God (...) [Levi the agnostic remembers]. For a moment I forget who I am and where I am. Pikolo begs me to repeat it. How good Pikolo is, he is aware that it is doing me good. Or perhaps it is something more: perhaps, despite the wan translation and the pedestrian, rushed commentary, he has received the message, he has felt that it has to do with him, that it has to do with all men who toil, and with us in particular; and that it has to do with us two, who dare to reason of these things with the poles for the soup on our shoulders.[84]

Besides such inspiring confidence, the frankness with which Améry denies himself any grand illusions may seem distressing, even 'bitter' and 'icy', to echo Levi himself. On the other hand the reference to Dante is not quite so inspired and cheerful as it at first appears, for what is more important than anything else to Levi is this partial line: 'as pleased Another' (*If This Is a Man*, p. 136), in which he immediately recognizes the reason for his being in Auschwitz. That strange Other causes the destructive programme threatening to crush them all. Here Levi and Améry are remarkably close, much closer than they would like to acknowledge.

However, they are diametrically opposed when it comes to determining the place Auschwitz will occupy in their lives *after* the camp. For Améry, his experience of the camp is a purely destructive one. 'We did not become wiser in Auschwitz. (...) We did not become "deeper" (...) better, more human, more humane, and more mature ethically.'[85] But for Levi, the camp was 'a university; it taught us to look around and to measure men'.[86]

Legitimate as the confrontation is, one feels that there is a subtext of subliminal hostility.

Primo Levi waxes indignant first against Améry's narrow definition of the (literary) intellectual, and he is right, for it excludes him as a scientist. But this dispute itself makes it clear how easily this choreography of vanities might have been avoided, if only the two 'grand old men' could have brought themselves to conduct a direct discussion. There was scarcely a scholar in the humanities who had as much respect for science as Jean Améry. His lifelong support for positivism was a longing for that 'other education', which Améry rated much higher than his own. The mathematician Jacques Sonnenschein tells us how, in flight from Gurs to their prison in Bayonne, he positively forced him to explain quantum theory. Also, his friendship with Ilya Prigogine in Brussels sprang from the same motivation. Conversely, Levi must have missed the irony when Améry, in his essay 'At the Mind's Limits', defines his intellectual as someone who – of all things – 'is well informed about Neidhart von Reuenthal, the courtly poet of village lyrics,'[87] giving an example that shows the 'uselessness' of his system of intellectual reference; it is useless for ordinary life and even more useless in the camp.

In addition, Levi objects to Améry's justification of counter-violence. Even as a Partisan he, Levi, had found the use of force extremely alien to him. Améry, on the other hand, would have given anything to be able to fight the Nazis with a weapon in his hand. There is, in fact, disagreement here, except that Améry revised his attitude to counter-violence in the course of time: he, who spoke of the 'redemptive character of revolt and violence in regard to the uprising in Auschwitz and Treblinka, and in the 1960s considered the "counter-aggression" of the freedom fighting in the Third World more legitimate, withdraws this justification in 1977 in the name of democracy.'[88] 'I admire Améry's (...) courageous decision to leave the ivory tower and go down into the battlefield,' Levi pays tribute to him, 'but it was and still is beyond my reach.'

However, his admiration does not go so far as his criticism, indeed his passionate resistance to the idea: Améry's approval of counter-violence, he says, has marked his whole life since Auschwitz, leading him to adopt

> ...positions of such severity and intransigence as to make him incapable of finding joy in life, indeed of living. Those who 'trade blows' with the entire world achieve dignity but pay a very high price for it, because they are sure to be defeated.

Levi is not willing to pay that price. Here he airs his rancour against Améry who took it upon himself to call him, Levi, a 'forgiver'.

In fact, Jean Améry was to Levi what Kleist, although in entirely different circumstances, was to Goethe. Levi picks up the scent of danger and possibly feels the undertow of Améry's intransigence, his pessimism, his destructive impulse – a self-destructive impulse that Levi sees confirmed in Améry's suicide.

As long as Levi lives, he invokes life as his most precious possession, defending it ardently against the pessimistic and suicidal Améry. Sebald, in his comparison, comments:

> It is almost as if Levi were primarily concerned, in view of Jean Améry's death, to assert himself – unlike (...) Améry, who had long been preoccupied with

possible ways of death – by once again attaching to life the importance which, he hoped, would preserve him from the ultimate act that he too already sensed in himself.[89]

Whether Levi himself did choose that 'way to freedom', whether he succumbed to the undertow that he so firmly believed he would withstand, is, as his biographer says, far from proven.[90]

It is certain that each of them preserves 'his' Auschwitz and the conclusions drawn from it later like a Grail, like an inalienable possession that must be defended against his adversary. Furthermore, just because they respect each other, the retrospective differences separating them take on emotional dimensions. In Primo Levi they appear openly on stage, even after the death of his rival Améry,[91] and in the case of Améry they are behind the scenes. The rival who 'came too late' publicly imposes silence on himself.

It is also certain that Primo Levi still lives on through discourse on Auschwitz today, while Améry's works, which created the opportunity for that discourse in the first place, went into it so deeply that we no longer feel it necessary to relate the discourse to Améry's name. The roles have thus, to some extent, been changed: although in 1965 Améry, with prognoses reaching far into the future (Bitburg,[i] the arguments between historians, the Wehrmacht exhibition, the Walser/Bubis debate), could claim greater aesthetic value for himself in the discussion of Auschwitz, he has disappeared again in today's culture of the Holocaust. Why?

Levi's account tells a true story with a beginning and an end, in chapters chronologically arranged; we can accompany him on his journey to hell, we can fear and hope with him. There is none of that in Améry; he will have no narrative; he will have no company, as he warns readers, appealing to their reason, against deceptive identification. Yet Améry also asks 'what is a man?' and when a man is not a man any more. He asks even more specifically what it is that constitutes the Jewish victim and makes more and more attempts to investigate its potential in borderline situations.

In Auschwitz, so he concludes, the Jewish victim comes 'At the Mind's Limits'; in the essay on 'Torture', if I may venture on an analogy, it is reached at the body's limits. Twenty years after his liberation, Améry follows an

---

i   A reference to the 1985 visit paid by US President Reagan, in the company of Chancellor Kohl of Germany, to German war graves (including those of SS soldiers) in a cemetery near the town of Bitburg, as a demonstration of German–American solidarity in the modern world. It aroused much controversy.

uncharacteristic Blochian impulse in writing, 'Thinking is almost nothing else but a great astonishment'[92] – astonishment at what one can become, flesh and death, astonishment at surviving your adversary's rage for destruction, at surviving at all.

Coming home to no home

As many as 25,437 Jews were deported from Belgium, 23,000 of them to Auschwitz. Hans Mayer is one of the 615 survivors. 'With a live weight of 45 kilograms, wearing a striped prisoner's suit,'[93] Hans Mayer comes home on 29 April 1945 to the world of Brussels that he left behind on 23 July 1943. His wife Regine, who had stayed in hiding in the city, is no more. Remarkably, he learns only six years later that she died of heart failure on 24 April 1944, exactly a year before he was freed.[94]

If he rehearses survival in reality, he rehearses death in fiction. He tries 'to conquer the world with words'. His attempts to do so are not primarily Breendonck or Auschwitz; he is threatened even more by the black hole into which he has fallen on finding that his beloved has so inexplicably disappeared. Whatever their names may be, those muses who accompanied the shipwrecked novelist on the rim of the abyss, whether Agathe, Beate or Odette, all that is left of the sense of love they once gave him is the 'crown of thorns'.[95]

CHAPTER 5

Living On – but How and Where? (1945–1955)
The original theme of suicide

Love's Crown of Thorns: variation 1

Not that there is any sign of the 'crown' itself. Only the 'thorns', both public and private, impel the writer to write again after 1945. The public thorns, those of the story, are indeed described – see Althager's account of 'The Fortress of Derloven' – but they are only a foil to the far more urgent, painful tale of 'private' thorns. The pain is shifted, transferred to an individual story of tragic love, where he may express it 'politically'. Whatever he puts down on paper in 1945 – from the fragments of his intended revision of his novel, mentioned above, to drama, narrative, even a screenplay – his martyrdom of April 1945, recorded in literary form, leaves out the torture in Breendonck and the humiliations of the camps, and even his knowledge of persecution and deportation; it is concerned exclusively with the pain of an abandoned man who does not even know where his beloved is. It is this personal wound, expressed again and again in new variations, that makes Hans Mayer's unheroic heroes contemplate suicide. All that is left of the magic of love is the ruin of a life; art in the form of a monologue *amoris causa* – black romanticism, love, death, the grave. In resorting to fine writing in the manner of Thomas Mann, he intends to persuade us that the Auschwitz chapter cannot touch the writer who survives.

Probably rightly, these manuscripts from the years 1945–1948, now in the Marbach archives, were not only unpublished but also kept secret by the author when he had become successful. However, they are valuable evidence for the reconstruction of his life, if only because the Austrian novelist of the 1930s, to whose career Hitler called a halt, is more determined than ever, in 1945, to resume his life as a writer. These works, or at least most of them, are concentrated exercises in writing, although not very innovative in either style or content.

This is particularly true of the Anacreontic work written in 1945, *Die Erzählung eines ländlichen Lebens* [The Story of a Rural Life],[1] in which the yearning of a country girl and a young countryman are presented alternately. Its mood, that of a superficial village idyll, is startling if we think of the background of the writer's very recent experience. Redolent of nostalgia, it reads like the evocation of a politically trivial world now out of reach.

Heinrich Greyt: variation 2

The 'play in three acts' entitled *Heinrich Greyt* is more dramatic: the wretched 'vagabond of love' Althager of the *Dornenkrone* changes from the author of pamphlets to a writer and informer driven mad by love.[2] The play is also topographically close to the early version of the Althager novel, set in Kirchleiten in the Tyrol, the very place where the Althager of *Die Schiffbrüchigen* follows the trail of his childhood. Agathe, Althager's girlfriend, also reappears here, this time as the wife of the Austrian writer Dr Heinrich Greyt, and we meet his friend-cum-enemy, Hessl, as the resistance fighter Franz Holler. A Jewish pianist, a priest, a deserter and a Gestapo officer complete the cast of the drama. The writer Greyt's honour is so deeply wounded by his wife's unfaithfulness and his friend Holler's betrayal of him that he hands over the woman he loves to the Gestapo. Mutatis mutandis, even in this sentimental story of a love triangle we are shown how quickly the intellectual comes up against the 'mind's limits' when the emotion of jealousy overwhelms him.

Quite different, because it breathes the air of the larger world, if no less politically disillusioned and pessimistic, is the story *Reise um den Tod in sieben Tagen* [A Journey around Death in Seven Days] of 1948.[3] A Belgian double agent, former Communist and fighter for Spain, steals from a Dutch millionaire, flees to Paris, 'the metropolis of ecstasy and euphoria', seduces a student, leaves her to go to the aid of the striking workers in Lorraine with the stolen money, and, after he has made up his mind to commit suicide, is shot by their Stalinist leader, who has discovered that he is a dissident.

Die Selbstmörder: variation 3

More ambitious in its narrative technique is *Die Selbstmörder* [The Suicides], intended to be a screenplay. Here Mayer experiments with a method between dream and reality which will determine the tone of his very last projected novella, *Rendezvous in Oudenaarde*, sketched out in the summer of 1978. The basic idea in both, the first and the last version of this subject alike, is 'the power of the imagination'. 'If the world is all my imagination, then within that general idea there are also particular ideas of "the world".' In this last exposé,

Améry symbolizes 'the dream as life'.[4] The same is true of the screenplay written 30 years earlier, in which the protagonists not only anticipate reality in their
respective dreams but also let their dreams dictate their experience of reality.
What follows is a 'new kind of structure', made new by its reflections, and he
sees it as a compromise between 'a treatment, a screenplay and a novella'. 'The
present film,' Hans Mayer continues in his introduction to *Die Selbstmörder*,
'is A PSYCHOLOGICAL STUDY [*sic*; author's note] arising from the action of
a crime film, its subject being a burning problem of our time, SUICIDE. This
action is not consecutive but builds up LIKE A MOSAIC. It is not the chronology of the police investigation that sets the tone, but the SUBJECTIVE LOGIC
OF MEMORY,' by which he means the 'psychology of remembering'. Even more
clearly he states, 'Everyone remembers what he wants to remember.' The formal
structure is also subordinated to the subjective principle, so that certain scenes
are narrated by various characters in various contexts.[5]

So even in his post-war fiction he remains faithful to the primal theme of
suicide. (The term used here is *Selbstmord*, literally 'self-murder', rather than
the alternative German word *Freitod*, literally 'free' or 'freely chosen death', a
distinction drawn again in his late book on the whole subject of suicide.) Further
points relating to *Die Schiffbrüchigen* are the names of the main characters.
Here we meet the musician Eugène, 'a composer of about 30, unsuccessful and
without any perceptible earnings. Fastidious and very cultured. Slightly built,
nervous, sensitive.' Although his name now takes the French form, he reminds
us of Eugen Althager. There is also an Odette, 'a young woman of 30, from the
border area between high society and the demi-monde', a reincarnation of the
singer from the first novel. Finally, there is Odette's divorced husband, Herr
Beaumann, 'the type of a not entirely reliable businessman of our time', who
anticipates the 'not entirely reliable businessman' Beaumann in the novel *Lefeu,
oder Der Abbruch* [Lefeu, or The Demolition].

However, the war is allowed into this screenplay, as it is into the revised
version of the novel. But by contrast with *Die Dornenkrone der Liebe*, Hans
Mayer experiments here with a change of perspective by exchanging the viewpoint of the Auschwitz survivor for that of a French soldier who has returned
home – 'I am POW No. 172364', says Pierre in his cry of desperation, and he
bears his creator's own Auschwitz number. From the point of view of a modern
historian it is noticeable that at this time Hans Mayer, unlike the later writer of
the 1960s, does not insist on the singularity of his status as a Jew but, on the
contrary, extends to other groups of victims his own suffering as an 'Odysseus
homeward bound' who is 'in search of lost time'. Whether the protagonist is a
Jewish prisoner in a German concentration camp, or a French prisoner of war

in the hands of the Germans, it makes no difference here – they have both lost their confidence in the world. On the other hand, that experience is not held responsible for the alienation, madness and suicide of the 'Odysseus homeward bound'. Once again, the cause is the supposed betrayal of love.

Kleist: variation 4

A variation of a very different kind on the theme of suicide is the novella *Das Ende des Schriftstllers H. v. Kleist* [The Death of the Writer Heinrich von Kleist], with the subtitle, 'Erzählung aus dieser Zeit' [A Tale of This Time].[6] In Hans Mayer's version of his story, the 34-year-old Kleist features as 'a former Wehrmacht officer', who with his friend Henriette Vogel, a woman who is little-loved and is sick and ready to die, goes to a 'modest inn on the Wannsee in Berlin' on a 'November evening in the year 1946', 'to prepare for their joint suicide the next day'. In 1945 the reason for Kleist's apocalyptic mood is not so much the collapse of Germany as his own failure as an author and poet. 'Cheerful' as the authentic farewell letter written by the real Kleist to his sister Ulrike claims to be, Mayer's Kleist faces his deed in a vacillating mood. 'It takes much goodwill to play the part of Tristan with this woman, he thinks.'[7]

At heart, he hopes for some outside act to save him and 'prevent his death'. This seems to him the ideal solution: 'The fact is that he wishes to suffer death without dying, to experience death in the same way as, when a boy, he often used to try catching the moment of falling asleep while still awake.' The planes of time are ironically breached when Mayer's Kleist gives himself up to such intellectual games as this:

> If I had been living on German soil, he thinks, in 1811 rather than 1946, then all anxieties (financial difficulty; trouble with the women whom one loves and at the same time hates) could have been drowned in a torrent of the tears of sensitivity.

His very German Kleist is dipped in Sartrean dye:

> In our days, however, all destinies go to extremes. You are 'cast into' them, *engagé*, as they say in that clever, that hated country of France. The days of a sentimental superstructure, which once rose so airily to the sky from the ground of the compelling force and economic power, are over. Today, talking will not do, and the mathematical equation, the answer to which demands my time of me, is: Eros, Thanatos, plus economic necessity = suicide.[8]

However, it does not turn out like that; the outside act, the unanticipated event, does occur, yet it kills rather than saves. So it is not suicide but a murder.

An NCO of the occupying power feels threatened by Kleist, who is firing into the air to try out his pistol, and the soldier kills the poet – in self-defence, as he thinks. The novella closes with an uncharacteristic arabesque striking a note of reconciliation:

> Heinrich von Kleist hardly had time to think. As life flows warm from his mouth, and the last cold wind (...) [of] this world roars around his head, he believes (...) that dying is not really hard.[9]

Die Eingemauerten [The Immured]: variation 5

Finally, there is what, for the time being, was Mayer's last attempt to tackle the theme of suicide – a comedy of its period clearly bearing the stamp of Sartre. The pseudonym of Jean-Paul Mayster and the title *Die Eingemauerten* [The Immured][10] do not try to conceal their origins. The cast of characters, the plot and the scene of the action (Limoges) are still the same as in *Die Selbstmörder*, but the emphasis is different, more precise; it aims to be existentialist. The home-comer Pierre, a hero *en situation*, turns back, like his predecessor Althager, into the concentration camp survivor who, after his first failed suicide attempt, now tries to kill his treacherous friend. However, as soon as he understands the madness of his jealousy he wants to set off for other shores – he speaks of 'the outline of a new world'. 'Let us break out of this musty crypt where we are immured,' he begs his beloved, but in vain. Their joint attempt to leave does not succeed; the 'immured' remain immured – except for the main character, who this time successfully takes the way to freedom, that is to say to death.

A new era has begun in Europe: in December 1945 Hans Mayer discovers the work of Jean-Paul Sartre. The individual is closely examined; he is the maker of his life, and in part at least of his story. *Die Eingemauerten*, the 'Immured', a kind of loan-word translation of *Huis clos* (1945), is Hans Mayer's first tribute to the master. Even the names of his protagonists are borrowed; not just Pierre but Olga and Mathieu too come from Sartre's early gallery of characters. Both plays depict antagonism between the alienated loner and the pitiless view of the outside world – 'Hell is other people,' as the (dead) Garcin announces in *Huis clos,* so that the image others have of us prevents us from retouching, in retrospect, the lives we have lived. Because others will not accept a lie, it becomes impossible for us to lie to ourselves. In Sartre's *Huis clos* – as also in Hans Mayer's *Die Eingemauerten* – a network of relationships of hopeful hopelessness is created. In such a 'theatre of situation', where the situations are created or caused by human beings, the product of war and resistance, emotional liberation and lost illusion, the characters represent 'freedom taken prisoner' in a world without God. 'How do they get out of the trap again?' asks Sartre in his essay 'What is literature?' of 1947. 'Every character has the choice of a way out, and that character will be worth no more than the way he chooses.'

Existentialism in France: Revolution of the mind? Fashion? Or the twilight of the 'esprit français'?[11]

It was not only as a dramatist that Sartre left his mark on Hans Mayer, who is particularly fascinated by the early prose works *La nausée* (1938) and *Le mur* (1939). These, he considers in this first essay on Sartre's existentialism, are works of art of 'terrible forcefulness'. 'What is ugly, indeed unpleasant and repulsive, is described with such fervour as to create a new aesthetic category for it.' He wonders whether not beauty but 'the intensity of representation alone' should be the crucial factor, 'the sole criterion of the beautiful in art'. Sartre owes his sensational success, says Mayer, to the fact that, like Freud 15 years before him, he is able to express 'discomfort in culture' so convincingly. 'In his books, Sartre gives the reader the opportunity of sexual gratification pertaining to the underworld, of a kind that has nothing to do with superficial sexual excitement.' However, Hans Mayer regrets that in France of all places, the land of Cartesianism, 'where the offensive of "existential", ultimately instinctual forces, free of ideas, is powerfully brought into play as an expression of the awareness of life', this must nonetheless be regarded as valid. Hans Mayer concludes these early comments on Sartre's existentialism:

> We do not believe that protests in the name of Plato will be able to check a very evident development. It is more likely that it will make a new and rational form of thinking possible. (...) But such a form of thinking would have to encompass the social reality of our world more broadly would have to take deeper root in the soil than *le rationalisme français* has been able to do.

'On the Psychology of the German People': revenge?

He gives us some idea of the 'new and rational form of thinking' that he envisages in his first work in the essay genre, which has its origins partly in Auschwitz-Monowitz. This is the programmatic text mentioned above which he finished in Brussels in June 1945, a bare three months after his liberation from Bergen-Belsen. It is a fine document, and not only because it exists in the first place and thus shows us the astonishingly 'objective' foundation on which Améry was to build the deliberately subjective essays in *At the Mind's Limits*, written 20 years later. Even more remarkably, unlike the emotional *fictional* works, it reveals a psychological vitality where one would least expect it. At the worst of times, Hans Mayer maintains an upright gait: an optimistic belief in the future, together with the firm conviction that analytical reason can solve even the most complex moral and socio-political problems, inspires him to draw self-proclaimed 'scientific' deductions from what he has just escaped. Here the pupil moulded by the neo-positivist educational principles of his mentors in the 1930s speaks; here too speaks the teacher he learned to be in Zirkusgasse. Like his mentor Langhammer before him, Hans Mayer raises his voice to educate the public. In this spring of 1945 he confidently takes the education of the German people upon himself. He knows that world opinion is on his side. He was never before as full of vitality and sure of prevailing as he shows himself to be here, and he never would be again.

For it is not as a victim, the only status allowed him in 1945, that Mayer describes and analyses the crimes of the Third Reich, but as a witness – one is almost tempted to say an impartial witness.

> The most tragic period in the history of the German people is beginning. The moment has come that Thomas Mann prophesied in his novel *Lotte in Weimar* when he put into Goethe's mouth these words: 'I fear that one day the hatred of the whole world may converge on the German people (...)'

He gives concrete examples: the Russian peasant demands revenge, so does the high school teacher from Warsaw, the American war widow, the British sailor, the Norwegian fisherman, not to mention the Jew exiled from Germany. 'The *vox populi* of the entire world (...) cries out for vengeance,' he says in this essay, written in Brussels in June 1945.

These, then, are the roots of Jean Améry's later essay on 'Resentments'. We become aware of the powerful path of thought and emotion that has been trodden from 'revenge' to 'resentment'. That pair of words in itself allows us to trace the evolution of Améry's thinking. The earlier term 'revenge' is symptomatic insofaras the kind of retaliation from which the victim of 1945 expects healing approaches the crime from the *outside*. In 1965 Améry is no longer speaking of revenge but of resentment, indicating that healing failed to materialize and that suffering caused by the lack of revenge has turned inwards as hopeless resentment.

Now back to Hans Mayer in 1945; is he too crying out for vengeance? No, he is not. On the contrary, he distances himself twice over, both from 'the mass instinct demanding revenge' and from 'the dulcet tones of *Realpolitik*'. 'We are guided by only two fervent wishes,' he concludes his introduction, 'to recognize the truth that lies somewhere very far behind appearances, and to prevent any recurrence at any time, on any pretext whatsoever, of the bloody venture that we have, miraculously, survived.' Incidentally, and this too is not what modern readers of Améry will expect, Hans Mayer celebrates his survival.

Neither guilt nor atonement[12]

Neither 'guilt' as a metaphysical concept nor the complementary concept of 'atonement', says Améry, has any validity. Trained in the Vienna Circle, the rationalist knows only the concepts of 'responsibility' and 'retribution'. And retribution makes sense only if those who are to be held responsible are capable of improvement.

> We may now, with some logical justification, look at what is known as 'the guilt of the German people' and ask the question: 'Do we have good reason, on the grounds of experience and analysis, to assume that on the one hand the German people are amenable to reasonable social arguments, and on the other are ready to abstain from further criminal actions out of fear of the punitive measures that may arise from them?'

As this question, applied to other civilized peoples, may be taken to imply a positive answer, another arises now: are the German people different in their nature from all those others? Hans Mayer does not really believe that the Germans have set out along a special path of their own. Under the Third Reich, he discerns three 'classes entirely different from each other'. They are the elite in governmental power, the mass of the people and 'the small class of intellectual opponents'. The perpetrators of Nazi crimes come from the governing elite. But what exactly, he asks, made them perpetrate those crimes? What form is retribution to take?

Deranged criminals

The ground in Germany had been fertile for such crimes, in an intellectual climate where the banners were inscribed with a maxim such as this: 'We Germans are heroic in bearing the sufferings of others.' He is citing a notorious remark made by Rudolf G. Binding in 1933. Hans Mayer understands it as a call to an entire generation to educate itself in atrocity. He holds none other than Friedrich Nietzsche responsible for this deadening of all human feeling. 'Since the rise of the Third Reich, sophisticated (...) cultural figures have gone to a great deal of trouble to persuade us that the influence of Nietzsche on National Socialism was based on a misunderstanding of the philosopher,' he says, rejecting such voices. According to them, says Mayer, his calls to atrocity had 'only symbolic meaning', relating

> ...to God knows what sublimations and other such insinuations. But we maintain, on the contrary, that when a man writes that one should strive 'not for

contentment but for power, not for peace but for war, not for virtue but for efficiency,' he means exactly what he says. There can be no clearer way of expressing it, and the leading German clique acted in precise accordance with those
maxims.[13]

He comments that 'the notion of exerting power divorced from any ideas and
aims' is one of Nietzsche's basic principles, and he anticipates possible protests
by adding, 'The fact that in Nietzsche's work there are also, naturally, remarks of
quite a different nature (...) does not alter this fact,' and that what he has quoted
is 'the essential part' of Nietzsche's 'personality'. 'For that reason, this man's
books should be banned, both his and those of all his biocentric successors, from
Klages to Spengler' (PdV, Vol. 2, p. 508).

National Socialism, says Mayer, is 'derangement as a constant psychological condition' and is merely the outcome of many years of a certain kind of
education. As for the perpetrators of the Nazi era, he can see only one punishment
that will fit their crimes: the 'integral physical extermination of all the leading
personalities in the Party (...) and the entire staff of the State Secret Police.'
This measure is not to be understood as a moral commandment but as a social
necessity, 'because these deranged criminals', if merely isolated, would continue
their mischief as before, because they are beyond the potential for any kind of
improvement (PdV, Vol. 3, p. 513).

Work will not make you free

It is in the relationship of the Germans to work that their 'education to be unfeel-
ing' is most clearly crystallized. To Hans Mayer, an obsession with work is a fatal
national quality: 'To be German means doing something for its own sake.' There
is hardly an ethos that could have suited the Nazis better; the German leadership
class, he points out, had skilfully exploited this national quality. 'Once again, in
exactly the same way as with the glorification of Aryanism, the old trick was a
great success: what the people already were was presented as the greatest good
to be achieved (...).' With the proclamation of 'a duty to work, as a replacement
for that suspect entity human rights, a stone truly fell from the heart' (PdV,
Vol. 2, p. 517). It was the only way in which what was psychologically useful in
the German people could be combined with political inevitability:

They armed for war with an expenditure of labour never before known. After
1935 the patient German people, who at the same time were possessed by a
sombre passion for work, were driven to a level of achievement that left them
hardly any time for love and none at all for thought. The German stood at his
workbench for ten hours, (...) 15 hours a day, and in the world outside others,

those who could see what was going on, calmly determined his fate. At the same time a constant hail of propaganda, monopolized by National Socialism, fell on brains anaesthetized by work and long unaccustomed to thinking. (PdV, Vol. 2, pp. 518–9)

There follows an excursus in which he stops to take breath and illustrate his thesis. No one – and by no means only 'the Germans' – is immune, he says, to such a 'monopoly of propaganda'. He uses himself as a demonstration:

The writer of these lines spent two years in German concentration camps, and at that time he could draw his information about the course of world events only from the German press. He had every qualification for immunity to the influence of National Socialist propaganda. (...) The Germans had persecuted and held him prisoner; they had killed some of his family. All the same, he could not in the long run withdraw from the effects of German propaganda. (PdV, Vol. 2, p. 520)

It is interesting that here Mayer speaks of himself in the third person, another indication that, in complete contrast to his later method, he wants to leave aside any subjectivity so that he can present a 'purely scientific' investigation.

Thus it was that on his arrival in Belgium in May 1945, he believed that the country had been shaken by constant uprisings, and he was greatly surprised to discover the extremely peaceful situation there. The reasons are simple. He had very soon realized that those of his comrades who, on principle, regarded all facts reported by the Germans as false, and every opinion they expressed as stupid, were mistaken, and were storing up severe disappointment for themselves. However, if one had accepted the Nazi press as a source of information, there was no way of telling truth from lies.

Here again, his analysis is based on empirical data. He himself, as a prisoner in Monowitz, circulated little questionnaires among the office employees of IG-Farben, so that he could assess the cultural horizon of the 'average German', to prove how little a man is able to understand 'the causal chain at the point where he intersects with it'. He adds, in defence of the German people, that 'it is therefore not surprising' if they could not distinguish between lies and the truth; they knew no better, they were brutalized and let atrocities take place before their eyes without protesting. 'The average German could do nothing to counter official terminology; he had to use it if he wanted to communicate securely and swiftly with the authorities' (PdV, Vol. 2, pp. 500–13).

Hans Mayer concludes from this that 'the German people as a whole were not guilty of the appalling atrocities committed in concentration camps and prisons.' However, he adds a reservation: even if as a collective entity they were not *actively* guilty, they did nothing to oppose those crimes in any way. He further concludes:

> The average German, one who, for instance, was working in industry side by side with political prisoners, did not beat them. (...) But, with a vanishingly small number of exceptions, such Germans did nothing to support the prisoners either (...) and *without any exceptions at all* they never publicly opposed the abuse of human beings.

Hans Mayer knows he can prove that they, the average Germans, 'knew' what went on.

> It is certain, and can here be reliably confirmed, that the workers and office employees in the Auschwitz IG-Farben factory knew very well that in Birkenau, five kilometres away, hundreds of thousands of Jews, Poles and Russians were being gassed, and some of them even burnt alive. In this exceptional case, then, about five thousand Germans had been aware of these most infernal of all possible methods of murder, but not one of them cried out: 'Stop! I will not go along with this any more.' (PdV, Vol. 2, p. 526)

This was so not only in Germany, he says; there was no shortage of eager collaborators in the occupied countries as well. Indeed, many Germans could have learnt something from the Flemish SS men. He sums up:

> The sin of the German people, if for once we allow ourselves to use that mythic term, their sin was a sin of omission. They incur no punishment for what they did. But they are told that they incur punishment for not doing what they ought to have done, for [so the educator deduces] they can be re-educated, they are responsible for their actions, and capable of improvement. (...) Let us not say: 'You are beasts, you are all radically evil beings because you freely elected those men Hitler, Himmler and Heydrich in 1932 and 1934.' That would be deviating too far from the truth. Those who elected Hitler in 1932 were not yet voting for Auschwitz and Birkenau. They had not deliberately approved such things, but they were either too cowardly or too deaf to prevent them. (PdV, Vol. 2, p. 526)

The reader of the Améry of *At the Mind's Limits* (German publication 1966) is surprised to find so much understanding and goodwill. As compared with his essay 'Resentments' (and in 1966 he nurtures those resentments like an inalienable possession), his analysis of 1945 is almost an acquittal. 'And if we now ask ourselves whether the German people are responsible for their actions, which in the sense used here means whether they are capable of improvement, then we can confidently say "Yes."' He has seen many nations and many lands 'in these years', he says. In the face of the Gestapo, in the face of instruments of torture, there were no major differences in their ability to resist.

> We have known peoples both better and worse educated. The German people were worse educated than any others. That is all. We must educate the people, and we must not make that education either too easy or too difficult for them. We will have to be very careful and very clever. (PdV, Vol. 2, p. 529)

His 'we' is not a royal 'we' attempting to conceal the subjectivity of his analysis, anxious as it is to be scientific. The 'we' here means 'we, the victims'. It also means 'we, the moral victors,' and above all it means 'we whose voices are now heard'. Hans Mayer's confidence can be explained only because he is absolutely sure that in June 1945 his hour, the hour of justice, has come. 'The German spirit' – by which he again means Thomas Mann above all – 'is ready' to wield the sword of humanity again.

> It [the spirit; author's note] had never given itself up – it had only withdrawn into darkened rooms in the face of power. It will be for us to liberate it in the full light of day, through effective action by the public.

The suicidal darkness of the first-person narrator in the early literary works is thus countered, in this discourse, by the confident emotion of the philosopher. In the letters of the late 1940s, darkness and light also balance each other out.

Letter of farewell to Knut Hamsun

In 1945 the hymn to Thomas Mann's 'nobility of spirit' follows the public letter of farewell to the Norwegian Nobel Prize winner Knut Hamsun, who in 1933, and even after the war when he faced court proceedings, spoke up without reservation for Hitler.[14] 'It is painful when we must accustom ourselves to hating and despising where we once loved and honoured.'[15] A whole generation of Germans had seen Hamsun as a great liberator; by coming to terms with National Socialist power he betrayed that same generation. Mayer asks, did he not know it? 'The spirit follows a dialectic of opposition: at the moment when an idea is realized in society, it opposes it. Not to have understood that is your great guilt,'[16] Hans Mayer tells Knut Hamsun. In a much later essay on Hamsun,[17] he draws a distinction in his verdict, by continuing to regard the 'enemy of civilization' as a 'Fascist' and an 'inveterate Nazi' in human and social terms, but trying to propose 'a process of literary *rehabilitation*' for him, particularly with regard to the two novels *Hunger* and *Mysteries* – much as it goes against the grain with him 'to separate aesthetics and ethics, art and politics' from each other.[18]

Where now? His fixed point: Maria Leitner

There was despair over what was past, and hope for what was to come – but where, and how, and in what way? It is not by any means to be taken for granted that he will stay in Brussels: his wife Gina, for whose sake he came back to that city, is no more. But there is his link with Gina's friend, the non-Jewish Maria Leitner from Vienna, who does not, in fact, live in Brussels any more but whom he knows from their days in Antwerp. In 1946 he is already confessing:

> In spite of everything, dear Mitzerl, my heart draws me to Austria, and it is quite possible that I may set off overnight some day. (...) I bear, and always will, the burden of my wife's death. It weighs on my conscience, because I did not always treat her as she deserved, even though I always loved her more than I can say. I ought never to have married her, in thrall as I am to a nature about which I could do nothing [He is referring to his many amorous adventures]. And yet I owe what little happiness I have known in my life to my marriage to Gina.[19]

In 1946 Maria,[20] to whom he sent these lines, was married to the Viennese Jew Rudolph Leitner (Rudi), who had been analysed by Freud before the war. In 1938 the Leitners emigrated to Belgium, and we first find them in Antwerp. The couple get away in 1941 to New York, where they will be safe from the Germans. Capable woman that she is, Maria goes into business, in the firm of Vogel, Leather and Furs. She earns for both of them, because her husband, although a qualified historian and an experienced publisher, does not succeed in finding a job after their emigration to the States. Rudolph Leitner suffers from chronic depression and withdraws from life. Maria is very anxious about his 'pitiful condition'. She has infinite sympathy for him, but there is nothing she can do to help him. The marriage fails and is legally ended on 23 January 1955, on the grounds of 'the adultery of the respondent with Hans Maier'. In suing for divorce, the petitioner (Rudolph Leitner) states that the marriage turned out unhappy soon after their emigration. The respondent, he claims, finally left him in 1948 and since then 'has been living with' Hans Mayer.[21] Besides working, she begins studying 'psychodiagnostics' in the autumn of 1949, financing her own studies and hoping that, in the foreseeable future, she will be able to stop working in business and set up independently as a psychologist.[22] However, she never puts this plan into practice, not least because in the end she devotes herself entirely to the needs of Hans Mayer. It is she who seeks to make contact with him again on her regular business trips – or 'missions' – to Brussels, Paris and Zürich.

Hans Mayer and Maria Leitner, Brussels 1948

The acquaintance between them becomes friendship; friendship turns to love. Between 1949 and 1952 they exchange letters almost daily, full of fantastical pet names in the Austrian idiom, longing, demanding, argumentative, reproachful, down-to-earth letters – but each is always confident that truth may be expected of the other. There is a quiet magic in this correspondence that deeply moves anyone studying Améry. It provides documentation, in particular, for the year 1949: a survivor of the concentration camps returns to nothing and struggles with the authorities for four years to have his official identity confirmed. The correspondence is a record of both work and emotions. It intensifies the pulsating here-and-now of the dark, difficult everyday life of the couple, now and then shot through with bright sparks. The moving aspect of the words the two of them find for each other does not lie in any exchange of utopian vows and promises in spectacular, rapturous ecstasy, but in the sober gravity of a situation in which they envisage the real possibility of a future – perhaps together? – and the serious nature of feelings that will prove reliable and resilient.

A lucrative commission from the Dukas press agency thus allows them to build castles in the air together; the cancellation of another such commission would finally send him, a man living on the edge of the abyss anyway, down into the depths of despair if she were not there to catch him. Something else that makes these letters surprising and delightful is the child-like Hans Mayer whom we encounter in them: an animal-lover who is playfully crazy about cats and suffers from the idea that his friend Maria, whose 'Haserl'[i] he is, makes her living from the furs and skins of similar animals. We come to know a man with a sense of humour – comical, exaggerating, sometimes malicious but always as sharp as a knife – and we also meet a man who likes life, is capable of enjoyment and can love the superficial. Within a very short time Maria is an indispensable confidante to her 'Haserl-Hanserl', who teaches her to like cats. She acted as a prop and stay to her first husband 'Rudi', and now she does the same for Hans, offering advice and above all practical help, money and ideas. In fact, she thought and wrote with him in an extremely active and productive way and did so to the end of his life. Without doubt, she was the *éminence grise* behind his work.

Maria believes in Hans Mayer, believes in his 'incisive intellect' and 'capability for precise thinking', and above all she believes in him as a writer of fiction. 'Come on, don't be downcast, we'll fix it so that you can write your novel too,' she comfortingly assures him in a letter from Prague on 4 November 1948, referring to the new version of *Die Schiffbrüchigen*. Although she is not immune to depression herself, she is always there, ready to sacrifice everything for him. However, it is not until 1955 that she finally moves from New York to Brussels, after the divorce from Rudolph Leitner in which she features as the 'guilty' party. On 2 April 1955 Jean Améry and Maria Leitner, *née* Eschenauer, marry at last in the Vienna-Währing registry office. He did not make things easy for her in the course of his turbulent life. He never set much store by fidelity, but he knew how much he owed her, and loved her in his own fashion.

He learns no more about the death of his first wife Gina, as mentioned above, until 1949. 'Muschi, whom I saw again, now gave me a full account of Gina's death: how she died, how she was found, how she was buried,' he writes in a letter to Maria on 2 May 1949.

> I cannot shake off the thought of it. May I be spared such visions; I do not have the strength to carry them with me through a life that is miserable anyway. I don't want to know such things, no.

In this context he also thought, he says, of his love for her, Maria: 'No doubt your own figure is entwined with the image of Gina in my mind, and so I love you more than I would ever have thought or hoped possible. It is, if you like, an "identification".' Maria, who was very fond of Gina, does not seem to be offended by this 'identification'. She suggests that he might come to New York,

---

i   A diminutive of *Hase*, hare.

but he firmly declines this invitation in terms that do not exactly flatter her. 'It is true that I have nothing to lose by leaving here,' he replies from Brussels, 'but I have nothing to gain by going there either.'

Nothing concrete, then, keeps him in Brussels, although, of course, there are certain friends who help him and stand by him – for instance, Ilya Prigogine, mentioned earlier, whose first wife Hélène Gofé comes to meet him and take him to the Association des Juifs in Brussels when he arrives from Bergen-Belsen. 'Hans is back,' she tells their few mutual friends, for instance, the chemist Kurt Schindel,[23] whom Hans Mayer met in Malines after being in Breendonck. Schindel's great attraction is that he can speak Austrian dialect with him.[23] The mathematician Jacques Sonnenschein also offers what help he can. Mayer had escaped from the camp at Gurs with Sonnenschein on 6 June 1941.[24]

Vienna? Bad Ischl? The 'indissoluble boyhood friendship'[25]

In 1945, Hans Mayer is thinking of all kinds of different *Örtlichkeiten* (localities),[26] for, of course, 'localities' are all that can be considered; there is no substitute for a native land, let alone any native land itself. No destination is ruled out; he even considers migrating back to Austria. Leopold Langhammer offers to smooth the way back for him by asking for 'help and support' from the administration in Vienna. Above all there is his friend Ernst Mayer, with whom he lost touch long ago, but they are now in contact again. 'You can hardly understand what extraordinary pleasure your swift answer gave me,' Hans Mayer replies, as soon as he is back in Brussels.

> Only when you are in the intellectual and human isolation in which I find myself here, in spite of all my supposed connections, will you understand what it means to me that I am not forgotten at home after all.[27]

His Viennese friend can hardly wait for their reunion:

> Your coming, our picking up that (...) firm net woven around our hearts by our shared youth and harmony of ideas, a net that even orgies of destructive rage and excesses of soul-destroying compulsion could tear, but could not destroy.[28]

At the thought of being able to spend a holiday in Bad Ischl with him, Ernst Mayer becomes enthusiastic:

> Think of it, Hans, perhaps we shall be able to spend several weeks together in that beloved landscape, we shall be able to experience the compelling harmony

of nature and spirit once more. Those two days we spent with each other in Lurg many days ago are still the best I can remember. (...) I know that one cannot bring back the past, and there is no need for me to conjure up the spirit of Hermann Hesse to keep us both from sentimentality, and thus probably disappointment too [Ernst writes to Hans Mayer on 4 April 1946].

I was often in Ischl in the course of my forced pharmaceutical activities, and knew that bitter and painfully sweet pleasure of exploring all the nooks and crannies of our youth: Egelmoosgasse, Kalvarienberg, 'Klein-Kammer' (where we always fancied (...) the girl visitors with their painted faces during the tourist season), and I must admit: despite any thought of disillusionment, a boundless longing for your company came over me. I wanted to walk those paths with you again, the one person with whom I share not only memories but feelings. If this wish should be granted, my friend, then new hours of complete happiness will be added to those many that I remember.

With a certain irony directed at himself, he senses that he may be 'overdoing it' in imagining how their 'conversations and arguments can be of more importance for the future than most of those popular diplomatic and economic discussions'. Ernst Mayer is determined to involve himself in the political development of Austria:

You alone will know how much I miss you in that respect, how I long for the day when, like an emotional poet of the Hainbund,[ii] I can take you in my arms.

Ernst Mayer is torn between duty and inclination. Much as he longs to see his friend, he knows it would be unreasonable for him to move back at once. For the Vienna of 1946 is 'fallow land run wild,' where there is literally a shortage of everything – for body, mind and soul. He cannot urge his friend to return; the first priority is, after all, his health, weakened by his time in the camps. So Hans would do better if, to begin with, he went to and stayed with his cousin Lili or his Aunt Herta in Bad Ischl. 'The landscape and good food there would very likely help your recovery in every way.'[29]

Ernst does not guess how undecided his friend really is. But whether he reimigrates or not, it matters to Hans Mayer to get his Austrian citizenship back. Only when he has an Austrian passport in his hands will he renounce his right to live in Austria. Neither a friend nor a mentor, however necessary they may be to his life, is as necessary as the *possibility* of being *able* to return to Austria; no one can make him change his mind. Hans Mayer does visit the country regularly at

---

ii The Hainbund (Fellowship of the Grove) was a group of eighteenth-century German poets based in Göttingen.

least once a year and will do so until his death, but as he explains in a retrospective article, 'without any idea of settling there,'[30] for 'you never go back to an inn
once you've been thrown out of it.'

However, in June 1946 he goes reconnoitring for the first time, as papers
from the Military Permit Office in Brussels show. Year after year he needs physical contact with his native land, the country he both loves and hates. 'I too feel
as you do,' he says, responding to his friend's birthday wishes:

> There is no one to whom I am so bound and by whom I feel so well understood.
> I too cannot imagine my past, my life without you. I see us sitting together on
> the school bench in Phorusgasse, riding hell for leather over the Kalvarienberg,
> together in Kärntnerstrasse, God help us, executing 'Wedetschuk', sitting
> together in the Münzamt and the Schottentor, together, if rather balder now,
> in Goisern, Vienna, Gastein, sitting at table in beautiful Rutzendorf – linked
> by a bond that can never be broken. The fact that the present situation does
> not allow us to make our spiritual and human intimacy a physical and concrete
> bond more often is one of the many evils of life. (J.A. to E.M. 24.11.58)

In 1971 he confesses:

> I sometimes have moments when I wonder if I should not come back at once in
> both the simple and the higher sense. If I should ever have the chance to retire,
> I would probably go back to Vienna after all. The retired Hofrat [Ernst Mayer;
> author's note] and the worn-out writer walking together on thoughtful paths
> through the Hauptallee or the Lainzer Tiergarten, would not be the worst of
> fates (...). (J.A. to E.M. 21.9.71)

By now he feels almost at home in the cities of the Federal Republic, whereas
Vienna is moving further and further away, he says, 'in the mists of myth and
legend' (J.A. to E.M. 25.2.71).

On 1 April 1972 he is invited for the first time to Vienna by the Austrian
Society of Literature, to give a lecture – we find him speaking ironically of the
'Return of the Prodigal' (J.A. to E.M. 23.1.72). 'We will walk our old ways
again, sit together in cafés,' he writes to Ernst Mayer, 'comparing the here and
now incredulously with yesterday' (J.A. to E.M. 12.3.72). In November 1977,
after the award to him of the Journalism Prize in May, he features for the last
time in the International European Discussions in Vienna. Very late and, in
fact, only through his success in Germany, he finds recognition in the Austrian
capital.

Yet, for all his longing, he can be an Austrian only in the 'sentimental'
sense, he says in 1976: an Austrian of the years between the wars, who knew

Vienna when it held an intellectual monopoly with Paris and Berlin, but who has also seen that intellectual city, as representing opposition, imprisoned by an anti-intellectual state in the ghetto of Austro-Marxism, 'to which an end was finally put in 1934 with the requisite energy symbolized by heavy artillery'. His own 'indelible' Austria, the Austria of the subversion of Freud and Schönberg, the Austria of the negation of force, the Austria that he had to leave in 1938, died with Hitler. He tries honestly to come to terms with this loss, but 'Austrian oblivion' makes it very difficult for him, for it is 'intent upon (...) stealing from me the last remnants of a past that, all things considered, is my dearest possession.'[31] 'Almost nothing,' he claims ten years before his death, 'links him any more' with the Second Republic, the Austria of the present,[32] although he carries its passport. However, the man who says he has 'learned to be homeless' is still bound to this country of his by so much that he wants to kill himself there and nowhere else.

Cologne? Comrade Heinz Kühn

In 1946 rescue comes from Germany itself: Heinz Kühn[33] – later prime minister of North Rhine-Westphalia, who himself emigrated in 1933 by way of Prague to Brussels, where he successfully escaped the Gestapo – sends the following letter to 'Comrade Mayer' on 7 July: 'I do not know if you have already been informed through official channels that you must prepare for speedy transfer to Germany.' He offers him an 'excellent job at North-West German Radio.' 'Your post is envisaged as director of the Cultural Word department. This is the department which is concerned less with politics (...) than with all that comes under the heading of literature and art.' It dealt with 'questions of adult education in the widest sense,' says Kühn. If for any reason this post should fall through, he could immediately take over the job of 'Cultural Editor of the *Rheinische Zeitung*' in Cologne, Aachen or Koblenz. The editor-in-chief Willi Eichler has authorized him, Heinz Kühn, to make this offer, he says. In addition, Hans Mayer can immediately

> ...make contact with the adult education organization here. The director, Education Officer Professor Nikolai, will entrust important tasks to you as his assistant, and you can begin giving two courses of lectures in September. I have suggested as the subject for one course, 'Problems in modern French literature' (...) and you can decide on the subject of the other course yourself. It would be a good idea for you to begin preparations at once in all the above-mentioned subject areas, so that you can start practical work here without delay. North-West German Radio is also situated in Cologne, so in any case you will be living here in the city, and in addition you will have an opportunity to help in building up

the educational activities of the Young Socialist Study Groups, the organization of which in the Rhineland has been entrusted to me.

Various arrangements must have been made shortly before this letter was written, probably with Kühn's wife Marianne, who unlike her husband uses the familiar *du* pronoun in addressing Hans Mayer. It is she who ends this letter by saying that she looks forward to his arrival in the near future, as if Hans Mayer's move were all settled.

Heinz Kühn writes to Willi Eichler in June 1945, and then, at greater length, on 11 November.[34] At this point Willi Eichler himself is still living in England, to which he has emigrated, and he has already asked for food parcels to be sent to 'Dr Mayer' from America. 'And now to something important,' Kühn begins. 'Dr Hanns Mayer, about whom I have already written to you, also intends to return to Germany (...) where he would like to be involved with me in working with young people in their studies.'

In the same letter to Willi Eichler, Heinz Kühn asks him to help Hans Mayer with a financial transaction between London and Cologne:

He has an uncle in London, who has sent him (...) large parcels as well as some money through a lady working in ENSA. The uncle, however, would like to send him a larger sum so that he can recover properly after the concentration camps of Breendonck, Auschwitz and Belsen, and get himself some new equipment, for he needs almost everything, especially if he is going to Germany. I would be happy to help in getting him there, since he acquired experience and valuable knowledge as a lecturer at the Vienna College of Adult Education [here Kühn is obviously using Langhammer's letter of recommendation] and is a very useful man in other ways as well. (...) He would like best to settle in the west and work with me there, although he has received a written contract of employment from his friends in Vienna to be director of a hostel for a school of adult education there. However, he does not want to be in the Russian zone of influence. It depends on making available to him the money that his uncle cannot send directly. I thought that it might be possible for you to send a comrade to this uncle, the well-known film composer Hans May, to receive the money from him, and you can then send it on here by way of Switzerland or some other means. Is there an opportunity of doing that kind of thing? You need not fear that this is a form of scrounging. Judging by all the letters from his uncle that I have read, he would be very happy to send the money. (...) However, he has no access to official means of transfer, since financial transactions with Belgium are not yet sanctioned. The uncle knows that he is to give the money to a gentleman who will present him with greetings from Hanns Mayer. The address is: Hans May – 42 Hatherley Court, Hatherley Grove, London W2. I would be very glad if you could help him.[35]

We do not know whether this sum of money ever reached Hans Mayer, but it is certain that Hans May the composer was indeed very fond of his nephew.

Dangerous games with identity

Apropos of 'Dr Hanns Mayer', Hanns Mayer did indeed credit himself with a doctorate after the war and even had notepaper printed with the title of Dr on it. He is also described, on the 'list of political refugees in Belgium' that Heinz Kühn sends to Will Eichler, as 'Dr Hanns Mayer' and a 'member of the Socialist Party of Austria (Vienna). 33 years old. Profession: doctor of philosophy and literature. Lecturer at the college of adult education.' It cannot be ascertained today whether Leopold Langhammer, who really should have known better, having met him when he was still a novice in the bookselling business, suggested this deception so that he could provide more protection for him, or whether it was the other way around, and whether Langhammer himself drew up his letter of reference in this way on account of Mayer's own fictions. The fact is that this fictional doctorate, his invented university studies, his also invented names and constant new spellings of them, all were to become a tragic trap for him in the late 1940s, as they had been in the 1930s over his certificate of citizenship. He does not know at this point how to disentangle himself from the fraud. It is, therefore, impossible for him to find legal ways of becoming an accredited foreign correspondent in Switzerland without the shame of having to deny the earlier data he had given on his identity. Instead of proudly displaying his self-taught achievements, the Hans Mayer of the immediate post-war period was to involve himself more and more in imaginary biographical data, until he found a solution in 1955 in his final choice of nom de plume. Nonetheless, all his life and even at the height of his recognition, Améry was to feel that his 'airy' schooling and non-existent university studies were a taint that clung to him. He always finds himself in great embarrassment if he is asked about his formal education. On the other hand, he is proud enough to reject the title of professor in no uncertain terms when Austrian friends apply to have it bestowed on him in 1972.

Hans Mayer also seems to have sent his manuscript 'Zur Psychologie des deutschen Volkes' [On the Psychology of the German People] to Kühn, but obviously it was never published.[36]

Immediately after the war he cannot have been seriously inclined to work for Germany or actually settle there. In fact, Cologne remains a city of transit for him, and from it he seeks 'a place to cross the border illegally to some western country or other'. Cologne has come to mean, to him, a centre for emigrants, a centre of 'criminals who have committed no crime'; Cologne is a city he wants to leave as soon as possible. No, he cannot stay here in 1946, tempting as the professional prospects that are offered to him may be. It will be 20 long years before he can venture on conversation with Germany. Undoubtedly Germany is his linguistic fatherland, but for that very reason it is a mobile homeland that he can take with him wherever he goes.

Lore's London?

On the other hand, for a little while he seriously considers London. 'And really, why not put down roots there, if rather late in the day?' he is still wondering in 1950. The country always stood up to Hitler. After all, it was the British who liberated him; how could he forget that? Moreover, he has family there: his cousin Lore, with whom he grew up; his uncle Hans, of whom he is particularly fond. When he comes back from the concentration camp his uncle sends him money and later remembers him in his will. Hans May's death in 1954 affects his nephew deeply. He decides to try England, and assimilates entirely after a few months, wearing tweed suits in heather shades. The International News Alliance has sent him there as a correspondent for a while. Before long he is familiar with the British press; when reading *The Times* or *The Manchester Guardian,* he actually turns first to the pages of Home News and Commonwealth News before taking a fleeting look at the rather brief accounts of what is happening among the savages: the French, Italians and Germans.[37] But no, this country is not for him either; it doesn't want to know about him, for all its goodwill it will not let him conquer it. The austerity in England is a deterrent: food rationing is still in force, the country is industrially backward, he is aware of 'the deep weariness of a people who have won the greatest war of all time and lost their empire', and finally of 'the unbroken continuity of the class structure in the state'. The British are too insular for him; it is impossible 'to be in England and in the wider world at the same time. This "second emigration" is not to be.'[38]

Sartre's Paris?

'To live permanently in Paris [is] about the only heartfelt wish I still have,' he writes in 1949 to his friend Maria Leitner.[39] As he sees it, only Paris is the world, and indeed the city is 'the sun of the world'.[40] He 'knew' Paris from books before first going there in 1941, when the city was living under the German blackout and was far removed from the *ville lumière* of his dreams – and at the time he was 'a man down at heel' and in flight. In 1946, when he visits the city for the second time, he is not down at heel any more, and the lights there are on again, although not for him, since he is in search of his beloved wife who has 'run away' from him. His third visit takes place under happier auspices, for he meets his friend Maria Leitner in Paris. 'In the years 1945–1948 (...),' he says in his account of it in the later *Örtlichkeiten*, 'after my return from the concentration camp, I lived partly in Brussels, partly in Paris.' He lets himself be carried away by the intoxication of liberation and the Resistance movement, by the 'dream of a new popular front and radical change', by France's 'extraordinary wealth and dynamic in the intellectual sphere', by existentialism, by Sartre and his 'Réflexions sur la question juive', by Camus, Simone de Beauvoir, Boris Vian, the *chansons* of Juliette Gréco, and by Aragon. However, he also knows that he will be unable to hold on to his mythical post-war Paris if he settles there; these are 'images' and 'sensory impressions', and he can preserve them only by protecting them from superimposed images of the new Paris of the Cold War. So he goes there merely as a 'spectator'. Paris will never lose its hold on him. It is also the home of his friend in exile the painter Erich Schmid. Shortly before his death, he wonders whether he ought not to have become a French writer. But he did not, and for good reasons.

Zürich and the Dukas press agency?

Zürich is also a 'world' in its own way. Hans Mayer says, reconstructing the situation as it appeared to him on leaving the camp in 1945:

> Germany is intolerable. Paris is brilliant and poverty-stricken. London maintains a dignity salvaged from its days of grandeur in the cold, rainy winter of limited heating and meagre food rations. Even Brussels, which has made a quick recovery from the disease of war, thanks to uranium from the Congo, seems at best an upstart compared to the Swiss cities. Here in Zürich, however, all is solidity (Ö, Vol. 2, p. 431).

In Paris you may be poor, he says, summing it up, in the London of Attlee's Labour government you must be poor. 'It is a matter of civic duty', so to speak (Ö, Vol. 2, p. 433). In Germany you are simply poor for no special reason, but appearing to be a scrounger in Zürich almost amounts to a criminal offence (Ö, Vol. 2, p. 433).

On 22 January 1950 Mayer will spend some months, at the invitation of Frank Dukas, in this rich city of Zürich, first as 'ghost writer for an established journalist', then on his own account for various very different Swiss newspapers, using a wide variety of pseudonyms. Chief among the papers for which he writes are *Die Weltwoche* and the *St Galler Tagblatt*.[41] Year 1948 onwards, he has already worked closely with the L. Dukas Press Agency, to which he was introduced by a mutual friend, the Boston psychiatrist Paul Stern, an author represented by the Dukas agency. It commissions and distributes nearly all his articles – both political and non-political – especially in Switzerland, but also in Holland, England, even Chile.

Lotte Dukas and later her son Frank make history in the Swiss press. They have founded a writers' centre in Seefeld in Zürich, which goes by the name of 'The Wasps' Nest' and soon becomes a secret meeting place for the Jewish intelligentsia. Visitors include Robert Jungk, Elias Canetti and Max Brod. Frank Dukas seems to have had a special liking for Hans Mayer, alias Jean Améry. An obituary of Dukas – he died in 2000 – records that 'a deep friendship linked him to Jean Améry, whom he represented as an agent for decades, as well as many others.'[42] Dukas too was Jewish, deeply scarred by a fatherless and difficult childhood. Like Améry, he was self-taught. 'Dukas was different,' Yves Kugelmann describes him in the *Jüdische Rundschau*. 'He thought faster than other people, was more sensitive, more amusing, sadder, more substantial.' There were obvious affinities between the two 'self-made men'. In these first years, Hans Mayer was making his living entirely by journalism, as Frank Dukas says in a letter to Friedrich Pfäfflin.[43] In the 1960s, he continues, he leaned more and more towards philosophical and literary activity, which was not the agency's business.[44] Zürich, then, is the city that nurtures him, the city where he visits editorial offices 'so that they will not forget him'.

The ethos of the German Swiss, whether here or elsewhere, intrigues him. He comes up against their 'complacency', which allows them to act as if it were to their personal credit 'that Hitler did not grab Switzerland'. The people of this 'paradise of full-cream milk chocolate, he says scornfully, are setting up as moral judges of the world, behaving as if there had never been any members of a Swiss pro-Nazi front. He cannot reconcile himself to this 'island of the blessed', this country without upheavals or divisions; its sombre self-satisfaction contradicts his 'mental concept of foreigners'. As a foreigner, he returns to a foreign place that is not quite so foreign to him now.

Brussels old and new

There is still his first place of emigration left. In fact, it is not in Paris but in Brussels that he meets Sartre, when the master comes to deliver a lecture there in 1945:

> Sartre and the anonymous X met only once, and the nameless X, when he was introduced to the great man, was too shy to utter more than a mere '*enchanté, Monsieur*'. Sartre could never have taken any notice of him; the water between them was far too deep. But he silently accompanied the great man for a quarter

of a century, saying nothing, alert and critical, loving and admiring him. (UW, Vol. 2, p. 269)

In the elation of his first success as an established writer, he will try a second time in 1966 and will again be rebuffed. This time he writes on behalf of Bavarian Radio, which has commissioned him to interview Sartre. Sartre declines, saying that he is *indisponible* [not available] for some months on account of overwork. '*Soyez sûr que je le regrette*,' [Be assured that I regret it] he automatically assures Améry and has the letter signed by his secretary.

Hans Mayer, then, decides in favour of Brussels, or perhaps it would be more accurate to say that he does not decide *against* Brussels, as he had against Vienna, Cologne, London, Paris and Zürich. A sparsely furnished room in the university quarter becomes his first lodging there. His greatest joy is 'a little cat' which delights him with its affectionate ways and the way it laps milk.

As long as he has no papers he can make no kind of claim. It is a tedious and laborious business to prove to the authorities that he still exists at all. His sole piece of evidence is his 'registration card' from Bergen-Belsen dated 24 April 1945, the day of his liberation, which bears the words 'Keep this card at all times to assist your safe return'. However, it does not enable him to travel. On 2 May 1945 the general secretary of the Austrian Freedom Front, Dori Meisemann, confirms his membership of the Resistance, his arrest on 23 July 1943, and, as he sums it up, writing in French, his deportation to Germany, 'from which he is returning. He was last at Belsen, and was liberated by the British troops on 15 April 1945'. He concludes by saying: 'We ask the authorities to be so good as to facilitate the regularizing of his situation.' A provisional Belgian identity card for war victims, especially for repatriated political prisoners, gives him the necessary legal status to stay in Belgium; his final 'Carte de Prisonnier Politique 1940–1945' is not issued until 14 December 1949, and legal status, by a decree from the Ministry of Reconstruction, follows on 29 December 1949. There has also been an official request for 'additional rations', both of food and clothing coupons. So that he can really get the help that he has been promised, he needs yet another 'Carte de Prisonnier Politique', which provides not just the usual personal details but also the length of his imprisonment. This entry gives the figure '647 days'. Finally he also needs an Allied Forces Permit to travel to Austria, a pass made out for him by the 'Bureau des Permis Militaires' on 24 June 1946 and extended until 15 August 1946. So it was three months before he could embrace his friend Ernst Mayer. On 25 October 1950 the kingdom of Belgium awards him a certified 'Croix du Prisonnier Politique 1940–1945'.

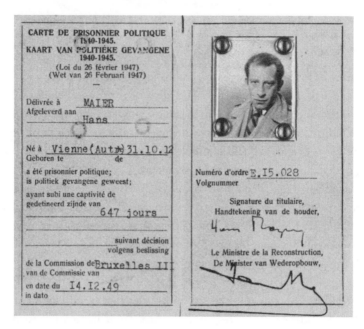

CARTE DE PRISONNIER POLITIQUE
1940-1945.
KAART VAN POLITIEKE GEVANGENE
1940-1945.
(Loi du 26 février 1947)
(Wet van 26 Februari 1947)

Délivrée à　　MAIER
Afgeleverd aan
　　　　　Hans

Né à　Vienne (Autr.) 31.10.12
Geboren te　　　　de
a été prisonnier politique;
is politiek gevangene geweest;
ayant subi une captivité de
gedetineerd zijnde van
　　　　　　　　647 jours

　　　　　　　　suivant décision
　　　　　　　　volgens beslissing
de la Commission de Bruxelles II
van de Commissie van
en date du　14.12.49
in dato

Numéro d'ordre E.15.028
Volgnummer

Signature du titulaire,
Handtekening van de houder,

Le Ministre de la Reconstruction,
De Minister van Wederopbouw,

Identity card: 'Carte de Prisonnier Politique' of 1949

'He is now at home in Belgium, in a vague kind of way,' he sums up the situation, 'he is at home in a certain form of everyday life, a network of habits.' *Habitude*, a word always written by Marcel Proust, for good reason, with a capital H, is a substitute for home to him. He writes in 'Verfemt und verbannt' that he feels as much at ease in the bars of Brussels as he once did in the cafés of Vienna. Brussels is his permanent place of residence – he constantly emphasizes the great gratitude that he feels for Belgium – but it is still a land where he is a visitor; the national disagreement between Flemings and Walloons has deprived him of any wish to 'become a naturalized citizen'.[45] But the best thing about Brussels is its geographical location: only a short journey from both Paris and Cologne.

The Adelboden sanatorium

First, however, Hans Mayer must visit Switzerland again, not because of the 'Rosa Blättli' [little pink paper], as he humorously calls the *St Galler Tagblatt*, but because of his heart is giving him trouble. 'The internist who happened to be here to convalesce (...) detected a considerable expansion of the heart and acute weakness of the heart muscle,' he tells Maria Leitner in a letter in early 1949, after suffering several heart attacks.[46] 'I myself have the impression that I shall soon in reality be at the point which we discussed jokingly in Brussels. I cannot say that this prospect makes me particularly uneasy,' he tells his friend. After

The Adelboden Sanatorium, 1949, Hans Mayer back right

mental proximity to death, he is now physically close to it – whether he fears or wishes for that outcome, who can say? He begs Maria, who is still living in New York at this time but is visiting Paris on business, to make haste to Brussels 'before it is too late'.

Mayer's friend arrives, but she cannot cure him. It is Switzerland that takes care of his health, even if he hardly feels grateful. In February 1949 the International Red Cross Committee sends him for two months of treatment to the Schoenegg sanatorium in Adelboden. He is glad he has been able to get a single room, and glad of the 'extremely good food', but complains that his room is cold, which makes it difficult for him to work.[47] And above all, his financial situation is bad; everything is 'wickedly expensive'. He has to hire ski shoes because of the weather, and they cost him 10 francs a week, so that 'in eight weeks' he will 'have to pay 80 francs just for the shoes'. And 'the other prices here, for coffee, chocolate, etc., are adjusted to the taste of English millionaires and thus a danger to the wallet'.[48] The portraits he provides of his fellow patients are not exactly kindly. His company, he says, consists of 'terribly estimable people' who are all 'so-called German Socialists' and address one another 'insufferably' as 'Comrade', using the familiar *du* pronoun. They are good-hearted, he admits patronisingly, but 'the Boche in them' is positively 'nauseating'. 'The main trouble is the landscape,' he says in the same letter. 'It is so beautiful that it ceases to be beautiful at all.' He describes the

> …neat and clean toy houses, gigantic and officially permitted mountains, inhabitants who are greedy for profit, if friendly – all of it there just to be called

"wonderful" by the British and Americans. I prefer the poor management and frugal human atmosphere of our own Lower Austria. Here we have the wonderful world of the tourist offices and the hotel WCs.

'*Non, pas pour moi*,' he sarcastically concludes. It is no use. Always a sworn enemy of health resorts, he cannot feel comfortable with his stay at the sanatorium and even speaks of it as a 'Swiss concentration camp'. He can hardly wait to be discharged. However, when Maria visits him and wins the approval of the 'terribly estimable people' around him, news that Hans Mayer naturally sends her in his next letter, he finds he can bear it there after all. 'Your "shockingly vain" little bunny felt mightily puffed up, and rejoiced to think that his little angel had won their hearts.'[49]

Journalistic confectionery

Hans Mayer's most important concern is to create a basis for making a living in journalism. In fact, he writes a number of pieces while in Adelboden, particularly for that 'little pink paper', the *St Galler Tagblatt*. He is also commissioned to write articles for *Newsweek*, for instance, one on 'Anti-Semitism in the USSR'. He finally declines this on ideological grounds, because he does not want to contribute to the escalation of the Cold War.

I would rather not write about anti-Semitism in Russia in the present circumstances. It may all be true (...) [he concedes] but at least it was not the Russians who made soap out of Jewish bones and extracted gold teeth from old people's bodies. I feel too un-Jewish to cry shame at once if told that the real name of a man called Schadenev is Finkelstein, but I am still too human ever to forgive the making of lampshades from human skin. At this time, anyway, one ought not to do anything to make mutual understanding more difficult, for none of us (...) has anything to hope for but this precarious peace – however poor a thing it may be.[50]

Every day, he is making new plans for his work. He needs to write at least three articles a week to earn enough for a minimum standard of living. He is ready to try any subject, whether it requires research or is merely routine: articles on the subject of scandals, politics, culture, royal families, countless 'random' uncommissioned articles which he sends around and which generally come back without finding any takers. In his letter of 12 March 1949, he mentions an article on the Russian statesman and lawyer Andrey Vyshinsky, another on 'the Sober Look', yet another on 'The Maid of Athens'. His high point in 1949 is a commission from the Dukas Agency to write five articles on Lola Montez, each of eight pages. 'I tremble at the mere thought of this commission.' It would enable him to pay his debts, with enough money left over, perhaps, to go to Austria.[51] The couple is euphoric. Maria plans to try selling the series in the United States (she does not succeed), they even have visions of a film based on the series. Dreams are not in short supply, but very few of these ventures bear fruit. No method should be left untried when it comes to earning a little money. Maria urges him to enter a competition in the *Aufbau*: 'I'd be surprised if you didn't win the first prize of 100 dollars.'[52] He sends in his *Kleist-Novelle*, but the first prize goes to someone else.

The correspondence between Hans Mayer and Maria Leitner in 1949–1950 shows, in great detail and in every nuance, how pitiless the everyday life of a journalist is, how much it is swayed by the market, how dependent it is on the goodwill of individual editors and agencies, while there is always the threat of rivals. Again and again, Hans Mayer fears for his fees, for commissions that sometimes (but not often enough) come in excess but generally fail to materialize, and then there are all the subjects that must be mastered. He can seldom do his own research. Maria, with whom he corresponds several times a week, is very well informed about his work and is much involved in it. Sometimes she writes pieces herself but signs them with his name; if he is not writing under a pseudonym, at times she does the requisite research. If he is in luck, as with the Lola Montez series, he does research in the Bibliothèque Royale; usually he 'invents' this or that or puts together material found in other journals. Financial insecurity is very hard to bear: in October 1949, when the Dukas Agency has committed itself to only one article a month, he fears he may not be able to pay his rent. He doesn't shrink from any kind of work – selling insurance, giving German lessons, removing furniture, running errands – he will take anything. Maria would like to open a bookshop with him, but where will they find the capital? This struggle for survival does nothing for his self-confidence.

At the same time – and this is what really matters to him most – he is trying to write fiction again and longs for encouragement. Without encouragement, he feels depressed. He confesses to Maria on 16 March 1949, still in Adelboden:

> I have wanted to set about the novella several times, but it usually ended with my opening the studies of Thomas Mann again and again, and the volume of Proust that I have with me for the nth time. *À quoi bon, ma petite*, others have done it already, much better too, and thank God for that. I am not jealous of the great men of letters, but do not want to copy them (...) and I will be content to read them with delight and admire them with an almost conspiratorial gratitude.

After six weeks in the sanatorium Hans Mayer once again 'experiences a very alarming heart attack,' as he puts it in his last letter from Adelboden.[53] Test follows test; if it is not his heart it is his teeth; there is talk of 'facial neuralgia', of 'extreme pain' that can be alleviated only by high doses of medication. Above all he wants to go 'home' to Brussels. If his Maria doesn't get him out of here soon, he threatens, he will 'run off' into the 'maquis' of the rue Veydt.[54]

He is discharged at the end of April. Back in Brussels it is mainly the 'debates' at the home of the Prigogines that reinvigorate him. Here, in the best of company, he can join discussions 'at the highest level' of the concept of Marxism or Heidegger's concept of historicity. He is still juggling his journalistic pieces – which hard as he works at them never seem to bring in enough money – and his writing of fiction, which is the 'most important thing'. Since he is not having success in making a living in either field, 'I have (...) in fact largely lost confidence in myself, and keep thinking, at every line I write, that it is useless.' He has come to the conclusion that his journalism is too literary and his literary fiction too much like journalism.[55]

CHAPTER 6

Jean Améry the Journalist (1955–1965)

The year 1955 sees the final change of name for Hans Mayer. He gives up experimenting with identities and from now on consistently calls himself Jean Améry, as if he had, in fact, found something like an 'inner centre' for himself, and one that could even express itself externally in the French anagram of his German surname.[1]

Améry's real originality as a writer lies in the very fluidity between genres to which he disparagingly refers in his letter to Maria, the interweaving of literary elements into his journalism and journalistic elements into his literary writing. As a journalist, he never lapses into wooden cliché, and his approach, whoever or whatever the subject of an article, is wide in scope. In investigating a phenomenon he always looks at the whole of it, finding particulars interesting only if they cast light on the essence of the subject.

He still sees himself, however, as a 'frustrated writer', and he speaks of his 'failure as a man of letters'; he regards journalism, whether he is writing on cultural or topical subjects, as a 'non-career, an anti-career'.[2] 'As for me,' he writes to his friend Ernst Mayer shortly after his forty-fifth birthday, 'I am tuned to the minor key. The balance sheet of my life shows little profit. What can still lie ahead? Nothing. I shall simply muddle along, intellectually, mentally and materially.'[3] He ascribes his 'failure as a man of letters' to his 'psychological and moral inability' to work for Germany. It means that until 1965 he must rely on the 'comparatively small Swiss German market in journalism to earn a living.'[4] He has to 'rack [his] brains to keep the commissions coming in (...), it is all difficult and laborious, and only half successful' (J.A. to E.M. 10.3.58).[5] In terms of quantity, he is not half but entirely successful, for in just under two decades he 'concocts' the 'surprising number of some 5000 newspaper articles, which added together would amount to about 15,000 pages.'[6] However, his 'concoctions' are well worth reading, for his expertise as a journalist is very impressive. He manages to impart colour of his own to the most colourless subjects. Furthermore, even when he may not diverge too far from the mainstream, his stylistic cogency still wins the reader over.

Portraits of famous contemporaries

His *Portraits berühmter Zeitgenossen* [Portraits of Famous Contemporaries], a series of articles published in the *St. Galler Tagblatt* over almost 15 years, are so succinct and informative that by the year 1961 they had also been published in book form, in three volumes. The first to appear, in 1955, was *Karrieren and Köpfe* [Careers and Minds], a well-designed volume of nearly 400 pages with photographic illustrations. According to the blurb, it is a collection of 60 short monographs on 60 'leading figures in science, philosophy, literature, the theatre, the cinema, dance, the visual arts and music'. In the manner of a mosaic, these 'models of the myths that we emulate'[7] add up to something like a picture of the times – a glimpse of the cultural constitution of the 1950s.

Vive la science!

It is Améry's 'envious admiration of science', an idiosyncratic relic of his positivist youth, that determines the structure and chronology of his *Portraits*. 'What can even a Nobel Prize winner like Camus throw into the scale to tip it his way against the conquest of interstellar space by exact science?' he laments to his Viennese friend Ernst Mayer. 'In the face of the reality of these times, which resides entirely in the field of science, we intellectuals whose interests are literary and philosophical cut only a poor figure anyway, whether we are successful or failures (...)' (J.A. to E.M. 3.11.57).

Consequently Améry, the intellectual whose interests are 'merely' literary and philosophical, makes 'The Philosophers' Stone', the heading of his first chapter in *Karrieren und Köpfe*, the foundation stone of the book, taking Albert Einstein, Robert Oppenheimer, Albert Schweitzer, the biologist Jean Rostand and the bacteriologist Alexander Fleming as subjects. However, the thinkers Romano Guardini, C.G. Jung, Bertrand Russell and Martin Heidegger also have their part in 'The Philosophers' Stone'. Only after them are 'tellers of tales' admitted to the company: Hermann Hesse, Thomas Mann and Ernst Jünger, representing Germany writers; François Mauriac and Colette representing France; and William Faulkner, Graham Greene and Somerset Maugham as well as (for the book sets out to represent a wide range) Pearl S. Buck and Agatha Christie, among writers in the English language. At the heart of the book, and in line with Améry's own deepest passion, is the chapter on 'The Committed and the Enraged': Jean-Paul Sartre, André Malraux and Arthur Koestler. He shows personal flair by including in his panorama the less well-known 'committed' figures of Richard Coudenhove-Kalergi[8] and Ilja Ehrenburg, who is the sole representative of Eastern Europe and is included here to counterbalance Koestler. The choice of musicians in the chapter 'A Wealth of Melodious Sound', including Stravinsky, Hindemith, Furtwängler, Menuhin, Horowitz and the singer Lily Pons, holds no surprises.

Jazz – heightened emotion

Jazz, to which Améry would devote a book of its own six years later, *Im Banne des Jazz*[9] [Under the Spell of Jazz], too finds a place here, with portraits of Louis Armstrong and Irving Berlin. As a former bar pianist, Jean Améry approaches his subject not from the musicologist's standpoint, as, he says, many much better-qualified writers had done before him, but from the perspective of someone writing about the *people* involved in jazz.[10] In his eulogy of Ella Fitzgerald – even at this time – he cannot refrain from a side-swipe at Adorno the musical theoretician, who saw jazz merely as 'the thudding negation of all real music.'[11] Is this perhaps at the root of Améry's dislike of Adorno as a cultural philosopher?

He himself proclaims his whole-hearted devotion to jazz and tells the reader why. Whereas, classical music, he says, is the *purification* of emotion, jazz is the *intensification* of emotion.[12] Jazz musicians, to him, are

> ...the last artists in the full sense of the word. While the painters, poets and operatic composers of our time adjust more and more to society, while to use a fashionable word they 'integrate' with it, jazz musicians live on the periphery of our mechanized world, a world that acknowledges only the 'standard of living'. They and they alone are still possessed by their art. In them alone we feel the hot breath of the daemonic artistry that once distinguished the great figures of literature, the visual arts and music.[13]

They are, he says, the last rebels, the last Bohemians, the last individualists, pitting themselves in their absolute artistic freedom against those who are part of the organized system.

Karrieren und Köpfe is rounded off by miniatures of painters, sculptors and architects in the chapter 'Colours and Stones'. Améry looks at the entire spectrum of artists from the Western world, from Picasso to Kokoschka, from Grandma Moses[14] to Henry Moore and Frank Lloyd Wright. He will return to the depiction of many of these figures in the future, for instance, Picasso, to whom six years later he devotes an 'Account' of the artist's life in five parts published in the *Weltwoche* of Zürich.[15] Here again Améry shows remarkable journalistic skill; not only is his 'account' very informative in casting light on art, politics and cultural history, it is also equally fascinating to read as if Améry himself had been present at every moment of crisis through which that 'natural phenomenon' Picasso lived.

Stars of the 1950s

These portraits are complemented by actors in 'The Footlights' and by dancers in 'Dreams Both Normal and Danced'. Améry also returns to actors in his microstudy *Teenager Stars. Idole unserer Zeit* [Teenage Stars. Idols of our times], the second book of this kind, with 20 more portraits.[16] Jean Améry did his job as a biographer so brilliantly that the first book was followed by this second volume, in which he conscientiously brought together 'the "stars" most popular with young people, all of whom aroused enthusiasm, frenzy, even ecstasy in audiences, from Frank Sinatra and Dizzy Gillespie by way of Brigitte Bardot and Eddie Constantine to Pascale Petit and Peter Kraus.'

Here again he performs his task with wit and elegance, looks into the sociological aspect of his subject, and anchors the cult phenomena so closely associated with its time in history. As with Heidegger and Russell, Koestler and Ehrenburg, Jünger and Thomas Mann, he likes to present contrasts. He sees Romy Schneider as an 'anti-Bardot' figure:

> The actress who played 'Sissy', the Empress Elisabeth, and the Bacchante of Saint-Tropez are worlds apart – as dissimilar as a garden tree and a skyscraper, a horse-drawn cab and a Nitribitt Mercedes,[i] Franz Lehár and Louis Armstrong, caviar and batter pudding, which if enjoyed in moderation is much to be recommended.[17]

Fan-worship of the teenage star Conny Froboes seems to him a dubious symptom of prim and proper German behaviour.

> She is a 'pure girl' (...) a picture of innocence (...). Youth is as safe with Conny as in a convent school. No whisky fumes, no cigarette smoke, no fashionable nonsense: the very best pre-war wares in sterilized post-war plastic packaging. Her conformism, or maybe we should call it Connyformism, is all that anxious parents and teachers could desire.[18]

Politically speaking, Améry issues a warning against this prim and proper attitude: 'We do not disapprove of it,' he protests. 'But we do not unconditionally approve of it either, for we know only too well how quickly the pendulum

---

i   Rosemarie Nitribitt, a well-known call girl between the wars, showed off her wealth by buying a black Mercedes with red upholstery, referred to as the 'Nitribitt Mercedes'.

can swing in the opposite direction (...).'[19] Améry had been passionately fond of the cinema even as a boy.[20] In fact, he is ashamed of himself for having to write such books: 'It makes people whose names you do not need to know consider you a lucky man,' he writes to his friend. 'I have a contradictory wish, one that it would be almost impossible to grant: I would like thousands of people to buy this book, but no one ever to get a sight of it' (J.A. to E.M., 15.11.59).

The tribute he pays to the principle of presenting a complete picture goes so far that the last chapter in *Karrieren und Köpfe* is devoted to the celebrities of the cocktail party circuit: society gurus and multimillionaires of the 1950s such as the Aga Khan and Barbara Hutton. He gives reasons for his selection and for the hierarchy in which he places them: he has left out the economy and politics because 'the gentlemen of the state chancellery offices' may decide our fate, but it is more than doubtful 'whether they shape the cultural face of our times'. And what about sport? Do not its heroes inspire 'the fantasies of a greater number of human beings' than many a poet? But he is afraid, he says apologetically, that he knows nothing about the subject.

Revelations

Although clearly a work written to order – something particularly noticeable in the apologias for Martin Heidegger and Ernst Jünger[21] – this book allows us a glimpse of the Améry of the future as a critic of his times, a man of letters and an aesthete. His reservations about Heidegger, for instance, become clear when he deputizes, so to speak, for Heidegger's critics, whom he, Améry, holds in high esteem. At one point the attack becomes particularly striking because it is hidden away, as if casually, in parentheses: 'Martin Heidegger speaks a language that cannot be understood by the methods of ordinary linguistic logic (the semanticist Rudolf Carnap has tried it, and broke down an essay by Heidegger into a number of meaningless or trivial sentences).'[22] His reservations are even clearer when he draws up his final balance sheet, expressing his doubts through the reported speech of an anonymous figure:

> Even purely political criticism has been made of Heidegger. It is said that his philosophy prepared the way for National Socialism, and his terminology in itself already belonged to the 'blood and the soil' school, to which it is added that as Rector of Freiburg University he clearly defined the National Socialist movement as a 'complete revolution in German life' (and meant it approvingly).[23]

Such camouflaging manoeuvres let him express his reservations so that he can then, diplomatically, make them appear relative. 'All these objections,' he concedes, 'appear to us justified only in part' – only in part, but still justified.

The case of Ernst Jünger is similar:

> Ernst Jünger (...) has been much loved and much hated in the course of his life. His friends see him as the prototype of 'the eternal German' whose nature could help the world to recover if it wished to. His enemies have tried to neutralize the influence of his ideas by countering them with other ideas, and after the war suggested that he should keep quiet. The brilliant nature of his unique character has both attracted and repelled.

The Améry of the time, let alone Améry as a Klett-Cotta author, does not count himself among Ernst Jünger's friends,[24] as we can tell from his consistent use of the term 'the eternal German' in an entirely negative sense.

Therefore, Jean Améry, writing what he saw as journalistic hack work in German, living in Brussels and travelling between Paris, Zürich and London, tacks back and forth for a decade – to be precise, from 1955 to 1965 – between the voice required of him by others and his own.

Gerhart Hauptmann, especially the negative aspects

What exactly he thought of 'the eternal German' we discover only eight years later in his monograph on Gerhart Hauptmann. Admittedly he also applies the epithet 'genius of the Germans' to Hauptmann, who was regarded in his time as a prince among writers. However, what Améry sees as his 'eternal German' nature is exactly a curious combination of literary brilliance and political barbarity, the paradoxical coexistence of intellect and power, and at the same time the gulf between them.

Améry celebrates the path of the rebel's life to a man in flight from reality in elevated tones, saying that Hauptmann was able to mediate 'like no other writer between his subject and supersensory events, between the ordinary day and dreams, between myth and ordinary life, mystery and mysticism'.[25] But when matters were serious, when Hitler's drums were beating all over Germany, when the Mann brothers had long ago emigrated, when Döblin, Feuchtwanger, Zweig, Frank, Toller, even the Prussian officer Fritz von Unruh and the Bavarian socialist Oskar Maria Graf had fled, not to mention Brecht, Hauptmann, that 'preeminent writer of the Republic', stayed on in the country. Gerhart Hauptmann remained in Germany, but his words had lost their force. In November 1933 he even made a statement approving Germany's break with the League of Nations.

Thomas Mann tolerated his conduct and was able to forgive him, not so his lifelong friend Alfred Kerr: 'From now on he and I have no more in common, not in life and not in death,' Améry quotes from Kerr's condemnation from exile in Paris. 'May thorns grow wherever he goes, and may awareness of his shame choke him. (...) Hauptman flatters the mob. (...) Hauptmann went over to the enemy (...). May his memory be buried under thistles, his image covered with dust.'[26]

In 1942, Améry writes, 'the Führer' sends Hauptmann a telegram of good wishes on his eightieth birthday, and 'has a valuable vase presented to him'. Hauptmann begins to guess how fateful his backing of National Socialism was only after seeing the destruction of Dresden – and then it is too late. New claims on him are about to be made by the other side: on 28 June 1946 Johannes R. Becher remembers Hauptmann's origins and on his death hails him as a social revolutionary and 'warrior in the fight against Tsarist barbarism', on his own behalf and that of the Republic that must now be founded again.[27]

Jean Améry counters this notion: for 147 pages he sings Hauptmann's praises, but the final passage is his own. 'He was none of these things,' he corrects Becher. 'Not a warrior. Not a rebel. Not a hero. He was a writer, no more. And he was – in the noblest and best but also the most tragically confused sense – the eternal German.'[28] In reality, Hauptmann ruffles his sensibilities. In a private letter he abandons the balanced opinion he has forced himself to give in the book and speaks plainly. '(I) toil away at the typewriter, trying to summon up the minimum of sympathy for Hauptmann that is necessary for the writing of a biography' (J.A. to E.M. 8.5.62).

Preface to the Future[29]

The 'eternal German' remains the theme of Jean Améry's life. *Die Geburt der Gegenwart*, translated into English as *Preface to the Future*, is his first work not written to order; from the first he conceived it as 'my great book',[30] written 'in a breathless rush', 'a luxury that I ought not really to allow myself,' he writes to the friend of his youth. 'The prospects of material success are so slight that I sometimes feel my honour as a professional writer is injured when I begin to do the calculations' (J.A. to E.M. 26.4.61). Indeed, with sales of 2800 copies, *Preface to the Future* was not a 'material success', but it did win critical recognition.[31] It was considered on a par with the reportage of Egon Erwin Kisch. 'Jean Améry shows us the way in speaking of the future. (...) He is an uncompromising diagnostician of our times, something of which we are in great need.'[32]

The book – 'fascinating, provocative, always striving for objectivity' – is ambitious and 'new', says the journalist Elisabeth Freundlich, returning to Vienna in 1950 from exile in the United States. Améry, she says, is sounding out no less than the whole of the Western world. He traces the way this post-war world is made, how it 'ticks', how he makes it 'tick' in her, the reviewer. It is not a history of culture, not a philosophy of culture, more like 'cultural reportage'.

Display of Améry's journalistic work. Exhibition at Marbach, 1982

It is concerned with presenting 'the intellectual disposition of a nation or a civilization as the projection of political, social and economic forces.' He sets out to offer information. What are the main trends? Who are 'the vehicles of the most important ideas'? What problems challenge the Western world most radically in the post-war period?

> Just what did existentialism mean in France in the post-war period? How did it relate to the complex of war, resistance and collaboration? What were the cultural effects of the Cold War on the United States? Why has German post-war literature produced no great work of fiction characteristic of its period? Why was the intellectual life of England so out of touch with that of the Continent? Where did psychology and sociology enjoy their stormiest development? Does the Hollywood film industry present a true picture of the Americans? Does the emphasis on creature comfort in our consumer society threaten to undermine traditional cultural values?

These, according to Améry, are 'some questions picked out at random.'

Inventory

The questions raised, naturally, are anything but random: they are neither mere research nor mere opinion; he is trying to paint a portrait of the time, filtered (discreetly) through his personal views. The entire post-Auschwitz era is studied in its political and cultural interconnections. Aesthetic activity is linked to the social, political and philosophical discourse of the decade 1950–1960. Améry draws up an inventory, shows what it was like and speculates on what it could be like. He creates his image of the present from the tension between past and future.

His specific understanding of culture as permanent self-discovery and self-invention, as an instrument of public education, unfolds fully in this first real book. He could equally well have called his account 'Faces of a New Euramerica'; 'Euramerica' is a neologism of his own. There is a great deal of activity in 'his' Western world. As Erich Maria Remarque told readers of his legendary war novel, *All Quiet on the Western Front*, his book sets out to be 'neither an accusation nor a confession. It intends only to attempt to give an account of a generation that was destroyed by war.'

Alternative memory

Yet we must not forget that Améry was a particular kind of representative of his generation, a representative whose alternative memory was unwelcome at this time in the German-speaking countries. It is noticeable that Améry restrains himself from expressing resentment against the Germans, at least on the surface.

However, *Preface to the Future* is a phenomenon in another respect too: not just because this Jew 'left over' from Vienna can leave aside his personal sufferings, but also because, although the Cold War is raging at its hottest, his new system of coordinates does not allow him to join the prevailing chorus of 'better dead than Red'. For all his condemnation of Stalinist terror,[33] Améry sees Nazism and Stalinism as

> …phenomena entirely incommensurable in historical, economic, intellectual and psychological terms. The atrocious nature of both does not allow us to draw parallels which never existed (...). The fact that untold numbers of human beings fell victim to both systems, that murders and torture took place under them both, the mind was stifled and human lives ruined, is merely that, a fact: it does not authorize us to reduce both phenomena to a structurally identical or even merely similar substratum.[34]

The East is not one of his subjects in *Preface to the Future*, not least because its cultural influence on the Western world is not yet perceptible, because its thinking, both philosophical and political, is too clearly ordained 'from on high'. It simply excludes itself from consideration. So he looks only at the cultures of the West, which he defines as a combination of art, history, politics and economics.

The 'engine' of a culture?

Preface to the Future, although one would not want to take the comparison too far, is in the nature of an antidote to Spengler's atavistic *Der Untergang des Abendlandes* [The Decline of the West].[35] Améry sets out not so much to look at his period as to understand it, sum it up, describe and analyse it. Where Spengler was concerned with decline and the will to achieve power, Améry is concerned with rebirth and the will to restore culture. Améry's new era is a democratic, egalitarian age of welfare which must first be studied without making value judgements. His diagnosis does not deplore the supremacy of science, mechanization, materialism, the cultural industry and industrial culture, but nor does it glorify mass civilization. It assesses it, presents it, sets out its pros and cons. As a democrat, and unlike Adorno, for instance, he sees the current absence of an elite culture, the progressive blurring of the borders between 'high' and 'low' culture, as first and foremost a chance to be seized.[36]

Améry is especially interested in the deeper driving forces, the 'engine' that impels a culture in one direction or another. He inquires into its understanding of itself, its narrative or 'myth', as he calls it, in which he sees the layers that make up national identities. It is curious that the rationalist Améry should make the term 'myth' the key to his analysis, for that anthropological term, removed from considerations of history and undoubtedly inspired by Levi-Strauss, is to serve as his yardstick of historical awareness. One might almost think that Améry is deliberately turning structuralist methods against himself and his own historical questions here.[37] With the aid of 'myth', he draws up the psychogram of whatever identity is concerned: sometimes the identity has an ideological sense of vocation, as in the case of the United States, sometimes a cultural one, as with France. To anticipate, both France and the United States – in that order – appear to Améry the vehicles of Western civilization after the Second World War.

France's cultural mission to the world

Germany no longer exists. Austria will soon deny its identity. Italy has lost credibility after 20 years of Fascism. Norway, Holland and Belgium are guilty of collaboration, and England is not interested in Europe. For Améry there is only one country to help Europe towards a renaissance, and that country is France.

It was the myth of the French Résistance that inspired France in the late 1940s, he says.

> [The earlier myths of] Marianne proud and smiling during the twenties and thirties, contrite and undernourished in Pétain's '*État Français*', were rejected after the autumn of 1944. What remained was the France of a new Joan of Arc who had read Marx and listened to the voice of De Gaulle broadcasting from London, the France which rose in rebellion against the foreign intruder with the worker's hammer, the farmer's sickle, and the writer's pen.[38]

Uncertain as the military significance of the Résistance might remain, its psychological significance was indisputable. 'The Germans, the English, the Americans, the Russians, all were soldiers. Each of them could plead a soldier's duty.' It was different in France, Améry thinks, where the existence of the resistance movement had presented before the people the choice of being potential heroes or potential traitors. The word 'commitment' acquired concrete meaning. It was given to everyone to shape his or her own fate within the collective destiny: he could – he must – choose, as Sartre put it. There follows a long list of great pre-war authors, all of whom have disqualified themselves in their own ways from becoming an example to the post-war youth of France.

> At this time there rose to the intellectual pinnacle of the nation a person wholly different, a crisis author. (...) a man of powerful originality, whose philosophy tossed the old categories of rationalism and irrationalism overboard and proposed exactly the intellectual attitude that would enable France, enmeshed in the specific problems of the resistance movement, to cope with her situation: Jean-Paul Sartre.[39]

Jean-Paul Sartre – First excursus

We may remember Améry's first meeting with Sartre in 1945; at the time he was particularly impressed by the author of *La nausée* (1938) and the dramatist of *Huis clos* (1944), who captivated and dazzled him.

Sartre's existentialism, strictly speaking, is anti-humanism, says Bernard-Henri Lévy provocatively, so far is his concept of mankind from the traditional humanist concept: it is not the realization of the 'New Man' that interests him, for in that sense even Stalin and Hitler could claim to be humanists – he is interested only in man as he becomes himself, man as a project, a hypothesis, man always re-designing himself.[40] 'To be a subject is not a condition but an action, a movement. (...) We do not come into the world as a subject, we become one.'[41] This subject is always moving, has no fixed point, and never rests. It is still the 'first' Sartre who ignores any metaphysical ideas of the essential, the Sartre who has not yet allied himself with Marx, let alone the Communist Party. However, it is no longer the Sartre of nausea disconnected from the world, of *Melancholia*,[42] the original title of his first novella *La nausée* but Sartre the idealist who has discovered the subject and freedom, the latter closely entwined with consciousness. At the same time, Sartre the materialist sees himself opposing a very different order: the order of things. There is no bridge between the subject and things, beyond reach from one another, strange and hostile as they are.

Jean-Paul Sartre

Sartre – the writer of the Resistance

In his chapter on France, Améry writes enthusiastically in his own person.[43] Yet unlike Malraux, Aragon, Mounier and Camus, Sartre took no active part in resistance, and indeed he adopted a stance at a tangent to the militantly organized Communists and the adherents of de Gaulle's government in exile in London. He was not at any time a traitor, he never collaborated with the Vichy government, but he was not a hero either.[44]

Thus in the choice between these two extremes – and Améry allows only those poles – the man who coined that axiom was not so far from reality. However, the points above are not unimportant in connection with a writer who builds his whole philosophy on authenticity. The fact that Sartre's real '*vécu*' was in such stark contrast to his philosophical principles could have damaged his credibility in Améry's eyes. In addition there was Sartre's arrogant attitude towards Camus, once an ally of his – and who did indeed prove a hero of the Resistance – whom he mocked with extraordinary virulence, going beyond all legitimate ideological differences. He did do Camus justice in his obituary of him, but too late.[45]

Sartre – the teacher of life

Améry says nothing about all this; he does not want to know.[46] On the contrary, he sides with Sartre against Camus, who 'unlike Sartre (...) broke radically with the Communists' but on the other hand refused to protest against the torture practised by the French police in the Algerian war. Sartre is his new faith, his Messiah, the elixir of life that he needs: 'He taught us to think, but even more to *live*,' he quotes Sartre's pupil Dominique Desanti. This comment obviously came from the heart. Whether Sartre really taught French youth to live is an open question, but he certainly taught Jean Améry to live in 1945. Sartre was his midwife; he was reborn with Sartre's help. Even if the past can no longer be changed, writes the former Auschwitz prisoner, the future, 'the real human dimension,'[47] is his; this new perspective imbues him powerfully with promise. 'I am becoming.' 'It depends on *me*.'

Because it depends on him, this 'great book', *Preface to the Future*, has to be written. It is indeed a great book and deserves to be rediscovered. Sharp in analysis, lucid in argument, frank in its only thinly disguised preferences, it not only represents a diagnosis of the post-war period which is historically still relevant, it also reveals the philosophical and political foundations on which his main work is built, and from which, finally, it will diverge over the course of the following decades. The fact that scarcely six years later, writing to a woman who had read the book and expressed enthusiasm, Améry dismisses this first piece of his in the essay genre as 'hopelessly behind the times' merely proves how swiftly the stages of his intellectual life succeeded each other.[48]

For even in this, in his pitiless revisions, in the never-ending self-critical procedures that become his method in writing the *Unmeisterliche Wanderjahre* [Years of Wandering] in 1971, the master has gone before him. There are indeed affinities of development and perception. For the French soldier-writer, meteorologist and later prisoner of war in Germany, Jean-Paul Sartre,[49] and for the survivor, Jean Améry, alike – if under completely different conditions – war and imprisonment mark an absolute watershed, become the catalyst for all their metamorphoses to come.[50]

The philosophy with which Sartre rewrote his life piece by piece took on the role, as we read in his war diary of January 1940, 'of protecting me against the melancholy, gloom and dreariness of war.' And a little later he wrote to Simone de Beauvoir: 'Everything turns naturally around ideas of liberty, life and authenticity.'[51] He notes:

> I do not try to protect my life after the event by my philosophy, which would be unworthy, or to make my life conform to my philosophy, which would be pedantic, but really life and philosophy are one and the same.[52]

It is exactly the same with Améry and already was in his youth in Red Vienna: for him as well, life and philosophy are inseparably merged. Very early, Améry recognizes that Sartre's strength lies not so much in his main philosophical works as in his exuberant moments of theory, always relating to a certain political context, reflected, for instance, in the later *Situations* series. If Sartre himself failed in direct action, then his genius for interpreting signs arose from that very failure, a form of interpretation with which he compensates very effectively for omissions in action.

Sartre – the teacher of thinking

Sartre's philosophical contribution to *Preface to the Future*, as Améry sees it, is reduced to three basic sentences:

> Man is only what he makes of himself.
> Man is free.
> Man is socially committed.

The first sentence contains the key, for it presents the basic idea of existentialism: existence precedes essence. Let us explore what this means. The Sartrean man was not created by God, for there is no creator to bestow on him an essence which he would be compelled or permitted to turn into living reality. He is a man who is constantly creating himself, and his essence is the result of his existence. He alone shoulders the responsibility. His reality consists in acting: he is nothing but the sum of what he has done; he is nothing but his life. (PF p. 27)

So, if man is only what he does and what he makes of himself, Améry sums up again:

Fundamentally man *is* nothing at all, but exists only in a continual process of self-realization. 'Being', the flinty *Être*, is not a property of man, but only of things; man consists of the sum of his past acts and of his future possibilities, his 'projects'.

From this, Améry further concludes that 'the future is the essential dimension of human existence' (PF p. 28).

Man is free, certainly, but freedom, responsibility, social obligation and solidarity condition each other, for man is free only within a given situation. That means, he says, quoting Sartre from the first issue of *Les Temps Modernes*, that:

we may not (...) regard freedom as a metaphysical force of 'human nature'; it does not give us permission to do what we want to do, nor to withdraw into some refuge of inwardness which would ultimately become a prison. We are free, but we do not do what we want to do. And yet we are responsible for what we do. We are also, of course, responsible for what we do *not* do. (PF p. 29)

The first idea for *Charles Bovary*

One passage from Sartre impressed Améry particularly deeply: 'I hold Flaubert (...) responsible for the atrocities that followed the Paris Commune, because [he did not write] a line to prevent it.' To illustrate such a sin of omission, an *acte manqué*, the early Sartre, writing in 1944, chooses none other than the upper-middle-class Flaubert, to whom the late Sartre of 1971–1972, understanding and forgiving everything, will devote the most empathetic 2000 pages of his opulent work *L'Idiot de la famille*. Améry, on the contrary, remembers Sartre's early work and his original condemnation of the author of *Madame Bovary*, which he quotes prominently in this first volume of essays. It left its mark on him for such a long time that in 1978, 20 years after writing *Preface to the Future*, he makes it central to his last work of fiction, *Charles Bovary*. However, there will be more on that at the appropriate point.

Sartre – the mouthpiece of the wartime generation

Man is socially committed – or, according to Sartre, he ought to be. What applies to Flaubert and the Commune is also true for all the French between the years 1940 and 1945, for everyone who 'did nothing to oppose the rise of international Fascism and who during the war merely sat by taking no part in the struggle, was responsible for the defeat, dishonour, and oppression.' Commitment alone does not constitute morality; we are committed anyway, whether we want to be or not; ethical conduct consists first and foremost in recognizing this commitment and acting according to it. Our personal value lies in 'our courage in accepting the fact that we are clamped to social realities and political events and our readiness to play our role in them.'

This, then, was the manifesto of the war generation who spent their crucial years in the world of the Resistance and collaboration. Because it is Sartre who wrote it, the influence of his philosophy in arousing awareness cannot be ignored. He pointed to 'the fearful burden of responsibility' on that generation and confronted those who failed with the pain that they tried to repress because he made it impossible for them to wash their consciences clear with some kind of determinist alibi.

Thus horror and promise are equally balanced in Sartre: horror because the past cannot be undone; promise because the future is always open before us.

'Le faux, c'est la mort'

Améry recalls Sartre's film *Les jeux sont faits*. As in *Huis clos*, we are in the realm of the dead here, for only after death is the game of life really over. 'Death is the end, it extinguishes, it is not a proper concern of man,' he dutifully quotes Sartre as if to make Sartre's advice his own, although he is obsessed in every one of his works, from *Die Schiffbrüchigen* to *Charles Bovary*, by death and suicide. '*Le faux, c'est la mort*,' says Sartre, and the same idea occurs in Améry's *Über das Altern* [On Aging], even though he changes his mind later.[53]

Sartre 'knows no partnership with death, no flirtation with it and its enticements' (GdG p. 39; PF p. 31). Perhaps 'denial of the enticements of death' can actually be learnt. At the time of *Preface to the Future* the magician Sartre seems to make even that possible. Impossible as it is to change the past, the future lies ahead of the former victim of torture. And Améry intones the invocation a second time. 'As long as I live, Sartre explains to me, I can still choose to change myself into a different, into a new person. (...) There is no limit to what I may still become' (GdG p. 40; PF p. 31). Existentialism and the Resistance become psychotherapeutic treatment for the French suffering from the political neurosis of defeat in 1940. Not only can he, Améry, still become anything, so can France. Perhaps 'there is no limit' to what the world itself may still become?

'The God that failed'

But not so; the system of coordinates has shifted. In France, the Resistance collapses as a national myth and is replaced by the 'myth of the cold war against Communism', not only in France but in the whole of Western Europe. Hatred of Stalinism, rising to its peak after the events in Hungary in 1956, becomes the new religion, documented in the historic book *The God That Failed*, in which Koestler, Silone, Wright, Gide and Spender give their views.

> The Gorgon's head of Stalin's terror state ensorcelled the neo-anti-Communists fully as much as it did such Communists as Aragon or Ehrenburg, who remained loyal to the point of intellectual self-annihilation. Whereas these latter were not able to whisper the faintest 'no', the former could only scream their 'no' without any qualification at all. Their view of history remained as distorted as that of the Stalinists (GdG p. 76; PF p. 69).

However, Améry sees a 'humanization' after the death of Stalin, one to which the 'cold war ideologists' close their minds out of personal hatred, and he is firmly convinced that the danger of war does not threaten from the East. For them, the new converts, 'there was not enough room on earth to accommodate the Communistic East *and* the democratic West,' Améry laments, and 'only the annihilation of the Communist hegemony, only *war* against this rule could bring about a solution and deliverance' (GdG p. 78; PF p. 72). Thus resistance of an entirely different kind comes to the fore in the West, with the United States as a world power at its head: hysterical resistance to the Eastern bloc. 'And all this tended toward war, to hot and bloody war, for the cold war, for which the crusaders provided the ideological weapons, made sense and could be justified only if it was a preparation for total war' (GdG p. 78; PF p. 72).

America's political sense of mission

If the Second World War left Europe in ruins, the United States is seductive in remaining intact, as if the catastrophe of our century had passed it by leaving no trace. It is 'the land of the longing heart, sought by the souls of millions of Europeans, the land of revelation and of happiness patently fulfilled, the land of power and the future,' in fact, the land of success and riches, as Améry says not without irony (GdG p. 81; PF p. 74). Hollywood beckons, with filmed versions of Henry James's *The Heiress* and Robert Penn Warren's novel of social criticism *All the King's Men*. On Broadway, Arthur Miller's *Death of a Salesman* and Tennessee Williams's *A Streetcar Named Desire* are playing. The book trade is bursting at the seams with 135 million paperbacks, New York's Museum of Modern Art is full of the latest abstract and tachist works, and the US classical music culture calls itself second to none in the world. So much for surface impressions.

The reality: the 'true' United Sates of the 1950s may show no traces of the war that has just been survived and won, but a glance in the main daily papers is enough to show 'that this country is at *war*' (GdG p. 87; PF p. 80). Worse still,

> ...this perfidious enemy (...) has even ensconced himself right in the middle of the country. He has infiltrated the press, literature, the movies, the army and the administration (...). He appears to have spun a monstrous web of espionage (...). He is ubiquitous and prepared, after completing some subversive activity, forcibly to overthrow the lawful government and thrust a free and peaceful people, prosperous and content with its lot, into wretchedness, war, and slavery. He is consistently engaged in his nefarious work, this enemy, 'the Red', 'the Communist' – and only constant preparedness for defence and unremitting vigilance can perhaps prevent him from carrying out his diabolical intentions. (GdG p. 88; PF p. 80)

Améry pinpoints the day of Franklin D. Roosevelt's death, 12 April 1945, as the day when the fronts were drawn between the United States and the Soviet Union, that is to say long before the rise of Senator McCarthy.

It is solely the defence of freedom that links the United States to the European West. It is well known what it wishes to be kept free *from* – Communism – but do we really know what it is to be kept free *for*? Suspicion and denunciations are out of all proportion to actual events, since the fervently desired insight into the state secrets of the 'enemy's' armaments never came. Only the damage remained; subversive tendencies were universally suspected, artists and scientists of high standing were hunted down in this zeal for cleansing. McCarthyism and a sense of mission became synonyms, there was a '*messianism* comparable in its claims only with the Communists and therefore bound to clash head-on with it,' explains Améry.

Nowhere in the democratic countries is the claim to know the way to salvation as 'clear and prescriptive' as in the United States, he says in 1961, a prophecy that is proving truer than ever in the early twenty-first century. Améry continues his analysis:

> The whole nation is convinced that there is only one correct, and in fact only one possible way for men to live together: the way that is sanctioned (...) in

its own constitution. Every other constitutional and social form, and especially one that is diametrically opposite to its own, can only be the political expression of something radically evil, inspired by the devil, a very hell on earth. (GdG p. 92; PF pp. 84–85)

Perhaps, suggests Améry, the generally accepted idea of the United States as the guardian of the West's frontiers is also the main reason why there was no left-wing protest movement in the United States in the 1950s. Whether or not there was an 'aristocracy of labor in America,' he says, it was a well-known fact that, as John F. Kennedy stated in 1960, '17 million Americans do not get enough to eat'. This 'inner unity of the democratic leadership', this 'voluntary "conformity"', has had devastating consequences not only on society but also on culture.

In the name of the Cold War

It is impossible to write a cultural and intellectual history of the United States in the 1950s, says Améry, of the kind that could be written of France. It is not the writers who have the say in America, but various 'experts'. French writers, Améry continues his typology, are the ambassadors of their country; American writers are outsiders and do not engage in the machinery of politics. Why, asks Améry, did not authors who showed much courage in the 1930s such as John Dos Passos and Erskine Caldwell, let alone the Nobel Prize-winning Hemingway, speak out against the terror of McCarthyism?[54] Although they were the authors of the golden age, he says, their political conformity weakened them artistically before their time. That was, he sums up, 'an American tragedy in itself'. The atmosphere of the Cold War nipped all cultural growth in the bud.

The abolition of death, the glorification of sex

What about Hollywood? American movies reflect the horizontal basis of thinking of the Americans particularly clearly – know-how in contrast to vertical European thinking which wants to know why. There is a great deal of killing, says Améry, in American films, 'but death is for the most part absent'. Death comes from outside, from 'the gangster with a gun in his hand who can be disarmed and wiped out. Death is never inside us, is not a part of ourselves' (GdG p. 117; PF p. 110). Consequently the murderer must always be a villain too; death is concealed. The metaphysical questions are left to 'experts' on transcendental matters, preferably theologians.

The quintessence of life is sexuality, that 'pandemonium of bosoms and thighs' exhibited in all its variants. 'Man in America (...) is surrounded by the

Dionysus cult of professional "models" in perpetual sexual blandishment or pro-creational readiness on every movie poster and in every newspaper advertise-ment' (GdG p. 118; PF p. 111). The sex cult is no less of a lie than the denial of death. In other words, sexual criticism, let alone social criticism of the prevalent American 'disorder', is a matter for American cinema even less than it is for American literature. Hollywood is the dream metropolis of the Cold War. 'Hollywood movies at mid-century (...) revealed while at the same time they concealed' (GdG p. 121; PF p. 114).

America's cultural contribution: sociology

The office of criticism is reserved, Améry says, for a new discipline, 'the field of sociology' (GdG p. 121; PF p. 114). Vance Packard lays the foundations of the interpretation of uncritical consumerism. David Riesman, with *The Lonely Crowd*, designs a typology of American conformists. After all, the functioning of the social machine must not be disturbed. William Whyte's *The Organization Man* also laments the danger of such an adaptation in the area of work of the corporations and big business firms. He is waging 'a rather vehement campaign against the whole concept of human engineering, but especially against the methods of psychotechnical and sociometric tests' (GdG p. 141; PF p. 134), which train young people to become de-individualized 'organization men', the technicians rather then the reformers of society.

The third canonical document on American society mentioned by Améry is C. Wright Mills's *The Power Elite*, which reveals that the loss of power by the middle class has been to the advantage of 'a top echelon of interlocking corporation directors, political heads, and army generals' who 'have developed a silent understanding, a convergence, for making crucial decisions which sweep the powerless citizen along as by the force of nature' (GdG p. 144; PF pp. 137–8). Even if politicians are in government, it is the chief executives, the 'Fausts of business', as Améry baptises them, who rule, who have the power to defend their privileges in their hands. Mills, who was anything but a Marxist, was firmly convinced at the time that the leaders of the big business compa-nies were the real warlords. In view of such manipulation, the question arises of just how democratic American democracy is. The possibilities of choice, which might serve as a criterion of freedom, prove on closer examination to be illusory.

Yet 'in this choice – illusory though it be – we have the whole difference'. Ultimately it all depends on this subjective sense of freedom to act. The sociolo-gist David Lerner has shown that the American 'model man' is 'obviously happy'. The standard happiness of the standard man seems to have been achieved in the

United States of the 1950s. And what about the 17 million who, as J.F. Kennedy said in his address on taking office, do not have enough to eat? 'We cannot do without American sociology,' Améry concludes his study of America, 'for it and it alone defines the "American mission", giving us at the same time a purchase for criticizing it' (GdG p. 153; PF p. 147).

England between Europe and America?

France's myth of the resistance and its political literature and America's myth of the Cold War and its economically oriented sociology are the axes on which Améry's post-war world turns. England might be expected to come between the two; after all, it is only ten minutes' flight by air from the French coast. But that is not the case. It is soon obvious how little the island belongs to Europe – with traffic driving on the left, judges wearing absurd wigs, and its non-metric system – England is an 'absolutely different' country, much stranger to any Continental European nation than the distant United States.

Between 1945 and 1951, it is above all the land of irreconcilable opposites: although it is the home of positivist and rationalist philosophy, it clings fervently to its monarchy. Although it is full of Victorian prudery, the most shameless sexual advertisements are on display in Soho. The English will protest in the street because the Russians send a dog into space but cannot bring themselves to abandon the death penalty. They made the first jet aircraft but did not open their first motorway until 1959. They won the war but lost their Empire. They celebrate the statesman Winston Churchill as a titan in wartime but reject him as prime minister when peace comes. As if that were not puzzling enough:

> [P]ost-war England created a welfare and workers' state (...) yet she preserved the most rigid class system in the Western world; it is a country where the first few words a person speaks reveal his economic and cultural status (...). (GdG p. 216; PF p. 214)

It is 'fair and brutal (...) backward and yet leads the time with giant steps', reasonable and superstitious, free and submissive, says Améry in his opening remarks.

Améry's picture of England, like his picture of the United States, is not exactly comprehensive and accurate, and he has no experience of living in those countries to back it up; with France it was different. He is excellent where he succeeds in summing up the light and dark sides in a few words, but irritating when he goes no further than cliché. His catchphrase about 'angry young men', which derives from John Osborne's play *Look Back in Anger* (1956), certainly falls short of doing justice to the English post-war literary generation.

What, Améry wonders, were these young writers, in fact, angry about? Are they like Sartre's heroes? Do they want to overturn the class system? Does England too have a national myth? Not the Battle of Britain, not the retreat from Dunkirk, not the epic of El Alamein either. The fact is that

> ... history, as it were, had revoked England's victory in the Second World War. England was the victor, and yet she had lost this, her greatest war. This was most clearly illustrated by the Labour victory in 1945, in the wake of which the war hero and British lion Winston Churchill was sent packing, as it were, duly adorned with laurel wreath and crown. In May 1945, the victory bells had pealed, but two years later India had to be relinquished. (GdG p. 221 f.; PF p. 219)

England's not so splendid isolation

After the victory, the liquidation of the Empire, Améry concludes that 'this formal victory, achieved at the cost of great courage and tremendous suffering, was essentially the greatest defeat in British history.' No historian could have expressed himself so disrespectfully on England's Pyrrhic victory at the time. Incidentally, Améry will later put together a monumental pictorial biography of Churchill in the year of his death (1965) – the last piece of hack work he will do – tracing the stormy career of that monomaniac, that brilliant 'artist-politician'.[55]

So what is England's 'national myth'? Is not the quiet revolution that began with Clement Attlee's welfare state in 1945, the way to social emancipation and equality, England's true hour of glory? The younger generation reacted with indifference to the Labour experiment, comments Améry; the revolution was only half-hearted (GdG p. 223; PF p. 221). To Améry, the fact that the Labour Party could not – and cannot to this day – part with the 'royalty religion' is reason enough for the angry young men to turn away from it, disillusioned. That may have been true of the angry young men themselves, but not for the majority of the population, who greeted Attlee's reforms as ushering in a New Jerusalem. The fact is – and here Améry is right – that, in spite of the fundamental reconstruction of society, the aristocracy and the middle classes still occupied all the key positions.

If we look at it closely, the angry young men reject everything that smacks of a philosophy of life, the 'ardent Fabian intelligence with its socialistic Sunday school enthusiasm', the tradition of the English gentleman embodied in the now old Somerset Maugham, 'the crushing arrogance of the landed nobility' as exemplified in Evelyn Waugh, as well as Stephen Spender's anti-Fascism. They also reject 'the gilt-edged idyll of the royal family', and the influence of Europe with such figures as Kafka, Sartre and Camus.

The British stand aside, turning inward, more insular than ever. Even the Cold War never becomes a national question. These young talents, says Améry, summing up the English scene, are 'rebels without a cause' in their principle of negativity. If there ever was an English myth, then it was the opposite of the 'myth of action' in France – 'a myth of negation' (GdG p. 236; PF p. 234).

Germany – an upswing through anaesthetization

If the British are choking on victory, the Germans positively thrive on their defeat. The political and economic revival of Germany proceeds at breathtaking speed. The country is taking part in the meetings of the European Parliament for consultation as early as 1950, the foreign trade of the Federal Republic flourishes. In 1950 there is also talk of rearmament. An army of 240,000 men is set up in 1959, and with the exception of the United States it is regarded as the most effective fighting force in NATO. The rumour of the German economic miracle has come true. The typical German anaesthetizes the pain of defeat by immersing himself in work.

> He made the economy his great personal and national business: all the pleasure he passionately takes in his work and its faultlessly operating organization, everything that showed as 'fanaticism' in political times, was put to the service of the economy.[56]

'Work makes you unfree,' as Améry has already recognized in his original essay 'Zur Psychologie des deutschen Volkes' of 1945, thus anticipating the Mitscherlich theses in *Die Unfähigkeit zu trauern* [The Inability to Mourn] of 1967 by many years.

First visit: Hitler never existed

> One who travelled in Germany for the first time after the war, as did the author in the summer of 1952, went through a completely foreign land in which nothing seemed to remind one of the Weimar Republic or even Hitler's Germany (GdG p. 161; PF p. 155).

He feels as if nothing had ever happened, Hitler had never been. And yet, 'Simulating luxury and joy in neon lights by night, they [the cities] looked in the pale light of day like dead animals with their guts pouring out. In the hollow windows horror actually dwelt' (GdG p. 162; PF p. 156).

To avoid having to act as prosecutor in his own case, he lets other critics speak, as he has done before. First he makes the journalist Dolf Sternberger his mouthpiece. 'What has become of those sturdy boys marching in six ranks and six columns?' he quotes Sternberger. Améry, firmly in control of the dramatic course of his dialogue, replies:

> Dear Mr. Sternberger, they are present! The two gentlemen at the next table, for instance, talking about some kind of business; they say 'injunction' and it sounds like 'order of the Führer' or 'classified'. They have the same look now they had then. One cannot trust the stylish cut of their clothes. Are not their civilian clothes and pigskin briefcases only a camouflage for uniform shirts, leather belts, and daggers? Are not their rubber soles an acoustic trick to dampen the tramp of their boots? (GdG p. 163 f.; PF p. 157)

No, these are not hallucinations, insists the writer, for 'after two or three days the visitor finds Germany quite familiar again.' Améry disappears, and the reporter engages once more.

Familiar? Who is speaking? Who is 'the author' writing this account? No one knows who this reporter is, where he comes from and what links him to Germany. But we know. We know that nothing is more sinister than that 'familiarity', as familiar as the horror that dwells in the empty window frames. He has already suggested it. 'They have the same look now they had then.' 'Then', as we remember, was Améry's last visit to Cologne in Germany in 1938 and was made against his will, a secret transit station on his way to the temporary freedom of Antwerp and Brussels.

Germany 1945, Germany 1952

This chapter, 'In the Shadow of the Third Reich', is Améry's second approach to that 'child of pain Germany', after his first attempt to write on 'The Psychology of the German People'. He, therefore, looks at present-day Germany in quite a different way from his analyses of the United States, England and France at this time.

However, what has happened? Where is the confidence of 1945, when Améry was still writing persuasively to acquit the majority of Germans of guilt, generously excusing the average German on the grounds of his 'bad upbringing', which he and those like him intended to set right?

His perception is darker in 1961, for 'the Germans' still show the signs of 'bad upbringing'. In spite of – or because of – the defeat of Germany, Améry's X-ray eyes see through the pretty neon lights: nothing has happened, nothing has changed, and that in itself is the tragedy.

The language spoken at the regulars' tables in cafés and inns, the language of the press, that language, both old and new, of 'the German army, enriched by industrial jargon and many English expressions' (GdG p. 164; PF p. 157), is the organizational German of the administrators: language as a refuge for what is suppressed.

A cultural miracle?

At the same time the book trade is flourishing. 'In 1951 West Germany published (...) 14,000 different titles, ranking second only to Great Britain (...) and this just six years after year nought.' A disproportionately large number of books are read in this new West Germany. There are very successful theatrical perform-ances too, even if most of the plays are by foreign authors – Anouilh, Camus, Tennessee Williams, Christopher Fry, T.S. Eliot, and the two Swiss playwrights Dürrenmatt and Frisch. German music has its triumphs too, with names like von Karajan, Keilberth and Jochum. So more than just an economic miracle is on its way, one almost seems to be witnessing a cultural miracle too.

The visitor's uneasiness is in the political sphere:

> We shall have to come to grips with the fact, itself full of consequences, that after the Second World War Germany lived without a legitimate ideology, with-out a national myth, the framework of which she could have supported with pure heart and clear conscience.

However, how should or could the Germans live in this vacuum? For most of them, the pinnacle of their lives had fallen with Hitler's Reich; the 'German' and the myth of the hero had been one and the same. Whatever his rank, wher-ever he found himself in the world, in peace but even more in war, his uniform 'turned him into a hero', Améry says, quoting from Erich Kuby's satirical retro-spective in *Das ist des Deutschen Vaterland* (GdG p. 171 f.; PF pp. 165–6). For what, the head of the German family asked himself, had he been condemned? For being happy for 13 years? Was that a crime? This was a case of aporia: in 1952 it was impossible to admit publicly to happiness tainted with blood, but it was also impossible for the German to obliterate that past from his conscious-ness without negating himself.

No revocation of history

What exactly, Améry asks, is that negation, that revocation of history – he had not yet reached that point in the 'Psychologie des deutschen Volkes'. Therefore, this chapter on the shadow of the Third Reich reads like an early version of his later essay on resentments (1966). In Améry's eyes, it was the one chance for the Germans to put themselves straight morally, not just in politics but also in cul-ture. 'The total negation of the Third Reich essential for the cultural existence of the nation in the post-war period would have been possible under one condi-tion only: that a considerable portion of the German people had revolted against Hitler, that a *German* revolution had taken place' (GdG p. 173; PF p. 167).

That revolution, even after the event, never took place. Instead, as Améry sees it, defeated Germany lives under the dictatorship of the shame ordained for it and takes refuge, *faute de mieux*, in virulent hatred of Russia, in the cold war, 'a direct continuation of Goebbels' attitude and propaganda' (GdG p. 176; PF p. 169), justifying Hitler's war in retrospect. 'Whatever one may say, the official anti-Communism which in the Western democracies was sanctified by democratic tradition and justified by democratic action, served in Germany to further the cause of the former Nazis' (GdG p. 176; PF p. 170).

Améry has heard a Belgian collaborator boasting, with the full understanding of Germans listening to him, of his heroic anti-Communist past in the service of the Führer. For the German soldier, then, there could be no 'complete break with the historically dishonourable, yet often individually honourable, adventure of the Third Reich'. In addition there is the fact that the worldwide Cold War merely helped to make National Socialism and restoration taboo subjects. We should not deceive ourselves, says Améry: Germany's Yes to Europe and the Atlantic alliance in 1952 was nothing but camouflage. Such is Améry's opinion in *Preface to the Future*.

German thinkers after 1945

Who are they? Adorno, Arendt, and Bloch, to name only those three, had been living and working outside Germany. But as for Heidegger, the most famous of those who stayed in the country, 'could his pronouncements serve as a focus for German thought after the war?' asks Améry; Heidegger, who as rector of Freiburg University had spoken 'in clearly positive accents about the Hitler movement as "a complete revolution in German existence"'. He does, in fact, become a centre of thought in the 1950s, as does Gottfried Benn, and rises to the status of a cult figure. This time Améry does not mince his words, as he did in *Karrieren und Köpfe*, but speaks for himself about Heidegger and 'the suggestively oracular appeal of his language, altogether suited to fill sensitive people with the intoxication of a hazy philosophical enthusiasm' (GdG p. 196; PF p. 191). This 'Magus of the land of the Teutons' was not 'the man to give new tablets to a people faced with the task of fashioning a democratic will'.[57]

There were other more likely candidates: Karl Barth, Romano Guardini, Reinhold Schneider and Friedrich Heer. The most radical, however, was Karl Jaspers, joining the discussion with his *Die Schuldfrage* [The Question of Guilt] of 1946. 'One would wish the Germans had read *Die Schuldfrage* with keener perceptiveness and in greater numbers,' writes Améry, and he goes on to quote from Jaspers:

People say that the [Nuremberg] trials are a national disgrace for all Germans. The reply is this: the German disgrace lies not in the trials but in that which led to them, in the fact of this regime and its acts. The Germans cannot evade the consciousness of national disgrace. They are wrong if they turn against the trials instead of their origin (GdG p. 197 f.; PF p. 193).

German writers after 1945

The list of writers who emigrated – here Améry quotes from Klaus and Erika Mann's book *Escape to Life* – is so long that we may reasonably wonder if any were left at all in Hitler's Germany. Améry has already mentioned the not very glorious part played by Gerhart Hauptmann elsewhere. Among those who did stay were Emil Strauss, Hermann Stehr, Richarda Huch, Ina Seidel, Hans Carossa, Ernst Wiechert, Gottfried Benn and Ernst Jünger – leaving aside those writers in favour with the Nazis – and it was they who dominated the 1950s.

The Jewish cultural figures who had given intellectual life a touch of the wider world in provincial Germany before the war were all gone. A Jewish writer himself, although never proclaiming the fact, Améry sets up a memorial to their honour: in philosophy he mentions Hermann Cohen, Ernst Cassirer, Edmund Husserl, and his own teacher Rudolf Carnap; in music Gustav Mahler, Arnold Schönberg and Bruno Walter; in the fine arts Max Liebermann and Ludwig Meidner. In literature he covers the entire political spectrum, with Rudolf Borchardt on the political right, Jakob Wassermann and Bruno Frank at the bourgeois centre, the left-wing radicals Ernst Toller, Arnold Zweig and the 'refined aesthete' Stefan Zweig. They might not have reached the 'supreme creativity' of a Rilke or a Thomas Mann, but they had given German literature between the wars a wealth of talent on the highest level, 'let us say from Hermann Kesten to Hermann Broch' (GdG p. 182; PF p. 176). Not only that, all German literary activity – publishing, journalism, and political essays – had been brimming over with a desire to experiment, with intellectual curiosity and vitality. Alfred Polgar, Alfred Kerr, Willy Haas, Samuel Fischer – they 'ventilated and cleared out (...) the folksily faithful, the grandly brooding, the ilk of Münchhausen [and] Will Vesper.'

A break with emigration

If there was a break, then, it was not with National Socialism, not with the authors who had stayed at home, but with the emigrants both Jewish and non-Jewish: Hans Henny Jahnn and Alfred Döblin are isolated, even a writer like Thomas Mann remains a controversial figure to the end. They had had their public between the wars, but for whom would they write after 1945 in a country that read Kolbenheyer and Hans Grimm?

To the new authors of the 'lost' generation, those who returned considering themselves entirely innocent of Germany's guilt, the writers who had emigrated were anything but a good literary example. They particularly did *not* want to be linked with them, as Alfred Andersch's manifesto for The Group 47, *Literatur in der Entscheidung*, makes abundantly clear.[58] To some extent, it was felt that the emigrants had left Germany in the lurch. Names such as Andersch, Richter, Böll, Koeppen, Eich and Schnurre naturally speak out against National Socialism, they speak of a clearance, they invoke point zero. In 1961 Améry already knows – as German literary criticism will not discover until the 1990s – that these metaphors coined for itself by The Group 47 have no substance.

No pact between reader and author

A cultural miracle has just been mentioned; in fact, the book trade was flourishing. Books were not only being bought but also read. However, does that mean there was a culture of reading that could be taken seriously? It all depends on *how* you read. You can pick up a book without letting it affect you. Then you are simply consuming it, and the cultural miracle, in analogy to the economic miracle, is to be understood in the sense of increased power of consumption.

However, you can also *live* a book, as literature was 'lived' in France. Nevertheless, the absence of any conception of itself by the German nation, in other words a national myth, as Améry calls it, made any kind of dialogue between author and reader impossible from the outset. Here again, Sartre sets the standard with his early essay *Qu'est-ce la littérature?* (1948), in which the dialectical interrelationship, the pact between author and reader, is raised to the status of a sine qua non if the act of reading is to lead to action. 'It has not been sufficiently considered,' says Améry, quoting Sartre, 'that a work of the mind is by nature an allusion. (...) The book, serving as an interpreter, establishes a historical contact among men in the same setting of history' (GdG p. 187; PF p. 181; cf. also Höller, Vol. 2, pp. 621–30).

If the book is to be an interpreter, Améry suggests, the author must master not only his own language but also the reader's. That was not the case after 1945; the author spoke the language of a new beginning, the reader the language of restoration. The new authors were read, of course, but after 1945 there could be no question of the reader's 'sharing with the writer a common experience in contemporary history'. People read merely to make it look as if they were in touch. 'The situation can be expressed in a paradox: since there was no public with a common mood ready for the authors, none could be created *by* the authors.'[59]

In France the fronts were clearly drawn; the French had a common enemy to be defeated together. In Germany, however, the fronts were far from clear after 1945. At most, resistance was imagined and 'transformed from the real into the metaphysical,' as in Heinrich Böll's *Wo warst du, Adam?* [Where were you, Adam?] (GdG p. 190; PF p. 184). The real content, however, is blurred even by the best authors, either mythologically exaggerated or, more usually, left out of consideration. No German writer faces his permanent share of responsibility for the concentration camps; the annihilation of the Jews is of no interest after 1945. The Germans had enough worries of their own. How, in these circumstances, were resistance and revolution that never happened to be portrayed? 'Under these conditions, how could German literature catch the accent of that activist humanism in which Camus, Malraux, Sartre wrote and lectured?' (GdG p. 190; PF p. 185).

Hope and the second generation

Much as Améry is concerned with the clichés of national psychology in this book, his prognoses, in part prophetic, are not taken from its contemporaries. If he thinks of Germany by night, it seems to him a country that must become aware of its regression before it can go forward again with the second generation. The act of remembering, neglected by the first generation in its obsession with work and its consigning of history to oblivion, will be performed, Améry still feels sure at this point, by the second generation.

In his eyes, then, the explosion of the economic miracle is – in political and cultural terms – an expressly German disaster. Améry laments in 1961:

> In their intoxication at producing and consuming the German people could forget their failures (...) their most recent past, and their future. The mass of the people were far too busy to think about the Third Reich, the unfought revolution, and the partition of the country. The German bowed respectfully in memory of Anne Frank. He observed June 17 as a day of mourning. But these were and remained ritual motions with hardly any relation to daily reality (...) The miracle became an institution.

However, he ends the chapter on Germany confidently:

> In time things will change. A generation will arise with nothing to hide or gloss over, a generation (...) who will not need to take refuge in business. The economic miracle in its hectic form will pass away just as the unpurged remains of the Third Reich will vanish. In a new people and through them a new Germany will arise, free from the shadow of the Third Reich (GdG p. 210 f.; PF p. 211).

CHAPTER 7

Drama of the Mind in Three Acts

The Autobiographical Trilogy

The 'poor misbegotten *Preface to the Future*', as Améry describes his writing to a friend of his youth in a moment of dejection (J.A. to E.M. 8.6.62), is a turning point and marks a change of direction. It lays the foundations of Améry's intellectual progress from freelance journalist producing articles on subjects chosen by others to essayist writing of only what he himself chooses. That is particularly true of his studies of Germany and France, opposite intellectual poles, which from now on will be central to his reflections. The fervour of the finale is positively breathtaking to readers attuned to mourning: here, in defiance of all indications to the contrary, he invokes the new generation, 'new human beings' in a 'new Germany'. The old ones, we remember, still bore 'the look of the past'. It is to the young that Améry gives his unstinting credo – a credo on credit,[1] so to speak – and it is to them that he must and will speak.

Prologue

A mere three years later, Améry's wish is granted. His original dream – ever since writing 'On the Psychology of the German People' (1945) – had been not just to reach a public but also to create one and ultimately improve and even educate it. In retrospect, that dream never came to anything; all he encountered was lack of understanding. How could it be

> ... that the vagrant wandering town and country in the years 1938–1945, the unassuming journalist writing for editorial offices in Zürich from 1948 to 1964, should now suddenly go to that Germany whose very language he had been unwilling to speak for some time after the war, to whose fate he was at the most indifferent (...).[2]

How can it be, Améry continues, that he is now actually 'speaking his mind on the internal affairs of the German state?'[3]

This is how Améry presents it in 1975. Yet we know that at no time was he ever 'indifferent' to the German language, let alone the fate of the German people. He had been writing stories and history in German and only in German, literally without interruption, and wished for nothing more ardently than to be taken on by a German-language-publishing firm. As early as 1945 he had been seeking a link with Germany (see Heinz Kühn) even if he did not claim one, and since 1960 he had been active as Belgian cultural correspondent in the literary department of South German Radio.[4] So why make this claim now? It is the retrospective angle that obliges him to adopt this attitude, for the credit that he so confidently gave to German youth in 1961 is now, in 1975 – the time when he records the 'German scene' as he sees it in *Örtlichkeiten* – long exhausted. Instead of accusing Germany or expressing the pain of his disappointment in the events of the post-Auschwitz period, he prefers to pretend he always felt detached.

Heissenbüttel and the consequences

The story goes that in February 1964 a meeting fraught with consequences takes place in Brussels, a sensational meeting. The well-known author Helmut Heissenbüttel meets the unknown journalist Jean Améry 'by chance'. Améry himself assiduously fostered this fairy tale in which the good German prince frees his poisoned Briar Rose from the curse. The then head of the Goethe Institute in Brussels, whose invitations he had hitherto persisted in ignoring,

Helmut Heissenbüttel

has requested, 'not without a certain urgency', his presence at a reading by Heissenbüttel. Améry describes him as follows:

> At the speaker's lectern stood a tall, one-armed man with steel-blue eyes. Their German radiance, however, was mitigated by the speaker's disability, so that there was something moving about it. Heissenbüttel read texts which were not immediately accessible to the visitor.

At the same time, he writes to his friend Ernst Mayer speaking of the 'alarmingly avant-garde Heissenbüttel', who induced a sense of inferiority in him because he felt so much a man of 'yesterday' (J.A. to E.M. 6.2.64).

Others who heard Heissenbüttel also had difficulty with his experiments in language; for instance, a young man who 'asked, in a very aggressive tone, the silly question of what it was really about (...) to which the speaker said quietly that it might perhaps be about death'. At this, 'the newcomer to the Goethe Institute immediately felt unbounded solidarity with the reader; where a man concerned himself with death, he belonged in his company' (Ö, Vol. 2, p. 470 f.). What would have been the reaction, one may ask, if Heissenbüttel's answer had been different? It seems to me that even more significant here is Améry's need to represent himself as saving the situation; his staging of the scene ensures that it is he who comes to the aid of Heissenbüttel when the latter is under attack, thereby earning a rich reward:

> After the reading there was a long conversation with Heissenbüttel in an intimate little restaurant. The great Auschwitz trial was just taking place in Frankfurt. I was feeling the need, which was more difficult to dismiss every day, to confront the Auschwitz complex, and I talked about it to Heissenbüttel.[5]

In another version, he describes Heissenbüttel as the 'key figure in his entire existence as a writer, (...) one of the German authors whom I particularly value in both literary and human terms, and to whom I am linked by something like friendship.' It had been a case of 'love at first sight'. Here again, he insists that the meeting was 'mere coincidence', and he goes on to describe how Heissenbüttel, in his capacity as a radio editor, invited him to write something for him.[6]

So much for the legend. Such a 'coincidence', of course, lends itself to a literary version of events in which the participants are surrounded by a softly radiant aureole. One can hardly imagine a couple better suited to the purpose than Heissenbüttel, wounded in the war, and the Jewish prisoner Améry. They really did have the power, at least for seconds, to demonstrate Améry's wish for 'a settlement of the unresolved conflict in the sphere of historical practice', realizing, if only for a brief moment, his dream of 'turning back the course of time' and 'finding a moral in history'.[7] Therefore, understandably, Améry feels great pride in making himself and posterity believe that he had been *brought* to Germany and, as a consequence, after mature consideration, had agreed to work for the German media. Such a chronological scheme of events flatters both parties: the Germans, who in recognizing Améry's value also appreciate the content of his diagnosis as well as Améry, of course, who feels rehabilitated through the German's recognition of his writings.

Who brings whom to the meeting?

In reality, however, it is Améry who takes the first step. He may not perceive it in retrospect, because he feels it demeaning to have been currying favour, indeed, it seems to him like prostitution to offer his torments at Auschwitz for sale on the German market. In fact, however, it was neither Heissenbüttel's assistants, as the first version claims, nor Heissenbüttel himself who urged him to write: Améry was the petitioner, Heissenbüttel his patron. The German prince certainly enables his Briar Rose to break the spell, but it is Briar Rose who must break it. Whether Améry sought a rapprochement with Germany of his own accord, or whether he was *brought* to Germany, is not just a simple question of chronology, and the depth of the wound inflicted on him by Germany is made very clear in his retrospective reversal of the facts.

If not now, when?

In fact, Améry had already taken steps towards 'casting his own words into the balance' on the subject of Auschwitz. The historical debates of the time, for instance, on the Statute of Limitations of 1960, which among other things promoted the 'extraordinary event' with Heissenbüttel, positively required him to take up a position. In 1961 Primo Levi had got in ahead of him in Germany with his own 'autobiographical account' of the world of the National Socialist concentration camp. In his testamentary work *The Drowned and the Saved*, Levi says of the German edition of *If This Is a Man*:

> The hour had come to settle accounts (...). Above all, the hour of conversation. I was not interested in revenge. (...) My task was to understand them. (...) Not that handful of high-ranking culprits, but them, the [German] people, those I had seen from close up.[8]

Whenever Améry speaks of 'documentary' presentations, distancing himself from them, as in his inquiries made to Schwedhelm and Heissenbüttel, it is a reference in shorthand to the book by Primo Levi, whom he also mentions as his comrade from Turin in the hut, the author of 'the Auschwitz book *If This Is a Man*'. Levi had thus, to some extent, laid the foundations for a dialogue with the Germans, going some way to meet them. Of course, Améry too wants to understand, but he is not so much interested in the psychology of the perpetrator of atrocities as in the devastation caused by that perpetrator to the victim – a perspective that goes nowhere at all to meet the Germans.

Hannah Arendt's book on the Eichmann trial (1961)[9] – which caused much controversy in Germany because of her assessment of the collaboration of the Jewish Councils, a polemic towards which Améry adopted a stance only later – also primarily focuses on the psychology of the perpetrator, in this case of a perpetrator of crimes on a huge scale, Adolf Eichmann. Although the trial took place in Jerusalem, 85 per cent of the German population followed the extensive account of proceedings in the newspapers and on television. She calls her work of reportage *Eichmann in Jerusalem*, giving it the subtitle 'A Report on the Banality of Evil', a term which to Améry, as a victim of Nazi torture to whom the sadistic intoxication of power that was at work in his torturers was as present as the day when he suffered it, seemed to call for passionate contradiction. To the end of his life, the conclusions to which Arendt came concerning a technocratic machine of destruction free of all emotion seemed to him only an affront.

Therefore, Levi and Arendt offer him double provocation, and Améry takes up his stance at a clear distance from both positions. Levi, who tries to 'understand', is, in Améry's eyes, a 'reconciler' – of course, not to be confused with the emigrants Martin Buber and Victor Gollancz, whom Améry dismisses as Jews 'trembling with the pathos of forgiveness and reconciliation' (JSS, Vol. 2, p. 123; AML p. 65). To wish to understand everything, the self-confessed aim of Primo Levi, says Améry, dismissing the idea rather too briefly, means wishing to forgive everything. He himself favours resentment, the 'slave morality' (JSS, Vol. 2, p. 148; AML p. 81).

Nor will he admit the deeper significance of Arendt's 'banality of evil' but contents himself with taking that banality literally: 'For there is no "banality of evil", and Hannah Arendt, who wrote about it in her Eichmann book, knew the enemy of mankind only from hearsay, saw him only through the glass cage' (JSS, Vol. 2, p. 62; AML p. 25). He sees Arendt's expression merely as an insulting trivialization, the idea of someone who had no part in these things and was not authorized to speak of them. The evil that his torturers had in store for him

... was not banal. If one insists on it, they were bureaucrats of torture. And yet, they were also much more. I saw it in their serious, tense faces, which were not swelling, let us say, with sexual sadistic delight, but concentrated in murderous self-realization. With heart and soul they went about their business, and the name of it was power, dominion over spirit and flesh, orgy of unchecked self-expansion (JSS Vol. 2, p. 78; AML pp. 35–36).

How can one speak of banality, Améry wonders, when an action calls for the utmost commitment? 'For at this point there is no longer any abstraction and never an imaginative power that could even approach its reality' (JSS Vol. 2, p. 62; AML pp. 25–6). In his polemical mood, Améry obviously fails to notice that Arendt's main aim, with her newly invented term, is to oppose the prevalent talk of exoneration in the media, which saw that ordinary, dispassionate man Eichmann as a horrifying monster. By confronting such a 'demonizing' of evil with her notion of the 'banality' of evil, she shows that the crime has to do with the many and not the few.

The Auschwitz trial

The background to these controversies is above all the great Auschwitz trial, beginning in Frankfurt on 20 December 1963, which created a great sensation. Améry also refers to it in his letters. Here again he is chiefly concerned with himself, with this 'all-decisive part of his life'. He cannot keep quiet about it. The German media were dominated for 20 months by the 'Criminal Proceedings against Mulka and Others', and they thereby acquired a social and didactic significance that was denied to the Nuremberg Trials held by the Allies. It was only with this trial that Auschwitz came closer to the general public. The place 'was now deliberately linked with the millions of murders of human beings by other human beings committed there. The trial pitilessly laid bare the crime before all eyes; that is its justification,' wrote Bernd Naumann in the foreword to his account of it, which Peter Weiss was to take as the basis for his much-discussed documentary play *Die Ermittlung* [The Investigation].[10] It was Hermann Langbein – the former Jewish Auschwitz inmate and a Communist Resistance fighter, actively involved in preparations for the trial (Améry met him almost a year later) – who provided a complete documentary account of it.[11]

Undoubtedly the Auschwitz trial in Frankfurt, which was attended by no fewer than 20,000 visitors, represents a 'watershed of memory'.[12] The historian Norbert Frei comments that after it 'nothing was as it had been before'.[13] Only with it and through it, he says, did the 'political climate of the past' change profoundly. Public reflection on Auschwitz begins here. The trial in Frankfurt, like the Eichmann trial before it, finally disposed of the mistaken belief that only a small clique, headed by Hitler, was responsible for the mass crimes. The year

1965 also saw the parliamentary debate on the Statutes of Limitations between Rainer Barzel, chairman of the CDU/CSU parliamentary party, and the SPD legal expert Adolf Arndt, who spoke passionately in opposition to it. Arndt's performance, writes Marc von Miquel, marked a change of political mood in the year 1965, even if the 'established' West German ideas of the Shoah came only 20 years later, with von Weizsäcker's speech on 8 May 1985.[14]

Auschwitz is the subject of discussion everywhere. It is 'his property', Améry believes, but the subject of discussion is not *his* Auschwitz. So he writes on 18 January 1984 to Karl Schwedhelm of South German Radio, for whom he is working as Brussels correspondent.[15]

> I am in the process of writing a reconstructed Auschwitz diary, not a documentary account, of which there are many already, but reflections in diary form on fundamental existential problems of the world of the concentration camps, and more particularly the reactions of an *intellectual*. I believe I told you that I spent years in various concentration camps, including Auschwitz. As the Auschwitz trial is now in progress in Germany, I wonder whether you might not like to include selections from this work of mine in a radio programme. I think that no one has yet written on the camps in this particular manner, focussing on the intellectuals in them.[16]

Heissenbüttel, since 1959 head of the Radio-Essay department of South German Radio, to which the director of programmes Dr Kehm passed on this query communicated to him by Schwedhelm, let Améry know on 30 January 1964 – that is to say exactly six days before his reading in Brussels – that he would definitely be interested in 'such a work', presenting 'the problem of the concentrations camps from a previously neglected viewpoint' and asked Améry for 'a short abstract of the structure and a few details, giving keywords'. No wonder Améry took the chance of going to Heissenbüttel's reading in Brussels; their preceding correspondence had been good preparation for their meeting. 'Perhaps I shall have the pleasure of hearing you in Brussels when you come to speak in the German Library,' Améry writes, indicating that he will be there (J.A. to H.H. 1.2.64). Furthermore, he was now actually dependent on Heissenbüttel's goodwill 'in [his] frantic hunt for commissions' (J.A. to E.M. 6.2.64), as he tells his friend Ernst Mayer. But the fact that this goodwill developed into cooperation was due not to chance but to the singularly responsive nature of Heissenbüttel and to the no less singular impact of Améry's work.

The 'discussion' with Heissenbüttel of 5 February 1964 in Brussels – he uses that expression in his letter to his friend and does not now speak of a chance meeting – went so well that 'much [work] comes raining down on me again, and my head could be said to be buzzing once more'. 'The poet and editor of the Essay programmes, Heissenbüttel', he tells his friend, has put a whole hour of air time at his disposal:

> Auschwitz: the Mind's Limits – on the life and problems of the intellectual in a concentration camp. That is a subject which, alas, I know only too well, and about which I have plenty to say. All the same, I would like to read a little literature. (J.A. to E.M., 6.2.64)

What exactly his friend sends him is not clear, but the emotions that overcome him as he reads are very clear indeed:

> It is painful reading, I can still hardly understand that I was one of the 'subhumans' who survived all that. I feel some dread of working on the subject: 50 manuscript pages; I shall have to spend many weeks reliving the years 1943–1945.

Although Améry hopes to achieve the status of a freelance writer with his work on Auschwitz, he cannot yet manage to do without his journalistic commissions: 'The silly and the interesting side by side: a history of Parisian *haute couture* (for the *Weltwoche*), a broadcast on the subject of mystification, and then probably a series about the 20 July assassination attempt on Hitler' (J.A. to E.M., 12.2.64). 'How am I going to manage to write a hundred pages by May?' he complains under stress:

> I know absolutely nothing about *haute couture*, and am rather in the position of a man who must write a book about Romanticism without ever having heard the names of Arnim, Schlegel and Brentano. *Quelle misère!* I am studying works on costume and gossipy articles about Balmain, Dior & Co. That does not chime well with the fact that I am reading Wittgenstein every evening when my eyes are already closing. (...) I will conclude, my dear fellow, being overcome by headache and weariness, since before writing this letter I was scribbling a 5-page article about the English science writer Ritchie Calder. (Between ourselves, only yesterday he was as much a stranger to me as *haute couture*). (J.A. to E.M., 3.3.64)

Améry is also anxious about the silence of Walter Verlag, the publishing firm to which he had sent 80 pages of his new book *Über die Unwahrheit* [On Untruth]: 'I shall have to see another serious book of mine come back, for I cannot rest much longer on the fading laurels of *Preface to the Future*.' When the rejection finally does arrive from Walter Verlag, he confides in his friend: '[I] suffered such a severe professional setback that many of the illusions I may have cherished about my position and my future prospects were badly shaken, if not entirely demolished.'

In addition to his professional distress, he is suffering physically; he has a stomach ulcer, recurrent heart problems, and problems even with his brain.

> To be sure, not epilepsy (as bourgeois convention sees it, Palmström would say), but related to epilepsy. So here I am with that sacred illness weighing me down, or rather weighing down my brain, and I could feel I was related to Dostoyevsky.

> Who would not be anxious? 'Anxiety felt in advance', so to speak.

> Will this 'irritation' develop further and prevent me from working? Or will medication perhaps help me, but leave me in a condition of mental semi-consciousness that cannot be concealed from either publishers or editors and readers, so that the career of A. the journalist comes to a swift end?

He concludes: 'One should not grow old. Is that an aphorism? No, but it is true! (P. Altenberg)' (J.A. to E.M., 4.9.64).

A star is born

All the same, a month after Heissenbüttel's acceptance of his proposal, Améry's essay is finished.

> I have just completed what I might immodestly call a very important radio programme: 'Auschwitz, At the Mind's Limits'. The essay grew into a kind of ontology of the intellect – I think that I have, in fact, said things that no one has said before, at least in this connection. (J.A. to E.M. 3.3.64)

He keeps his friend up to date with the logistics of his work – a striking feature is the complete absence of any discussion of the content, particularly when it is part of 'his' subject.

Améry is instinctively confident in what he is doing, asks no one for advice, does not exchange comments with anyone. No one can follow him where he goes; it would be presumptuous for any unqualified person to encroach on his domain. So his 1964 study of Auschwitz, which had begun in 1945 with 'The Psychology of the German People' and continued in 1961 with 'In the Shadow of the Third Reich', now emerges like an erratic block. The reader too is convinced that not a word can be changed; the text, in contrast to its early predecessor, seems to be a single whole, as if he could not have written it in any other way. Now that we know the early versions, however, we also know how long an incubation period the work had. There is no discussion of its content with Heissenbüttel either. Heissenbüttel receives the work – like all its successors – pronounces it good, understands and praises it:

> What you have written is (to my mind) one of the most important contributions ever made to this subject. Your analysis goes beyond the immediate context and becomes a fundamental study in which the failure of the mind, so to speak, gains a new philosophical quality. (13.5.64)

He asks Améry to read the essay on air himself – 'only then will it carry the greatest possible conviction' (13.5.64). Heissenbüttel immediately sees the explosive power in Améry's intense 'objective–subjective confessions'. They were, as Gerhard Scheit writes in his afterword, something entirely new in the context of the crimes of the Nazi era (J.A. *Werke,* Vol. 2, p. 650).

Finally the essay is broadcast on 19 October 1964 in Stuttgart, under the title of 'At the Mind's Limits. Essay on the Intellectual's Experience of Auschwitz'. However, there is a contretemps when the essay is published in print before the broadcast goes out. Améry had sent it to his Swiss agent on the express condition that it should not be printed until after 19 October, but the agency did not comply, and so the essay appeared in the Zürich *Weltwoche* on 5 June, when a dossier on the subject of the concentration camps was being opened.[17] Heissenbüttel is forgiving, and Améry is glad of his magnanimity and yet more pleased with so much appreciation even if he sometimes has 'the feeling that all this is too little, too late' (J.A. to E.M., 3.6.65).

Act I: *At the Mind's Limits* (1966)

Auschwitz and the intellectual

The special problem of the intellectual, if it is one, in measuring the reality and effectiveness of his mind against the extreme situation of Auschwitz, of hardening its power or declaring it useless, is, in fact, an entirely new concept in the discussion of Auschwitz at the time. For Améry, of course, it is an old one – and in that sense not a special problem, because the intellectual's encounter with the power of political reality has always been a common denominator in his cognitive interest. Althager, the prisoner in Breendonck of *The Fortress of Breendonck* (1945), is already testing the power of his mind in the face of torture by his ability to transcend that torture with his 'fictions'. In 1945, then, when he was rewriting *Die Schiffbrüchigen*, Améry's mind still knew *no* limits.

In 1964 the question remains the same, with the crucial difference that after 20 years of meditation Améry comes to the opposite conclusion. Now it is the *powerlessness* of the mind that he shows; he reveals his previous ability to transcend experience as purely esoteric, a trivial *ludus*. Améry concludes his consideration of Auschwitz in the essay 'At the Mind's Limits' with a quotation from Karl Kraus: 'The word fell into a sleep, when that world awoke.' There is worse to come; the mind is not only no help to the intellectual in a camp, it also 'led straight into a tragic dialectic of self-destruction' (JSS Vol. 2, p. 36; AML p. 10). For the original rebellion against SS logic led very quickly to unconditional subjection to it.

> The power structure of the SS state towered up before the prisoner monstrously and indomitably, a reality that could not be escaped and that therefore finally seemed *reasonable*. No matter what his thinking may have been on the outside, in this sense here he became a Hegelian: in the metallic brilliance of its totality the SS state appeared as a state in which the idea was becoming reality. (JSS Vol. 2, p. 40; AML p. 12)

Certainly, there were intellectuals who were capable of transcendence, intellectuals whose faith or ideology enabled them to 'spiritually unhinge the SS state'. It was not so with the sceptic humanist agnostic: 'For the unbelieving person reality, under adverse circumstances, is a force to which he submits; under favourable ones it is material for analysis. For the believer reality is a clay that he moulds, a problem that he solves.' Furthermore, if the unbelieving intellectual analyses the reality of Auschwitz retrospectively, he must come to the conclusion that he has not solved the problem, that it has overwhelmed him entirely. 'In Auschwitz we did not become more human, more humane, and more mature ethically (...). We emerged from the camp stripped, robbed, emptied out, disoriented' (JSS Vol. 2, p. 52; AML p. 20).

The phrase 'At the Mind's Limits' shows in itself what method of thinking the author is pursuing 1964 onwards. As a rule, he thinks and writes against himself and only incidentally, as he lays out his thinking before the reader, requires the reader too to think against himself, which often provokes resistance. The subject of this first essay could hardly have been personally more explosive. We only have to imagine for a moment what 'the mind' means to the self-taught Améry. He has worked hard at it for himself and cultivated it; it is his only chance to overcome his economic, psychological and above all political situation. It is his one chance of making sense of the senseless. The mind is also a synonym for literature; it means home to him, it is his life, and it is so much more real to him than what we call reality. Alfred Andersch clearly saw that idiosyncrasy. 'Report on the return of the mind as a protagonist' is the caption under which he introduces Améry.[18] To Améry, and this holds good for all his works, the mind is in fact a protagonist, a 'you' and a 'he', often one and the same; his 'I' is a real person, the only suitable and reliable interlocutor on whom Améry can depend, with whom he can argue. The story of Améry's life is always a history of the mind: this mind – as Améry draws up the balance sheet – fails him in Auschwitz, abdicates, says goodbye. Just when it would have been most necessary, it lets him down. It capitulates in the face of violence, an appalling betrayal.

Subliminally, the whole weight of education and culture is there in the back-ground. Is not Germany, land of poets and philosophers, the land of judges and executioners instead, of the notorious German *mésalliance* between mind and power? 'At the Mind's Limits' is certainly also a history of the fall of the intel-lectual, but a second glance is enough to show that it is strictly autobiographical – and written in the author's heart's blood. It is about the person of Améry, about *his* mind, a mind that met its limits in Auschwitz; it is *his* story entering into his own auto-demolition in this first chapter. We only have to read the essay once against the grain to realize that here, in his thinking against himself, Améry is demolishing and destroying all that had previously constituted his nature.

It is strange that no one heard the bitter irony directed against himself, urg-ing on Améry's not so sovereign discussions. The intellectual described here, also a man of letters – for, of course, this is a pitiless self-portrait – is not celebrated as a higher being, as Primo Levi wrongly assumed. Far from it, he is scorned – his uselessness revealed. The 'cultivated man' in Auschwitz, who thinks of the poet Detlev von Liliencron at the mention of the syllables 'Lilien', who 'is well informed about Neidhart von Reuenthal, the courtly poet of village lyrics' (JSS Vol. 2, pp. 24–25; AML p. 2) but struggles desperately with bedmaking in the hut, who is entirely at the mercy of the physical and even linguistic violence of those in authority over him, this intellectual is a poor, even despicable creature, positively ridiculous in his helplessness. There were moments in the camp, he says, in which he wondered whether he did not deserve to be despised. The one thing his analyti-cal mind enabled him to do was to seal his own self-destruction, for in Auschwitz, Améry says firmly, the mind is good for only one thing: to obliterate itself.

The title of the essay, 'At the Mind's Limits', is a euphemism, dealing as it does with the intellectual's limitations in Auschwitz, for the limits collapse with the death of the mind. He writes near the opening of the essay:

I recall a winter evening, when after work we were dragging ourselves, out of step, from the I-G Farben site back into the camp to the accompaniment of the

Kapo's unnerving 'left, two, three, four,' when (...) a flag waving in front of a half-finished building caught my eye. 'The walls stand speechless and cold, the flags clank in the wind,' I murmured to myself in mechanical association. Then I repeated the stanza somewhat louder, listened to the words' sound, tried to track the rhythm, and expected that the emotional and mental response that for years this Hölderlin poem had awakened in me would emerge. But nothing happened. The poem no longer transcended reality (JSS Vol. 2, p. 12; AML p. 7)

The death of the mind is synonymous with death itself. We must remember that Améry's life story, his 'autobiographical trilogy', begins with the story of his death, or at least the death for which he was predestined. He will have been aware of the euphemism. He himself aimed to push back the boundaries, at least verbally, to the point of extinction, for all his subsequent work concerns the revival of the mind. The mind, 'the word', as Kraus calls it, has perhaps really just fallen asleep 'at its limits', perhaps it is only an apparent death.

So much for the wider context of the origin and future of Améry's first essay. Heissenbüttel was the first but not the only one to assess the value of his comments at their true worth. After the broadcast, which 'curiously enough found some echoes in Germany, particularly in religious circles' (J.A. to H.H. 23.11.64), the Munich publisher Gerhard Szczesny, who was also editor of the *Club Voltaire*, got in touch. He wanted to reprint the essay that same year, with contributions from such illustrious figures as Ludwig Marcuse, Ulrich Sonnemann, Karl Löwith, Alex Comfort, Ernst Topitsch, Hans Albert, Rolf Hochhuth, Günter

Frankfurt Book Fair 1966; left to right: Gerhard Szczesny, Jean Améry, Karlheinz Deschner

Grass – and Heissenbüttel. In the contents list of that issue Améry gave the sections of the essay 'At the Mind's Limits' subtitles, which clearly show where he saw the emphasis lying: 'Auschwitz and the intellectuals', 'The failure of the aesthetic imagination', 'Rationally analytical thinking led to self-destruction', 'The attitude of the agnostics and those with religious or political convictions' and 'The mind proved useful only for its self-abolition'.

The fact that Gerhard Szczesny noticed Améry was fortunate, for it was he who a little later offered to publish the complete collection of essays. Améry received a rejection from Suhrkamp Verlag, to whom he had sent the first three, giving the following reason:

> Unfortunately we have for some time been planning a book on a similar subject, and we already have contracts with the authors for this book. It is possible that the two publications would stand in each other's way (...) There is no doubt [Suhrkamp's letter consoles Améry] that in more favourable circumstances we would have published your essays.[19]

Indeed, a few years later, when Améry had long since opted for Klett, Suhrkamp Verlag would try to lure him away. However, Améry remained loyal to his publisher and not least to his editor Hubert Arbogast. In 1965 Krauskopf Verlag published an abbreviated version.[20]

A slightly abbreviated version was also published in Paris, in *Documents*, this time in French translation – Améry's only French publication,[21] and in it

Left to right: Günter Kunert, Hubert Arbogast, Maria Améry, 1982, at the ceremony for the award of the first Jean Améry Prize.

the text is divided up under different subheadings, obviously those that Améry thought more suitable for French readers.[22] The fact that no more came of this publication of his in Paris, which could have marked the beginning of a continuous reception of his works in France – they were published there in translation only 20 years after his death[23] – must have been a great disappointment to Améry, for he had longed to take part in that country's intellectual discussions. There were ideas, even in the sixties, of translating *Jenseits von Schuld und Sühne*, but they remained ideas, so that Améry remained an entirely unknown writer to the French during his lifetime. However, at this time he was still struggling to make a name for himself in the Federal Republic of Germany, and Heissenbüttel remained the base from which he took off. Originally he had 'simply wanted to become clear about a special problem: the situation of the intellectual in the concentration camp,' as he recapitulates in his first foreword (1966) to *Jenseits von Schuld und Sühne*, 'but when this essay was completed, I felt that it was impossible to leave it at that' (JSS, Vol. 2, p. 20; AML p. xiii).

The single useful starting point: the 'I'

'Your kindness in accepting my Auschwitz essay encourages me to make a request,' Améry resumes his correspondence with Heissenbüttel two months after delivering the first essay. The spell is broken, he has been in 'search of the time that was impossible to lose' (JSS, Vol. 2, p. 20; AML p. xiii), and now that search has come to an end. It is clear to him that he is still at the very beginning of his 'Auschwitz diary', that he has by no means exhausted his subject. Not only does his articulation and expression appear as he writes it down, his method also imposes itself.

> If in the first lines of the Auschwitz essay I had still believed that I could remain circumspect and distant and face the reader with refined objectivity, I now saw that this was simply impossible. Where the word 'I' was to have been avoided completely, it proved to be the single useful starting point. I had planned a contemplative, essayistic study. What resulted was a personal confession refracted through meditation. (JSS, Vol. 2, p. 20; AML p. xiii)

A radical change has been completed. From now on he is not a journalist writing articles commissioned on subjects chosen by others, but a self-confident essayist dwelling on subjects close to his heart.

Améry's request shows how far the project is flourishing in his head already. He tells Heissenbüttel:

> I have been planning, for some time, to write a book containing considerations of the complex of the Third Reich, in which, however – as in the Auschwitz

essay – I would like to keep going beyond the documentary aspect and into the realm of fundamental analysis and existential problems. I intend, among other subjects, to write on torture, solitary confinement, emigration, the loss of one's home, the fact of resistance, and life under the occupation.

It is surprising how early the dramatic structure of his 'considerations' has already been established, and yet in the execution of the project the emphasis is to shift in one important point. He is still speaking of 'the complex of the Third Reich', offering a view from outside, a perspective in which Heissenbüttel's experiences are contained but not his own. The insider's view of the victim, particularly the Jewish victim, is still left out of this inventory, at least terminologically. Is it shame that keeps him from addressing the problem of his Jewish identity, which in the book proves to be the real vanishing point of his confession? Or is it fear that he might alienate Heissenbüttel? Self-consciousness on the subject, even fear of contact with it, is the order of the day in 1964. Améry is still courting Heissenbüttel's favour. He continues his petition:

> I kept hesitating to write such a work because I simply doubted whether I could venture upon it from an economic point of view, since I would have to devote much time to it, with no guarantee that such a book would find customers to buy it.

Today we know that, directly after its publication, it was widely acclaimed. The climate was ripe for it; readers had been awaiting just such a voice as his. To have recognized that is not the least of Heissenbüttel's merits.

The tiresome question of money plays a vital part in all his 'business' correspondence – with radio, television, publishing houses, lectures, public discussions. Améry is positively obsessed by the amount of his royalties, and not just because as a child he suffered financial need as the son of a war widow, and later as a self-taught freelance, or not just because he and his wife are at present trying to secure themselves a reasonable income – it is above all concern for the future of his wife that troubles him, as if he had always had an idea that he would die prematurely or by his own hand, leaving her without financial means. In 1964, however, he is still struggling to earn a basic living, and that in a time when most of his fellow victims of the camps had already been assured of financial compensation from the German state. He does apply to the Austrians, submitting a file on himself, but in vain; the state will not admit responsibility for anything. He will not turn to the German authorities; perhaps his pride forbids it. It is bad enough to be taking the story of his sufferings to market in Germany. 'If you were interested in one or other of these subjects for the radio, perhaps as a continuation of my Auschwitz broadcast,' he concludes the same letter to Heissenbüttel, 'I would feel that I had some financial cover, and would make the venture.' Heissenbüttel is indeed interested, and Améry does make the venture. Meanwhile, Heissenbüttel commissions a study of Jean-Paul Sartre's *Les Mots* from him and plans to broadcast other minor pieces originally intended for Hessian Radio.

Less than welcome approval

Ernst Mayer expresses delight to the new star – not without some reservations, for he is under the impression that his friend will now think himself too good for him. To this Améry energetically replies:

> No, I am neither a writer who has 'made it', nor one who can properly look back on a successful work. (...) I am over 53 years old and already feel my powers waning slightly. With my only moderate state of health, I am still as economically insecure as a beginner, and cannot lay claim to any work that really corresponds to my hopes.

The fact that his name is known to various newspaper or radio editors is, he says,

> ...far too little for a man on the threshold of old age, who rightly or wrongly makes serious demands on himself, without which he could not live at all. Anyone who sees that as clearly and realistically as I do, and suffers from depression that cannot be called a psychological phenomenon but is the subjective reflection of objective facts – well, it hurts rather than cheers him when his closest friend tries to conjure up the magic of an illusion, however good his intentions.

However, he sets him right: 'We should pride ourselves intellectually on the most pitiless honesty, and I would rather you had said, with that honesty: you are a poor sort of fellow, my friend, and so am I' (J.A. to E.M. 8.1.66). He objects that he does not have even 'a few reasonably good references for the jacket of a book' and speaks of his own dissatisfaction with himself. How could his friend have believed, for even a minute, that he had become a 'glamour boy' of literature, who would perhaps 'risk his oldest friendship for the sake of some chimera'? Even if he receives honour of some sort, he himself thinks nothing of it: 'I believe, I know, that I am nothing' (J.A. to E.M. 8.1.66), and he assures his friend: 'We have no time and no strength to waste on doubting each other. Nothing has changed between us' (J.A. to E.M. 8.1.66).

There is method in his severe self-criticism; he makes it difficult for everyone by citing his self-distrust, for his friend, his readers – and himself.

At the body's limits

Euphemism was mentioned above, Améry's stylistic decision to stop 'at the limits' of the mind, limits that do not exclude its revival. However, before introducing that revival, he looks one last time at a still more violent and indeed mortal blow, one that annihilates the mind entirely. 'Torture' is his subject and the title of the new manuscript that he places before Heissenbüttel in January 1965. 'I am very curious to know how you like this essay. I myself think that I have dealt with this subject from points of view that have not yet been considered' (J.A. to H.H. 13.1.65). In fact, the essay deprives Heissenbüttel of speech. 'At the moment I can say nothing specific about it, only in general that – as with your first essay – I think it truly excellent. Please believe me that this general judgement is meant absolutely seriously' (H.H. to J.A. 27.1.65). In a later letter, where he asks Améry to read the text for the broadcast himself, he praises it in more detail.

> What makes the quality of your work so good, the direct link between personal experience and objective analysis, can, I think, be conveyed to a listener only by the man who has experienced these things and written about them himself. You have done that with the utmost possible conviction. (H.H. to J.A. 12.3.65)

This essay too has, as we know already, an earlier version in 'The Fortress of Derloven', the fragment written in 1945, in which there is a general description of how his character comes to be tortured. The story of his arrest, his own torture and his recovery is meticulously described there, as if these crimes could be factually represented in language by the fictional person of Althager. It will be remembered that Althager does not give his comrades away. He not only withstands the torture but also tricks his torturers with invented messages and plays a trump card with 'fairy tales' that can only lead them astray in their attempt to disrupt the Resistance operations. His alter ego Althager presents 'the absolute triumph of mind over matter'.

Not so Améry in the 1965 essay. In his reflection on the incident, matter triumphs over the mind, not the material Auschwitz but the material body. In this point the pupil differs fundamentally from his mentor Jean-Paul Sartre, for in *L'Être et le néant* [*Being and Nothingness*] Sartre explicitly states that 'even torture does not deprive us of our freedom'. It is almost as if Améry were rhythmically imitating the process. With blow upon blow, Améry comes to the heart of the matter: 'Everyone went about their business,' he says of the 'business room' in the Belgian concentration camp of Breendonck, 'and theirs was murder' (JSS, Vol. 2, p. 56; AML p. 22). The reader walks through the camp with him, through the 'damp, cellar-like corridors', the 'prison cells', 'heavy barred gates before one finally stands in a windowless vault in which various iron implements lie about'. The nature of the place and the items in it become autonomous; they speak for themselves, no further commentary is needed. 'There I experienced it: torture.' 'It', torture, happened to him; it has reified itself, taken on an independent existence. It has also reified the individual demoted to the status of an object, violating him. 'Torture is the most horrible event a human being can retain within himself' (JSS, Vol. 2, p. 57; AML p. 22). Only after this peak of damage has been reached does he work it out – politically, verbally and psychologically.

Politically, Améry evokes the prisons where torture is inflicted in other times and in other countries, for instance, in Russia, Hungary, Spain, Algeria, Vietnam, Poland, Romania, Yugoslavia, South Africa, Angola, Congo, the list could go on forever. But Améry cites these possibilities of comparison only to demonstrate their futility. Torture under Hitler, he insists, as it did already in 1945, remains singular, for 'torture was the essence of National Socialism (...) it was precisely in torture that the Third Reich materialized in all the density of its being' (JSS, Vol. 2, p. 59; AML p. 30).

Verbally, however, the author sees things quite differently from the way in which, in 1945, he not only saw them but also presented them in his unpublished novel. Although the content in 1945 was broken, the flow of language depicting it was not. Twenty years later, the refraction of experience is reflected in the refraction of the language. Metaphors and comparisons are nothing but a kind of all-purpose glue because no power of imagination is adequate to verbalize such a monstrous experience.

> Not because the occurrence (...) goes 'beyond the imagination' (it is not a quantitative question), but because it is reality and not fantasy. One can devote an entire life to comparing the imagined and the real, and still never accomplish anything by it. (AML p. 25)

However, for the very reason that Améry studies the problem of the incommensurability of the imaginary and the real in this way, he manages to express it after all, finding the words to establish the difference between *Death in Venice* and death in Auschwitz.

He succeeds by setting out from the stage just preceding torture, the 'first blow', torture's primal scene. It is psychologically responsible for the qualitative leap in the violated individual. That first blow brings it fully home to the prisoner's consciousness that he is helpless before his torturers. No doctor, no mother, no friend will make haste to help him. 'But with the first blow from a policeman's fist, against which there can be no defence (...) a part of our life ends and it can never be revived' (JSS, Vol. 2, p. 67; AML p. 29). It contains in the bud all that will come later, torture and death; its character is indelible. All the trust in the world, as Améry says, has gone with it (JSS, Vol. 2, p. 67; AML p. 29). For, as Améry further reasons, varying Wittgenstein's dictum about the limits of his world: 'The boundaries of my body are the boundaries of my self. My skin surface shields me against the external world. If I am to have trust, I must feel it only when I want to feel' (JSS, Vol. 2, p. 67; AML p. 28). When the skin surface is brutalized, when the victim's fellow man becomes his counter-man, the programme is destruction.

> Now there was a crackling and splintering in my shoulders that my body has not forgotten until this hour. The balls sprang from their sockets. My own body weight caused luxation; I fell into a void and now hung by my dislocated arms, which had been torn high from behind and were now twisted over my head. Torture, from Latin *torquere*, to twist. What visual instruction in etymology! At the same time, the blows from the horsewhip showered down on my body, and some of them sliced cleanly through the light summer trousers that I was wearing on this 23 July 1943. (JSS, Vol. 2, p. 73; AML pp. 32–3)

That was how it happened; that was how it happened to him.

Even if the *how* of pain eludes verbal communication, at least this much can be established of *what* it is: pain is the ultimate physical experience. 'Only in torture does the transformation of the person into flesh become complete' (JSS, Vol. 2, p. 74; AML p. 33). It is as if the torture victim experiences his own death. The mind has not simply reached its limits here, the mind is systematically liquidated by the torturer.

> A slight pressure by the tool-wielding hand is enough to turn the other – along with his head, in which are perhaps stored Kant and Hegel, and all nine symphonies, and the World as Will and Representation – into a shrilly squealing piglet at slaughter. (JSS, Vol. 2, p. 77 f.; AML p. 35)

Again, this is the point where even the body reaches its limits – a desolate accounting, leading to an equally desolate prognosis. 'Whoever has succumbed to torture can no longer feel at home in the world' (JSS, Vol. 2, p. 85; AML p. 40). The 13 years that Améry still has to live are marked by this knowledge. 'One who was tormented is a defenceless prisoner of fear. It is fear that henceforth reigns over him' (JSS, Vol. 2, p. 85; AML p. 40). The shame of annihilation, a sense of being a stranger in the world, can never be done away with. In the preface to an article for *Amnesty International* (1977), the complaint in his own name becomes one made on behalf of the political prisoners of 1977. Again, he does not try to describe the indescribable, 'because the quality of feeling of physical suffering cannot possibly be communicated,' and yet it matters for words never to fall silent, for them 'to be heard, if it must be so, to be heard crying out'.[24]

Welcome approval

Dark as his meditations on the past might be, the present in which he has made his breakthrough as an author is bright. Although he may not wish to acknowledge it, he relishes the novelty of public attention, of esteem, approval, and fame. He enjoys this late arrival in Germany far more than he really likes. His joy is great when Hans Paeschke, at the time editor of the *Merkur*, asks him to contribute regularly to the journal, since he is 'enthusiastic' about his publications on literature and cultural criticism (H.P. to J.A. 27.4.65). Paeschke mentions his *Preface to the Future*, of which he has learnt from the *Times Literary Supplement* in London. He offers Améry the choice of a whole range of subjects – Europe, contemporary literature in Germany and/or political and psychological theories in France. Améry even feels that now he can pick and choose and expresses reservations, partly because of a lack of competence on the subject of Europe and partly because of a lack of funds. Much as the subject, for instance, of 'an analysis of a cross-section of modern literature' attracts him, he could write on it, he says, only if it were also to appear reprinted elsewhere. All he can offer Paeschke unreservedly, he says, is the 'continuation of [his] confessions and meditations'

Left to right: Elias Canetti, Rudolf Hartung, Jean Améry

(J.A. to H.P. 4.9.65). Paeschke says that he regards the essay 'Torture', which Améry describes to him as 'a study in the existential psychology of power' (J.A. to H.P. 2.5.65), as 'one of the most important and most intensely felt' statements that he has read recently. 'Confession and analysis are combined here in the same way as in post-war Germany, which had tried to achieve such a combination, but succeeded only in exceptional cases' (H.P. to J.A. 11.5.65). Elias Canetti also writes Améry a personal letter, saying how much the essay shook him. 'Only with some timidity – for you might consider this presumption – do I add that I have never before read anything in which that experience appears intellectually so well dealt with' (E.C. to J.A. 5.4.66).

Merkur to the end

Améry's essay on 'Torture' makes history: Heissenbüttel broadcasts it on 3 May 1965. Paeschke publishes it in June, 'in slightly abbreviated form'.[25] This publication opens up a close collaboration with the editor of *Merkur*. Between 1965 and 1978, Améry is to write about 60 pieces for the journal: essays, reviews, commentaries, film criticism, open letters. With Heissenbüttel, Hans Paeschke becomes a constant companion and friend. Their correspondence, running to 814 pages, is evidence of a closeness that, in contrast to Améry's relationship with Heissenbüttel, is expressed in extensive discussions of content, a *dialogue ininterrompu*, as Paeschke calls it (H.P. to J.A. 21.3.77). His last letter to Améry was written seven days before Améry's death, on 10 October 1978.

Adorno – friend or foe?

Adorno too takes notice of 'Torture' in the *Merkur*, so much so that he even makes it central to his lecture of 15 July 1965 on 'Metaphysics and Death after Auschwitz', saying that 'Jean Améry (...) expresses the changes in the strata of experience brought about by these things in a truly admirable manner.'[26] In a later letter to Ernst Fischer, Adorno says expressly how highly he 'esteems' Améry. 'I was deeply impressed by his essay on torture' (quoted from a letter from E.F. to J.A. 31.1.68). He even says that he wants to write to him and asks Fischer to put them in touch. 'If you can help us to establish a friendly relationship, I would be very grateful to you (...)' (quoted from the same letter from E.F. to J.A. 31.1.68).

How can we explain the fact that in the later, printed version of the 'Meditations on Metaphysics', in his *Negative Dialectics*, Améry's name and every mention of the essay have been deleted, although the reflections there on 'perennial suffering' of body and mind are clearly inspired by him?

Of course, Améry never knew of Adorno's short-lived esteem for him. What influence such a public acknowledgement might have had on Améry's life can hardly be imagined. With Adorno behind him, he could have taken quite a different stance in the German post-Auschwitz period, and the student-Left would have glorified him as well as Adorno. Nothing of the kind happens: instead, he tries to win its favour, assesses himself against its chief ideologist, feels that he is ignored and ignores it in his own turn. He writes to Ernst Mayer:

> The day before yesterday, I heard a lecture here by Adorno, and was introduced to him. A disagreeable, coldly arrogant gentleman, who in addition, despite the radicalism and internationalism of his opinions, looks almost comically like the stereotype of a German professor. The lecture – on the sociology of music, delivered in excellent French – was very remarkable, but I liked the man so little that I could not really enjoy it. (J.A. to E.M. 5.3.66)

This antipathy then transfers itself to a sharp polemic against 'dialectical pirouettes' – or, in fact, against the jargon, not against dialectics per se. Adorno's disciples, he says, may succeed in 'making the roles of victim and torturer interchangeable as they please, and propagating this idea with the most progressive airs and graces'.[27] Although he is working on the essay, he admits to his colleague Horst Krüger: 'I keep clashing with the important but extremely irritating figure of Adorno, who would greatly benefit from a thoroughly positivistic course on banality' (J.A. to H.H, 5.10.66). Putting it more simply, we can say he wishes Adorno had the courage to call victims victims and perpetrators perpetrators.

Adorno was obviously unhappy with Améry's criticism, for in a letter to Fischer he expresses his pleasure that, in spite of everything, Améry feels 'well inclined' towards him, which he, Adorno, had not expected after Améry's critical remarks in the *Merkur*.

For Améry, it is Fischer's dialectical language that is 'exemplary', because unlike Adorno's it 'does not resort to contorted esotericism' (J.A. to E.F. 27.1.68). 'I have admired not only your wealth of knowledge and the assurance with which you express your view, (...) but also, and perhaps above all, the way in which you expound your thinking,' he writes, congratulating Fischer on his work *Kunst und Koexistenz* [Art and Coexistence]. 'If one is wearied by reading Adorno and other neo-dialecticians of the same stamp, one is struck by your plain, straightforward style – never lapsing into mere simplicity – and it is also so very attractively and precisely cogent' (J.A. to E.F. 14.11.67).

Améry's praise for Fischer by comparison with Adorno seems to Rowohlt Verlag such a good marketing point that the publishers think of using it for advertising purposes. Fischer apologizes to Améry for this indiscretion, to which Améry replies: 'I am sorry (...) for your sake, and not my own, if that particular sentence should appear anywhere. Adorno is certainly ill disposed to me anyway because of my essay in the *Merkur*' (J.A. to E.F. 27.1.68).

In a later letter, Améry amplifies:

> Another word on Adorno. There is a respectful distance between him and me, the distance suitable between an author who, even if he can claim considerable mitigating circumstances, at the same time has only desperately few publications of any stature to his credit, and a thinker who moulds his time and is the creator of a great body of work. My deep respect for Adorno's achievement may be taken for granted. But the fact is that neither deep admiration, nor the distance owed by respect, ought to limit one's right to criticism. The work of Adorno is mighty; however, I cannot agree with everything in it. (J.A. to E.F. 7.3.68)

Fischer obviously passes this on to Adorno, who replies to Fischer expressing great relief:

> It seems to me more important, and it really pleased me, to think that Améry, whom I value highly (...), is kindly disposed towards me. After his essay in the *Merkur*, I did not expect this. As soon as I am more myself again, I will write to him, and if you could do something to help us in forming a friendly relationship I would be most grateful to you.

Adorno's letter to Améry was never written. Fischer did what he could by continuing, in the same letter to Améry:

> You know how much I agreed with your essay, and also how highly I think of Adorno. It cannot be denied that he has his weaknesses, but nor can one deny his importance in the intellectual climate among the young people of Germany. If this incident could help to establish friendly relations – without giving up the right to criticism – between you and Adorno, that would be a happy outcome. Never mind controversies one way or the other – we do not have too many men such as Adorno and yourself, and we need a republic of intellectuals more urgently than ever before. (E.F. to J.A. 31.1.68)

There is some comfort, if it be comfort, in the fact that because Améry was never to climb the heights of student esteem, he was also spared falling from those heights as low as Adorno did shortly before his death.[28]

No 'republic of intellectuals'

Primo Levi, Hannah Arendt, and Theodor Adorno – all of them were atheist Jews whose thinking was influenced by Auschwitz. Each in his or her own way might have been predestined to conduct a dialogue with Améry. But exactly where an affinity might have been felt, proximity leads only to withdrawal into petty hostilities. One wonders how far, in Améry, this is due to rivalry and feelings of inferiority. The differences of opinion between them are real enough in philosophical dispute; it is regrettable when that dispute becomes an excuse for settling personal accounts. Entertaining and pleasant company as he can be personally – everyone who knew Améry socially spoke of his Viennese charm – he remains deeply scarred, indeed tormented, at heart. In his understanding of himself, whatever honours he receives he is still in the position of the victim: a David pitted against far too many Goliaths. That, or something like it, is the way that Améry must have perceived his role in the coming decade in West Germany. He leaves out of account the moments of happiness that he certainly knew as well; they are too ephemeral for him. He can define himself only through unrequited love, and those he would like to reach, the left-wing young of Germany, put up barricades against him.

Canonized by Ingeborg Bachmann

The essay on torture also makes history by impressing Ingeborg Bachmann, who gives Améry a moving memorial in her finest story, *Drei Wege zum See* [Three Paths to the Lake].[29] The 'strata of experience' (Adorno's term), expressed with such virtuosity in Améry's essay, have cast their spell over her too. The narrator tells us of the protagonist Elisabeth:

> She read, by chance, an essay 'Torture', by a man with a French name, although he was an Austrian and lived in Belgium. (...) She wanted to write to this man, but she did not know what to say to him, why she wanted to say something to him, because it had obviously taken him many years to bring terrible facts up to the surface. (...) This man was trying to track down what had happened to him in the destruction of the mind, and discover in what way a human being had really changed, and lived on although annihilated.

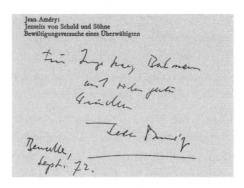

Jean Améry's dedication to Ingeborg Bachmann

Inhalt

Extract from Ingeborg Bachmann's (barely legible) notes in her copy of Jenseits von Schuld und Sühne [At the Mind's Limits], dedicated to her by the author, Sept. 1972

Bachmann did not write him a letter, but she wrote her story instead, which concerns, among other things, a love relationship between the journalist Elisabeth Matrei and a man called Trotta,[30] an 'exile', a 'desolate man', an 'expatriate among the living,' who after his death 'slowly drew her down with him into downfall'. It is not difficult to gather, from her style here, how Bachmann changed her Trotta character into an Améry character. Améry could hardly have wished for a more sensitive reading. Yet she hardly does him justice, because she passes over the very point that distinguishes Améry's analysis more than any other. Bachmann, who immediately speaks of 'the destruction of the mind', fails to notice in her paraphrase the fundamental difference between the disabling of the body and the disabling of the mind. 'The limits of my body are the limits of my self,' writes Améry, but when the body is violated and the self overwhelmed by pain, there is no self any more, there is no mind any more, the self is all body. Naturally, in Améry as elsewhere, physical destruction subsequently leads to psychological destruction, but that is the subject of reflection, it is not equated with a premise from the first. Améry is well aware of this and other instances of blurred boundaries, which do not prevent him from defending Bachmann's volume of stories against the attacks of the press. 'Trotta returns,' he says, enraptured and indulges in the reminiscences of one who suffers from traditional homesickness and gives himself up to the 'magic of old Austria'. Bachmann ennobled him with her fictional idea, not least because she calls him an 'Austrian' as the most natural thing in the world, as if he could claim that nationality without any further ado.

Without knowing it, Bachmann thus rehabilitates the real Améry, and by means of this literary detour he can win back a little of the homeland that was so unmistakably denied him by the Nuremberg Laws.[31] We can tell how deeply wounded he was by the indifference of his fellow countrymen from a letter to Fischer:

> But what you said to me about my work was good and moved me, not least because your voice (...) spoke to me from Austria (...), the land of my origin, where indeed almost no one else cares about me, and leaves me to act my part as a Federal German writer, a role which does not suit me. (J.A. to E.F. 13.6.71)

The eternal exile of writers[32]

The next essay that he writes for Heissenbüttel's essay programme deals with this loss of his homeland. Although torture remains an indelible act, the pain can be moderated, physicality dissipates, and as for the mind, it returns to itself. 'Necessity teaches us to think,' Améry says, quoting Ernst Bloch.[33] 'Thinking is almost nothing else but a great astonishment' (JSS Vol. 2 p. 83; AML p. 39). After reaching the nadir of extinction in the torture essay during the Nazi period, he now begins to live on. After 'flesh' and 'death', he must now face the question of how such a wounded self can adjust to what is called normality. 'As for the continuation, I have the following plans,' he writes to Heissenbüttel. 'Another essay will have the title "How Much Home Does a Person Need?"[34] and will look at the problems of lasting exile' (J.A. to H.H. 3.2.65). The essay on exile is delivered to Heissenbüttel on 7 July. He thinks he ought to warn Heissenbüttel that 'it does not have the same forceful impact as Auschwitz and Torture' (J.A. to H.H. 14.7.65). Heissenbüttel does not agree, saying that the thematic impact is achieved by the way he brings these subjects together in working on them, in a way 'which for present ideas is very radical and unusual' (H.H. to J.A. 14.7.65). Heissenbüttel is referring to the complete subjectivity with which Améry studies an objectively problematic situation.

Améry's sketch of exile, for that is the subject of his reflections on home, differs fundamentally from the glorious picture constructed in anti-Fascist West and East Germany. He moves away even from his own positions, or rather illusions, those, for instance, that he expressed so solemnly in 1945 on Thomas Mann and the continuity of the German spirit. The reality of exile – for him, anyway – is very different; it is, in truth, in defiance of all rumours of the enrichment brought about by cosmopolitanism, a miserable condition. Améry's thesis is simple and carries conviction: 'One must have a home in order not to need it.' However, if you no longer have a home, because you have been hunted out of it, you need it all the more. What does a home mean? Reduced to its basic content, it means security (JSS Vol. 2, p. 94; AML p. 46). Security is provided only where you know and recognize the signals, where you trust and are familiar to those you know. But where something entirely unexpected, truly scandalous, happens, where trust is so thoroughly broken, you become lost. Your home has irrevocably become enemy territory, which in turn means that not only do you lose your home, you are also shown that you appropriated it illegally, you never possessed it. Such a politically forced loss of home must lead to self-destruction, for it goes hand in hand with the systematic dismantling of all that meant something to you from childhood on. In addition and above all, there is your mother tongue which has turned into the language of murderers. Re-immigration becomes impossible, and all that is left is the writer's eternal exile.

For some four decades Améry has lived in the Francophone area, his reading has been up to 80 per cent French, and yet it is still German that 'overwhelms' him when he is agitated. And not only then – for he can write on the subjects anchored in the language itself only in that particular language. 'Isolation in Brussels may mean protection in a certain sense, but it is also sometimes a torment,' he tells Horst Krüger (J.A. to H.K. 11.1.73) 'He is living in a ghetto,' Améry suggests in the year of his death, 'all his thinking, all his endeavours are directed to the place which he cannot reach through a kind of historical error, yet he thinks and hopes that he can soon correct it'. Once an emigrant, always an emigrant, that is his final assessment – you are alien to what is foreign. As he did in the 1930s, Améry develops a materialistic philosophy in his concept of his native land. His being, writes Gerhard Scheit, determines the consciousness – but it is the being of a man once persecuted and tortured. Exile is fear, home is safety; those are the precise definitions that Améry uses to counter the romanticizing of exile on the left and the homeland on the right (Gerhard Scheit, Vol. 2, p. 663). It is not his home in itself that interests him but the possibility and above all the need for a home that concerns him.

Longing for 'redemption'

Heissenbüttel is still on his trail and does not even flinch from the next scene in Améry's thought-drama, although he is personally challenged there. For here Améry returns to his original theme, the theme that he put off confronting for 20 years: how do I feel now about Germany and 'the Germans'? 'A fourth [essay] will be entitled "Resentments",' he writes to Heissenbüttel, and he prepares him for what is to come with the warning, 'It is "strong stuff", I hope not too strong for your listeners. But it is like this: such an essay can either be written with complete honesty or not written at all' (J.A. to H.H. 24.11.65). Heissenbüttel sets his fears to rest by accepting this essay too for his programme.

In 'On the Psychology of the German People', his work of 1945, Améry exonerated the 'average Germans' to some extent of collective guilt. This early piece expresses a sense of vocation; he feels called to educate the German people. His hour never came. The need to recognize that sharpened his gaze considerably, and now there is no trace of any sense of vocation, for 'the education' with which he hoped to correct history has demonstrably failed. His thirst for revenge, originally externalized, which might have been cured by drastic measures of post-war justice, turns incurably inward 20 years after Auschwitz, in the form of resentments. Incurably so because in 1958, for instance, a German businessman takes it upon himself to tell the author that the West German government corrected the 'historical mistake' long ago through its policy of reparations, and moreover the Germans no longer bore the Jews any grudge (JSS Vol. 2 pp 125–6; AML p. 67). How dare he continue to feel resentment in the circumstances? He must expect a lack of understanding if not actual disapproval.

Améry 'dares' to do it, he does venture to express resentment despite the warning. For Nietzsche, from whose definition of resentment Améry distances himself, and to the psychologists, resentment is the hallmark of a clinical condition, the symptom of a warped mind. For Améry, exactly the opposite is true. To him the 'warped state' of the mind of the Jewish victim of the Nazis 'morally as well as psychologically is of a higher order than that of healthy straightness'

(JSS, Vol. 2, p. 127; AML p. 68). Only in becoming aware of this unconscious process, only in conjuring up ghosts with the aim of taming them, can the future be realized for him. His resentments are there, he explains, so that the crime may become reality for the criminal. Resentments are not to be confused either with a desire for revenge or with atonement, he continues; they insist solely on recognition. 'The experience of persecution was, at the very bottom, that of an extreme *loneliness*. At stake for me is the redemption from the abandonment that has persisted from that time until today.'

Waiting for requited love

This is the turning point in the essay on resentment, the reason why he had to write it in the first place. A negative – resentment – is postulated, but the postulate is presented in a positive light – redemption. So this essay, if our ears are attuned to this dissenting voice, at the same time becomes the converse of a 'tirade of hatred', as most German readers saw it.[35] At its heart, it is a fervent appeal to the Germans ('The Germans' was the original title of the essay in the Szczesny edition), a longing for 'redemption', and one that does not shrink from emotion. This is, strictly speaking, one of two passages in Améry's entire oeuvre where he allows himself to indulge in such a 'counter-Enlightenment' concept as redemption, the longing for requited love that could 'redeem' him from this enduring sense of abandonment.

Cross-check the idea in reverse, and we see that only where there is love can resentment arise. The difference between victim and perpetrator must not be dialectically neutralized, even here. Where the perpetrator confesses to his crime, where the resentment of the victim is recognized as legitimate

> ...the overpowered and those who overpowered them would be joined in the desire that time be turned back and, with it, that history become moral. If this demand were raised by the German people (...) it would have tremendous weight, enough so that by this alone it would already be fulfilled. The German revolution would be made good, Hitler disowned. And in the end Germans would really achieve what the people once did not have the might or the will to do (...) the eradication of the ignominy. (JSS Vol. 2, p. 143; AML p. 78)

The opposite of symbiosis

Even when he was writing this essay, Améry realized how far he was giving himself up to the Utopian ideas in it. The evidence for that is readily accessible in the form of an exchange of hostilities with the writer Hans Egon Holthusen, one of the major right-wing intellectuals of the 1960s, whose stylishly written apologia, 'Freiwillig zur SS' [Volunteering for the SS], provokes Améry into making

Hans Paeschke

a statement in the *Merkur*, if reluctantly and, therefore, belatedly.[36] He finds Holthusen's essay doubly offensive: first because of its unusual length, which lends it a certain weight, and second, because it was bound to be objectionable to Améry that Paeschke, who less than a year before had asked for permission to reprint his essay on 'Torture', had now commissioned Holthusen's confessions. Paeschke, enjoying the media event that this causes, forces Améry to reply.

It is with distaste that Améry picks up his pen. He writes to Paeschke:

> You are kindly disposed, and yet you make life so difficult for me! When I read your letter I was so discouraged that I seriously considered leaving the open letter alone. But then I said to myself (...) that I had no right to do that: if you publish a book about your misfortunes for the general public, then you have certain responsibilities. (J.A. to H.P. 9.2.67)

Furthermore, when he has composed his answer, he is concerned not just to put Holthusen in his place; behind the scenes he feels he must even justify himself to his patron Paeschke before the latter publishes his answer to Holthusen.

Holthusen's retrospective is an autobiographical piece in which he looks benevolently at the foolish 'greenhorn' he had been when he volunteered for the SS in 1933. He never went along with National Socialist ideas, and 'the motive' of anti-Semitism, as he delicately puts it, 'was something that I had, as it were, faded out'. Vanity and defiance, he claims, had induced him to volunteer for the SS, and he hopes to be forgiven this 'negligence'. Now and then, when it cost him little, he offered a helping hand. What is he setting out to do with this account? He wants to show 'what actual human reality can be concealed behind such a label as "SS volunteer"'. He intends to plead 'for the right of the individual, in all circumstances, to have been a loner, with all the contradictions, inconsistencies, human and intellectual weakness that that entails'. This is his defence against the young intellectuals of the 1960s who take it upon themselves to condemn him for his political past.

Nothing could illustrate the source of Améry's resentments and their legitimacy better than this futile confrontation with Holthusen's retrospective survey. Obviously there are 'individuals' within the mass, and 'individuals' are rejected by the same mass. Améry too was a loner, only he stood on the other side; he was not protected by the crowd, but 'alone' and 'abandoned', at the mercy of the same crowd to which Holthusen willingly belonged. Améry's response, which he entitles 'Questions to Hans Egon Holthusen', adopts a casual tone of amusement.[37] 'Dear comrade of my own generation,' he addresses his colleague, who was his own age. He cobbles together the points they have in common, and where none exists, he pretends to understand. 'I read your essays (...) not without sympathy at first', he comments, only to take aim all the more ironically at Holthusen's smug attitude. 'You volunteered for the SS. I went elsewhere, not in the least of my own volition.' But, he asks, 'what did you really learn from your mistake of that time?' Améry tackles that subject too in his essay on 'Resentments', which steal up on the victim only because, even where there is an appearance of acknowledging responsibility and guilt, it merely pays lip-service to that idea, and there are no consequences to the perpetrator's concept of himself, or at least not in the case of Holthusen, who thinks he is acquitting himself of guilt in his account. It is nothing but a calligraphic exercise in self-exoneration, there is not a grain of uncertainty in his view of the present and the future. Améry continues:

> You lose your sense of equilibrium (...) when you speak angrily of the clever children of the welfare state with their nickel-framed glasses and Brecht haircuts (...). Those clever children must indeed be true members of the intelligentsia, like those others with horn-rimmed glasses and curly black hair, of whom there was so much talk at that time. Has your error not taught you that it is not permissible to allow yourself to describe your own feelings and not your adversary's in such a way?

The contenders Améry and Holthusen thus represent a first example of a German Jewish paradigm, like Friedländer and Broszat later, for instance, in their correspondence on the Historians' Quarrel,[i] or Bubis and Walser in their debate on the implications of Walser's 'Sonntagsrede' [Soapbox Speech].[ii] What Améry's exchange with Holthusen shows, above all, is that there can be two clearly distinct memories, two kinds of memory, two ways of writing history, and that where the subjective premises of this discrepancy cannot be expressed clearly, there can be no real exchange of ideas.

The psychoanalysis of being a Jew

In his fifth and final essay, 'On the Necessity and Impossibility of Being a Jew', Améry looks at the fact that Jewish memory is and must be at the opposite pole from German memory. He sends this essay to Heissenbüttel on 7 February 1966. Améry hopes 'that some of the philosophical implications of this work will be interesting enough to address even those listeners not directly affected by the problem' (J.A. to H.H. 7.2.66). In fact, here Améry is not merely trying to probe his own concept of himself as a Jew. The analysis of the formation and construction of his own identity is also offered as a model for other variants of historical and social heteronomy, for Améry will recognize the Jew in himself only in those terms. It is the same, although with the conditions reversed, with the necessity and impossibility of being a German, and finally if indirectly with 'the impossibility of being a German and a Jew', which was the title he gave to an early draft of the essay (J.A. in a letter to Suhrkamp 10.8.65)[38] Heissenbüttel welcomes this final essay as Améry's 'most outspoken', and he is right in thinking that 'here at last we [find] the key' to the other four essays' (H.H. to J.A. 11.2.66).

The contradiction between necessity and impossibility is, in fact, at the centre of all these studies. Améry is principally concerned with the necessity and impossibility of continuing to live – after Auschwitz and more particularly after his torture. There is also necessity and impossibility in his relating to his homeland. But only as he determines the position of his Jewishness do all these necessities and impossibilities come together, not least because they have their cause in the Jewish nature imposed on him from outside. Améry's Jewishness is an absolute vanishing point; everything runs towards it.

However, because Améry knows nothing of Jewish tradition, let alone the Jewish faith, that is equally impossible. It is defined solely by his historically

---

i   The dispute concerned the way the Holocaust should be interpreted in Germany.
ii Martin Walser's acceptance speech on the award to him of the 1998 Peace Prize of the German Book Trade led to a dispute with Ignatz Bubis, head of the Central Council of Jews in Germany, who accused him of anti-Semitism.

determined nature, by the Nuremberg Laws, and consequently he sees 'being a Jew' as something deliberately different from religious Judaism. Althager in *Die Schiffbrüchigen* already felt it necessary to show solidarity with 'the hunted'; he already knows that he will have no alternative but to accept the 'verdict of history' and at the same time rise up in revolt against it. 'To be a Jew,' as Améry defines it in 1966, 'that meant for me, from this moment on, to be a dead man on leave, someone to be murdered, who only by chance was not yet where he properly belonged' (JSS Vol. 2, p. 154; AML p. 86). He speaks of the degradation that such a death threat entails. 'Our sole right, our sole duty was to disappear from the face of the earth' (JSS Vol. 2, p. 155; AML p. 86). To him, a 'Catastrophe Jew', his Auschwitz number has become the basic formula of his Jewish existence. Being a Jew can thus, even after the event, be only a negative fact, something foreign, 'a creeping sickness', but a negative that can, however, not unlike resentment, also become a positive.

In revolting against being a Jew, Améry makes the identity imposed on him from outside into his own idea of his identity; he is the existential outsider as Hitler marked him once and for all, one who is mutating into the intentional outsider. In his own name he now transforms the self imposed on him from outside into a self that he has chosen, bringing his own political suffering into action for the good of all the humiliated and insulted. He overcomes the misfortune of being a Jew not in denying it, but in a deliberate, indeed self-confident acceptance of a moral mission in being allied to all those oppressed and deprived of their rights, as Althager was already putting it in 1933. Every essay in the collection is not just, in the literal meaning of the word 'essay', an attempt, but a search under the influence of this paradox. As self-questioning, they question the time, they are manifestations of history, and at the same time they put up resistance to it.

Jean-Paul Sartre – second excursus

Améry's point of departure in 'On the Necessity and Impossibility of Being a Jew' is Sartre's *Betrachtungen zur Judenfrage* [*Réflexions sur la question juive*; English translation: Anti-Semite and Jew], in which the French philosopher devotes 80 pages to drawing up the 'portrait of the anti-Semite'. In so doing Sartre provides, as he indicates in his subtitle, a 'psychoanalysis of anti-Semitism'. Améry's own reflections read like the correlation of Sartre's; the Austrian author draws up his own 'portrait of the Jew'. 'It was not the anti-Semites who concerned me,' he says, adopting his stance towards Sartre, 'it was only with my own existence that I had to cope' (JSS Vol. 2, p. 164; AML p. 92). So in 'On the Necessity and Impossibility of Being a Jew' he succeeds in psychoanalyzing his own experience of 'being a Jew', how it came to that point and where it would lead. A basic thesis defined in negative terms is in common to them both. 'It is not the character of the Jew that makes anti-Semitism (...) but on the contrary it is anti-Semitism that makes the Jew.'[39] From this, Sartre concludes:

> If there was no Jew, the anti-Semite would invent one. (...) Anti-Semitism is a deliberately chosen attitude of the entire personality, a comprehensive attitude not just to the Jews but also to mankind in general, to history and society. It is simultaneously a passion and a philosophy.[40]

Deluded as that passion and philosophy may be in the case of anti-Semites, it could not be more real for the Jews exposed to them.

Sartre's reflections are bold, if only because they are the first document in Europe to tackle the Jewish question as early as 1945, for in post-war France memories concentrated solely on the political aspect and the Communist Résistance. As in Germany, although for other reasons, to mention the word 'Jew' and most of all the term *déportés raciaux* was to break a taboo of the highest order. So Sartre's remembrance of the wretched situation of the Jews before, during and after the war was a daring venture in itself, and his appeal to the Jews to return to France was a singular and generous act of solidarity. It was this essay above all that bound Améry to him so closely over a long period. Whatever charges we may make against the *Réflexions sur la question juive* from today's point of view – and Bernard-Henri Lévy lists them all – they weigh light in the balance against the liberating effect that they had on the Jewish intellectuals around Sartre. One such intellectual was Claude Lanzmann, who later directed the 12-hour film *Shoah* and whom Bernard-Henri Lévy cites from the immediate post-war period: 'On this earth (...) there was at least one man in our vicinity who understood us.' Sartre broke the silence with his essay. It was, says Bernard-Henri Lévy, a thunderclap in the strange atmosphere of France, a 'bizarre mixture of false shame, hypocrisy, and – of course – covert anti-Semitism (...).'[41]

Dis-similation, not as-similation

It was a thunderclap to Améry as well. He did not really need to adopt Sartre's definition, since he had anticipated the same insight already in *Die Schiffbrüchigen*. However, he takes the idea further. For Sartre's Jew, there are only two alternatives: either he faces the anti-Semite, takes his Jewish identity as a fact, a situation in itself – you are a Jew if others think you are Jewish – or he flees from the anti-Semite, denies him. But the Sartrean Jew who wishes to assert and maintain his Jewish identity in post-war France can never in his life be happy.

The republican model of a solution to the problem by assimilation merely, in the name of human rights, allows a man to figure as a *citoyen*, not as a Jew.

Sartre rejects this abstract form of universalism and pleads for difference. So does Améry, the non-non-Jew, who until his death speaks not of assimilation but of dissimilation. 'What had to happen,' he asked, 'for me not only to dare to speak of my Jewish identity today, but to say, at every opportunity that offers, "I *am* a Jew"?'[42] What happened was the same difference that he experienced physically between 1935 and 1945. From now on only that identification holds good; anything else would be a lie. So Améry too faces his Jewish identity, fully and entirely embraces it, and at the same time rebels against it by showing, with his sensitivity to every form of injustice, that in the present and the future it can be seen in a positive light. 'Redemption by Revolt' is the heading of his review of Jean-François Steiner's historical novel *Treblinka*.[43] It is no coincidence that the word 'redemption' occurs in this context for the second and last time, for it is the armed revolt of the Jews in the Warsaw ghetto, in Sobibor and Treblinka, that is here called an 'example to lift the heart' and described as proof of 'how that people (...) won back its humanity.'[44]

Améry's essay on being a Jew also makes history, and like the essay 'Torture' it finds a place in one of the most controversial of post-war novels, Alfred Andersch's novel *Efraim* (1967).

A fundamental document of our time

'That seems to be the last chapter in our series,' Améry writes to Heissenbüttel, 'and I could understand it if your listeners want to hear no more about either Nazis or Jews for another 50 years. Even I have had enough of the subject for the next half-century!' (J.A. to H.H. 4.3.66) There could be nothing worse for him, he says, than 'to be made into a professional Jew or a professional concentration camp inmate' (J.A. to H.H. 17.3.66). However, that 'worst' thing does, in fact, happen to him, since when he wants to stand back from the subject, as he does later in his essay-novel *Lefeu oder Der Abbruch*, he is not allowed to do so. Only the 'professional Jew and concentration camp inmate' is in demand. His mere presence – whether at lectures, platform discussions, seminars, in adult education colleges and at radio stations – was a sign of political correctness. After Suhrkamp and Kiepenheuer & Witsch decline to publish the five essays, he entrusts them for publication in book form to the publisher Gerhard Szczesny. 'My book of pain is now published, and I hope it will lure a few dogs out from behind the stove, even if they bite' (J.A. to H.P. 17.5.66). He hoped, as mentioned above, to lure out the dogs with the equally biting title of *Resentments*, but the publishing house decided against it at the last moment; it obviously seemed too threatening.

Reluctantly, Améry bowed to the judgement of the publisher and resorted to the title *Jenseits von Schuld und Sühne* [Beyond Guilt and Atonement], which in the variant *Weder Schuld noch Sühne* [Neither Guilt nor Atonement] had already appeared in his 1945 manuscript text 'On the Psychology of the German People'. The new subtitle was 'Bewältigungsversuche eines Überwältigten' [The Attempts of a Man Overwhelmed to Come to Terms']. 'This title,' he explains to Szczesny, 'is objectively accurate, for it is about an existential condition situated in the valley beyond guilt and atonement, and also indicates the content' (J.A. to G.S. 2.6.66). Within a very short time he becomes the star author of the publishing house of Szczesny, a second printing is necessary, which does not, however, keep the publisher from having to declare bankruptcy a year later.

A spectacular effect

Today we can see the situation better: the book is a hit, appearing at exactly the right time. Améry is applauded not only as a 'long-term analyst' but also as the 'analyst of the moment' (A.A. to J.A. 21.2.71). His meditations stand apart from all existing attempts at explanation, whether Marxist or totalitarian, historical or psychological. Améry unerringly follows his own idiosyncratic path through every individual question raised, a path where only what he has experienced and his introspection have the last word, with a subjectivity that is never satisfied. But woe to any readers who fall into the trap of 'unthinking' identification with the victim – this is nothing but 'inadmissible sentimentality', and they will incur the author's displeasure. *At the Mind's Limits*, the title of the book in English translation, consists of monologue, for all its intention of featuring as dialogue. Améry himself even calls it 'autistic' (J.A. to H.K. 5.10.66), a book that casts a bright light, with monomaniacal obsession, on every imaginable hiding place in the softening of condemnation. Here a writer has demanded and encouraged the utmost from his reader. It is almost as if he were anxious to alienate the reader, sometimes with his pitilessly radical approach, sometimes with a pathos that frequently tips over into self-pity.

The fact that such a thoroughly demanding book had such a wide and profound reception proves that in 1966 Améry had found his public. Suddenly all doors are open to him and many hearts as well. He dines with Alain Robbe-Grillet, with Ernst Bloch, meets that 'wonderfully vital old man Ludwig Marcuse', revels in recommendations from Günter Grass and his own 'twin brother', the Leipzig literary critic Hans Mayer, who propose him for election to the Berlin Academy.

He is positively overwhelmed by letters from readers, some of them very personal, particularly from women, asking for absolution – and perhaps more.

His correspondence swells and cannot be dealt with but for the clever and loyal Maria. I have already mentioned the tireless Hety Schmitt-Maas, a town councillor in Wiesbaden and press spokeswoman of the Hessian Ministry of Culture, who in her eagerness to make matters right put Améry in touch with Levi and Langbein. It is she who also introduces Mary Cox-Kitaj, an American academic specializing in German literature, to the Amérys. Améry suggested that Mary should introduce the paperback edition of *Jenseits von Schuld und Sühne*, and we shall meet her again in the final chapter. Another and not exactly well-balanced relationship, beginning at about the same time (1967) and leading to a voluminous if rather one-sided correspondence, is with the Viennese psychologist Inge Werner, whose last letter to Améry is dated April 1978. She was later to be the model for the distraught poet Irene in *Lefeu oder Der Abbruch* (1974).

Elias Canetti and Ernst Fischer have their say

Other illustrious voices are heard: Elias Canetti tells us how, after reading Améry, he found that 'many of [his] intellectual certainties, which were not so lightly won' seemed to be built on shaky foundations. 'That is perhaps the utmost praise one can give a book.' Améry's 'purity of thinking', his 'incorruptible holding fast to a fate that is both complex and exemplary', seems to him unique.

> I dare not go into the ideas that concern me in connection with your book. Who would be competent to do so, who would not seem to himself like a chatterer if he tried to express to you a somewhat different opinion, with so much less to base it on?

Canetti's comment on the Jewish chapter is revealing:

> It strikes me that the Jew, as he is presented in your last chapter, is mankind itself, as it should be today, aware in memory of the past of the menacing catastrophe, having shaken off all deceptive certainties and comforts, feeling the catastrophe in its skin and bones, a prophet in his own physical being. The world has never before known such prophets, and one dares to hope that through their mere presence, they can do something. (E.C. to J.A. 16.8.66)

Fischer too sets his 'emotion' down on paper:

> That admirable distance preserved in the mist of events, that speaking of the unspeakable, when you reflect reflection always casting itself back into the permanent present of a past that was a terrible crime against human

nature, that energy of the intellect that is able to analyse even torture, and can uncover the deep connection between power and degradation and mortal fear, that confrontation of a home pursuing the fugitive not just in dreams but in fact, to crush and devour him (...) apart from that, [he concludes his declaration of friendship] endearing as you are in every line, we may learn from you the art of concentrating honesty, understatement, and the interweaving of experience and knowledge into prose of the first rank. (E.F. to J.A. 27.3.68)

Alfred Andersch's appreciation rises to the following prognosis and may be taken as representative of the unanimous high regard that the cultural press showed to the volume: 'It will certainly remain one of the fundamental documents of our time,' he writes. 'What you say in the first two chapters is the crucial factor, something to be found in no sociological or metaphysical analysis of the concentration camps. (...) The book is unreservedly the fixed point to which all further thinking must relate if it is not to be mere talk.' He writes admiringly of the 'clarity of Améry's language', saying that it has 'a kind of functional exactitude'. 'It will be some time before political and philosophical thinking understands the importance of your book,' he ventures to predict, 'but it is unthinkable that it will not be understood' (A.A. to J.A. 24.7.67).[45]

Without doubt, the book belongs to the canon of works on the Shoah, even if it did not even found the genre. So much so that we no longer think it necessary to indicate the originator of its contents, which, as Andersch foresaw, really have become the basis for 'all further thinking'.

Act II: *On Aging* (1968)

An incurable illness[46]

Améry's own further thinking – 'What are we humans? A dwelling of grim pain' – first moves in another direction, away from history and back to humanity per se. On 18 December 1966 he sends Heissenbüttel an exposé entitled 'The Incurable Illness. Essays on Aging.' As in *At the Mind's Limits,* the point of departure is subjective but because he wants to achieve a balance between confession and objective analysis, he hides the I behind the initial A. 'I am eager to know what you think, particularly as I do not have authority on the subject on my side, as I did in my writings on the condition of the victim' (J.A. to H.H. 18.12.66). Heissenbüttel disagrees, in a later letter; it is his opinion that Améry's authority on the subject is just as great in this case. 'People do not like to speak of the subject that you discuss, and it is difficult to speak of it. I think it is praise if I say that you have made this clear at the very beginning' (H.H. to J.A. 5.7.67).

If the first book is primarily concerned with a historical phenomenon, its counterpart in the second book is anthropological. But the link between the two central themes, which really have nothing in common with each other, is far closer than it appears at first. Améry himself provides information on the biographical dimension. After escaping, as he puts it, 20 years of

> ...hard labour writing articles (...) I could think of writing what was really on my mind. And as a late beginner I stayed with the autobiographical theme. This posed first and foremost the crucial personal problem, the crux of my existence, with aging at the centre. Obviously the mere fact that as a man in the middle of his sixth decade of life, I found myself at the point reached by others at the age of 30 or 35, was reason enough for me to feel aging particularly painfully. I was at the beginning, and at the same time, letting the reins drop, I was galloping towards the end. In view of such a state of affairs, it did not even need a dangerous state of physical health to make the problem of my aging the subject of my writing.[47]

Influences

Améry speaks in his foreword of the heterogeneous influences that he has 'transformed and assimilated' in his project.[48] He mentions Simone de Beauvoir's *La force des choses* [translated into English as The Force of Circumstance], the essays of Sartre's pupil André Gorz, *Le vieillissement* [Aging], the 'riveting essays of the physician and anthropologist Herbert Plügge on the philosophy of physicality' in *Wohlbefinden und Missbefinden* [Feeling Well and Ill], Vladimir Jankélévitch's *La Mort* [Death], and finally Proust, 'whose eerily magnificent phenomenology of aging, presented in the final volume of the *Recherche*, was around and in me for many years.' Proust serves him as a 'symbolic figurehead' (J.A. to H.P. 19.11.67). The author of *The Magic Mountain* also determines the literary character of *On Aging*, as does Roger Martin du Gard's depiction of his dying father in *Les Thibault*.[49]

Autobiography Part 2?

Améry asks the rhetorical question of how far his book on aging, which 'entirely omits everything private and anecdotal', can be part of his autobiography. The private and anecdotal are indeed excluded, and yet he speaks – through Proust, Mann, Beauvoir, Sartre, Gorz, Jankélévitch, Plügge and Roger Martin du Gard – in his own name on *his* relationship with *his* time, *his* space, *his* body, *his* society, *his* death. He takes himself as the prototype of an aging human being and sets out to explore its conditions, possibilities and impossibilities by way of 'introspection, observation and empathy'. Under cover of objective meditations on time, space, society, civilization and death smoulders a subjective lament for his own lack of future. With age, Proust writes in *Le Temps retrouvé*, it is as with death. Many meet it with complete indifference, but not because they are braver than the others, only because they have less imagination.

Between profit and loss to the self

Like the first volume, the second is also divided into five parts. 'Existence and the Passage of Time', which in abbreviated form also appeared in the *Merkur*, distils a depiction of *temps vécu* from Proust. Améry opposes subjective experience to the objectively measurable quantities of time and space: for a young man, time is essentially a synonym for the future, moving and realizing itself spatially. For the aging man there is no future any more; he has become a creation of static time without space. Proust and Thomas Mann become Améry's mouthpieces for his own time as he has lived it. Here again reading = living.

In the second chapter, 'Stranger to Oneself', he leans on Simone de Beauvoir and Herbert Plügge. Aging as a purely physical phenomenon is influenced by ambiguity. The alienation that physical decline brings with it produces a curious mixture of profit and loss to the self. Profit because physical ailments – *nolens volens* – make a man more familiar with his body. Loss because with the same painful awareness of the body comes a form of the dissociation of the self. Aging is experienced as an attack on the individual, who still feels young. The third chapter, the heart of the book, analyses the source of aggression. Here social aging is defined through the Sartrean 'Look of Others'. Now all that matters is the moment of reckoning. *Les jeux sont faits*: society grants no more credit to the aging person, he is nailed down to what he has done or not done and is a human being without potential. The fourth chapter is concerned with 'cultural aging', the acceleration of changes in technology and culture, the inability of the aging to read and learn the new signs of the times. A, who no longer understands the world, becomes anachronistic and reactionary. What else? The last chapter is entitled 'To Live with Dying'. No high flights in the sphere of metaphysics can avail; after aging comes dying.

Revolt and resignation

A glance at the subtitle, 'Revolt and Resignation', will suffice to show the thematic link with Améry's first book of essays. In searching for a title with his new editor Hubert Arbogast of Klett Verlag (later Klett-Cotta), who looks after him with the utmost care from now to his suicide,[50] various alternatives of this phrasing are tried out: for instance, 'Revolt in Resignation'. However, they agree on the conjunction 'and', on parity and the equal status of revolt and resignation, as coming closer to the paradoxical attitude to life, the movement of the argument in conflict of *On Aging*. With this we are immediately *in medias res*: was it not also revolt and resignation that moulded Améry's stance towards his Jewish identity? 'I understood,' he writes in his last essay in *At the Mind's Limits*, 'that while I had to accept the verdict as such, I could force the world to revise it. I accepted the judgement of the world, with the decision to overcome it through revolt' (JSS Vol. 2, p. 161; AML p. 90).

Aging and being a Jew

Mutatis mutandis, the judgement of the world must also be accepted in the process of aging. Aging as an incontrovertible fact cannot be avoided, but one can revolt against old age. In this work too Améry stresses existential aspects: as mentioned above, the 'look of others' that makes the aging person what they are, just as it is the look of the anti-Semite that makes the Jew a Jew. Even if there is no connection between 'being a Jew' and 'aging', the attitude the author adopts to these very different phenomena creates such a connection. Revolt against the given facts guides the process of regaining 'dignity'.

> [The aging] do not lose themselves in the it's-all-the-same-to-me of a normalcy without self, nor do they look for refuge to the madhouse, nor do they deceive themselves with a mask of youth, nor with a deeply deceiving idyll of aging (...) they are as society prescribes: what they are, a nothing, and yet in the recognition of being nothing still something. They make their negation in the look of the others into something of their own and rise up against it. They embark on an enterprise that cannot be accomplished. That is their chance and is, perhaps, the only possibility they have of truly aging with dignity. (ÜdA. p. 86; OA p. 77)

The parallels between being a Jew and aging go as far as metaphor: Améry stigmatizes both phenomena as 'incurable illnesses'. It takes a certain amount of imagination to follow him in his associative equation of aging with being a Jew. Of course, the two phenomena, even in his mind, are separated by an insuperable gulf; one is a historical and the other a biological condition. The revolt against being a Jew allows for the discovery of a new identity and for all its negativity can be seen in a positive light. Aging, on the other hand, has no compensations to offer apart from the satisfaction of refusing to live a lie.

Aging and torture

The closest connection between Volumes 1 and 2 in Améry's autobiographical trilogy is to be seen in the connection between torture and aging. Strictly speaking, Améry's treatise on aging is a pendant to his essay on torture, this time outside the historical context. To establish such a correspondence may seem perverse. How can torture, that singular violation, be even approximately compared to a 'natural process' such as aging? It can and it must because these phenomena, although qualitatively so different, are associated with each other in Améry's mind and his analysis. This is done without in any way trivializing torture, although the experience of aging undergoes considerable dramatization. To Améry, aging is anything but a natural process:

> For aging is not a 'normal condition' (...) a norm is a matter of objective insight. That applies to aging just as much as to death. (...) We find it in good order if our neighbour ages and dies: ourselves we always remove from the course of life and death. (ÜdA. p. 43; OA p. 33)

Time may obviously pass

> ...*but to meditate about time is not natural and is not intended to be so.* It is the work of human beings who are horrified, who are no longer at peace with themselves because their disquiet does not leave them in peace. (ÜdA. p. 36; OA p. 26)

To him, then, aging is an entirely different and eerily covert form of 'violation': aging is a scandal against which we must protest, useless as any objection may be. In 1969, when he is asked in the *Internationale Frühschoppen* about torture in Greece, yet again he expressed his horror at the idea of torture being used as a political instrument. 'The torturing of a human being by another human being contravenes all concepts of humanity in its directly personal injury of one by the other.'[51] He also experiences aging as a directly personal injury, even as 'the ultimate disability' (ÜdA. p. 37; OA p. 26).

Torture from outside – torture from within

However, the parallel ends here, since the motive for brutalization and the degree of it are structurally entirely incompatible. Torture never comes from within oneself, it is never 'physically one's own', as Herbert Plügge says.[52] It comes 'from others', the brutalization comes from outside, another human being has put his mind to annihilating my own humanity; he degrades my 'living flesh', making 'butcher's meat' of it. Not so with aging. Biological decline is anchored in human beings themselves. The enemy here comes from within.

Yet as Améry sees it – for this reason the book was difficult reading even for those who admired him most unconditionally – the process of aging is all loss and is indeed long-drawn-out 'torture'.

Whatever there is in consolation that is recommended to the aging – how to come to terms with one's decline and fall, even if possible to be able to gain assets from it, nobility of wisdom, serene resignation, late tranquillity – it all stood before me as a vile dupery, against which I had to charge myself to protest with every line. (ÜdA. p. 10; OA p. xxii)

His analysis, writes Améry, has become an act of rebellion against presenting old age as heroic or transfiguring in any way, for its 'contradictory premise was the total acceptance of inescapable and scandalous things' (ÜdA. p. 10; OA p. xxii). It is obvious that biologically conditioned 'torture', torture without a torturer, in no way becomes real torture.

Améry's line of thought, so systematically opposed to himself, to society, and to the world, shows in both cases how his refusal even to begin to reconcile himself to the realities creates autobiographical continuity where it is least expected.[53]

However, aging has a certain 'ambiguity', and here it diverges from the absence of ambiguity in torture. But this ambiguity moves gradually into the contradiction that can never be resolved, the primal contradiction of death.

We become I and not-I. We possess an ego clothed in our skin and may at the same time find out that the limits always were fluid (...). We become more alienated from ourselves and more familiar with ourselves. (...) Alienation from oneself becomes alienation from being. (ÜdA. p. 61; OA p. 52)

We are 'already about to be the negation of our self'. (ÜdA. p. 62; OA p. 52)

Death comes as the end

'I am on the final lap of completing my book about aging and death. I have just reached death,' Améry writes to the philosopher Heinz Robert Schlette.

My wife wants to know no more about the subject since she copied a text in which I claimed that it was 'the negation of the negation of negation'. That is too much for her healthy mind, and I fully understand her; but on the other hand I must add that the essayist may not have a healthy mind. So stern are the customs (...). (J.A. to H.R.S. 31.3.68)

In this book he is concerned not with legally recorded, historical death, but with organic and biological death, death in life. The man who revolted must now be resigned to the inescapable fact that his life is nothing but a permanent process of dying – physical, social, cultural. Although to Améry the atheist, death literally represents the unthinkable; it is at the same time

> ...the only thing that's true (...) since it is the future of all futures. Every step we take leads us to it, every thought we think breaks down on it. Its completely empty truth, its unreal reality is our life's meaningless fulfilment, our triumph over life only mastered in the nothingness of our border crossing. (ÜdA. p. 117; OA p. 109)

At the same time, however, it is false, writes Améry, quoting Sartre: '*Le faux, c'est la mort.*' To sum up: 'It is the false, since we cannot think it, and the true, since it is fully certain for us' (ÜdA. p. 128; OA p. 121). As abstract as these ideas may sound, for the author they could not be more concrete. A is interested only in the when, where and how. He knows death, he has met with death when it came from outside in the form of death by gas, of murder. That dying, as Améry describes death in Auschwitz, 'was terror' (ÜdA. p. 123; OA p. 116). Now death comes from within, is 'angor', anguish associated with great physical anxiety (ÜdA. p. 123; OA p. 116). To say that he feels fear at the prospect, writes the I, now unconcealed, no longer hiding behind the mask of A, would be an understatement, 'Instead I say that I *am* fear' (ÜdA. p. 124; OA p. 117). So he thinks back to the 'good death by murder that didn't want to know me at all. No nicer death, as a matter of fact – not everyone has the chance' (ÜdA. p. 125; OA p. 118).

Reading this, one stops short – indignant. Améry is the first to know how 'unacceptable' it is ever to think such a thing, which does not prevent him from thinking it to the end. 'A. is up to his neck, up to his mouth, in thoughts of death (...) One should leave him alone' (ÜdA. p. 134; OA p. 126).

The darling of the media

Karl Korn's review in the *Frankfurter Allgemeine Zeitung* (23.11.68), entitled 'How the existentialist ages', sets the tone.[54] 'A caustic and extremely clever book,' he writes, has just been published. Its 'fundamental thesis' is 'highly original'. The 'revolt' to which Améry calls in this book, says Korn, is not so much a revolt against aging and death as one 'against the feeble reaction of lies and lying', against hypocritical 'serenity' and 'the yearning for harmony, husbanding one's forces' to avoid facing the reality of death. A year later Korn writes a letter to Améry asking, 'Please allow one who is not personally acquainted with you to knock at your door,' and introducing himself as one of Améry's 'admirers' (K.K. to J.A. 25.11.69). He would like, he says, to ask him to write for the *Frankfurter Allgemeine Zeitung* (FAZ), although without wishing to 'steal him from his old colleague Paeschke'. A second attempt is made, this time by the editorial office of the FAZ's literary review, in a letter from Karl-Heinz Bohrer (K.H.B. to J.A. 3.1.72).

However, first, comments reach him from Horst Krüger, author and co-editor of *Die Zeit*, with Heissenbüttel and Paeschke the third in the league. He writes emphatically to Améry: 'This is the best thing you have ever written' (H.K. to J.A. 9.1.68).

> I consider it even better than your essay on torture. I hope you will not make light of my extremely positive judgement. It was not made easily, but rather, if I were to analyse the depths of my own psyche, arose from secret resistance. It expresses admiration for the writer Améry in whom – beneath the surface – some resentment plays a part. I heard, not without envy, how well you are able to approach a subject, go into it and find the right words for it, a task in which I have failed (...).

But perhaps, he writes, correcting himself, he has not failed, it is simply not his subject, in contrast to Améry whose comments owe much to his own 'logic of life'. That logic enables Améry to write with great consistency about something that is entirely alien to him, Horst Krüger. He praises Améry's entirely new tone, and indeed his new 'structure of thought' in approaching the subject. 'When we write on old age and death, we strike a pastoral note of "wisdom" and "serenity", in any case always promoting harmony, that is to say, in essence, covering up a tainted subject.' The 'German spirit', Krüger generalizes, 'does not like to look into dark corners and unpleasant rifts (...).' He congratulates Améry that he has succeeded

> ...in cleansing a tainted theme, washing and drying it, opening it up and then thinking it through cleanly. It can be relished thus. In such an honourable way, one could confront the subject. You have truly made a breakthrough with this book in the philosophical and moral sphere of the essay. (H.K. to J.A. 9.1.68)

It is indeed a breakthrough. The first edition of 5000 copies sells out in four months, a second edition follows, and within a short time a third is contemplated (Letter from H.A. to J.A. 21.5.69). In his preface to the fourth edition, Améry confronts the critics who cannot recognize themselves in the black hues of his picture of old age. Alas, he says, he has nothing to retract.

> If I have learned anything in the last ten years, it has led me instead to accentuate what I said at that time rather than to modify it. Everything has been a trace worse than I had foreseen: physical aging, cultural aging, the daily approach, sensed as a burden, of the dark journeyman who runs along at my side and urgently calls

to me as to Raimund's Valentin with the uncannily intimate phrase, 'Come, little friend ...' (Preface to the fourth edition, ÜdA. p. 12; OA p. xix)

The book is now in it seventh edition, receiving nothing but praise. In 1970 Améry is elected as an extraordinary member of the Berlin Academy of Arts. In 1970 he wins the Critics' Literary Prize of the League of German Writers.

Heart attack

Breakthrough or not, it is followed by a breakdown. His public success does not bring stabilization, let alone peace, but an abrupt fall. His first will – 'My last will and testament' – is written on 24 March 1968, that is to say directly after he wrote *On Aging.*[55] He must have known, for it is his opinion that 'we depend on reality as it depends on us' (J.A. to E.M. 12.4.68). No sooner is the book published than the 'dark journeyman' also appears. Améry suffers a heart attack. The bow has been bent for far too long: the *Merkur, Die Zeit*, the 'little Swiss papers', and a little later the *Frankfurter Rundschau*, the *Neue Rundschau*, as well as the *Süddeutsche Zeitung* are all trying to recruit him. Finally, there are the many radio stations: South West Radio (SWF), West German Radio (WDR), Bavarian Radio, Radio in the American Sector (RIAS), and later North German Radio (NDR). There are his reading tours and public discussions, for instance, the 'Nuremberg Conversations' to which he is invited. He writes to Ernst Mayer:

> My dear old friend, I am drained, *hélas*. Nuremberg (where every day I was not in bed until three in the morning, and getting up again at seven), then a visit from Heissenbüttel, and an *Express* article in double quick time. In Nuremberg Helge Pross (professor of sociology) had me on toast; I still feel quite dazed. Dear Ernst Fischer, whom I was so much looking forward to seeing, was not there because of illness. Conversations here and there: Robert Jungk, Hilde Spiel, Peter Härtling, Rolf Schroers, sociologists and political scientists and left-radical students, very clever. But I think I am no longer up to such demands on me. (These fellows have German vitality and can hold their liquor; how is a poor old 'Jew' to keep up?) In addition there are female admirers who would like to leap from literature straight into life. Too late. All of this, of course, is just confidence tricks and Vanity Fair. (J.A. to E.M. 28.4.68)

After his 'descent into the abyss' of aging comes 'full-blown depression: fear of life and fear of death united in a dull sense of surfeit, of battle-weariness' (J.A. to E.M. 29.10.68). He mentions a 'grave mental crisis', saying that 'it is not entirely without foundations: (...) after so many years of toil, I saw a faint gleam of success, and (...) then, as it were, my whole book rose up against me and hit me on the head' (J.A. to E.M. 8.5.69). Maria speaks of the worst nervous breakdown he has ever suffered, and how in Oostduinkerke on the Belgian coast, where the couple went every year for a working holiday, he felt like throwing himself down the stairwell from the fifth floor[56]; 'He does not want to get better, he would like to die,' she tells Ernst Mayer. She confides in him that she has '*very grave concerns*' for 'Hansi's state of mind'; he refuses 'to let any psychiatrist or psychologist into the house for fear that he might be taken to a psychiatric hospital, which I myself intend to prevent at all costs' (M.A. to E.M. 25.4.69). The fact is that the heart attack leaves him physically and mentally prostrated for several months. After that, they speak in the Améry household of 'a new system of dating (in our private lives); b.h. and a.h. (before and after heart attack)' (M.A. to E.M. 8.4.69).

Act III: *Years of Wandering* (1971)
Questioning himself, questioning the time

In this state of crisis, after two acts and ten scenes, Améry writes Act III of his drama of the mind. He sees it at present as his last 'essay in self-questioning' and thinks it his 'most personal' mental reconstruction, although as usual it leads to a fury of mental auto-demolition.[57] His financial situation has improved, and as a staff writer for the *Merkur* he now receives a regular monthly salary of 200 DM. Again, Heissenbüttel is the first to be told about the new work. Améry points out that there are six 'separate essays' this time, and they 'are more closely linked together' than was the case before, for the motifs of alienation and historicity, for instance, merely indicated in the first essay, are fully developed only in the subsequent writings (J.A. to H.H. 28.4.68). It is not only the most personal but also the most autobiographical book in the trilogy, both a justification and a self-interrogation. Here a man is sitting in judgement on himself. Who was I? What have I become? Why have I become what I am? *At the Mind's Limits* and *On Aging* showed the way clear to the *Unmeisterliche Wanderjahre*.[iii] Améry first had to call his festering wounds – Auschwitz, torture, resentment, being a Jew – by their true names in isolation and expel them from his system, before a chronological account of his career could be simulated, with its political locations – Vienna, Paris, Cologne – and the breaks within, of 1938 (exile), 1943 (torture), 1945 (liberation) and 1966 (professional breakthrough), all interwoven. The 'six essays that represent the development of the mind in that period through a personal example, my own' are also to be understood

---

iii   'Years of Wandering', with a reference in the German title to Goethe's seminal
      Bildungsroman entitled *Wilhelm Meisters Wanderjahre*.

as an intellectual biography of the twentieth century, in which history is ultimately experienced only, in the words of Theodor Lessing, 'as giving sense to the senseless'.[58]

'Survey of a period'[iv]

Améry looks for signs of the life he had lived in his philosophical landscapes of former experience. In the process, he will speak of 'irrationalism (at the time of our 'forest walks'), of neo-positivism, existentialism and structuralism. It is all very closely related to the subject, and presented in a very literary language', he tells Heissenbüttel in his exposé. It is impossible for him to escape the intensity of reflection with imagination, thinking with feeling. Indeed, we may say that a close connection between philosophy and literature is even more obvious than in the first and second volumes, so organic is the interweaving of quotation, memory and invention, so inspired the vigour that imbues Améry's ideas. Paeschke is delighted. Améry conveys something 'that only an Austrian can convey in this situation. So much new is said here about the existentialist context of logical positivism!' he enthuses.

> Essay, did you call it? *Ecce poeta!* I would reply. If the first works were moving because they came from the torture of individual experience, we now have a writer well aware of all his stylistic means, with everything that also belongs to the temperament of the game. Am I wrong in feeling that you wrote this all at once, in a kind of delight in discovery? Towards the end, [he refers to the second chapter] Apparent sham questions (...) before you return to the immediate personal situation, I even momentarily had the impression that you were putting all your cards on the table at once, as if your delight in language was racing ahead. (H.P. to J.A. 4.3.70)

A Bildungsroman[v] turned upside down

Paeschke obviously does not yet know about the mood of the closing: the chapter on 'Expeditions beyond the Rhine' reads like an elegiac continuation of the 'Resentments' essay in the first volume. After considering a wide variety of titles, Améry finally decides on this ironic reference to Goethe's *Wilhelm Meister,* for despite alleging that he has not mastered anything, the first-person narrator presents a Bildungsroman. After all, it traces the path from darkness to light, the progress of the 'fool' Hans Maier to the enlightened philosopher Améry,

---

iv *Ein Zeitalter wird besichtigt,* the title of a volume of memoirs by Heinrich Mann.
v Goethe's *Wilhelm Meister,* to which Améry's *Unmeisterliche Wanderjahre* (see above) makes punning reference, is the great example of the Bildungsroman genre.

from the 'great refusal' as *flight* to the 'great refusal' as *action*. Admittedly it is
a Bildungsroman in reverse, for its aim and purpose is not to be integrated into
society, but to live a life of alienation outside it.

Not that he had intended that from the start. On the contrary, at first this
autobiographical novel reads like a surprising renaissance. A first-person narrator asks himself questions and exchanges the falsehoods of the past for the truths
of today. In the process a whole spectrum of ego-constructs comes to light,
entangled in role-playing that must be constantly redrafted. The vagaries and
confusions of the forest enthusiast of the Alpenland, venturing close to Fascism,
are taken ad absurdum. The 'aesthetic of irrationalism' is exchanged for the 'aesthetic of rationalism'. At the end of his twenties he 'mocked Heidegger, in the
company of Carnap'. At the beginning of his thirties, he is deeply shaken when
Heidegger emerges historically the victor. 'You knew not what you did', the narrator, now almost 60, derides the young man.

After receiving the first two instalments, Heissenbüttel expresses his astonishment. 'It is clearer this time than on the first occasion that you always faced
whatever confronted you with great confidence,' he says, revising his earlier
verdict.

> The reflection that your years of wandering represent gains its colour from the
> fact that you were not and are not a sceptic. For me, it now becomes clear that
> the three books fundamentally form a unit. They can be read separately, each
> for itself, but the work gets its true depth only when they are seen in relation to
> the others and in their changed perspective. (H.H. to J.A. 24.2.70)

To this Améry replies: 'It is true that I was not a sceptic – I was only too
lacking in scepticism. The other instalments, however, will trace how I became
a sceptic, so that I am entirely sceptical today' (J.A. to H.H. 15.5.70). Both
are exaggerations; in fact, the coordinates of his 'false' socialization, which
he determines in the *Unmeisterliche Wanderjahre* with enviable clarity, never
existed quite so clearly. The walker in the forest was nothing like the 'fool' he
likes to make him out here, nor was the reactionary young man so 'dull-witted'.
Here we have a desire for stylization at work, drafting a psychodrama in which
he aims to present fictions of a self, reflecting the fall and rise of our epoch.

An artist of transformation

He experiences a great awakening only with the Nuremberg Laws. At this point, if
we wish to stay with the chronology, *At the Mind's Limits* has to be interpolated,
for his torture and time in the camp are left out of this third book. In fact, the

Unmeisterliche Wanderjahre form the framework and background to his first book in the trilogy; they provide what came before and after, as Gerhard Scheit says in his afterword to the new editions of Améry's works.[59] Looking back to his chapter on France in *Preface to the Future,* we learn here all about Améry's first encounter with that country. In 1945 Sartre's existentialism appeared to him, risen as he was from the dead, a 'very personal philosophy of the hunger for life'. Sartre's philosophy of freedom not only made sense of his past but also promised a future. For if the essence of existence came first, he could construct his tomorrow as if his yesterday had not broken him. He had projects; he could redesign himself and make demands on the world. But what he values most of all in Sartre is his concept of *dépassement*, his belief in a 'permanent revolution against his Self', his insistence on constantly making his own choices, and finally his call for what Améry calls a 'moral of historical will regardless of whether history (...) says yes or no'. In Sartre's defeats by history, Améry sees at first only the triumph of humane protest. Sartre is not only a father figure with whom to identify, he even provides Améry with a method of reconstructing his own mental biography. Just like Sartre himself in *Les mots*, conjuring up his childhood and youth so that he could destroy them all the more thoroughly, Améry conjures up his Austrian forest wanderings in order to put his ability to transform himself to the test, thus demonstrating how his aesthetic existence can cross the boundaries drawn by history.

Homo absconditus

Euphoria is followed by a hangover: if Sartre began as Améry's philosopher of the hunger for life, then Sartre's turning away from humanist existentialism towards an ever more rigid Marxism and Maoism contributes to his weariness with life, as we shall see in his last book, *Charles Bovary* (1978). It is not only Sartre who betrays him – all of France stands accused of betrayal: France's celebration of the structuralism of such writers as Foucault, its farewell to the Enlightenment as a mystifying entity set up by the bourgeoisie, his sabotage of the moral subject as a means of oppression – this tendency to turn from Cartesianism to a dehumanized, a-historical, arbitrary France plunges Améry entirely into despairing disorientation.

Even beyond morals and history, whatever they may be, he continues his soliloquy, Where is mankind?

> This poor bundle of all too vulnerable flesh, intangible emotions and impressions, this poor human skin that wants only to protect itself from icy cold and burning heat. One can never make enough allowances for mankind, whose physically vulnerable existence crushes and devours him from within. (UW, Vol. 2, p. 236)

Here Améry's self-demolition reaches its final point. In a grand gesture, the rescuer now speaks up – 'Alienation is existence in a world without love' (UW Vol. 2, p. 345) – the Pascalian awareness of our pitiful animality is to be saved, if only in the negative sense. 'Here he is addressing not only the inner connection with the two preceding books,' Gerhard Scheit explains in his afterword to *Unmeisterliche Wanderjahre*.

> This place marks the point from which Améry conducts all his intellectual confrontations. The philosophical recourse to 'the body in pain' lends these confrontations (...) a weight that is still singular within the left-wing journalist of the sixties and seventies. (Gerhard Scheit, Vol. 2, p. 765)

No place anywhere

> I am just describing our youthful desire for forests and what it means when examined in the light of today's perspective. And then I become aware how totally questionable every consideration of history is, and by very roundabout ways I return to Lessing's *Geschichte als Sinngebung des Sinnlosen* [History as the bestowal of meaning on the meaningless].

Améry can hardly believe that the allegedly politicized young people of 1968 chose Hesse's *Siddartha* as their cult book.

> We are supposed to go on thinking historically, and not say to ourselves: vanity of vanity, all is vanity. And senseless. And without any rules. But with dialectic, of which I have had no wish to hear any more for a long time, perhaps we may master even such a foolishly kaleidoscopic pattern. As for me I can say only that it was all stupid, all failed, all lost, from the irrational excesses of Leo [Leopold Langhammer; author's note] to the most sophisticated neo-positivism. Everything is confused and past. Sartre himself is silent. To whom does this time belong? The murderers of Vietnam? The would-be Stalins in the Kremlin? Chairman Mao? I am sometimes so exhausted by the vain hunt for firm standpoints and productive ideas that in the evening I am just about capable of taking a Simenon off the shelf. (J.A. to E.M. 11.12.69)

The 'most certain of truths', he says, were becoming increasingly doubtful to him. What began with such hopeful ardour ends in the most hopeless lamentation:

> The business of disputing with himself was all that still saved his intellectual dignity (...). Once there had been right and wrong, good and evil. He would no longer be as comfortable as he had been in the dungeons of the Third Reich. Nothing could be substantiated as true, he found no shelter anywhere in what was good or even merely right. (UW, Vol. 2 p. 347)

A forced relationship with Israel: 'I came, I saw, I lost'[vi]

Améry had been disappointed in love not only by Sartre, and not only by France. Germany, which he had approached with so many reservations, too had betrayed him, indeed betrayed him doubly – at least the Germany that he had always claimed for himself, pre-1933 Germany, a land of culture and education, and even more painfully the Germany of the 1960s which at first seemed to him so well disposed. The great disappointment of the post-war period is the student-Left. Not only do the students not want anything to do with him, they go over to the other side: in their understanding of democracy, in the matter of violence, above all over Israel, which wounds him deeply in 1967 after the Six Days' War.

> He had always marched on the left, but now the strength of his legs was failing, because the left-wing obsession with history addressed him in the international press, and succoured by all progressive minds in universities and churches made it clear to him that the tiny country on the Mediterranean had transgressed against peace and the law, saying why that was so, and suggesting that it would do well to strangle itself, difficult as that undertaking might be. (UW, Vol. 2, p. 348)

He will see only covert anti-Semitism in the anti-Zionism of those institutions. The 'dismal failures' of students, for he is concerned principally with them, lump it all together in their sterile constructs of thought which, as he thinks, would do away with his own experience of suffering under National Socialism with a single stroke of the pen.

Améry insists on his own solidarity with Israel, although it is not entirely without its problems: 'I will not rejoice too early at Israel's victory,' he writes to Heinz Robert Schlette, prophesying even after the Six Days' War that the victory on that occasion 'cannot easily lead to a genuine peace. It is terrible to be conquered, but nor is it pleasant to be obliged to play the conqueror' (J.A. to H.R.S. 16.6.67). He feels the Palestinian assassination of Israeli athletes during the Munich Olympics of 1972 like a personal threat. The Yom Kippur War of 1973 casts his mind into turmoil. He wonders, 'why is this land of Israel, which I do not know (...) the only nation (...) whose existence as a state really matters deeply to me?' And he is indignant to think that it has 'no other friend on this earth but Nixon's terrible America' (J.A. to E.M. 27.11.73).

His identity as a 'Catastrophe Jew' makes him a Zionist against his will. Only with the founding of Israel, he says, have Jews all over the world learned to

---

vi   UW, Vol. 2, p. 316.

walk upright again. He confides to Paeschke that only the news from the Middle East interests him, and he is 'in a state of confusion – above all in what affects (his) position on the left' (J.A. to H.M. 27.11.73). He is even more confused after his first visit to Israel. On a postcard from Tel Aviv he speaks to Ernst Mayer of a 'state of consternation', and to Paeschke he says:

> My head is full to bursting point of contradictions and the problems of Israel, which – just as in the case of Austria – unfortunately are in some way mine too. I am really half crazy, and barely capable of articulating my state of confusion. (J.A. to H.P. 31.3.76)

He follows the events concerning the hostage-taking and freeing of the plane in Entebbe with bated breath, as if his own fate depended on the outcome.

The circle is closed

The turning point of his reflections, covering the period from 1930 to 1970, becomes the breaking point. In terms of time and space it is his immediate present, the multifarious misunderstandings of the 'failed revolution' of 1968 in France and Germany,[60] that are too much for him. 'The walls stand speechless and cold,' he says, distancing himself from the lines of Hölderlin in the opening of his Auschwitz cycle, *At the Mind's Limits*, in the coda to the *Unmeisterliche Wanderjahre*. The walls here literally indicate the 'four walls of (my) study', and metaphorically the philosophical structures he hates so much. 'Whoever is at the mercy of these walls will feel a deep longing to keep silent' (UW, Vol. 2, p. 349).

'Life is not what one has lived,' says Garcia Marquez in his memoirs, 'but what one remembers.' An autobiographical trilogy suggests a chronological sequence of the events of a life. Not so with this drama of the mind. Améry remembers it backwards, reversing the chronology, beginning not at the beginning with his origin and birth but with the death to which he was promised. For him, in the beginning was Auschwitz. Act II explicitly leaves Auschwitz out, but it lingers on, as if still part of his aura, seen in aging as death in life. In Act III, finally, the author soars to his vital origins. The renaissance is deceptive, only now has he reached the full height from which he longs to fall into silence. All has come full circle; at the beginning and the end alike, if in very different circumstances, the mind comes up against its limits. The work of auto-demolition seems to have been completed.[61]

CHAPTER 8

Jean Améry
as a Writer of Fiction

Snapshots

Améry's self-demolition is still 'only' literature and has not yet come to coincide with the biographical facts of his own life. However, demolition assumes previous construction, and in reality Améry's rise from being a 'journalist concocting articles' to becoming a 'moral authority' much sought after by the cultural public now proceeds apace. 'Over the last few weeks', says Horst Krüger humorously, 'it has often seemed to me as if J.A. were like a financial share traded on the stock markets of the world at rates rising to dizzy heights' (H.K. to J.A. 14.4.71). There is rejoicing in the Améry household over such a demand for his work. 'It would be merely coy of me (...) if I did not admit to being glad of this late-found *succès d'estime*' (J.A. to E.M. 21.9.71). His books are translated into other languages and are in particular demand in Japan. 'Well, imagine that!' he laughs at himself, 'To think that someone can unexpectedly come to fame and fortune like this. Soon I shall be a Japanese classic!' Of course, he cannot yet be called a classic, either in Japan or anywhere else, but there is no lack of appreciation even at the time, and it prepares the ground for his present classic status. Above all, Alfred Andersch, in his 19-page 'Anzeige einer Rückkehr des Geistes als Person' [Announcement of the Return of the Mind as a Protagonist],[1] praises him as a persistent subjectivist and self-negating seeker after truth, to whom 'autobiography' is synonymous with 'self-criticism', and as a uniquely profound, keen-minded, inspiring, sensuous and even 'amusing' writer of fiction. Paeschke says, in the same year, 'I can think of no one else in Germany today who is so active on all intellectual fronts (...) as an essayist and cultural critic' (H.P. to J.A. 21.2.71).

Honours

Améry's birthdays, first his sixtieth and then his sixty-fifth, are marked with great ceremony by his friends, the press and his publisher. Even federal Austrian chancellor Bruno Kreisky wishes him 'many more healthy and creative years'. Obviously pleased, Améry replies that on receiving this message, 'The troubled story of my love for our country suddenly assumed a more cheerful aspect, looking to the future' (J.A. to Bruno Kreisky 3.11.77). Mayor Leopold Gratz of Vienna, Deputy Mayor Gertrude Fröhlich-Sandner and Federal Minister of Education and the Arts Fred Sinowitz also send congratulations:

> I always find recognition from people in my native land valuable and encourag-
> ing, and if it comes from elevated official quarters then there is an added ele-
> ment of happy surprise, for in my youth I would certainly never have allowed
> myself to dream that anyone in the official and public sphere would ever take
> any notice of my modest person. (J.A. to Fred Sinowitz 3.11.77)

Furthermore, he receives honour of a more personal kind from the Federal Republic of Germany, where authors send greetings – Peter Huchel, for instance, sends a 'wonderful poem'. After reading the *Years of Wandering,* Ernst Klett sends him a warm appreciation, speaking of the book's 'charm, melancholy, dis-cretion, resignation and elegance' (E.K. to J.A. 28.5.71). Six years later, Michael Klett sends an equally personal letter, speaking of his own status as a 'late-born German'.[2] Améry's editor Hubert Arbogast, also joins in the congratulations, missing no opportunity to say how much he appreciates him: 'These days you will be reading what an excellent man you are so often that I, and others like me, will find it very difficult to add anything ourselves.' However, he does have something to add that no one else would have dared to say: he wishes that Améry would retract his gloomy prognoses in *On Aging*, having disproved them in real life. Now, he suggests, it is time to change his attitude and 'make up his mind to say yes' (H.A. to J.A. 26.10.72). A pious hope, no more.

In July 1972, before his sixtieth birthday, the Bavarian Academy of the Fine Arts awards Améry its prize for literature, praising him as 'a brilliant essay-ist, a master of the German language, a sensitive critic'. The citation mentions his 'extraordinary' work, 'in which the radical and pitiless analysis of his own person is combined with the analysis of an age,' and declares that 'the Bavarian Academy wishes to honour it here today'. By an irony of fate the certificate is signed by Hans Egon Holthusen, the then president of the academy and author of the confession 'Freiwillig zur SS' [Volunteering for the SS]. In his speech of thanks, Améry does not shrink from expressing the uneasiness he feels as a writer of the Left in being honoured by a right-wing body.

On the other hand, the award soon afterwards bestowed on him by the Federal German Cross of Merit, First Class, with which he is decorated on

7 November 1972 by Federal President Gustav Heinemann, 'in recognition of special services to the Federal Republic of Germany', is welcome as an unexpected birthday present. He thanks the country with great delight:

> It is like a dream to think of receiving a German distinction, and it seems to me even more like a dream that I am now able to accept such a distinction with a happy heart and an easy mind.

Or is he only dreaming, after all?

> What I would once have thought scarcely possible has happened: a new and truly different Germany has come into being since 1945. This new Germany, Mr President, is well and fittingly represented by your own person, and I am happy that the certificate of this award bears your signature (4.1.71).

Yet there is some discontent in the Améry household at his being the object of all this attention: 'I am hunted down more than a man's strength can endure: "society" makes its claims, and if you have ever ventured as far out as I have, then you must accept that fact' (J.A. to E.M. 23.9.73), which does not prevent him from complaining bitterly of having his miniature apartment besieged for days on end by 12-man strong camera teams.

Everyday life in Brussels

After five moves from furnished room to furnished room, the Amérys have an apartment at last. 'It's amusing,' he writes to Ernst Mayer, 'that I had to wait until I was 51 years old before living anywhere worthy of a human being' (J.A. to E.M. 8.5.63). The reason was probably his gift for adapting comfortably to places unworthy of a human being – 'above all a hotel room!' The new apartment is not in a hotel, but in an ordinary terraced house and unfortunately has to be reached by way of a steep spiral staircase. There is no lift, a disaster for both of them: his heart and her knees protest – but another move would be even worse. The address is 56 Avenue Coghen, in the Uccle area of Brussels, a good part of the city. The two-roomed apartment could hardly be more modest and is not designed for grand purposes, although the living room aims for the bourgeois style of the 1960s, with the obligatory teak shelving, coffee table and two armchairs 'for occasional visitors'. Gauloises and cognac form part of the basic household equipment. Apart from Erich Schmid's dark oil paintings – 'the pictures of Schmid are part and parcel of my life: I can no more imagine life without Schmid's pictures than my room without the emotions I experience in

Maria and Jean Améry outside their front door in the Avenue Coghen, 1976

it'[3] – and a stack of the latest new books on the aforesaid coffee table, the over-whelming impression conveyed by these 60 square metres is one of austerity: every last centimetre serves some purpose. Maria types in the corridor, on a writing surface wedged between two built-in cupboards containing the writer's private archives. He, who by his own account picks up his pen mainly 'when lying horizontal', turns his bedroom into a study where he writes busily.

In its 'diabolical rhythm', the Améry household has a supremely ascetic approach to work. Maria runs the place as general manager, secretary, financial administrator and planner of their travels. Neither he nor she has any family, 'unless I include a blackbird that has taken up its quarters at night on our kitchen terrace for the last two years' (Maria Améry to Hety Schmitt-Maas 1.2.68). It is surprising to find that with all their busy activity they still preserve a certain childishness; they can fool around and even make silly jokes at times. There is no comfortable homeliness, no family in the conventional sense; we have already seen how Améry disliked the idea of childbearing, exemplified by Agathe in *Die Schiffbrüchigen*, but they have substitutes in the form of small soft toy animals which they call their 'rag children' – easy to care for, reliable, able to stimulate the imagination. They like toy rabbits, squirrels and monkeys best. In correspondence with Ernst Mayer and his mistress Erni, they speculate at length on how these creatures are faring; the animals send each other greetings, dictate their own comments to the writers of the letters and receive presents.

Jean and Maria Améry are a 'working team', a 'cultural export–import' business

Jean and Maria are a 'working team', a 'cultural export–import' business, 'in which of course my husband is the productive partner,' Maria Améry points out (Maria Améry to H. S-M. 1.2.68). Her own domain is the course of their daily life: 'He was a child in all practical matters; I had to do everything' (Maria Améry to Erich Schmid 20.12.79). She records all their incomings and outgoings – so that we learn, for instance, how much his various physical ailments, including suicide attempts, have cost them. Domesticity of every kind is anathema, even housework and cooking. They eat out as a matter of course, usually at their local bistro du coin. Now and then they are invited out, but only very rarely do they ask any visitors to come and see them. Although they set a high value on social intercourse, in principle it takes place outside their home.

Mens sana in corpore insano

Among the things Améry cannot do without are cigarettes – 'I am smoking more than ever myself, which can be regarded as a kind of slow suicide' (J.A. to H.P. 9.2.75), or as he puts it more cynically to Ernst Mayer: 'I (...) am increasing my nicotine consumption; one can rely on such treatments to prove mortal!' Black coffee and an inexhaustible arsenal of analgesics and narcotics, stimulants and sedatives are all part of his 'treatment'. 'It's a good thing the little tablets take effect so quickly these days. Don't talk to me about medical poisoning, I'm just grateful to those chemicals for bringing me relief,' Améry makes his character Lefeu say in 1973 (L, p. 81), for after all, one 'must do something to encourage

Römerberg Conversations 1976. Jean Améry and Erich Fried. In the background,
Wilfried Schoeller and Leonhard Reinisch

a heart attack and cure oneself of memory' (L, p. 45). He never, incidentally, needs to go to any particular trouble to encourage a heart attack, as his letters to Maria in 1946 tell us. His heart has never really been in good working order since his internment in the concentration camps.

In fact, ill health is the norm for him; even as a schoolboy he was sent into the country because of his 'weakness of the lungs'. His body is 'susceptible to torment', sometimes imaginary, generally real. Friends speak of his pathological observation of himself, of hypochondria as his usual state of mind and constant theme. To Améry, the ideal of the well-balanced mind and body, *mens sana in corpore sano*, is merely an unfortunate misunderstanding. How can the mind be healthy in the same sense as the body? Essentially, the mind is 'uneasiness, a tormenting question, sensitivity, irritability', 'If it is a mind at all, the mind is always disturbed' (L, p. 91). 'The entire history of the intellect teems with artistic achievements wrested from a deficient organism, and they may indeed have been achieved only as a manifestation of the suffering body.'[4]

Although the Avenue Coghen is the Amérys' permanent home after 1963, there is no lack of *déplacements*. There are the tours of Germany 'singing for his supper', which Améry dislikes and which he also calls 'business trips of the mind' (J.A. to H.P. 26.9.76, and also 15.12.77). There are visits to the Berlin Academy, where he is in touch with his namesake the literary critic Hans Mayer and with the authors Peter Huchel, Elias Cannetti, Günter Grass, Günter Kunert,

On holiday in the French Pyrenees, 1964

Uwe Johnson and Peter Weiss. There are his lecture tours to foundations, adult education colleges and universities all over the Federal Republic, his partici- pation in discussion groups such as the Nuremberg and later the Römerberg Conversations – there was a culture of such discussion groups which is hardly imaginable today – not to mention appearances on radio and television sev- eral times a month. The media is a part of Améry's legacy. When the walls of Brussels crowd in too much, the Amérys go to the coast of Belgium for a change of scene, for instance, to Oostduinkerke. And every summer they go, with books and typewriter, to take a room in a boarding house in Austria for four to six weeks, usually somewhere such as Bad Goisern in the Salzkammergut resort area, almost always in the company of Améry's old school friend Ernst Mayer and his partner Erni. Or they go to France, if not to Paris then to the south, fol- lowing some kind of trail.

However, is there any part of his life and work in which he is not follow- ing a trail? 'I really live only in the past,' he admits to his friend (J.A. to E.M. 23.9.72). 'That is how we remember him,' says North German Radio editor

Hanjo Kesting, who broadcast Améry's novel *Charles Bovary* with him.

A small, slight man, moving gracefully, holding the inevitable cigarette, (...) emphasizing what he says with energetic gestures, spreading his fingers. His gaze under drooping eyelids is tense and concentrated, sometimes retreating into itself, then beaming cordially again. Irresistible charm, a little helpless, a little ironic. Mockingly ignoring the impositions of daily life. Never a loud word. Anything coarse was like a rent in the fabric of the world. A man of the intellect. A comprehensive education, living in books, pictures, films, conversations. But he was as if released at the wheel of a car. A belief in progress *and* humane scepticism – both at once. Light and dark mingled, as they were in the century of what we call the Enlightenment. It is not impossible to imagine him in a full-bottomed wig of the time of Mozart and Voltaire. A combination of grace and demonic energy. Clarity of the mind, but buried under the features of suffering and despair.[5]

A rebel treading a path between lightness and gravity, between the conception of a juster world in this life and a devotion to the apocalyptic. We know the portraits in Stephan Steiner's book *Jean Améry (Hans Maier)* – together they add up to a record in images.[6] There is hardly a face that puts the time it has lived through so cruelly on display as the ever deeper ravines digging into Jean Améry's features. It is a physiognomy that demands to be read. Améry's texts also offer themselves for the interpretation of that face.

Young Törless and his years of wandering (1971)

'It would be idle (...) to argue the point,' writes Heissenbüttel, wondering whether the work of Jean Améry should be called philosophy or *belles-lettres*. He himself only ever wanted to be an author 'who made it superfluous to draw such distinctions'[7] – and also to be an author as actor, we may add. Améry's *Törless aus Robert Musil* [Törless, from Robert Musil] (1971)[8] is a hybrid somewhere between philosophy and *belles lettres* – a fictional pendant to the chapters on Austria in the *Years of Wandering*, and again it is a work of prose in which he assumes a role, assessing his own potential vagaries against the confusions of Musil's character the young cadet Törless. Even his *Gespräch über Leben und Ende des Herbert Törless* [Discussion of the Life and Death of Herbert Törless] becomes self-criticism.

More precisely, Améry turns Musil's philosophical and psychological novel into a parable of modern history, interpreting Musil's text, as Volker Schlöndorff does in his film version of 1966, as a prophetic study of the intoxicating qualities of power and violence. Beineberg and Reiting become, in his presentation, the representatives of dictatorship, Basini the paradigmatic victim on whom the dictators test their own power.

The 'aesthetics of barbarity'[9]

Musil depicts his character Törless leaving cadet college, after becoming an accomplice in the tormenting of his fellow student Basini, as a young man hungry for knowledge and in search of 'the answer to all riddles'. Where Musil is primarily concerned to present his readers with a meticulous account of the cadet's adventures 'as they broaden the experience of awareness', Améry gives a political turn to Törless's amoral attitude. He thinks his way further into the character and shows how such an alliance of youthful 'idealism' and an intellectual reversion to the wild, aesthetics combined with terrorism, absolutist thinking with moral neutrality, can impel the Austro-Hungarian trio – Beineberg, Reiting and Törless – to experiment on another human being. The 'slaughtering block' to which the esoteric youths ritually lead their 'boyishly attractive' victim Basini is not itself vile, but if anything the opposite; in the task they have set themselves, to find out 'how far one can go', it represents something 'sacred'. In Améry's view such a structure of motivation, characteristic as it was of the mentality of the Fascist Austrian intelligentsia, was bound to lead to Hitler and his genocide.

Améry presents the life and death of Herbert Törless in the form of a retrospective dialogue from the point of view of two former students of his. So we learn of his career as a mediocre journalist and his early membership of the National Socialist Party. He is impressed, says his friend, by the 'link' in Hitler's ideas 'between technically brilliant organization, physical boastfulness and degenerate Dionysian irrationality' (*Törless*, p. 192). 'The Basini experience', he says, '(...) left its mark on him for life' (*Törless*, p. 193). Törless, he explains, made his Aryan victim Basini into 'his' Jew. 'Once he told me, diffidently: "Basini seduced me as Mephistopheles seduced Faust, as a Jew seduces a German."' (*Törless*, p. 189). His friend wants to know more details and asks him about his share in the responsibility for mass murder, to which Törless replies: 'Am I my brother Basini's keeper?' (*Törless*, p. 189). After the perfect model of bourgeois youth had made himself the outsider in the torture chamber, his friend continues, it was only logical for his separation from society to drive him into the arms of the brownshirts. He did what they told him just as he had once done what the torturers Beineberg and Reiting told him. 'He saw the evil that can never be banal. However, instead of turning away in horror, he considered that evil a threshold that one must cross in order to enter into the mystery' (*Törless*, p. 194) – the mystery into which he entered 'through the methods of clear reason'. As a man of many abilities but without qualities, as a misunderstood genius, as a complete failure, he has hidden from the world because he felt soiled.

In terrorizing Basini he crossed a threshold of shame and transgressed all civilized norms; from now on society is no more to him than a fool's game played with marked cards.

> The real Törless was the man, his health shattered, already in a state of psychological decline, economically on the brink of the void, who in his dismal abode read to me, in 1946, from the notes for his work, which was never completed. (...) The war, then just over, became in his eyes (...) the apotheosis of the madness of the world. (*Törless*, p. 195)

The strange aspect of Törless's conduct, his friend goes on, was his 'total indifference, his coldness, his soullessness'. He has, says his friend, killed every human feeling in himself, every kind of sympathy, all sense of pity.

If ultimately Améry is filled with abhorrence for the life of Törless, despite the fascination that it exerted on him, he is anxious to reclaim him at least in death. In his continuation of Musil's story, Törless atones for the torture of Basini with his own death, which becomes an act of self-punishment. Törless has indeed become his brother Basini's keeper; that is how Améry causes his friend to close his account of it. 'He died of him' (*Törless*, p. 197).

No rationalism without sympathy

We are reminded of Améry's own encounters with the natural sciences, with the idea of letting criteria of pure efficiency rule one's thinking and with positivism, for he too, like Törless, was convinced at the age of 20 that the 'logical structure of the world' could be deduced from mathematics. If the Améry of the pre-war years had had the option of being, like Törless, a voyeuristic writer, a 'vivisector', would he have withstood that temptation? The Nuremberg Laws took the decision out of his hands, instead making him the paradigmatic victim himself. It is not difficult to see Améry's fictional narrative about Musil's character as another autobiographical variant of Althager, the *morbus austriacus*, who in his time exchanges the aesthetics of irrationality for the aesthetics of rationalism and finally, as a failure, sees no way out but indirect suicide.

However, the *Törless* story reveals a new emphasis in Améry's thinking. It is not only Althager and Törless who lose their staunch faith in instrumental reason, but also Améry. Once again he ranges himself with Thomas Mann, thinking with 'spirit, body and soul'. Rationalism without sympathy can only foster brutality, or at best it pleads for the status quo, becoming 'an outspoken affirmation of suffering that, because it is affirmed, ultimately loses the quality of suffering'. Améry's controversial criticism of the artist Dürer, in whom he discerns, at the same time as he is writing *Törless*, 'a form of indifference to what is humane',[10] may also, with the requisite adjustments, be regarded as his criticism of Musil. Dürer and Musil both show their knowledge of human misery, but it is a kind of knowledge without reflection, let alone sympathy; neither Dürer nor Musil protests against that misery.[11] Musil's *Törless* appears to Améry an Austrian illustration of R.G. Binding's observation that 'we Germans are heroic in bearing other people's suffering', the National Socialist motto par excellence, as Améry censures it as early as 1945 in his essay on 'The Psychology of the German People'.

Venturing into literary fiction

Améry's next work of fiction also addresses the problems approached in *Törless*, again, among other things – although under different auspices – presenting the relationship of madness and reason in fictional form. His Lefeu consoles himself, he writes to the friend of his youth, by '*not* sacrificing reason to his visions' (J.A. to E.M. 26.1.74). To Améry as a writer of fiction, the *Discussion of Törless* was, in fact, a mere exercise by comparison with his high hopes for his next book. In *Lefeu oder Der Abbruch* [Lefeu or the Demolition],[12] an essay-novel or novel-essay, as he puts it with reference to Hermann Broch, he is venturing 'for the first time after many, many years into something like "literary fiction" again' (J.A. to E.M. 26.1.74). Three years earlier, he has already had a clear idea of it: the central point is to be

> ...a fictional character for whom, perhaps, my friend Erich will provide the model. And now I think I know that at heart I was not meant to be a pure thinker, but a thinking novelist. But will my novel be able to stand up to all that is now considered prose? Has not too much happened since I wrote *Die Schiffbrüchigen*? Nonetheless, and despite some hesitation, I will make the venture. I keep thinking of Proust: 'It was high time to begin the work. But was there still time enough...?' (J.A. to K.M. 16.11.71)

Who is Erich Schmid?

This is not the first time that his imagination has turned to the painter Erich Schmid. Even when he was working as a journalist in Switzerland, Améry had sung Schmid's praises in the *St. Galler Tagblatt* of 5 April 1959, under the title of *Die neuen Mönche. Bildnisse (un)berühmter Zeitgenossen: Unbekannter Maler E.S.*

[The new monks: portraits of (non)-famous contemporaries. Unknown painter E.S.]. The portrait was to be the beginning of a series parallel to the famous *Careers and Heads*. In fact, Schmid was not entirely without fame and, particularly in the 1960s, achieved a certain reputation with exhibitions in France, Belgium, Switzerland, Canada and the United States. In 1985 he had a retrospective in Paris, and in 2002 there was a special exhibition of his work in the Palais Ferstel-Harrach in Vienna.[13] The two men knew each other from Vienna, where Schmid studied psychology before turning to his studies of art (1930–1934) and where he had been analysed by Wilhelm Reich (1925–1930). As Jews they both fled into exile in Antwerp, and as Jews they were both deported to the internment camps of Gurs and St. Cyprien.

After escaping from Gurs, Améry joins the Austrian Resistance in Brussels. Schmid makes contact with the French Resistance in the Lyon area. His parents and his brother are murdered in Auschwitz, he himself survives in hiding.

In 1945 their paths diverge. Schmid returns to Paris after a seven-year odyssey and earns a living as a concierge in the rue Rollin (which Améry renames in *Lefeu* the rue Roquentin, in the manner of Sartre's *La Nausée*). Améry decides to settle in Brussels, where he makes his living from journalism. In a Swiss newspaper article, Améry describes Schmid as 'a monk of our time', a man who keeps

Erich Schmid in his studio

the 'threefold vow: his poverty is obvious, he shows chastity in withstanding worldly temptations, and he is obedient to the artistic law!'[14]

Besides his painting – Kokoschka and Kubin were his masters – Schmid lives with an American woman, and he is also very close to Améry. 'Hans was my best friend – the only man I could talk to – and now there is a void,' he tells Améry's widow Maria. In reading *Örtlichkeiten*, which Maria sends him, he is overcome by longing: 'To us, pursuing our parallel ways, this is all so intimate and intense that it is almost painful to experience it again.'[15] In fact, after Améry's suicide Erich Schmid dies alone in the rue Rollin. For half a century the material for his

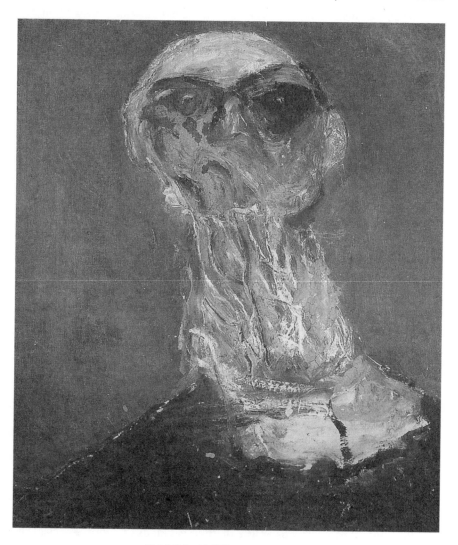

Erich Schmid: 'L'Oiseau de malheur'

pictures was drawn from that quarter in the fifth *arrondissement*, with the cob-blestones paving its narrow alleys, its wine shops and flower stalls, its butchers' and fishmongers' shops. These rather aloof pictures, varying between the figura-tive and the abstract, remain to bear witness to his life.

> Cities without names, streets without people, buildings without faces. The space in which he himself lives is reflected in his pictures, and in them, particularly in his still lifes, one can breathe again the atmosphere of his small one-room studio apartment.[16]

What also remains, most strikingly, is the painter's alarmingly distorted self-portrait, a dark work in the expressionist surrealistic style, painted in 1956 as *L'Oiseau de malheur* [Bird of ill omen], the central metaphor for Améry's novel.

A novel about an artist, with evocative images

It is Paris versus Brussels; Améry's new prose work also takes inspiration from that contrast, for he comes to see the choice of Paris as a home, a choice that he did *not* make in 1945, as symptomatic of courage and a refusal to compromise. Améry is not ready for the 'monastic life' on which Schmid, with his own decision, embarks. Instead, Améry wants a public, success and fame, even if those aims take him to Germany. The fact that a vagrant painter, highly educated and trilingual, 'says No in Paris, and by doing so achieved in his lifetime a part of what moves me', and that he 'led a life (...) which I myself did not have the courage to choose' arouses his admiration. Althager the nay-sayer from *Die Schiffbrüchigen* is resurrected in Lefeu the nay-sayer, by comparison with whom Améry the narrator at first sees himself as a contemptible yea-sayer. But the artistic figure of Lefeu/Schmid merges with the artistic figure of Lefeu/Améry – how could it not? – and 'contrary to my intentions the autobiographical element once again intruded' (L, p. 172).

Of course, the book has a much wider context. Améry made some notes when he was preparing for a reading in Mainz[17]: the book, he says, takes 'crisis as its subject', it is concerned with the 'waste society'

> ... humanity consumed and used up. This waste (enticement – pseudo-satisfac-tion) is symbolized by what I call the lustre of decline (...). Why does Lefeu want to fall into decline? – On a superficial plane of thought because *death* is the lustre of decline, and *death* (sickness and death) is a lively affair – on a deeper plane, see Fire-Rider.

There was to be 'no "construction", no "characters", the action of events and thoughts all in the language, the rhythm. All kinds of poetic aspects.' The essay, he says, will not be inserted into the novel, the events themselves will lead into it just as it leads back to the events. In the process, he uses the technique of montage. Another theme is the crisis of language, 'which as an item of consumer goods like other goods (...) is used up'. The answer, however, cannot be further linguistic destruction or the establishment of 'linguistic autonomy', but a new kind of creativity (creativity without constraint – but not unbridled), emphasizing the sensory nature of the statements made, for instance, by interweaving two languages. He has already spoken, in an early letter to Paeschke, of his 'dream' of writing in two languages, with 'German and French alternating' (J.A. to H.P. 12.4.68). With *Lefeu* at least, that dream became reality.

Andersch calls this novel-essay a 'very difficult' book, 'of burning intellectual relevance, (...) uncomfortable, (...) tragic, making great demands on the reader.'[18]

The genesis of no other book by Améry is so thoroughly documented. In summing up, he hopes that *Lefeu* will be 'an account of my own existence, my own thinking' (L, p. 184). In the first place, this novel-essay derives from Améry's unpublished novel of his youth, *Die Schiffbrüchigen*, written in 1934–1935. If the nay-sayer Althager is the original model for Lefeu, then his friend Hessl is the model of a yea-sayer, the original of Beaumann, 'formerly of Meyersohn and Son' (L, p. 47). The novel's philosophical and political premises also have their origin here, for instance, in addressing the decline in values and, above all, in reflecting on linguistic confidence and linguistic scepticism. In 'Why and How', the seventh chapter of the book, he establishes a discrepancy between intention and realization, a subject later reflected in his correspondence with Heissenbüttel.

The essayist as novelist

The essayist Améry, hitherto used to ruling supreme over language instead of letting himself drift with it, had not expected to be taken unawares as he wrote. The *Lefeu* project, he says, assumed a form in its writing that he did not intend, and in his hands it imperceptibly condensed into a complex of images of longings and memories.

'Lefeu – Feuermann – the Fire-Rider – oiseau de malheur – feu Lefeu [the late Lefeu]'[i] – all these strands of narrative and aesthetic horizons of experience could hardly be more economically and at the same time sensuously interwoven. 'The existential factor is concrete,' comments Heissenbüttel (H.H. to J.A. 2.3.75). The skilfully interwoven strands on which Lefeu has so daringly kept his balance

---

i Améry is indulging in wordplay on the name of his character Lefeu, whose surname literally means 'the fire', and whose original German name was Feuermann, 'fire-man'. The Fire-Rider (German, *Feuerreiter*) is a strange, sinister character in a poem by Eduard Mörike. Finally, *le feu Lefeu* = 'the late Lefeu'.

until now suddenly break. The break comes when Lefeu recognizes himself as Feuermann. It is also a break in language. The words '*I remember*', printed in italics, draw from the narrator a long 'suppressed cry of mingled pain and laughter' (L, p. 121 and p. 124).

The Lefeu of the first four chapters is still very Sartrean, confessing to feeling nausea in the face of success, competition, all that he calls 'the lustre of decline' (L, p. 20). Considering the gleaming new architecture of the Paris-Seine steel and concrete apartment blocks, bringing threatened demolition to the building where he lives, he defends the organic dilapidation of his 'high-rise cavern' as the last bulwark of a counter-world worthy of human dignity. The individualizing value of dissolution is, as he sees it, a protest against functionalism. He pays tribute to reason, he trusts language, he builds on the sense of what is said, swears by the verifiability of words. A humanist who is an *engagé en situation*, Lefeu likes to adopt a partisan stance. His confession of faith is to educate the human race.

Feuermann

However, at the sight of the sprawling gasworks of lou Gaz de Lacq – a complex not so far from Lager Gurs, the Gurs camp – all is over for Lefeu and his trust in humanity. It is Feuermann who breaks out of him, and as Feuermann he swears revenge on the perpetrators. Lefeu entertains fantasies in which he raises fires in the city of Paris that he both hates and loves. He explains to the Düsseldorf art gallery owner:

> I am a landless man (...) I was twice expelled, first from the rolling hills, (...) then from the high cavern (...); a man has a home, but he is not born in it, he must look for it, lost in dreams (...). (L, p. 147)

His desire for an act of revenge is incompatible with his declared faith in reason. Waking from his amnesia, Feuermann/Lefeu, the man of fire, knows better:

> As I tried to link the idea of arson to revolutionary hope, as I understood, although late, that the counter-violence I was to exert was the only possible answer to the violence I have suffered personally from that evil, I face the question of whether individual motivation is really, as Sartre thinks and as I more or less automatically used to maintain with him, the natural intermediary of supra-personal, historical constraints. (L, p. 162)

This, then – with five years yet to pass before he writes his *Charles Bovary* – is the time when Améry is no longer 'automatically' inclined to 'maintain' the theses of Sartre on counter-violence.

Améry frees himself from his mentor and turns action into art. He does not set fire to Paris but paints a picture of a burning Paris and then burns that picture. 'Paris brûle. Il brûle et ich brülle'[ii] (L, p. 165). He has learned to put a name to the 'black core' of his unhappiness. 'Here I have the whole complex that I buried in the last depths I can still reach of my existence' (L, p. 124). Since 1945 everything he did and everything he did not do has been solely determined 'by the fact that I could not survive my survival' (L, p. 161) 'Survival was an absurdity' (L, p. 161). The painter Lefeu kills his art and – at least in a transferred sense – kills himself. Not as a phoenix, more as the central figure in an auto da fé.

'Lefeu. The Fire. Or Feuermann' (L, p. 23). This first chain of association is connected from the start with the fire of Auschwitz. On p. 121 the series of metaphors implodes – the flames flaring up from the gasworks complex extinguish the former *maquisard* Lefeu, who has made a Frenchman of himself, and resurrect Feuermann *père* in Stuttgart in the person of Feuermann *fils* – resurrecting the father who takes out his Iron Cross, First Class, with shaking fingers, whose hands later clench and stretch in death, before – like the sobbing mother – rising to the legendary grave in the air.

Feuerreiter [Fire-Rider]

But Feuermann does not come alone, he comes with a 'mystical companion' (L, p. 127), a 'Fire-Rider' [German *Feuerreiter*] galloping at full speed, into whom he is finally transformed. Améry weaves Mörike's poem, which also has associations with painting but in a very different context, line by line into his Romanesque vision. The verses about the *Feuerreiter*[19] are from Mörike's novel *Maler Nolten* [Nolten the Painter]. Feuermann as Fire-Rider is close to madness in his pain, like his model, who is another clear case of self-destruction, for the 'raging rider' dies in and by his own fire. However, in Améry, Mörike's pathos strikes a grotesquely tragi-comic note instead: 'So let my misfortune die and be extinguished in the flames' (L, p. 168), declaims Lefeu, having poured out some petrol in a garage to set light to his picture.

> And my trousers only slightly charred. (...) I just feel sick (...). I am perfectly unharmed [German *heil*] apart from the sickness. *Heil*, I say. *Heil! Heil!* (...) Il n'est pas blessé, absolument pas. C'est plutôt le cœur qui flanche. (L, p. 168)[iii]

---

ii This short half-French, half-German sentence contains a pun on the French verb *brûler*, to burn, and the German verb *brüllen*, to roar or bellow.

iii Besides the French part of this speech [He is not injured, not at all. Rather it is his heart that flinches.] there is a pun on German *heil* = intact, uninjured, and the Nazi salutation familiar now from the phrase *Heil Hitler!* = hail! (as a rather archaic greeting).

'Feuermann is no more, so Lefeu should not exist either; the logic is unassailable' (L, p. 131).

Oiseau de malheur

At the vanishing point of all these transformations is the *oiseau de malheur*, the bird of ill omen, 'a (...) self-portrait transported to the metaphysical sphere. (...) All things considered, it is an unfortunate bird, distantly related to the Fire-Rider's bony horse' (L, p. 145–6). Lefeu calls for 'the hour of shame in Stuttgart to be cancelled out', for 'a shameful survival to be extinguished', for a finale – and here is the point of Améry's narrative structure – that was already implicit in his name, Le-feu. So the circle closes: *le feu Lefeu*, the late Lefeu, retrospectively tells the story of his death.

The truer truth of the emotive

With the metaphors of the Fire-Rider and the *oiseau de malheur*, the novelist is testing out the demolition not only of Lefeu's building but also, above all, of language, sentences and even words. He leaves the plane of what is strictly verifiable, letting pain and desperation hunt him down. At first the world still seems to fit into an order of being which is reflected in language; the Vienna Circle and the early Wittgenstein still stand sponsor. Lefeu counters his lover Irene's 'crushed ruins of language' (L, p. 8) with Wittgenstein's credo: 'One must stand by the sense of the sentence (...). One can say of that sense that it is the path of verification' (L, p. 8). The world, Lefeu informs the not very receptive Irene, is 'all that is the case, and *only* what is the case. (...) Language reflects what is so in the world' (L, p. 72). And of Wittgenstein himself, the narrator says, 'He understood what can be understood of the world and of language. But when he no longer understood, but wanted to go on understanding, he said what cannot be understood and lost all three: himself, language and the world' (L, p. 72).

One point was not anticipated in the outline of the novel: Lefeu/Améry also loses himself, language and the world, and again it is Wittgenstein who, willy-nilly, shows him the way out of the restraints of verification. Language both realizes and, to coin a word, ir-realizes; it is both a bridge and an insuperable gulf, and yet, says Lefeu, the attempt to communicate must be made again and again. The poet Irene, who tries to reduce Lefeu's reasoning to absurdity with her apparently senseless verses about poplars, stands in contrast to him.

However, after his journey of initiation by way of lou Gaz de Lacq, which has 'fulfilled its function in the system of coordinates of his existence' (L, p. 129), Lefeu turns his back on neo-positivism and asks Irene, as the prophetess of dissolution, for forgiveness. She has already exposed the wounds of Auschwitz in her strange world of alien words, at a time when Lefeu was still trying to suppress them. He has learned to distinguish between the rational and the emotive meaning of language. 'Forgive me for not doing justice to your babbling' (L, p. 127), he soliloquizes in an imaginary dialogue with Irene, who has killed herself. '(...) For a long time, my friend, I was not sure of the meaning of what you were saying, and I have much to apologize to you for. The poplar avenue, for instance' (L, p. 152). He has now understood that the poplars conjured up by Irene are the same as the poplars lining the gasworks complex up to the way to Auschwitz. But how could he recognize them while he would not acknowledge his own past?

In fact, Améry as novelist is no longer so certain of himself in the matter of language. 'Words, whatever their relationship to reality, are to be suppressed for the sake of reality and mortal honour' (L, p. 123). But to keep silent means, for Améry, concealing the truth. Language is wrong 'when it raises itself up and wrong when it flatly cuts itself off' (L, p. 125).

Améry's uncertainty is not confined to language; his moral demands on his autonomous subject are beginning to totter as well. 'He voluntarily accepts (...) the word of reality as the last word, and thus renounces (...) the establishment of the sovereign ego' (L, p. 95). This establishment, which Améry proclaims in his essays as a sine qua non, is presented as a problem in the novel – aporia again. Does not the title itself – *Lefeu oder Der Abbruch* [Lefeu or the Demolition] – say it all? We are presented with an alternative and must choose between the subject of Lefeu *or* demolition as a cipher for destruction. Is this a synonym whereby Lefeu brings himself into line with demolition?

Améry describes himself as an obdurate cultural conservative who has difficulty with the experimental and dismisses these 'interwoven textures' as wordplay. 'However original they may be', they do not concern him, they cannot meet his needs, 'when it is time to stop work, you close the books with a sigh of relief.'[20] *Lefeu oder Der Abbruch* is still virgin territory to most readers of Améry. But the rediscovery, or discovery, of Jean Améry the writer of fiction is long overdue. Not that we should decry the way in which readers concentrate on his moral discourse as an essayist, but as an author he should be restored to the battlefield of literary fiction with his own experimental novels; it is his rightful place. Deconstruction is his express programme in the title of *Lefeu oder Der Abbruch*, summing up and revealing an Améry who understands and feels, an Améry who can turn to the anthropological history of his times. The logic of reason is placed beside the logic of the senses, not, 'I think, therefore I am', but 'I feel', and, above all, 'I suffer, therefore I am.'

Lefeu oder Der Abbruch – 'a summary of his own life'?

Lefeu oder Der Abbruch is, in fact, the summary of his creative work. What Améry praises in Heinrich Mann is true of himself: 'This work is distinguished not for the modest industry of a craftsman, but for its powerful and brilliant excess.' He speaks of the 'carnality of his prose', the steeply towering style with its periods chasing each other, the dynamic syntax that demands the utmost from the reader.[21] And *Lefeu* is also the sum of his own work literally, because it includes all that is past and still to come in his work – not just *Die Schiffbrüchigen*, the autobiographical trilogy, not just *Charles Bovary*, but also his last project for a work of fiction, *Unterwegs nach Oudenaarde* [On the Way to Oudenaarde]. Here we have the Jewish artist and intellectual, the broken stranger who leaves reality for the madness of dream images dictated to him. Life as a dream – a dream that, of course, is a nightmare – becomes a nightmare of a life. We should not delude ourselves: only those who know Améry's novels really know him. In his essays, an implacable super-ego forbids him to follow paths of thinking and feeling that could endanger the line of his argument. The novelist, on the other hand, can allow equal rights to statement and contradiction, besides entering hallucinatory spheres and striking subtly different notes, from tragedy to comedy, from pathos and irony to the grotesque. Améry shows himself, with fewer reservations here, as an 'ego for which there is no guarantee'. The medium of the novel also allows him to delegate his ego to fictional protagonists, before the first person pronoun cuts in with its categorical imperative.

The book should really have been called *Lefeu **and** the Demolition*. Améry is thinking inclusively. He continues to keep the subject autonomous and the language sensuous, he stands by reason, but in the same breath he introduces its dissolution. 'We must occupy the field of formal logic in thought, if we are to be able to move out of it into more fruitful realms of the mind.' Lefeu's identity consists of the present *and* the past, progress *and* regress, the particular *and* the universal. He asserts himself and history, the ego *and* the id, to the point of self-assertion *as* self-extinction. The positions are played off against each other, they cannot be dialectically cancelled out.

In 1974, many readers smiled pityingly at his excursions into fiction. Today we know that he was ahead of his time even as a novelist. Time has now caught up with him – but it does not yet know it; to quote Améry himself, 'I tell myself that this book will have its time,' he writes in the year of his death, 'even though it will hardly be in my time' (J.A. to H.A. 26.6.78).

Faith in language versus the dissolution of language

Even Heissenbüttel initially has reservations 'which he finds hard to formulate in writing,' he tactfully adds (H.H. to J.A. 2.8.72). However, it is easy enough to formulate those reservations, because Améry's excursion into the upper reaches of literary fiction parodies Heissenbüttel's own concept of literature and language and thus was hardly likely to meet with Heissenbüttel's blessing. Indeed, the discomfort was mutual. After his first reading of Heissenbüttel's novel *D'Alemberts Ende* [D'Alembert's End], which he had originally wanted to review for *Merkur*, Améry himself found that he had to give up – citing his own 'antiquated nature', as he put it to Paeschke, and blaming himself.[22] 'I feel vaguely that this is an important book, but I am left entirely at a loss over long stretches of it. Il m'arrive de me dire: Mais je ne comprends rien à rien'[iv] (J.A. to H.P. 28.8.70). He also blames himself in his letter to Heissenbüttel, saying how sorry he is 'about his own alienation from progressive German literature,' and he reminds his friend of his predictions about 'cultural aging'.

The reciprocal lack of understanding is awkward for them both. Améry makes many attempts at damage limitation by articulating the problem: 'I know (...) that my "theories of art", in so far as I have any, do not coincide with yours' (J.A. to H.H. 18.7.72). Heissenbüttel still keeps his distance, although he knows that Améry had also shaken his head over his experimental poetry. When, in the year of publication of *Lefeu oder Der Abbruch*, his (and Franz Mons's) *Antianthologie* [Anti-Anthology] is torn to shreds by Ernst Klett in *Merkur*,[23] Améry can only agree with the sarcastic reviewer[24] – and word of his opinion must have been passed on. But such evidence was hardly necessary – the caricature of Irene, the poetess of the poplars, Lefeu's opposite number, in which Heissenbüttel recognizes himself, is painful enough for him. He retreats into silence and avoids any discussion of the matter. There was a rift, one that was probably never entirely healed.

In fact, it is not so surprising that matters come to this pass, much more surprising is the fact that they do so only at such a late date. One cannot say that any ill will, tactlessness or actual disloyalty is involved. This is a case of different concepts of art; the gulf separating the two artists is much too deep. Originally, Améry had even taken up a position opposed to that of thinkers such as Heissenbüttel and Vormweg, yet their linguistic experiments were the initial spark inspiring his new novel. He says in a letter to Paeschke:

> In the November issue of the *Merkur* I read Vormweg's essay, un vrai délire! [he adds sarcastically] If I only had more time, then some day I would look hard at the madness of trying to see the point of language *in* language. (...) But flat common sense can't do anything about that. I am vaguely thinking of continuing the

---

iv   I find myself thinking: I don't understand any of this.

contest by means of *production*; producing something that I would like to call a novel-essay, taking absurdity *ad absurdum*. (J.A. to H.P. 16.12.71)

In April 1972, even before drawing up his outline, he had sketched out Lefeu's problematic situation – 'a labour of Heracles' – as follows:

> Revolt of logically pure human reason against the tyranny of conceptual poets. Revolt of humanism against the devotees of form and structure, a campaign of one who believes in language against those who are determined on linguistic dissolution. (J.A. to H.P. 27.4.72)

He could not know, before writing his *Lefeu,* that it would not turn out at all like that, or that Améry's new narrative style would assert itself against his will, bursting out of the trammels of reason. Just as Lefeu asks Irene's forgiveness – did Heissenbüttel miss seeing the retraction of the parody in the novel? – Améry now asks Heissenbüttel for his. 'Today, now that I myself have my *Lefeu* behind me, I have a chance of approaching your work in a very different way.' He himself finds parallels between Heissenbüttel's *D'Alembert* and *Lefeu,* not just in the collages but also thematically, particularly in his treatment of the subject of death. 'In fact I feel that somehow or other we are converging. As far as I'm concerned, it is a fact that the language in *Lefeu* to a certain degree negates the theoretical sections about what language is' (J.A. to H.H. 5.1.73).

It is in that very battle that the intensity of this work of art resides. Those familiar with Améry will know very early what they have here. For instance, Paeschke says that the first chapter draws him into 'psycho-physical sympathy'. 'The text is compelling, it exerts a real power of attraction. If you can succeed in wresting subjects and objects from the wake of that attraction, it will be a great achievement,' he writes after reading the opening chapter (H.P. to J.A. 23.3.73).

Similarly Arbogast, who has already seen the outline, abandons himself entirely to Lefeu's 'visions'.

> It was not edifying (...) but it was fascinating, and follows one into one's dreams. The way you connect the painful and sometimes unappetizing aspect of the accusation with a manner of presenting it that can bring the *frisson de beauté* from decline is truly exciting. And so is the violent subjectivity, breaking out again and again only to collapse into itself – the narrator's interior monologue picks up the painter's interior monologue, and both are really one.

He praises the 'flow of the language, now reflecting, now narrating, now ironic, and sometimes almost rising to song' (H.A. to J.A. 26.4.73). Canetti too thinks so, saying he read the book three times at short intervals because he found it so gripping. Grass says he is impressed.[25] Even more effusive is Alfred Andersch:

> I have read *Lefeu*, or rather devoured it, I am *in raptures!* One of the greatest German books since the war. The triumph of the *furor reflectionis* at full throttle. Credibility, the intensity of the descriptions of human beings (...) you have written a wonderful book (24.2.74).

The reviews do not share that opinion, at least as represented by Reich-Ranicki in the *Frankfurter Allgemeine Zeitung*. Schütte counters his colleague's verdict with a full-page tribute in the *Frankfurter Rundschau*, praising *Lefeu* as 'a Proustian masterpiece'.[26] There had been unedifying quarrels with *Die Zeit*, which gave Améry a choice: either they would review his book *or* they would send him further work in future. Améry, still expecting to make his breakthrough as a novelist, chooses the review rather than more work from *Die Zeit*. Everything seems to be conspiring against him.

> Lefeu's fate is also dialectical. With this book, on the one hand I have brought my friend Schmid's lack of success on myself, and on the other I have made a kind of mystical trouble for him: the building in the rue Rollin has been sold, and it may be that Lefeu will have no roof over his head within the year (J.A. to H.A. 21.2.74).

For Améry, it is only this damning review that counts, 'an unpleasant shock,' he says, trying to make light of it. But, in fact, this is the beginning of the end, or more precisely a new beginning of the ultimate end. The 'world' has sat in judgement on his 'life's work', and has condemned it. 'I have no kind of even approximately normative aesthetic. (...). Quality in literature does not mean the quality inherent in a work, only the relationship between a work and those who receive it,' he writes to Günter Kunert (J.A. to G.K. 24.6.74). Furthermore, because 'those who receive it' have rejected his work – Améry never shrank from logical deductions – he literally tears his own copy of *Lefeu oder Der Abbruch* to shreds. The mutilated book, in Maria Améry's private archive, is now in the DLA, Marbach.

The 'demolition' of Jean Améry

No one wants to know about him as a novelist, he is regarded only as a 'victim to be put on show, an example of Jewish suffering,' Améry complains in a letter to Inge Werner (J.A. to I.W. 21.12.75). His identification with Lefeu goes so far that he feels writing the book has drained him entirely. It is all the more remarkable that he disputes that very point in his reply to Günter Kunert's letter of consolation. Nothing in his 'writing of that preposterous failure', he complains, went as he had expected, his 'calamitous heart's blood' played 'as good as no part' in the work.

> If all my early works were in their essence autobiographical, here I was confronting someone else, I had a living man before my eyes, and I was trying to portray him. – If I spoke of autobiographical elements in my afterword, events crowding in on him, it was out of consideration for my model, whose feelings I did not want to hurt. (...) (And incidentally, the afterword was not an afterword but was conceived as a direct continuation of the essayistic part of the work.)

It was due to a misunderstanding, he says, that the publisher printed it in italic. 'There is almost nothing of me in this book,' he insists. 'So none of my "heart's blood" was flowing' (J.A. to G.K. 24.6.74).

The way to un-freedom

With or without his heart's blood, whether the book is autobiographical or not, ultimately the facts speak for themselves. Améry finishes writing it on 16 February 1974, and on 20 February 1974, like his character Lefeu, he attempts to take his own life. Three months before the savage review in the *FAZ,* and even before the publication of the novel in March 1974, his friend the chemist Kurt Schindel

Améry's mutilated copy of Lefeu oder Der Abbruch

finds him in a coma. Beside him is a note for the police saying that he has tried to take his life with sleeping pills because, for reasons of ill health, he can no longer exercise his profession as a writer: 'J'essaie de mettre fin à mes jours moyennant des somnifères.' To ensure that he will be believed, he cites further reasons in the note, speaking of 'une maladie cardiaque qui est douloureuse et ne me permet pas l'exercice de mon métier d'écrivain,' and signing it Hans Mayer, alias Jean Améry.[27] Especially touching are the mysterious addenda decorating this formal letter, scribbles that he added in a semi-comatose state. We can decipher the word 'Ischl', set down on the paper three times, one after the other, as if magically conjuring it up – you need a homeland for dying, as he knew even with this first attempt. Later he grants his own wish for one, when the attempt is an attempt no longer.

Schindel has him taken to the hospital of St. Jean in Brussels by ambulance, with blue lights flashing. 'I still remember just how I felt when I came round after what was later reported to me as a 30-hour coma. Fettered, drilled through with tubes, fitted on both wrists with painful devices for my artificial nourishment,' he writes in his next book, *Hand an sich legen* [translated into English as *On Suicide*][28] (Hasl p. 71; OS p. 78). It is nine days before he is discharged from

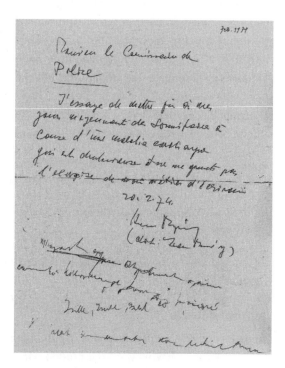

Note to the police written before his suicide attempt of 20 February 1974

hospital, and there is also an account of this, which makes difficult reading. The aggressive tone of what he wrote on this scrap of paper (supplied by Maria) tells us that the hospital is an inferno to him – in short that he considers the saving of his life as an unreasonable humiliation and that indeed 'the rescue, about which the physician boasted, belonged to the worst that had ever been done to me – and that was not a little' (Hasl p. 71; OS p. 79). In his book on suicide published two years later (1976), with the subtitle 'A Discourse on Voluntary Death', he says he hated the nursing staff and speaks of being at their mercy, 'as if I were already a thing' (Hasl p. 71; OS p. 79).

Only a few people knew about it. Andersch, for instance, says that 'One's first reaction, naturally, is (...) to shake you. (But the tubes and cannulas won't allow that.) (...) You have no idea at all how much you are needed, but it is so!' (A.A. to J.A. 17.3.74). Arbogast is even more forthright. 'You cannot abandon us, you cannot abandon yourself like that, you, to whom people have begun to listen at this time of general devastation as to a moral authority, the voice of conscience (...)' (H.A. to J.A. 27.2.74). His work on *Lefeu,* he writes, had 'something both euphoric and murderous' about it. 'You have gathered up your entire existence to engender this jet of flame, it must necessarily leave a sense of emptiness behind.' But that sense of emptiness, Arbogast assures him, is the pre-requisite for a new beginning.

It is a long time before Améry is able to function again. Ernst Klett had already diagnosed this mixture of fragility and toughness in him. Améry takes stock of himself and after all tries to salvage something that, as he sees it, cannot really be salvaged, but he wants to have made the attempt. He offers a Bavarian Radio editor the subject of *Lefeu* as a film. It is a work, he says, positively predestined for the screen, and he supplies the outline for a screenplay with literary reflections reduced to a minimum, concentrating entirely on the visible course of events:

> [T]he decay of old Paris, the building of the new city (Quartier de la Défense), the painter's relationship with his psychopathic lover, the landscape of the Basses Pyrénées, all of Swabia with the 'Fire-Rider', the visions of the burning city – a wealth of visually dramatic possibilities – my imagination is running riot. (J.A. to Wolf Seidl 16.4.75)

Erich Schmid's provocative paintings form the backdrop. The proposition is seriously considered.

The Baader-Meinhof débacle

Of course, he is needed – urgently needed. Améry is in public demand, and again he responds to it. Horst Krüger, having just seen him on television, comments on his performance:

There is no one else in this country who can think in public as seriously, as profoundly, and with such awareness of problems as you. Outsiders feel as if you wanted to compensate for 20 years of silence (...) and in doing so you show that you have no rivals. (H.K. to J.A. 14.4.71)

He writes even more enthusiastically later: 'You have developed the skill (...) of speaking philosophically in front of millions, conducting the process of reflection itself before the public eye. No one since Jaspers has mastered that art' (H.K. to J.A. 27.3.73).

Perhaps that is why Heinrich Böll, 'the good man of Cologne', turns to him. Böll's denunciations of the vicious campaign by the Springer press against the Baader-Meinhof group, when it was already crushed, now make Böll himself the target of a witch-hunt. 'I am very sick,' Böll writes to Améry. 'The conduct of the Springer press is criminal, and I myself – I can say this only in plain terms – I am utterly exhausted' (H.B. to J.A. 18.6.72). Améry immediately comes to Böll's aid, announcing his solidarity in advance with an article in the *Süddeutsche Zeitung* (15/16 June 1972).

On 17 November 1974, the witch-hunt catches up with him as well. During a discussion on the Internationaler Frühschoppen TV programme[v] on the subject of 'Life as a throwaway consumer item?' one of the subjects addressed is the hunger strike of the Baader-Meinhof prisoners, and Werner Höfer invites Améry to state his own views

Höfer: I understand that you are not without sympathy for these people, who may now be starving themselves to death? What would you say to them? Jean Améry, you have to limit your comment to one word only.
Améry: Forgive me for taking so long to think about it. The question you ask is a very difficult one.
Höfer: Would you say give up, come to your senses?
Améry: No, don't give up.

The consequences of such an ambiguous remark could be foreseen. Even if his recommendation does not refer directly to the terrorist activities of the Baader-Meinhof group, but only to their hunger strike to obtain better conditions of imprisonment, in the eyes of the law it makes him a subversive

---

v A popular talk show in 1953–1957, transmitted at peak viewing time in the early evening.

sympathizer. Now *he* is the witch being hunted. No one knows, no one wants to know, that he, a man of the Left, has, in fact, spoken out against any kind of revolutionary terrorism in the Federal Republic of Germany, particularly in the last few years and in defiance of all fashionable trends.

'I see nothing here that could be interpreted as sympathy with the actions or ideology of the group,' he defends himself. 'How could I possibly feel solidarity with people who give political backing to the Palestinian terrorists while I, a Jew, fear for Israel's last stand?'[29] The law is the law; investigatory proceedings against him begin, and three months later, on 21 February 1975, are withdrawn again after causing him the greatest psychological stress. His *Örtlichkeiten*, on which he is working at the time with the West German Radio editor Manfred Franke, shows traces of this stress.[30] But at least he can now move freely again.

Albert Speer's lucrative remorse

Just before this incident, there had been another 'scandal' concerning the *Spandauer Tagebücher* [Spandau Diaries] of the Nazi minister Albert Speer, to whom he wants to convey the message that he too, he above all, is 'beyond guilt and atonement'. Once again, Améry occupies the middle ground, neither on the left nor on the right. As 'a former personal employee' of Speer's armaments factory in Dora-Nordhausen, he urges him in an open letter:

> ... to keep quiet, if only out of a sheer regard for human decency (...). It seems to me as if the former perpetrators of such acts have no moral right to indulge in their emotional outpourings in public. Remorse and atonement can be dignified only if they are felt privately, without grand gestures on the public stage (*Frankfurter Rundschau* 6.10.75).

He gains a good deal of sympathy, and there are protests against the purchase of the book – 'No 38 marks for Speer' – but he also gives offence.

Ernst Klett, for instance, protests against his objections, whereupon Améry writes to Klett.

> I think, dear Herr Klett, that as a star writer and witness for his own defence Speer needs no support; the public listens to him, he makes its flesh creep enjoyably, and the sun shines on him as if hundreds of thousands of souls had never perished miserably in the places that he ran. (J.A. to E.K. 15.11.75)

Erich Fried does not agree with him either and responds in an open letter of his own in the *Frankfurter Rundschau* of 16 October 1975. 'Today Albert Speer and those like him, of all people, should be required to use their own experiences, their own guilt, in helping to warn us of what is now approaching (...).' Améry considers that the *querelles juives*, as he calls them, are better settled among the Jews themselves. In a private letter, he tells Fried what he is really concerned about: there is a worldwide move towards the rehabilitation of such criminals, and it should be resisted. There are several examples:

> [u]p to and including that same Herr Speer, the elegant seeker after profit, who is becoming the flagship of the rehabilitation fleet. Herr Speer shows his remorse in a very lucrative way. It is enough to sicken us to think of those he destroyed, and also of the young people of Europe now growing up, who if faced with a display of such self-satisfied remorse are likely to say: Ah, well, that's the way of the world.

Speer's conversion, he considers, 'is the most macabre of all macabre jokes, *humour super-noir*' (J.A. to E.F. 26.10.75).

However, more drama is yet to come: three years later he will sit at the same table as Speer, not without 'a heartfelt groan', as we learn from Rolf Schroers, president of the Theodor Heuss Academy (R.S. to J.A. 7.12.77). The occasion is a seminar on the very question that troubles Améry: 'Hitler – a revivalist movement?' The participants are boldly chosen; their argument is deliberately confrontational. Concentration camp victims Eugen Kogon and Jean Améry face former Nazi officeholders Werner Stephan (of the Reich Propaganda Ministry), Thilo Graf Werthern (tank commander and holder of the Knight's Cross) and Albert Speer. The object of this experiment, as cautiously expounded by Schroers, chairing the discussion, is to 'gain information even if it cannot be reduced to a common denominator'.[31] Little information is, in fact, gained; the participants confine themselves to historical accounts of what happened. Each plays his part objectively, courteously, in a civilized manner, until Améry, who has been holding back for some time, deliberately disrupts this amiable harmony:

> I did not intend to argue with former Minister Speer. It was inconsistent of me to come here at all, but sometimes it is wrong to be consistent. If I have been inconsistent once, then now I will be inconsistent again.

As he saw it, it was high time to break through this *entente cordiale*, which made him uneasy. Once again he states his earlier position, talks about the murderous slave labour done in the underground galleries of Dora Nord and the armaments minister's visit of inspection to the place. He, Speer, says Améry, must have seen the mountains of corpses, the skeletons that they had to climb over when the camp was evacuated. Had light not dawned on him at that time? Kogon, composed, a practitioner of *Realpolitik*, intervenes to protect Speer: we must look to the future. Améry insists on his point of view: where is the future to come from 'if the slate is not wiped clean first?' Kogon, diplomatic as ever, now stands up for Améry: he welcomes the fact 'that you are sharper and more absolute on this point. I would say that the two ideas complement each other.' And when Speer begins to speak again, according to a retrospective account, Améry rises and leaves the hall.[32] Speer's public 'conversion', which was no such thing, would have been hard to bear anyway because he sticks to proclaiming his innocence, which had already been confirmed at the Nuremberg trials. His professional work, he claims, was entirely non-political, he has never read *Mein Kampf*, he knew nothing about the Wannsee Conference, let alone the way its decisions were implemented. It does not help that he states himself to be in retrospective agreement with Améry's open letter, saying that he has 'internally accepted' the criticism of him.

And so nothing changes. The man in the dock is not the penitent Speer who saw what was done at the time, but Améry, the vengeful victim who witnessed those things. The latter would happily have dispensed with such confirmation of his point.

A Werther of the 1970s

This experience was not calculated to deter Améry from his next project as a writer. In fact, he makes the 'new' beginning that Arbogast had suggested, coming up with the theory that justifies his failure in practice. His next book is entitled *Hand an sich legen. Diskurs über den Freitod* (1976) [translated by John D. Barlow as *On Suicide. A Discourse on Voluntary Death*, published in 1999]. It 'follows on from *On Aging* and *Lefeu*', as he tells Arbogast. Most of all it follows on, we may add, from the setback he has just suffered. At the same time, he describes it as his 'most abstract' and 'emotional' work, and we can see why (J.A. to E.M. 18.11.75). He is sure that it will 'make up' for his novel's failure (J.A. to H.A. 21.2.75). Améry keeps his promise: *On Suicide* is a sensation, a 1970s parallel to Goethe's *Werther*. 'My book on suicide has sold astonishingly well, some 9000 copies in six weeks' (J.A. to H.P. 15.10.76). Its success came to seem positively uncanny to him.

'Lessing's first brother'

Despite the 'silence of the grave' surrounding *Lefeu*, Améry's stock is high. Michael Krüger invites him to be co-editor of *Akzente* (M.K to J.A. 7.5.76). He regretfully declines, out of loyalty to Paeschke and *Merkur*. He becomes an honorary member of the PEN club, and a little later a corresponding member of the German Academy of Language and Literature in Darmstadt.

The city of Vienna awards him its Prize for Journalism, an honour that Améry takes as a rather backhanded compliment, since he thinks of himself as predestined for the Prize for Literature, but that goes to H.C. Artmann. On 29 March 1977, when he is already at work on another narrative project, the Senate of the Free Hanseatic City of Hamburg awards him its Lessing Prize, which comes with the sum of 15,000 DM. At the presentation in the Imperial Hall of Hamburg City Hall, he is praised as a latter-day Lessing, a

> ... valiant humanist who all his life has defended the worth and dignity of the individual against the overwhelming power of society – which, however, he does not despise as a mere sombre entity. Améry demands as determined an opposition to aging and death as to every form of tyranny. As a survivor of Hitler's death camps, he has summoned up the power to survive his fate free of resentment and emotional expressions of reconciliation, delivering a reminder to those who are only too oblivious of the past and also a warning to posterity.

The Lessing Prize, he says in writing to Hans Paeschke, is 'balm to my many psychological and mental injuries. But you know what such pleasures are like: their analgesic effect does not last long. Pain, a faithful companion, soon returns.' Paeschke calls him 'Lessing's first brother', and 'a Laocoon' who 'creates sweet sound, in thought and in style, out of his constant suffering' (H.P. to J.A. 16.8.78).

Sartre's failure

Clothed in sweet sound, that suffering now flows into the fate of poor *Charles Bovary, Landarzt* [Charles Bovary, country doctor],[33] Améry's next work of fiction. To some extent, his speech on the occasion of the Lessing Prize forms its basis. What he has never allowed his own readers, the ability to identify with him as they read, is like an elixir to Améry himself: 'I lived with Emma Bovary, knew and loved her brown hair, suffered with her and her poor Charles when her tormented body writhed in the agony of death by poison (...)' (UW, Vol. 2, p. 233). In his new narrative, Charles is to be the star, not Emma; he revises Flaubert's *Madame Bovary* in favour of the betrayed husband. Améry gives the life of the country doctor who never really lived it fully the voice that was denied him by Flaubert, in his autocratically elitist belief as a narrator in art for art's sake. 'Aesthetics and ethics are two forms of a single doctrine,' Améry says as early as 1955, quoting the philosopher Coudenhove-Kalergi. 'Aesthetics teach what is beautiful *around* us, ethics teach what is beautiful *in* us.' He is concerned with this symbiosis in his rehabilitation of that 'simple man' Charles Bovary.

His farewell to Sartre, already indicated in *Lefeu*, is completed in his 'Bovary Passion'. Now, with his *Charles Bovary*, he opposes the authorial commitment once so hotly advocated by Sartre – 'I hold Flaubert (...) responsible for the horrors following the Paris Commune because he wrote not a word to prevent them' – which Améry himself made the aesthetic and ethical heart of his *Preface to the Future* in 1961. Despite his own scepticism, Jean Améry also defends the ever-controversial claim of the committed writer to change society by his writing in his later essay on 'The power and powerlessness of intellectuals'.[34] In 1968, Jean-Paul Sartre's commitment still seemed to him incontestable. Sartre did indeed end his childhood memoir with the often quoted confession, 'For a long time I took my pen for a sword, but now I know how little power we have.'[35] However, he made an unmistakable declaration of intent in opposition to that idea. 'Nonetheless, I write and shall continue to write books. It is necessary, and in spite of everything it is useful.'[36] That does not dismiss the obvious dilemma of the intellectual who writes; the 'nonetheless' sounds the alarm. Jean Améry manages to make something positive out of this crisis. It is, he writes, having reached a climax, the place where

> ...intellectuals find, in acknowledging their powerlessness, the traces of their undeniable influence. They will then have the power to continue with their mission, which is to contest and control, to let the mind and thus humanity assert itself. No one could be Robespierre or Trotsky. Everyone still has a chance to be the Zola of *J'accuse*.[37]

With the portrait of *Charles Bovary, Landarzt*, the last chapter of which – at first[38] – culminates in a *J'accuse*, Jean Améry takes that chance, deputizing, as it were, for his mentor Jean-Paul Sartre, who according to Améry threw it away in his book on Flaubert, *L'Idiot de la famille* [translated into English as *The Family Idiot*]. In his review of that book, Améry speaks clearly:

> In this extremely elitist, indeed esoteric work our author, who does not wish to be a bourgeois intellectual any longer, but a man of action and servant of the revolution, has in a certain sense denied his recent work on *The Intellectual and the Revolution*.[39]

These are harsh words from that great admirer of Sartre, Jean Améry. He accuses Sartre of treachery, of betraying his social role as an intellectual. With his work on Flaubert, Sartre falls back on the role of the bourgeois philosopher that at heart he always was. The critic of the bourgeoisie, says Améry scornfully, has chosen a writer from that bourgeoisie as his hero. Améry goes on the offensive, planning to counter Sartre, who calls his Flaubert *un roman vrai*, with his own version of a 'true novel'.

Flaubert/Sartre/Améry: Charles Bovary *as a reply to* The Family Idiot?

There is no longer any 'identification as if with a father', after 30 years, no 'confident desire for veneration', he no longer sees 'the teacher' as 'providential'. In his essay 'Sartre: Greatness and Failure',[40] Sartre's greatness is one with his failure. We should note that here it is genuine failure, not rhetorical, as in the *Years of Wandering*, where Sartre's defeats by history are made to appear the triumph of protest. Here, Améry understands failure as moral failure:

> Two facts have really brought this to my mind: first Sartre's public declaration that he will not vote for Mitterrand in the second round of the French presidential election, since the whole election is a bourgeois affair designed to mystify, and the authentic revolutionary can only ignore it; the other, my reading of the third volume of Sartre's work on Flaubert, a book that shows the (...) philosopher in full possession of his penetrating intelligence and visionary power. On the one hand, then, we have almost childishly defiant political affectation, absolutely blind to reality – on the other, unbroken brilliance.[41]

'It is a deeply disturbing and sad spectacle to see this man clinging to what are now indefensible ideas of absolute revolution.'[42] Since 1968, says Améry, these false ideas had increasingly led Sartre away from reality, and indeed into a mistaken frame of mind, his visit to Baader in Stammheim[43] being a striking example. 'The normal intellectual will wonder (...) what Sartre might hope to discover from Baader. How not to bring revolution about, how it cannot be brought about in a country with a democracy that is still working?'[44] The 'unbroken brilliance' that Améry discerns in this last essay on Flaubert by Sartre is both praise and criticism. Certainly *The Family Idiot* is a titanic undertaking, he says, 'one that tries to unite phenomenology, psychoanalysis and Marxism theoretically,'[45] an 'inspired use of ideas in a work of literature',[46] and it undoubtedly shows Sartre at his finest. Yet in Améry's eyes, it obviously represents only the reverse of his 'mistaken frame of mind'. The brilliance that Améry discusses here is to some extent an accusation. It can be 'unbroken' only because its origin lies in the blindness to reality that he has mentioned. With his two chapters 'The Reality of Gustave Flaubert' and 'The Reality of Charles Bovary', Améry explicitly sets out to consider the reality that Sartre has misappropriated. This external construction in itself suggests that *Charles Bovary* was conceived as a response to *The Family Idiot*. It is not, thus, by chance that this last book before Jean Améry opts for suicide is dedicated not to Flaubert but to Sartre. It is a final showdown, a settling of accounts with the master he has loved for so long. We can conclude, from reading Améry's version of Flaubert, that this love was not a happy one.

Testament

Charles Bovary is Jean Améry's last testament. The case so strongly brought against Flaubert as a violator of reality is primarily an arraignment, constantly repressed in the discursive narrative, of Sartre who, as Améry sees it, is 'blind to reality'. The withdrawal of the arraignment is not to be understood as retracting its social justification; instead it represents an ultimate kind of desperation, 'a turning point', says Helmut Heissenbüttel, making it possible 'for a man toying with the project of self-destruction to consider it and then carry it out'.[47]

Here I am anticipating something that has yet to be shown. To say that Sartre's *The Family Idiot* cannot be linked with Améry's *Charles Bovary* because Sartre did not analyse *Madame Bovary* properly is an invalid objection: Sartre's three-volume text, just less than 2500 pages, refers again and again to the author of *Madame Bovary*, and then there are his appendices to *The Family Idiot*, exclusively considering this novel.[48] For instance, we find Sartre saying in an interview that 'Emma is stupid and bad, and the other characters are no better, except for Charles, who finally, as I discovered only later, represents one of the author's ideals.'[49] In the first volume, Sartre rates Charles higher than the characters of Homais and Larivière because, in his love for Emma and inherent innocence, Charles is the only one capable of going further than the others.[50] Elsewhere, Sartre speaks of the 'powerful, dreamy stupidity of the child Charbovary' – here 'stupidity' means a form of divine proximity to nature – 'who, as a man, will have the incomparable honour of dying of his love'.[51] Again and again he mentions the power of attraction that Charles Bovary exerts on Flaubert. 'Charles Bovary is not Gustave, although several times he becomes entirely absorbed in that character.'[52]

Sartre in search of Flaubert, Améry in search of Charles

So why the counterblast? Is Améry simply running his head against an open door? The answer is to be found in Sartre himself. In his novel, he says, Flaubert is anxious to present a negative portrait of Charles: '(...) During his school years he tries to paint him not as he is, but as he is not.'[53] In addition, Sartre accuses Flaubert, as Améry himself does later, of inaccurate historical perception. On the whole Sartre goes some way to meet Améry's criticism in pointing out the ambiguity of his own enterprise. As relating to the content, he says, it is a flight from the political present to the present of Flaubert's day; however, where Marxist and psychoanalytical method is concerned, he is contributing to the solution of modern problems. To reconcile these two dimensions, claims Sartre, he has had to fall back on empathy.[54] The striking aspect of Sartre's references and observations is not the difference between his and Améry's evaluations – they have some quite surprising points in common – but his fundamentally different point of departure. Whereas Sartre is in search of Flaubert's reality, that is to say the psychological reality of the author of *Madame Bovary*, which he tries to deduce from detailed analysis of his work and his society, in *Charles Bovary* Améry concentrates solely on the social reality of the fictional character. Améry aims to present a 'true' portrait of Charles Bovary, Sartre to present a 'true' portrait of Flaubert.

Sartre is trying to expend the maximum imagination, empathy and indeed vision on producing a 'total' picture of Flaubert the man. He refrains from all moralizing prejudices that could divert him from this reconstruction. His highest aim is to discover the secret of Flaubert the writer, in complete contrast to Jean Améry, who sides from the first with Charles and against Flaubert. His method in this process of rehabilitation derives from Sartre in so far as each of them, Sartre and Améry, defends his protégés against their adversaries like a lawyer. Both Sartre's work, particularly the first volume, and Améry's read like the records of a trial in court. In Sartre, those on trial are first Flaubert's own father and then the almighty father of creation, whom Flaubert himself opposed all his life. In Améry, the creator of *Madame Bovary* himself is in the dock, not for allowing Emma to occupy the foreground in his fictional masterpiece, but for robbing Charles, a simple man, of his human rights.

A plea for Charles, the intellectual proletarian

We can tell that Gustave Flaubert is not just the peg on which Jean Améry hangs his hostility to Sartre, from an essay[55] of seven years earlier, written by Améry on the hundred-fiftieth birthday of the 'master novelist of Bovary', in which he is already pillorying Flaubert the prosperous bourgeois who denounced the communards of 1871 as 'mad dogs'.[56] Here he still shrinks from his own partisanship, restoring the equilibrium: despite his middle-class prosperity, he says, Flaubert was also the 'Cyclopean destroyer of bourgeois cowardice, stupidity and avarice, creator of the apothecary Homais and the merchant L'Heureux, those characters in the novel who appear ridiculous to abhorrent.'[57] In this essay he presents a 'balanced' view; the novelist Flaubert's point of view is preserved. *Madame Bovary* is the first great novel in world literature that presents incidents in a bourgeois setting with total objectivity and no moralizing intention at all, but then turns dialectically to complete subjectivity.

> The characters, from the unfortunate Emma Bovary to such minor figures as the Abbé Bournisien, stand before us in all their pitiful nakedness, creatures who are nothing but what society has made them. On the other hand, the mysterious phenomenon whereby the author transforms himself into the characters he has created means that the reader identifies, willy-nilly, with each of them. (...) If there is any point in the concept of realism in literature, it lies in this congruity of objectivity and subjectivity.[58]

Flaubert's brilliant success in merging the two in *Madame Bovary* makes him, says Améry in 1971, not just the progenitor of the modern novel, but also of the *nouveau roman*.

As a literary critic, Améry pays tribute to such skill; as a moralist he is indignant. Anticipating his own presentation of Flaubert seven years later, he is already speaking of 'poor Charles Bovary'. In *Charles Bovary*, Améry exposes Flaubert's apparent 'objectivity' as a myth. It is as if Améry had made Georg Büchner's words his own in describing Flaubert's novel thus: 'One must love humanity to be able to see into the unique nature of every being, no one must seem too small, too ugly, only then can he be understood.'[59] However, this itself, says Améry, is the difficulty; Flaubert is misanthropic, does not love mankind, refuses to understand Charles Bovary, who is too small and too ugly for him. It is not only class-consciousness that stands between him and Charles, for as a country doctor Emma's husband has a certain position in society, if a modest one; rather there is an intellectual arrogance, a 'sense of aristocracy', to quote Büchner again, that is tantamount to 'the most shameful contempt for the Holy Spirit in mankind'.[60] In rescuing that 'simple man' Charles Bovary, Jean Améry gives voice to an intellectual rather than a social proletarian, a humble man – in fact, a typical underdog.

Ethical defence = aesthetic defence

Améry's aim (see the outline of *Charles Bovary*)[61] is a double one. He is attempting both social and aesthetic rehabilitation. In other words, the defence of Charles Bovary as an individual and a bourgeois subject is necessary on artistic grounds. As Améry sees it, Flaubert's grotesquely clumsy Charles Bovary is not a credible character, he lacks all aesthetic probability. Améry writes:

> It is simply impossible for a (...) husband passionately in love to deliver his most precious possession up to her lover with the blindness of a donkey. (...) The effect is positively grotesque when Charles meets the woman supposed to be Emma's piano teacher, and she tells him that she does not even know his wife

– when he allows himself to be fobbed off with a few mendacious excuses which are not even properly thought out. I claim that no such person as Flaubert's Charles Bovary ever existed. And I ask – and answer – the question of who the real country doctor Charles Bovary was.[62]

Améry's narrative begins with a passage taken word for word from Flaubert's novel, where Charles, directly after Emma's agonizing death, makes arrangements for her funeral. In Améry's version, however, this passage sounds quite different because of the attitude taken in the narrative: under the chapter heading 'Dirge', we read, 'I am determined to (...) I will find the strength (...) I will (...)' (Ch. p. 9). With this declaration, with the use of the first person, and the modal verb 'will', Charles shows that he is an individual who not only expresses his wishes but also expects them to be carried out. In the original, Charles can admit his own intentions to himself only in writing and behind closed doors. In Améry this clear declaration of his will becomes a challenge to Charles Bovary's creator. Similarly provocative is the quotation from Proust with which Améry prefaces his *Charles Bovary*, leaving it in French: 'Les maris trompés qui ne savent rien, savent tout, tout de même.' The Proust quotation is well chosen for the very reason that it precisely describes the span of time in Améry's narrative here supplied, or rather re-created, for the literary character of Charles – the period of time giving knowledge to the man who apparently knew nothing. Flaubert never lets Charles's potential show. He even strangles it by making him die in silence after his beloved wife.

C'est la faute de Flaubert

However, first the despairing husband utters the famous sentence, the only one that Flaubert allows him to articulate himself: '*C'est la faute de la fatalité*' [Fate was to blame]. This sentence stands in direct opposition to the 'I will' remarks that Flaubert allowed his Charles only in writing but with which Jean Améry makes him begin his lament for his dead wife. The line that Améry traces, from a declaration that it was all the fault of fate to an announcement of Charles's intentions, shows the same development expressed in the Proustian quotation from blind resignation to the discovery of his own will. This discovery culminates, in Améry's final chapter, with Charles's '*J'accuse*':

> Charles discovers that he is someone of whom Flaubert did not want to take notice. Belatedly, he has suffered his Passion, and only Améry shows the reader that it alone, not Rodolphe's indifferent playfulness or Léon's puerile love, could have done justice to Emma's unconditional readiness to venture anything.

Charles thus rises higher and stands before us on a par with Emma; they are now both the tragic heroes of the bourgeois tragedy of *Madame Bovary*.[63]

But what justifies Améry the writer's interference with the work of Flaubert the writer? To quote Améry himself:

If I presume to take his character out of the hands of Flaubert the master novelist and transform him, I can justify that only if I succeed in addressing the problem of the 'bourgeois subject' through the question of probability.[64]

As Améry sees it, Flaubert's lack of political conscience lays his novel open to attack for its aesthetics and casts doubt on the novel's often-quoted realism. Améry devotes two long, essay-like passages to this debate, incorporating them into his narrative: Chapter 3, 'The Reality of Flaubert', is presented in counterpoint with Chapter 5, 'The Reality of Charles Bovary'. The two chapters give his work its theoretical superstructure, which, of course, does not alter the fact that here the arbitrary stance of one narrator – that is to say, Améry – is played off against that of another, Flaubert. The difference is that Améry's arbitrary stance is in support of the downtrodden Charles, attacked by Flaubert out of a purely bourgeois dislike which – and this is at the root of Améry's criticism – is not anchored in any kind of social criticism.

In the name of the bourgeois subject

It is not just Charles whom Améry reassesses, but also Homais, in Flaubert a man who ridiculously parrots received ideas, while Améry makes a potentially enlightened figure of him. Here Améry reformulates, as mentioned above, what the novel says in the spirit of his speech on receiving the Lessing Prize,[65] which he was writing at the same time as *Charles Bovary*. The bourgeois subject, scorned by Flaubert as a stupid, narrow-minded monstrosity, is to Améry primarily a *bourgeois citoyen*. Charles, Améry complains, was let down by his creator because in devising his character as a man who always dutifully does his work in society, he failed to see a man who 'maintains the values of a certain period of history' and 'ushers in a better future'.

Améry is not setting out to make the immoralist Flaubert into another Zola. What repels him is the way apparent objectivity turns to vicious irony, for instance, in the middle-class Homais who, despite his opportunism, is a supporter of progress. Flaubert sees him as a ridiculous puppet.

In the artist's overweening pride, Gustave Flaubert refused to recognize that such characters as Homais were those who promoted bourgeois progress, the

precursors of those who voted for the Radicals in the Third Republic, historically well placed to prefigure those who joined Zola and Clemenceau in defending Captain Dreyfus. (Ch, p. 69)

In his treatment of Homais and other such figures, says Améry, Flaubert
is hunting down the entire bourgeois Enlightenment, not out of anything like
economic determinism but out of hatred, even self-hatred.

As a self-appointed aristocrat, Améry claims, Flaubert uses his world (including the lower-class maidservant who is commended in *Bovary* for her 45 years
of service) as mere stage-setting, like a backdrop. He has no understanding of
a bourgeois subject. Charles Bovary, although a doctor and a representative of
middle-class social values, remains the 'clumsy wretch' that his wife sees in him.
If Flaubert's genius is kindled by Emma, says Améry, it is only because with her
he can escape from reality into words. 'Her excess is his, her mystique of passion is analogous to the writer's mystical immersion in his art' (Ch, p. 75). All
the same, in his novel Flaubert remains the realist he is celebrated as; we have
a case of 'realities that can be inter-subjectively experienced, and that he can
approach as little as someone who is deliberately seeking them out'. Gustave
Flaubert incorporates them into his novel in two forms, as money and as the
desires of the flesh. Emma may choose her 'gift for beauty', but nonetheless she
will feel the force of the capitalist laws of money and they are her *'fatalité'*.

Charles the representative of liberté, égalalité, fraternité

Flaubert expressly appoints not Emma but Charles the victim and representative
of that Fate. Why is he presented as ridiculous from the start? His beginnings as
'Charbovary', his school imposition of lines, writing out 'ridiculus sum', already
point the way to his contemptible end. Flaubert did not allow him any kind of
existential freedom, although that was part of the code of bourgeois society and
the Declaration of the Rights of Man. Why may Emma fulfil her passion although
Charles must merely suffer his? Why has not Charles – and here again we see the
unmistakable influence of Sartre – 'been able to make something of what he has
been made?' Why does Charles not do something to put an end to Emma's escapades
but even encourages them? Why does he not resist the humiliation that he suffers
after the failure of his operation on the boy with the club foot, when better-known
physicians such as Larivière would accept such setbacks fatalistically?

Flaubert was a conscientiously realistic narrator in describing rural festivities, the wedding party, the ball at Château Vaubyessard. He leaves the ground of
realism when he turns exclusively to Emma's fantasies, at the same time refusing
to allow Charles both inner and outer realities. A poor fool cannot be a poor fool

for 24 hours of the day. Even if Flaubert denies him the human right of thinking, he might have claimed at least the right of feeling. Améry quotes as an example the scene in which, after receiving Rodolphe's letter finally rejecting her, Emma calls for that letter even between fainting fits. Flaubert will not allow Charles to draw any conclusions of his own about that, let alone any rebellious ideas.

Améry provides him with the ability to rebel. In a virtuoso intensification of feeling, Bovary the defendant blames his accusers. The accusation against Charles, however, is of his own imagining: Charles accuses himself of the murder of his wife's lovers. No sooner has he enlightened the confused judge about this mistake than he indulges in more wishful thinking, involving alternative realities. His rebellion finally leads to his rejection of Flaubert's high-handed stance, in which the ideals of the French Revolution are trodden underfoot:

> I accuse you because, in your stupid hermitage, you listened only to the fine sound of your words, but never looked at me with the eyes of a man able to feel for me. As for *liberté*: you denied it to me. As for *égalité*: you would not suffer me, a man of the lower middle class, to be the equal of upper middle-class Gustave Flaubert. As for *fraternité*: you would not be my brother in misery, but preferred the role of tolerant judge. I accuse you before the tribunal of the world for the abhorrent indifference with which you discarded me at the end. (Ch. p. 152)

Short Letter, Long Farewell[vi]

Formulated more cryptically, his accusation reads thus:

> I accuse you of breaking the pact you made with reality before starting to write my story; for I was more than merely what I was, like every living man who daily and hourly stands up to others and the world, denying what he was and becoming what he will be. (Ch, p. 151)

This last sentence postulates, in shorthand form, the uneasiness that Améry feels about Flaubert's novel, an uneasiness deriving from the early Sartre, who in 1946 declared his creed: *Existentialism is humanism*. What Améry says here is ambiguous, for his remarks both address Sartre and criticize him, they play off the early Sartre, who gave Améry the courage to live, against the late Sartre, who took that courage away from him again. Jean Améry appropriates the existential method as his own in writing his *Charles Bovary*. Améry too fixes his gaze on the country doctor's limitations by portraying his 'constitution' as 'Charbovary' and by giving Charles the

---

vi   English title of a novel by Peter Handke, translated by Ralph Manheim, Farrar, Straus, 1974.

chance, with his interior monologues ('Dirge'; *'Ridiculus sum'*; 'The bourgeois as lover'; *'J'accuse'*), to step outside himself, 'to deny what he was, to become what he will be', that is to say a passionate lover, Emma's equal. This metamorphosis makes Jean Améry's Bovary an entirely new Charles, his book an autonomous story. On the other hand, the same story, particularly in the interpolated essays, becomes a polemic against Flaubert and also, above all, a polemic against Sartre.

Améry responds to Sartre's 2136 pages with 162 of his own. Sartre's expansive work impels him to keep his as short as possible. He replies to Sartre's empathetic recreation of Flaubert with wholeheartedly partisan backing for Flaubert's fictional character Charles. He knows that although Sartre as a writer was working on his version of Flaubert, which had him psychologically under its spell, he was subscribing with grim obstinacy to a blindly proactive attitude, representing himself as a supporter of absolute revolution who does not shrink even from a policy of violence, hence Sartre's visit to Baader in Stammheim. To Améry, this uncompromising stance in Sartre's political actions appears to be the price he is ready to pay for his 'delirium of interpretation' in *The Family Idiot*.

In *Charles Bovary*, Améry is taking stock of his position. By turning himself into the early Sartre, he offers his former teacher his hand 30 years later on, in his final parting from him. Sartre has taken existentialism but not humanism into account in his Flaubert novel. Too much understanding for the psychological needs of the 'victim' Flaubert, that upper-middle-class citizen, bars Sartre's way to the social victims in Flaubert's own work. In his everyday life, the 70-year-old Sartre sets up as defending counsel for the proletariat; in his life as a writer he declines to do the same for the oppressed. Not that Sartre would have taken any offence on reading Améry's Charles – quite the contrary, his goodwill has already been mentioned – but the problems of the bourgeois subject in a democracy no longer interested him. Ultimately Améry's attack on Sartre, then, is political, not to say ideological. With every fibre of his being, Améry subscribes to Enlightenment[66] ideals of democracy. He wants to preserve the literary concept of the useful citizen of the state as a potential microcosm of that Enlightenment. Ever since 1969, on the other hand, Sartre has been proclaiming himself more and more clearly as an adherent of the ideals of absolute revolution. The more radical his political stance becomes, the more esoteric and apolitical are his literary works. Jean Améry, deputizing for Sartre, tries to bridge this gulf by presenting his Charles in humanist terms and giving him a touch of the existentialist.

Monsieur Bovary, c'est moi

One last thing should be said of *Charles Bovary, Country Doctor, Portrait of a Simple Man*. For the very reason that this book is a polemic against both Flaubert and Sartre, two authors who are very close to Améry's heart, it is also a deeply autobiographical work. The Charles for whom a language of his own is devised to help him find himself is also Jean Améry speaking to us. Making his own last plea before the tribunal of the world with this book, Améry anticipates his own dirge, staging his suicide in literary terms. Charles Bovary dies in his book not 'only' of a broken heart; like Lefeu, he does something positive to ensure his death. But just as Jean Améry, a Jew of the diaspora, speaks in the fictional character of Lefeu, the homeless man, the outsider, the persecuted, a freedom fighter, so also he speaks in the fictional character of Charles. As with Imre Kertész, he sees being a Jew as ultimately tantamount to belonging nowhere, to the 'loneliness of the mind' after Auschwitz, a loneliness that can be fought only individually, as 'a form of existence and an ethical task'. He makes accusations here before the tribunal of the world, in the name of all who are deprived of their rights, and in their name he proclaims art a hopeless but all the more necessary medium of their fight. They fall fighting, they take their own lives, but their declarations of war survive.

'Wait to hear the sound of the echo. Is it hollow? Does it ring clear?'

How will the critical tribunal react to his new venture into fiction? Améry considers it the 'most exciting' and 'lightest' of his books. He is confident and even daringly contemplates prefacing the work with 'an imaginary review' in lieu of a foreword. It is a damning review, of course; we recognize the model. 'There is no end to this nuisance,' he begins:

> An essayist who was always overestimated in that capacity (...) now commits a second offence. Years ago he wrote a useless book and gave it the fashionable subtitle of a novel-essay. Here an idea that might then have been laid to rest becomes intolerable. The author misuses a masterpiece, Flaubert's *Madame Bovary*.[67]

The author could not care less about Flaubert, Améry continues, he presumes to present the incidents from the point of view of Charles, he interferes with Flaubert's chronology and operates 'with brazen self-righteousness', using flashbacks and anticipations, 'just as the fancy takes him'. He is very high-handed with the essay sections and does not even stick to his master Sartre. In short, 'The end product is an impossible book. It is not worth reading a page, even a line of this concoction.'

It is only because, this time, he is so confident that he can allow himself to imagine such a bad review. The interest shown while he was writing the work had lulled him into a sense of security, although it was not always uncritical: Gisela Lindemann of North German Radio says that Charles speaks Améry's language but not the language of the 'simple man' he is. Hanjo Kesting (also of North German Radio) does not agree; he is extremely sympathetic to the book and its author and as early as 27 November 1977 is making detailed suggestions for a staged reading. Paeschke too seems confident: 'The book will probably help you to make a public break-through as a novelist,' he ventures to prophesy (H.P. to J.A. 1.3.78). To which Améry replies, 'I must ultimately succeed in introducing the Germans, who always think of me only as an essayist, to a different Jean Améry' (J.A. to H.P. 4.3.78). And he writes to Arbogast: 'May Fate be kind to it, kinder, I hope, than to my beloved *Lefeu*. (...) Fundamentally, I am *not* pessimistic this time' (J.A. to H.A. 26.6.78).

At the end of August 1978 Améry is glad to have the printed book in his hands, thanks Arbogast and does not attempt to hide his excitement:

> The design is very fine again: the choice of *that* Magritte [it is the 'Perspective: David's Madame Récamier' (1991)] – fits the narrative almost uncannily well. (...) Let us wait to hear the sound of the echo. Is it hollow? Does it ring clear? I ought to be blasé by this time, but unfortunately I am not. (...) I know and recognize only the aesthetics of reception. If this work is well received, then and only then will it have been a good one. Twice now, first with *Lefeu* and now with *Charles B.*, I have tried to show German readers that I can write literary fiction, and I once really thought that I could. But as an attempt *Lefeu* was about three-quarters unsuccessful. If *Ch. B* fares no better, I would probably have to say that I was mistaken all along. *En cas de malheur*, [he concludes ambiguously] I would drop the whole idea. Hence also my hesitation over the *Rendezvous in Oudenaarde*. (J.A. to H.A. 29.8.78)

Amidst all his forced optimism, Heissenbüttel's 'enthusiastic verdict' raises him instantly to a 'childish mood of euphoria' (J.A. to H.A. 5.1.78), but he fears the 'trials and tribulations [of] literary life'. As we now know, the reception of this work is no less than a matter of life or death to him. Taking part with Hanjo Kesting in a political discussion of 'Our historical obligation' with Martin Walser on 1 October, 14 days before his suicide, he pleads with uncharacteristic insistence to be allowed a quarter of an hour on the 'Literary Matinee' programme. 'I would very much like to show the Germans that I am not "just" an essayist; I am getting tired of the label' (J.A. to H.K. 10.8.78).[68] The discussion evening in Hanover turned out a disaster:

> The occasion was what it was. You know that better than anyone, and were visibly suffering. It was not laziness that made me keep my mouth shut, but a sudden realization that I have as little to say to that audience as they want to hear from me.

He ought not to have come, he says, he is 'out of place' at public events of that kind. 'The reasons would be a long and sad story, one that I hardly like to tell myself now, let alone you' (J.A. to H.K. 3.10.78).

He did not tell the 'sad story' to anyone but instead tried to convert it into action once and for all.

> Wherever *échec* threatens constantly, in the form of failure in the *Abitur*,[vii] bankruptcy, or a diatribe by a leading critic (...) voluntary death becomes for everyone everywhere a promise full of potential. (Hasl. p. 43; OS pp. 42/43)

He 'hesitates', falters, 'absolutely must see how *Ch. B.* is treated,' but nothing would annoy him more than to write down that story, 'which matured over a long time'. Then he returns to the *leitmotiv* of his last letters: 'Je ne suis pas un homme qui s'obstine!' he says in the same letter to Arbogast – he is not an obstinate man! – 'and if people do not want to know about an essayist writing *belles-lettres*, then he will not put himself forward (...) However, I will at least work out the outline' (J.A. to H.A. 29.8.78).

Exactly a month before his death, he describes himself as a 'man who is changing', and it is as a changed man that he seeks recognition by the public (J.A. to H.P. 18.9.78). He might even have found it, but he does not wait long enough. The response to *Charles Bovary, Landarzt* did not by any means ring as clear as he had hoped. Two days after his suicide, a review by F.J. Raddatz appears (*Die Zeit* 20.10.78): 'An amusing game with ideas,' the critic calls this 'biography of a potential hero', even praising it as a 'bold experiment', although his (and not only his)[69] unmistakable conclusion is that 'Améry does not show himself to be a writer of fiction here'. That, and only that, was what Améry wanted. So here was the confirmation of his worst fears, the 'hollow echo' that inspired him with such horror. Hollow enough to make him take the last step?

No more *Rendezvous in Oudenaarde*

At the height of his conception of himself as a writer of *belles-lettres*, as if in a trance, Améry devotes himself to the outline of a novella, *Rendezvous in Oudenaarde* (J.A. *Werke*, Vol. 5, pp. 11–23). It is his last declaration of war, a defiant delusion, an apotheosis in which he insists – without thought of losses (what did he still have to lose?) – on taking his rightful place in literature. It is

---

vii *Abitur*: the final school-leaving exams taken in German schools. Améry is quoting the sad story of a boy who became suicidal on failing this important examination.

based on the idea of 'the power of the imagination', but, he claims, 'At the same time it should be of a realistic and fantastic character.' Such at least is his intention. Here Améry leaves his own stamp upon realism. If he took Charles Bovary from fiction and 'perfected' him ethically and politically in line with the ideals of the French Revolution, he does the precise opposite in *Oudenaarde*: here reality is not brought close to fiction and recreated under its influence; the fiction itself is declared to be reality, indeed fiction and reality coincide perfectly. In *Rendezvous in Oudenaarde* we feel that Améry's life itself is trying to be a work of art.

Final declarations of love

In this furious flight forward, Améry the would-be improver of the world takes leave of its imperfections on this side of the grave, resorting entirely to the world beyond: to literature. In *Oudenaarde*, he is in hot pursuit of categorical imperatives in social practice, whether they are of an existentialist or a Marxist character. Almost in imitation of Sartre, whom he pilloried so sternly for his work on Flaubert, Améry too now lives out his 'delirium' to the end, indulging his passion and hurrying to meet his only 'beloved' – Litta, Littera, in other words literature. Here, without guilt or shame, he makes his accusations behind the mask of his doppelganger Vanderleyden[viii] – again, a significant name, denoting his always existential relationship to the heroes of his interior world, as if they were the criterion of everything. The result is a headlong declaration of love to his lifelong companions along his way, the books to which he had already in part set up a memorial in the *Bücher aus der Jugend unseres Jahrhunderts* [Books from the Youth of our Century] (J.A. *Werke* Vol. 5, pp. 243–503).

Oudenaarde, like *Lefeu oder Der Abbruch,* goes back to Améry's literary origins, to the film-like dream sequences of the *Selbstmörder* [The Suicides] of the year 1945. Like his predecessor Charles Bovary, Vanderleyden is spellbound by his love for a dead woman. Litta is, so to speak, the esoteric counterpart of Charles's Emma. In its 'magically beautiful moorland landscape' of the Flemish Ardennes, this novella is Améry's first and only tribute to Belgium.[70] As the background to the story, Améry has in mind the 'imaginative Belgium of Paul Devaux with its abandoned stations, its brick houses standing in the cold moonlight, its naked women mysteriously gazing ahead(...)' (Ou., Vol. 5, p. 11 f.).

It is remarkable that the country in which he lives for 40 years leaves its mark only on his final work. *Rendezvous in Oudenaarde* is also a tribute to his first wife Gina, but its real homage is to literature:

---

viii   The character's name echoes the German word *Leiden* = sorrows, suffering.

The *reality* of literary figures is to be substantiated. Hans Castorp is more real than any uncle, Niels Lyne is more of a companion on our way than any acquaintance; the characters from Herman Bang, Proust, Flaubert, Joyce, Musil, Thomas Mann, etc., *do* exist. And there are the authors, long dead, with whom we have an intimate personal relationship through their works. They all symbolize the dream as life.[71]

The 'tender, shadowy memories of literature', he suggests, have a higher degree of reality than the present that now seems stale to him.

Unio mystica

Heissenbüttel, who accompanied Améry to Oudenaarde when he is sketching out the novella, probably knew best what kind of state he was in. Reading had always been an experience 'more significant and profound than the experience of life,' to him, says Heissenbüttel. 'A text was more real than reality for this author.'[72] He was so fascinated by the outline of the novella that after Améry's death he seriously considered writing it himself.[73] The projected *Oudenaarde* novella which was never written, either by its creator or by the guardian of his memory, is the most striking evidence of how much the world of literature made up Améry's world *tout court*. Atmospherically it takes its inspiration from Jens Peter Jacobsen's story *Ein Schuss in den Nebel* [A Shot in the Mist], to which it also owes its grand finale.

It was going to describe the progressing alienation of the protagonist Vanderleyden, who works in Brussels as a translator and, like his author, is haunted at night by dreams of his wife who died young. 'He has news of Litta. She wants to meet him.' The meeting is to be on 1 November (All Saints' Day!) outside the Gothic Town Hall, with its delicate architecture, in the historic little town of Oudenaarde. In the full knowledge that he has 'only' been dreaming, he sets off in his car. Although it is not a long journey, it proves very difficult. So he wanders through the multilingual and 'dangerous' country of Belgium, more than once led astray by Flemish place-names on signposts, and spends a 'wild night of love' with Emma, although thoughts of Litta make him feel guilty.

Will [Litta] forgive him? Will she be waiting for him outside Oudenaarde Town Hall, when he has been 'unfaithful to her the night before with the doctor's young wife? Flashback: he was often unfaithful to her, he was unfaithful to all women; he did nothing but damage; he bears some of the guilt for Litta's early death from heart failure.

Oudenaarde Town Hall

Not only are 'fantastic' admissions made here, they should also be seen as distinctly 'realistic' or in this case autobiographical in character. Deep in the landscape, as twilight falls, he longs for the release of Jacobsen's 'shot in the mist'. But his wanderings lead him on to further meetings: for instance, with Rüstrüp (Castorp), who introduces him into the Sanatorium Einfried, with many Scandinavian gentlemen, and a Madame Clawdnowa. Vanderleyden changes course and meets 'Bangenis (Herman Bang)', 'Nagelson, the protagonist of Hamsun's "Mysteries"' and finally Keller's Heinrich Lee, Goethe's Werther, Flaubert's Bouvard and Pécuchet, Hauff's Hasentreffer, Fontane's Effi Briest, Leopold Bloom and Dedalus. They all give him news of Litta. The police are after him for breaking the speed limit. On 1 November he finally reaches his destination, he is racing towards Litta who lures him on, smiling. 'V. thinks: there is a shot in the mist.' The union of Vanderleyden and Littera – the *unio mystica* with literature – takes place in death. Améry has come home; he is safe here.

Passions of the mind and the body

This late Romantic rationalist – 'where is it written that enlightenment must be without emotion?' (JSS, Vol. 2, p. 19) – who monomaniacally circles around the close relationship between love and death, is never intent on self-portrayal even in his essays on Auschwitz, torture or aging. Indeed, that is what distinguishes him so fundamentally from other writers on the Shoah such as Primo Levi. He is concerned in all his works, and most clearly of all in his fictional narratives, with an analytical dissolution of reality, for only in such a dissolution can he track down its deadly effect. In *Lefeu*, in *Bovary*, and finally in his sketch for *Oudenaarde*, only this 'dreaming in thought' makes it possible to discern what is not visible. Here he is able to sound out the basic questions of existence. Proust did it before him. Such is the stature of Proust's *Recherche*, he writes on the centenary of Proust's birth, that it looks not at the concentration of reality but at its dissolution. A dissolution that in his own *Oudenaarde* project also aims, at all costs, to be realistic. 'Nothing happens that is inconceivable in reality (which can only be everyday reality). (...) The characters from literature appear in such a way that we can believe them to be real' (J.A. to H.P. 4.3.78).[74] Even the shot fired by the guardian of the law, hitting Vanderleyden at the moment of his meeting with Litta, becomes real only through its literary accreditation. Life can be recognized only in works of art.

This, really, is his last stop – the last stop of an enlightened supporter of the Enlightenment who has come to realize that its deficiencies can be removed only by subjectively and aesthetically radical means. So he remains true to the dreams of his youth, probably the only constant factor in his turbulent life – he still expects literature to tell him all about the world and himself. The idea of a homeland, even a political one in the manner of Bloch, resides only in the light of literature, in the world of books. In this sense, Améry the neo-positivist and champion of verification presents, in his dream novella *Rendezvous in Oudenaarde*, the reality of unreal literature. That was his first credo, and it is his last.

They are all projected forms of death, the 'phenomenology of fear',[75] and all of them, despite appearances, are thoroughly de-romanticized, shot through with irony, a confession of the 'body that is vulnerable to torment'. The higher viewpoint of eternity is never suggested as any compensation. Whether in Törless, or Lefeu, or Charles, or Vanderleyden, they are passions of the mind and the body in pain, where even the world of literature on the other side of the grave finds, without exception, its brutal end in the ephemeral world on this side.

CHAPTER 9

Last Things

The unnatural nature of natural death

Is what we call 'natural death' really so natural? Améry asks in *Hand an sich legen. Diskurs über den Freitod* (1976) [in English, *On Suicide. A Discourse on Voluntary Death* (1999)]. Is it natural for Thomas Mann's Lieutenant Joachim Ziemssen, 'a soldier, and brave', to die so young? (Hasl. p. 35; OS p. 32). Or for Schiller to have been mown down at the age of 46. What about Büchner and Kafka? Or even Adorno when he was 60? 'Here as much as there, the continuity of a creative existence was chopped to pieces so that (...) we tend to object, like Voltaire, who protested against the earthquake of Lisbon (...)' (Hasl. p. 35; OS p. 33). For a man dying but 'still very lucid', no death is natural, even when nature causes it.

If even 'natural' death is a taboo subject, then suicide appears positively monstrous. To Améry's mind, it is also monstrous in the temptation it represents. It hardly needs to be said explicitly that suicide is Améry's preferred manner of death. He has always thought of it like that, in unbroken continuity 'since childhood', as he recollects in an interview with *Die Zeit* (13.8.76). He knows what he is talking about, because every one of the virtual situations enumerated so casually here corresponds to a real experience in his life:

> Wherever *échec* threatens constantly, in the form of failure in the *Abitur*, bankruptcy, or a diatribe by a leading critic, or the crippling decline of one's creative powers, or sickness, or (...) love, or (...) trembling anxiety (...), here voluntary death becomes for everyone everywhere a promise full of potential. (Hasl. p. 43; OS pp. 42/43)

'Voluntary death' is the form of words he chooses, not suicide, not 'self-murder', for voluntarily chosen death cannot be an act of murder; it is, by any criterion, the most comprehensive 'No' uttered by the nay-sayer who countermands the logic of life in carrying out his act. Our only scope for action is to get in ahead of the guillotine blade that will fell us in any case. Furthermore, he cites the French suicidologist Jean Baechler, who in his book *Les suicides* of 1975 describes suicide as 'specifically human'. Only human beings have consciousness, and without consciousness there is no suicide; animals, for instance, do not kill themselves.

Suicide – an inalienable human right

Améry's book *On Suicide* represents to him 'the last attainable stage of enlightenment'.[1] It is a free act deserving not condemnation but respect. Society, inclusive of suicidology, would point to the law of the preservation of the species and when the suicidal person has made up his mind to kill himself is intent on keeping him from doing so. It teaches mankind to accept 'that what is, is'. Améry will have nothing to do with such 'shrugging acceptance' of creation in the name of the logic of life. The suicide, 'the man who is extinguishing himself is, so to speak, reversing creation.' His inner world, the dark 'world of the unhappy man', to join Améry in quoting Wittgenstein, must be illuminated, his state of mind 'before the leap' to the point where he takes the 'way to freedom' must be evaluated.

> [Suicide is] the retraction of all the lies of life that we have suffered, and are able to suffer only by virtue of those lies (...) [because] voluntary death is more than a pure act of self-abolition. It is a long process of bowing down, of approaching the earth, a summing up of many humiliations.

Death itself, on the contrary, is 'an accursed inconceivability' (Hasl p. 25; OS p. 19) which the writer, through introspection and empathy, 'can imagine as partially conceivable' (Hasl p. 32).

Améry does not want his book to be taken as an apologia, let alone as a plea in favour of suicide – Michael Krüger was not the only one who, having read the book, spoke his mind to its author. To someone who asked for a signature in a copy after his last reading in Marburg, Améry is said to have pointed out firmly that it was not an instruction manual. Améry justifies himself in his reply to Krüger:

> I have made no demands. What I was trying to do was to circle around the trans-social situation of an outsider, which of its nature is beyond psychology and sociology, and to do so as an 'a-social' person. No one can, should or may draw any conclusions from it about society. (J.A. to M.K. 31.12.76)[2]

Yet he is appealing to society, he requires it to accept the freedom to commit suicide as an inalienable human right, and not to condemn the person who contemplates or commits it as a pathological case. 'Suicide is (...) hardly more of a scandal than poverty and sickness' (Hasl. p. 56; OS p. 60). It is not to be condemned as the act of a sick man, a misfit, but as the rational answer to oppressive circumstances, when the ego has a right to want to stop exposing itself to them, 'a resounding no to the crushing, shattering *échec* of existence' (Hasl. p. 57; OS p. 60). When a man is contemplating suicide, the popular wisdom holding that 'one must live in the end' is not in force; for him, as for Kleist and Chatterton and many of the nameless, life is 'not the highest good of all' (Hasl. p. 21; OS p. 14).

To whom does a human being belong?

The potentially suicidal Améry, for whom God is dead, takes the decision in full responsibility for himself. Should not he, and only he, have a right to decide how to deal with what is his own possession – life or death? It is true that voluntary death as an individual act will never be performed entirely without reference to society, but the person carrying out that act is alone with himself, 'before which society must fall silent'. After all, a man belongs to himself, and never more so than at the moment when he decides not to belong to himself any more.

Of course, there is the Other, 'the "you", specifically, without whom I could never be an "I"' (Hasl p. 93; OS p. 107). This Other, Améry writes, is both murderer and Samaritan, hell and blessedness. He is bound to him, needs him. Much was 'very good', the 'honourable moments' did exist up to the *instant suprême*. Here, however, he takes the leap, breaks the contract with the Other, an act to which 'the great, towering accumulation of *échecs*' drive him after all (Hasl 102–103). However great the pain of parting may be, the suicide dies reconciled. The claim that only a man 'who has no more hope of love' (Hasl p. 98; OS p. 114) commits suicide is an idea that Améry energetically rejects. 'The wrong love at the wrong time from the wrong other can just as easily lead to suicide as a lack of demonstrated love' (Hasl 98; OS p. 114).

It is this very point that goes against the grain with Paeschke:

What caught my attention as I read, even in grief, is the isolation out of which you have written this. A conclusion drawn from Sartre's terrible saying that hell is other people? (...) If this is the case with the Other, ought we not to conclude that the You does not exist, and nor does love? You keep coming back to the I that must assert and preserve itself (...).

He counters Améry's 'inclination to death' with the idea of 'love in death'. 'Your isolation,' he concludes, 'thus verges on solipsism' (H.P. to J.A. 5.3.76). Deeply wounded by this accusation, Améry replies: 'If even you see me as a solipsist (...) – what will the critics say?' He has in no way suppressed the Other. He contradicts Paeschke:

> You say I keep coming back to the 'I', but I am not the one doing that, it is the ontologically fundamental condition of mankind that drives us all into this blind alley – unless we are religious believers (...). Yes,, love exists. But it has little chance (...) only a mystic can persuade himself that the shadow-fencing of the I with himself would die through it.

And, he goes on: there is no 'sweet death', nothing but formulaic phrases conjuring it up, 'all my efforts have been put to dispelling the misconception that death is the "brother of sleep"' (J.A. to H.P. 13.3.76).

How free is the way to freedom?

He was still calling voluntary death a 'fool's story' in *On Aging*; in *On Suicide* it becomes the apotheosis of self-determination. Améry conjures up ideas that he owes to the Enlightenment, not gentle and soothing but harsh and disturbing.

> As a method of death suicide is still free from constraint: no cancer is eating me up, no heart attack threatens me, no uremic crisis deprives me of breath. *I* am the one laying hand on myself, dying after taking the barbiturates. (Hasl. p. 11)

In condensed form, 'The man contemplating suicide deprives himself of himself' (Hasl. p. 33).

Yet Améry is always aware of the contradictions in his position: yes, 'voluntary death is a breath-giving *Road into the Open*,[i] but it is freedom itself,' it promises freedom from something but never *to* something, for death and suicide are pure negation, says Améry, the anti-metaphysician. 'What is free is not freedom, but the road is the road to freedom' (Hasl. p. 123). Only the decision to take it is free. 'At the moment when a man says to himself that he can throw his life away, he is free' (Hasl. p. 113).

A frenzy overcomes him: his project will enable him, with this last act, to wrest some sense from the absurdity of life and death.

> A requirement of life is here (...) the demand to escape a life lacking in dignity, humanity, and freedom. And so death becomes life, just as from the moment of birth life is already a process of dying. And now negation all at once becomes

---

i *Road into the Open* is the title of a novel by Arthur Schnitzler [*Der Weg ins Freie*, 1908], tr. Roger Byers, California 1991.

something positive, even if good for nothing (...) What counts [concludes Améry, the intellectual] is the option of the subject. (Hasl. p. 128; OS pp. 153)

To this, Améry the sensual man replies, 'But the survivors are right; for what are dignity, humanity, and freedom in preference to smiling, breathing, and striding?' (Hasl. p. 128; OS p. 153).

This is barely credible. Are philosophical abstractions being played off here, in the peroration, against humanity's most vital functions? Is this a recantation of the merits of voluntary death as against life that must be suffered? Not at all, and a second look is informative. The vital functions – the *smiling, breathing, striding* – are 'only' a literary quotation, the title of a poem by Franz Werfel. So he is not taking anything back, rather he is raising what is intellectual into the aesthetic sphere, for the real 'option of the subject' is literary, and moreover the heading of the final chapter, 'The Road into the Open', is already preparing for that. As with his model Heinrich Mann, for Améry 'the mind always comes first'.[3] The point made later in *Unterwegs nach Oudenaarde* – where literature is declared the truer reality, and only literature, so to speak, authenticates life – is already present here in *On Suicide*.

'Life and death: two unknown quantities'[4]

So much for the theory, the high tone: the 'privilege of humanity', the *'acte suprême'*, the 'option of the subject', a wonderfully edifying story. In fact, hardly any other work by Améry is as full of life as this book. He enthuses:

> Suicide is something great and mysterious. One can never do it justice, and if I hear of people who have been more 'successful' at it than I was, my thoughts on the subject sometimes seem like mere games played with ideas. (Letter from J.A. to Ben Gurion 27.4.78)

Yes, the freedom to choose a voluntary death exists, the *ars moriendi*, and these five penetrating essays conjure it up repeatedly. It must exist, for the very reason that Améry the survivor claims it insistently for himself. To deny it to him in the usual way by saying that although he survived Auschwitz it has at last caught up with him makes him a victim again and denies him the ability to 'make something else of what was made of him' for the second time.[5] Nothing was determined in advance. Once humiliated and permanently wounded, he sets out to prove this like a man possessed. 'You shall not sway me. My death will be my own business.' His work, the essay of his life which fruitfully nourishes itself not with plenty but with loss, is indeed an *essai*, an attempt to survive his ever-open wounds by writing.

But the other story is his knowledge of the conditional nature of that freedom, of the compulsion to commit suicide as a 'contradiction of life' and of the irresistible way he is drawn to it. This is Améry's open secret. 'The leap into suicide is a paradoxical and absurd attempt to escape the loneliness of "natural" death and at the same time to experience it to the full' (Letter from J.A. to Uwe Schultz 3.12.76). In a radio broadcast a year later he speaks of the 'revolt against the loneliness of death, and suicide is presented as the only way of tricking death by means of death, removing loneliness by means of loneliness'.[6] However that may be, in truth death and life are both unknown quantities to him. One can talk about them, think of them, but they cannot really be 'thought'.

Art as life, life as art

Losing oneself in the many thousand pages of Améry's letters, notes, essays, one begins to have a sense of a distance that cannot be bridged. With that, paradoxically, respect for his artistic achievement grows, for his own art in thinking ideas through to their bitter end requires rigorous control and owes much to such a sense of distance.

We can tell how closely his theory and practice are related, how urgently Améry's literary work calls for realization in real life from *On Suicide*, which was certainly written with some presentiment of the closing act. What was ultimately a reflex action in Améry – setting up the dynamics of its chronology – proves impossible and the failed suicide precedes this 'book of dis-consolation', as Günter Kunert calls it. Améry's writing provides guidelines for life – or death – to the same extent as it works on and appraises real life. 'All your books are stages in an uncommonly painful self-analysis,' said Ernst Mayer after reading *On Suicide;* they are chapters of an existential phenomenology written with 'pitiless determination to spare yourself no torment and omit no source of shame in your merciless exploration of your own mind' (E.M. to J.A. 11.11.75).

'Man thinks, multi-causality guides'

It is true about 'torment', his friend is right there, and he is right about shame as well. Yet it is irritating to find Ernst Mayer taking this 'metaphorical' book so entirely at face value, when, as with others before it, there is something like a theatrical performance in its dramatic sweep of thought. It is not a directly autobiographical document; it is a construct, it is self-stylization. Heissenbüttel emphasizes the literary quality of *On Suicide*, calling Améry a 'concrete thinker' because he 'employs the pictorial and attractive features of language like concepts' and in turn 'makes those concepts into metaphors'.[7] Améry's *On Suicide* is a book of both revelation and concealment. It is, absurd as this may sound, and beyond all Blochian connotations, his ultimate realization of Utopia.[8]

For some time Améry the man – as opposed to Améry the thinker – has not been living a very bright and cheerful everyday life in the Avenue Coghen. At best it is a matter of ups and downs, grey on grey, dragging wearily along, oppressive to the point of being depressing – it has none of the dramatic, blade-sharp profile that distinguishes his lively, leaping book on death.

No necessity

When the time really comes, everyone has seen it coming and indeed thought it was bound to come. No one claims to have been surprised; it had been only a matter of time. Not only could his suicide have been foreseen, people think they also know exactly *why* he killed himself, they immediately range him with the long series of Auschwitz survivors, with Celan and Szondi, to mention only the most famous. They talk of 'a heavy fate' and establish the fact that such was his, they see only the inevitability of it.

Both true and false.

On a sheet of paper headed, 'How it all began', Maria surmises, on 5 May 1980:

> Even in 1948 Hans was having motor difficulties, he would drop things, put them in the wrong place, he kept sweating all the time – when I raised my hand to stroke his hair he would flinch as if fearing a blow – and standing in line to buy cinema tickets, for instance in Paris, was out of the question. He had been made to keep standing in line in the concentration camp. Crowds repelled him...he kept losing things, the left luggage ticket, the Metro ticket, and then in Frankfurt in 1977 he lost 2000 DM in a taxi along with several thousand Belgian francs. In July 1975, in the spa hotel in Goisern, he kept talking about suicide. August 1975, he became aggressive, clashed with a German over smoking by the lake (...).[9]

In an imaginary letter to him, she writes:

> Auschwitz number 172363 – for that number sealed your fate. (...) But there was so much else; it was all in you from an early date. It was no coincidence that as a very young man you loved only the poetry of those poets who wrote of decline, melancholy, and death.[10]

That is true, for Améry's 'inclination to death' – as he calls it, after Auschwitz – is already manifesting itself in his very first literary work. Initially it takes the form of flight: 'Being destined for death is enough to destroy one's pleasure in pleasure, and finally to make death seem better than one's wretched, tedious existence. You see, I am optimistically and "positively" disposed, as always' (J.A. to Inge Werner 21.12.75). He scarcely writes a letter without mentioning death – Améry's store of quotations on the subject is inexhaustible. 'We live so short a time, and we are dead so long,' he quotes Wilhelm Busch.[11] The following lines of verse by Karl Kraus are his *leitmotiv* in the year of his death: Es *dauert nicht mehr lange, mir ist so bange* [It will not be long now; I am so much afraid], and then he adds to his friend, 'Isn't it strange – we long for our final peace and yet we fear it. The stupid *creature* is in us and puts the deepest yearning of the spirit to shame' (J.A. to E.M. 30.7.78).

Then death features as the idea of freedom and self-determination: voluntary death is already one of his themes in *Die Schiffbrüchigen*. It is also true that Améry is among the first to insist on the close relationship between writing and living; his collected reflections nourish themselves on 'what has been lived', *le vécu*. He not only draws *on* his life but also makes his radical Utopias into real-life scenarios, and part of his staging of them is that publicly, and at every opportunity, he is answerable for them (or in this case thinks of being answerable for them) *with* his life. For instance, he stages the following scene, one that he often likes to quote: 'So a student recently asked me: why did you write that book about voluntary death, and then why didn't you kill yourself? I told him: just you wait.'[12]

So he sets traps for himself, perhaps *wants* to set traps for himself to bar all his possible ways of escape, from the start. It is as if he had laid a bet with himself, and his self-respect forbids him to lose.

The inevitability that people mention – particularly the idea of a single motivation for that inevitability, Auschwitz – was never inevitable at all. That hypothesis will not hold water. The *possibility* of suicide was, in fact, always vitally necessary to him, but *committing* it was not. He could have committed suicide much earlier – see 1943 in Breendonck, see 1974 after *Lefeu* – or indeed much later, perhaps not at all; even that consideration, however improbable, cannot be excluded. In 1976, just after the publication of *On Suicide*, he himself decodes the relationship of theory and practice in remarking to Paeschke: 'Man thinks, multi-causality guides his actions' (J.A. to H.P. 15.10.76).

Why? On the necessity and impossibility of being a writer

In 1970 – directly after the success of *On Aging* – doubts creep in again.

> Talent is like this: if you do not have it to a high degree bordering on genius, like Thomas Mann, for instance, (...) it is almost better not to have it at all.

> I was (...) too gifted to be anywhere nearly satisfied with being an average human being, but not gifted enough to give up the joys of ordinary life, the best of which is to be satisfied with oneself (...). Well, it will soon all be over, and as they say, then it will be all the same – how could it be better put? (J.A. to E.M. 1.11.70)

His 'self-denunciation in doubt' of 1977 gives more basic information, for it conveys the naked fear of existence, loss and isolation:

> I am a man of 65 who has tried all his life to think as well as he can, to act as far as his powers would reach, and now I am more at a loss than a young man of 20. The world daily, hourly confronts me with new problems, intellectual, political, emotional. I am no longer master in my own house. (...) All my systems of coordinates are breaking down, and with them an 'I' who has long ago learned to distrust himself.[13]

His last major setback occurs, as we know, in 1974. *Lefeu*, his 'life's work in miniature format (for I never trusted myself to write on the grand scale anyway)' (J.A. to E.M. 17.1.75), the book that 'has cost so much blood, sweat and tears' (J.A. to E.M. 8.10.72), 'has sunk' without trace, as he thinks, and that makes him wonder 'how I myself and a few clever people could have been so completely wrong'. In the same letter, written in January 1975, just under a year after his second suicide attempt, he tells Ernst Mayer: 'I do not like it here below any longer. (...) A small wave washed me up on land for a brief moment. Now it has ebbed away.' We can tell how deep the wound went in his final stock-taking of himself as a writer, his introductory speech to the German Academy of Language and Literature: 'I was called an essayist,' he mocks himself, 'and was severely criticized for crossing the border in *Lefeu oder Der Abbruch* and venturing into the field of *belles lettres*, in which, after all, I had my literary origins.'[14] It is only by that criterion that *he* assesses his success.

Perhaps it is something to do with Germany, with the German language? Again and again he thinks of

> ... the chance I might have had if I had seriously begun to communicate in French in 1945. The French language inhabits a better, brighter intellectual sphere than our German, which is more suited to poetry (particularly of an expressionist nature) than to discursive narrative prose. In my case, it means that the 'novel-essay' genre which I wanted to create, failing in the attempt, might have been [more] successful in French. (J.A. to E.M. 28.9.75)

Best not to play the author any more, to climb down for good, and after all, Sartre, now a sick man, is also condemned to silence.

So his mother had been right in her depressing prognosis: 'You'll never amount to anything.' He takes her verdict as his own. 'It has been a life that came to nothing after all' (J.A. to E.M. 17.1.75).

If the reviews of *Lefeu* in 1974 and of *Charles Bovary* in 1978 had come up to his high expectations, however, he would *not* have taken his life at this time. At least, Maria Améry's search for clues suggests such a conclusion: the lack of appreciation of *Charles Bovary* as a literary work seals his failure as a writer of fiction for the second time. This was undoubtedly the crucial moment, for he makes his decision dependent on the public reception of his *Bovary*, with which he identifies entirely. *Bovary* was 'the final test case,' notes Maria Améry in her reconstruction. ' "If the Bovary book goes wrong I know what I have to do." When the book was ready (I believe around the middle of August)' she explains further, 'he waited with positively morbid irritability for some discussion of it, in particular throughout September.'[15] The lack of interest shown by the critics is, for him, the worst humiliation of all, and he plans to pre-empt it with his act.

Yet he was still full of plans, Maria Améry goes on, he wanted to go to Darmstadt with her to make his maiden speech at the Academy and then go on to the meeting of the Berlin Academy. Above all, 'if the Bovary book had been at all successful, he would also have written *Rendezvous in Oudenaarde*,' says Maria Améry in the same document. Finally, he also wanted – see his last major essay for Rowohlt – to work on a concept of the new Left.

The Left without a home

The system of coordinates that is now falling apart applies, not least, to the world situation. The radical liberal that he is, without any doctrine of salvation, always expressing a spirit of contradiction and criticism, we know that at the end of his life he also feels let down by his intellectual home, France. He thinks that with the collapse of the *French* Left, the country, taking an anti-Cartesian turn, has given up its cultural mission to the world.

But poor conditions in *Germany* perhaps contribute even more directly to his mood at this late point. Améry writes to the North German Radio editor Gisela Lindemann, just 11 days before his suicide, when she sends him the transcripts of his last broadcast for the station, the occasion when he was meant to discuss 'German guilt' with Martin Walser and never opened his mouth:

> My obvious superfluity has not been weighing on my mind too much, but I have asked myself whether it was not by a mistake of fate that in 1945, when I was still relatively young, I did not resolve to be a French writer. A famous poem by H.M. Enzensberger occurred to me (my memory stores up poetry very well): 'What have I to do in that country?' The answer is, a good deal. (J.A. to E.M. 5.10.78)

Améry holds himself partly responsible for the disorientation of the *German* Left – he has always been very adept at self-denunciation. We read in his 1945 work 'Spoken into the Wind', accusation and self-accusation: 'I imagined that the world belonged to us, the defeated who had now become victors, the utopians whose wildest dreams seemed to be suddenly overtaken by reality'[16] (IdWg. p. 258). The Cold War, the restoration of the status quo in Germany with such figures as Globke and later Filbinger, brought this euphoria to an abrupt end. He turns another way and cultivates blindness in his left eye until the 'second rape of Czechoslovakia' (IdWg p. 264) 'What a shameful failure!'

The *new* Left is equally bad. A 'betrayal of the intellectuals' – it is no coincidence that at the end of his life he promotes the German translation of Julien Benda's *La trahison des clercs* (1927), writing a preface for the Hanser Verlag edition in which he recommends it to German readers.[17] As early as 1969 – see *Widersprüche* – he is reproaching the Left for its lack of a sense of history and its irrationally fetishist concepts: it has lost its sense of reality, he says. It acts as if it were involved in an apocalyptic class struggle under a pitiless dictatorship, its language is Manichaean, and it opposes the lies of power with a mendacious vocabulary of its own.[18]

Its anti-Zionist stance is an 'existential threat' to him, although he is also much troubled by the machinations of the Israeli hawks. In March 1976 he writes briefly of his visit to Israel: 'Need does not teach what is good. The hatred that breaks in waves around it does not make it better, or improve its diplomatic and military hopelessness in any way' (J.A. to H.P. 27.2.76). He feels about Israel as he feels about Austria – what a curious comparison! – there will always be 'a dissonance that cannot be resolved' (J.A. to E.M. 17.1.75) – 'You can be sick with dislike of the country if you belong to it. But you do not stop loving it in a perverse way.'[19] He will 'resolve' that specifically Austrian dissonance, on 10 October 1978 in Salzburg, with his death.

'A man and his body'

He is not a stoic, Jean Améry confesses to his friend. Nor is Ernst Mayer himself; their correspondence over 30 years sometimes reads like a wry exchange of medical case histories. Every other letter ends with the hope that nothing will go wrong because he always 'has to fear for the way his body works' (J.A. to E.M. 16.2.72). Then again, if one thinks of the amount of work that Améry contrives to do in this poor state of health – eyes, mouth, teeth, stomach, veins, there is hardly an organ that was not affected at some time or other – he appears positively heroic. In 1974 there is even a mention of *lupus erythematosus*.[20]

The 'main disorder' is his 'calcified heart', which gives him a lot of trouble, he 'feel(s) it all the time', and it leaves him 'puffing miserably at the least expenditure of strength' (J.A. to E.M. 24.4.66). For years, he says, the doctors had diagnosed his various heart troubles as 'cardiac neurosis', and 'I felt very comfortable with the role of a neurotic who was not in any danger. That's all over now' (J.A. to E.M. 8.7.61). Since 1961, although really it is since his release from the camp, his heart has not functioned well, the doctors speak of 'coronary insufficiency' and the beginnings of *angina pectoris*.

So it is obvious to read his remarks on the books of Herbert Plügge, specialist in internal medicine and neurologist, particularly the chapter on 'the condition of those with heart infarctions' (in whom he obviously sees himself), as a self-portrait.[21] Plügge speaks of the loss of an easy, uninhibited attitude that accompanies severe illness. Maria Améry adds: 'And what about after failed suicide?'[22] 'With the pain of a man with heart trouble, a man who "has a bad heart",' Améry comments, his world changes

> ... and it is illuminating here to see how much consciousness really is, as Merleau-Ponty says, *conscience engagé*, how much the world is perceived *à travers notre corps*. The man with heart trouble finds himself at odds with the world. (...) All steps are too high and too steep, the legs get heavier and more shapeless by the minute, the street more uneven at every metre.

And then there is a kind of mourning in the image of a severely ill man. 'He no longer asks for a diagnosis or a prognosis, often not even for his family.' His worldly connections are shrinking, 'gradually, barely imperceptibly, he leaves his body on the inside. In this process the body changes, lagging further and further behind, into a mere *husk*.'[23] To the sick man, his existence is made transparent when he reads the works of Plügge. 'He comes to "the finding of himself" in the literal sense.'

Finding himself means, in this connection, something more like the possibility of *losing* himself by his own free choice: 'Physical decline depresses my morale, and if I still believe that I no longer fear death as something "other" (...) I still have a terrible fear of excessive suffering' (J.A. to E.M. 24.4.65).

'Yes, love does exist'

He knows his way around the 'wanderings and confusions of passion', he has 'known plenty of them in his own life,' he says in a letter to the friend of his youth Ernst Mayer, they are 'both uplifting and depressing'.

> Uplifting because in spite of suffering, or better, through suffering, one feels alive, depressing because at our age we are bound to feel we are no longer

entirely able to deal with them. I think of my friend Prigogine, who told me in the days of his marital difficulties, 'I don't have time for living out novels anymore!' (J.A. to E.M. 1.2.62)

Not that Jean Améry would have had time, but he steals it for himself, for sometimes 'the novel overwhelms us' (1.2.62). It 'overwhelms' him on 8 March 1968.

That was the day when a visitor from Wiesbaden comes to see him, the Hessian press spokeswoman Hety Schmitt-Maas, an artist at bringing people together – she has introduced Améry to Levi and Langbein. Now she introduces someone else into Améry's life, a woman, and his meeting with her was to have fateful consequences. Yet it all begins so innocently: she asks if she may bring a friend to Brussels with her. An American Maria, or rather Mary Cox-Kitaj (1924–1997), an academic teaching German, M.A. of Chicago University, now assistant professor of German at Idaho University. She has 'begun another course of study in Frankfurt'. Hety has known Mary since 1945 when she was working for re-education in Wiesbaden in 'American military uniform'. 'Of the Americans "occupying" us at the time, I found her one of the few who could understand something of what had been and was still going on,' says Hety Schmitt-Maas to Maria Améry in preparation for her visit (23.2.68).

Mary Cox-Kitaj is 44 in 1968, the mother of two children aged 13 and 10 and has been a widow for two years. She was married to the Viennese Jew, Bill Kitaj, whom as chance would have it Maria Améry had also known in Vienna.

Mary Cox-Kitaj

Bill is said to have been a linguistic genius, a lecturer in Russian and French at Idaho University. In 1966 he died in an accident on a research visit to Moscow. Mary Kitaj is also the aunt of the famous painter R.B. Kitaj, who died in Los Angeles in 2007.[24] 'She is writing a book on Germany for American students,' Hety Schmitt-Maas continues her introduction:

> One chapter in the book is about the 'past with which the Germans have not yet come to terms'. So she has been getting literature from me, and as you know, Améry, Levi and Langbein were all part of it! (Hety Schmitt-Maas to Maria Améry 23.2.68)

Mary, she adds, would be very glad if she could talk to M. Améry.

Their friend assures the Amérys:

> I know you will like her, and it will be good for her to speak to you. On television Jean Améry apparently mentioned Bill Kitaj (think of that!) and yesterday she returned me *Jenseits von Schuld und Sühne,* and our conversation then showed me that she (...) has entirely accepted and understood the book! (H.S.M. to M.A. 28.2.68)

Then she returns to describing the start of her friendship with Mary.

> I think the path leading from her experiences in Germany at that time to Bill Kitaj was, in a way, only logical. Whether she is prepared to talk about him I can't say in advance – it would be good if she did, but that will depend on what kind of contact you all have with each other. (H.S.M. to M.A. 28.2.68)

The contact is good, very good, even too good. After her visit, Maria Améry writes Hety Schmitt-Maas an effusive letter of thanks; she hopes that it will not be their last meeting. Cox, a former sergeant, she says, called directly after her return, 'a brave and clever woman, it was a pleasure for us to meet her'. Jean Améry adds a handwritten 'Very best wishes', particularly to the 'truly refreshing Sergeant Cox' (14.3.68). In April they meet again at the Nuremberg Conversations, this time without Maria Améry; in May, on her own, Mary visits Brussels and 'Mops' – as Maria Améry likes those close to her to call her – once again thanks Hety warmly 'for introducing us to Mary' (M.A. to H.S.-M. 25.5.68).

Not until a year later does Améry let his friend into the confidence of his 'remarkable story': 'To make a very long and complicated business short and simple, a love triangle has developed between Mops, Mary and me. I expressly say *love*' (8.2.69). So there is happiness for Améry as well and has been for hours, days and weeks – even months. 'It would be positively untrue,' he tells his friend, 'if I did not admit that sometimes now I am very happy (because so is Mops),' he says, summarizing the situation in February 1969.

Then on 2 April comes the heart attack mentioned above. This love is 'certainly not ideal for a cardiac patient,' but he refuses, 'in agreement with Mops, to live in future only for my sick heart and brittle arteries' (J.A. to E.M. June 69). In his good moments, that is to say pain-free moments, he feels euphoric, he is impelled to visit Mary in *her* world; he wants to conquer the American West. The last 18 months 'have been a great joy', a 'gift', particularly because it is one that he has been able to 'share with Mops, for such affairs in one's later years often end in tragedy' (J.A. to E.M. 10.4.70). That at least, he says, *he* has been spared.

Two months later he goes on his first visit to America, with his wife Maria. He is both fascinated and repelled by the 'truly Wild West' – wonderful landscapes, vast lakes, snow-covered mountain ranges like moon landscapes, stony deserts, grassy steppes. In Yellowstone Park he even buys a Texan hat and poses as an 'Austrian-Jewish cowboy', see picture! But besides the mighty scenery, there are 'the ugliest imaginable towns, forests of gasoline pumps, outsize supermarkets and towering exhibitions of pop art' (J.A. to E.M. 10.4.70). The people are a mystery to him, a mixture of warmth and efficiency, or such are his

Jean Améry in Yellowstone Park, 1970

impressions (28.6.70). Long live old Europe, what luck that all those years ago he didn't have the chance of emigrating to the States.

In the autumn of 1970 Mary and her two children Kathy and Paul move to Brussels. She now devotes herself entirely to her dissertation, having registered at the Université Libre de Bruxelles. Its subject is 'Thomas Mann's ambiguous relationship with the United States of America'. Améry sees a joint venture in this project and immerses himself in the work. 'Because of the oldest love of my life, I take more interest in this dissertation (...) than in my own work, and will be proud if Mary has her diploma in the bag some day' (J.A. to E.M. 6.10.70). Two years later, on 16 December 1972, Mary does indeed have her doctorate 'in the bag'. So far, so good.

That hope is fulfilled, but the other and greater hope fails. No one is spared anything. The 'happy passion' turns into a very unhappy one. Tensions escalate, reaching a first climax in January 1973. It is particularly tragic for Maria, who has shared Améry's life and now finds herself excluded from the *ménage à trois*. The newly exclusive relationship with Mary means that she and Jean have to think up new, surreptitious ways of meeting – a network of lies both small and large, in fact, the usual old story, which in no way detracts from its tragedy.

This time it is Ernst Mayer who appeals to his friend Hans's conscience: Mary has her children and her work, whereas Maria has only him to bring meaning to her life. To break his long connection with Maria would be like destroying her. Can such a decision ever make him happy? The 'sanctity of egotism' is not compatible with his own claims for morality.

They are all unhappy, in their own different ways. 'Passion leads to suffering' was Améry's refrain, remembers Paul Kitaj, Mary's son.[25] Jean tries to part from Mary, throws himself into *Lefeu*, and after completing it intends to take his life (February 1974), an attempt which, as we know, did not succeed at this point – failure all along the line, in life, in love, in death. To a man tired out with wandering, he writes to Paeschke, that last resting place is as much *l'ultime espérance* as it was for Heinrich Heine (15.12.77).

The situation is visibly deteriorating. He clings to Mary. 'She became the real centre of my failure of a life. *The Old Man and Passion* – there's another book title for you' (J.A. to E.M. 21.10.76). Sarcasm or no sarcasm, he sees no way out.

In 1976 Améry writes from Idaho:

The plain truth is that I can't live without Mary. Mops knows that now, and has understood. I will never leave Mops, I am most deeply bound to her, but nor can I do without the narrow beam of light that brightens my very gloomy years so late. (J.A. to E.M. 10.5.76)

He has been toiling for years so that Maria will not be left penniless. He begs his friend for understanding. As for Maria, he can only hope 'that my dear, good companion will accept that passion and heartfelt affection can exist side by side' (J.A. to E.M. 18.5.76). She, Maria, grits her teeth, stays with him and goes on typing and revising his work.

In 1977 Mary leaves her post at Idaho University and desperately looks for a new way to earn her living in Europe. Améry tries to find a teaching position for her at a secondary school in Austria and then in Germany, but in vain. Yet she does move to Germany – without a job, without money. Maria, manager of the Amérys' finances, is supposed not to know about her husband's surreptitious attempts to provide help. He knocks on many doors, even that of his 'Nobel laureate friend Prigogine. He was very generous, but our intimate friendship of many decades has certainly suffered from this affair' (J.A. to H.P. 8.7.78). However, since 'fate' still has him 'by the throat', he applies now to Paeschke and Arbogast, begging them to become involved as go-betweens. He asks them more and more frequently to withdraw small sums from his account with the publishing firm and forward the money to Mary; he even, in dire need, asks them for an advance. Mary just about manages to keep her head above water in this way, until Michael Klett, in response to Améry's pressing request, comes to their aid and employs her as an editorial assistant in the English foreign languages department of Ernst Klett Schulbuch Verlag, the educational publishing side of the firm (March 1978–December 1978). To Paescke, he says: 'M.K. was *wonderful*' (Undated letter from Vienna).

In delirium, badly shaken by the damage he is doing – 'I have made all the women in my life unhappy' (J.A. to E.M. 30.7.78) – Améry writes to Michael Klett: 'A couple of words say it all: thank you. You have done more for me than perhaps you yourself can guess' (J.A. to M.K. 14.2.78). In his exuberance he employs language that approaches denial of his past, as if Michael Klett's kind deed could make up for all that Germany had done to him.

In 1976 he thinks, Mary 'saved his life' when after a final farewell 'she wrote again after all'. In 1978 their love contributes to his suicide. 'The wrong love at the wrong time by the wrong other can lead to suicide, just as the lack of it can' – he already knew that in *On Suicide* (Hasl p. 98).

When?

At Christmas 1977 he tells Paeschke: 'It is very wretched. My Christmas festivities as gloomy as they could be only in a kitschy novella, and 1978 (...) looks unpromising' (24.12.77). The year 1978 proves even worse than it promised to be. He is like a hunted man, despite the acclamations and honours. Above all,

Michael Klett at the Book Fair, 1972

he is tired of 'playing the Auschwitz clown'; he is referring to his broadcast on North German Radio on 1 October. He wants to move on into *belles lettres*.

The summer is passed in the usual company of Maria, Ernst and Erni, in Bad Goisern, Austria. September and October are occupied by the publication of *Charles Bovary*. In this connection, the publishing firm sends him on a marathon reading tour, in the company of Mary, as it later turns out: from 10 to 24 October he must 'sing for his supper' from *Charles*. The journey was to have taken him from Hamburg (10.10.78) to Kiel (11.10.78), Neumünster (12.10.78), Oldenburg (13.10.78), Marburg (15.10.78), Mannheim (16.10.78), Heidelberg (17.10.78), Karlsruhe (18.10.78), Stuttgart (20.10.78) and Schwäbisch-Hall (24.10.78), stopping for the festivities of the Frankfurt Book Fair, including a dinner with Michael Klett on 21 October. 'Many thanks for your invitation,' he replies before setting off. 'I will be very happy to be there' (J.A. to M.K. 9.10.78).

However, he is not there. Maria Améry speaks of a 'depressed phone call' from Neumünster on 12 October 1978. Three days later Améry breaks off his reading tour in Marburg, where he is visiting friends with Mary. He had seemed 'composed', according to his hostess, no one had noticed anything wrong with

The Österreichischer Hof, Salzburg

him. He must have made his decision that afternoon; there had been talk of his wish to see the Salzkammergut.[26]

Where?

Even earlier Améry had said nostalgically to the friend of his youth: 'I would like to come home in my old age. (...) I belong in our hilly country'(25.5.76). On 17 October his 'hilly country' was at the Österreichischer Hof in Salzburg. He could hardly have chosen a grander setting for this final act.

How?

Améry now literally sets to work on this death of his, giving himself up to the last to his extravagant aesthetic of death, as he described it in 1976 in *On Suicide*. What he has to say about that 'star writer' Stefan Zweig sounds almost like an anticipation of his own obituary.[27] So at least he would have wished it to read. 'The greatest masterpiece of Zweig, the successful and popular, the darling of the gods' – Améry had been all those things in his own time, even if he was incapable of seeing his public role in that way – '[was] his voluntary death in 1942' (J.A. *Werke* Vol. 5, p. 420–1). Stefan Zweig's suicide, he thinks, raises him above his work and gives that work a new dimension.

Is Jean Améry's suicide on 17 October 1978 not also his own last 'masterpiece'? Does not *his* suicide give a new dimension to his work? His literary example is not Zweig but Kleist,[ii] as it always was. He would have liked to choose Mary Cox Kitaj as his Henriette Vogel, [28] Eros and Thanatos.

---

ii   The writer Heinrich von Kleist died in a suicide pact with Henriette Vogel, shooting her and then himself in 1811 on the banks of the Kleiner Wannsee near Potsdam.

Salzburg, 16.10.78

An die betroffenen Polizeibehörden

Sehr geehrte Herren:
Ich, Unterzeichneter,

HANS MAIER (genannt: Jean AMÉRY)

Schriftsteller, wohnhaft in Brüssel, 56, Bd. Cayhen,

erkläre hiermit, daß ich mir freiwillig, im Vollbesitz meiner geistigen Kräfte, den Tod gebe. Ich bitte um sofortige Verständigung meiner Frau, bzw. Witwe, Maria Maier, geb. Eschenauer, derzeit und bis zum 19. ds. im Hotel Regina, Wien Währingerstrasse (Telephonische Nachricht, wenn irgend möglich.) Es liegt mir sehr daran, daß dies ohne Verzug geschehe, so daß meiner Frau überflüssige Ferngespräche von Belgien aus erspart bleiben. Ich gehöre keiner Religionsgemeinschaft an und würde die Einäscherung meiner Reste jeder anderen Bestattung vorziehen; sollte allerdings meine Frau eine Beerdigung verlangen, ist ihrem Wunsche stattzugeben. ./.

Eine größere Summe Geldes, (Rund 4.000.–
DM) und etliche belgische Franken sind nach Bezah-
lung der Hotel-Kosten und allenfalls auflaufender Spe-
sen meiner Witwe auszufolgen. Der Betrag liegt
in einem Briefumschlag auf meinem Tisch. Mein
Reisepaß liegt dabei.

Dies verfügt mit herzem Dank und Entschuldi-
gung für die Umstände, die er bereitet.

[signature]

Ehrenmitglied   (Mitglied des PEN der BRD
des oest. PEN   "   "   der Akademie der Künste,
                                        Berlin
                           "   "   der Deutschen Akademie
                                        für Sprache und Dichtung,
                                        Darmstadt
                           Preisträger des Bayer. der Akademie
                           der schönen Künste 1972
                           Lessing preis d. Stadt Hamburg
                           1977,
                           Preis für Publizistik d.
                           Stadt Wien 1977)

Die Ehrungen führe ich ausschließlich an,
dass meine Witwe entsprechend rücksichtsvoll
behandelt werde.

Tel. Nr der Hotel Regina: Wien 427681

Letter to the police authorities, written on the day of his suicide, 16 October 1978

Jean Améry prepares everything meticulously; nothing is left to chance. His farewell letters are ready. In his best handwriting he apologizes to the hotel management for giving them 'trouble'. He tells the police that 'I am taking my life of my own free will, in full possession of my mental powers.' He asks them to inform his 'wife, or widow' at once; she is at the Regina Hotel in Vienna until 19 October. On the table he leaves an envelope with a considerable sum of money to settle his hotel bill 'and other expenses'.[29]

He leaves a letter for his editor Hubert Arbogast.

A brief word from the night: forgive me the inconvenience I am probably caus-ing you. I hope Michael Klett will forgive me too: I was a bad investment. But he is kind and clever. And his father will understand, even better than he will, that a man can want to lay down his tools.

He sends greetings to his 'friend Heissenbüttel' and then turns to Arbogast again:

But above all to you, *cher ami*, thank you for so much. How sad that it is end-ing now. I leave with a sore heart, but I know that I cannot do anything else. I stood erect as long as my powers would allow. Now they are dwindling, and I must go.[30]

The other letter is for his wife Maria:[31]

Beloved little heart, my darling, to whom I kneel in guilt as I die –

I am on the way to freedom. It is not easy, but it means release. Think of me without resentment, if you can, and without too much tormenting pain. You know all that I have to tell you: that I loved you endlessly and yours is the last image before my eyes. You see, my heart's darling, I have come to the end of my strength and cannot bear to watch my intellectual, physical and psychological decline. And think of the fine poem by Christian Wagner that you once cut out for me.

I have lived an upright life, with the exception of those vile years, and I will die an upright man (well, by means of stuff that can be reduced to powder). You are all I am concerned about. It is some small comfort to me that you are financially reasonably secure, if on a modest basis. I feel, like poor Charles, 'ter-rible' when I think of you, and am wretched. But you have always understood me and so, on this last evening of my life, I hope that you will also understand me this last time.

Please, please do not feel angry with me – indeed I feel now as if I could guess that you will forgive me in the end. A shimmer, a faint presentiment of peace of mind.

Go to Vienna, dear heart, where you have close friends. Thank you for everything, for so much, for the Jean Améry who existed only through you and with you.

I kiss you with deep love.

Your Pink

(Please don't throw our 'rag children' away ...)

P.S. Mary. She came to Europe on my insistence. Her flight back to Pocatello ought to be assured, and something for her first weeks there. My dearest wish is one I hardly dare to express: it is that some day you might embrace her as a sister again.

Afterwards

He was expected not just in Mannheim but at the Frankfurt Book Fair as well. When the news from Salzburg broke in Frankfurt, the world of books there held its breath for a moment. There was not a single obituary that did not praise the essayist Jean Améry's moral authority to the skies.[32] Irony of ironies, only the *BILD-Zeitung* gives him the epitaph he had so longed for: 'Suicidal novelist Améry lay dead in his hotel – poisoned!' (19.10.78).

In 1938 Jean Améry is hunted out of the country like the spawn of the Devil. In 1978 he is buried there as 'the darling of the gods' in a grave of honour in Vienna.[33]

Gravestone, Vienna Central Cemetery

Appendix

List of abbreviations: titles of works

In order of appearance

Sch	*Die Schiffbrüchigen* (1935)
PdV	'Zur Psychologie des deutschen Volkes' (1945)
GdG	*Geburt der Gegenwart* (1931)
PF	*Preface to the Future*, tr. Palmer Hilty (1984)
JSS	*Jenseits von Schuld und Sühne* (1968)
AML	*At the Mind's Limits*, tr. Sidney Rosenfeld and Stella P. Rosenfeld (1999)
ÜdA	*Über das Altern* (1968)
OA	*On Aging*. tr. John D. Barlow (1994)
UW	*Unmeisterliche Wanderjahre* (1971)
Törless	*Törless aus Robert Musil* (1971)
L	*Lefeu oder Der Abbruch* (1974)
Hasl	*Hand an sich legen*. Diskurs über den Freitod (1976)
OS	*On Suicide*, tr. John D. Barlow (1999)
Ch	*Charles Bovary*, Landarzt (1978)
Ou	*Rendezvous in Oudenaarde* (posthumously, 1978)
Ö	*Örtlichkeiten* (posthumously, 1980)
IdWg	'In den Wind gesprochen' (posthumously, 1979)

List of abbreviations: initials of persons and institutions

Institutions

DLA	Deutsches Literaturarchiv, Marbach am Neckar
SDR	Süddeutscher Rundfunk (South German Radio)
SWF	Südwestfunk (South-West Radio)
WDR	Westdeutscher Rundfunk (West German Radio)
NDR	Norddeutscher Rundfunk (North German Radio)

Persons, letters to and from

A.A.	Alfred Andersch
J.A.	Jean Améry
M.A.	Maria Améry
H.A.	Hubert Arbogast
H.B.	Heinrich Böll

K.H.B.   Karl-Heinz Bohrer
E.C.   Elias Canetti
E.F.   Ernst Fischer
E.F.   Erich Fried
H.H.   Helmut Heissenbüttel
E.K.   Ernst Klett
M.K.   Michael Klett
K.K.   Karl Korn
H.K.   Horst Krüger
M.K.   Michael Krüger
G.K.   Günter Kunert
H.K.   Heinz Kühn
E.M.   Ernst Mayer
H.P.   Hans Paeschke
H.R.S.   Heinz-Robert Schlette
E.S.   Erich Schmid
H.S.-M.   Hety Schmitt-Maas
I.W.   Inge Werner

Notes

The literary estate of Jean Améry is in the Deutsches Literaturarchiv (DLA), Marbach am Neckar.

All the unpublished manuscripts and letters are in the archive in Marbach and can be viewed there unless there is a specific note to the contrary.

Chapter 1   Village Idyll (1912–1924)

1. Jean Améry's birth certificate is in the name of Hans Maier; in the class register of Bad Ischl elementary school it appears as Hans Mayer for the school year 1920–1921 and as Hans Maier for the school year 1922–1923. In the class registers of the grammar school in Gmunden the name is given as Johann Mayer for 1923–1924 and 1924–1925. At the beginning of the 1930s his name appears in print as Hanns Mayer, for instance, in his capacity as editor of *Die Brücke*. Jean Améry himself inclines to the form 'Hans Mayer', which I will use in the following pages.
2. This 21-page manuscript, now in the DLA, Marbach, is entitled 'Gasthof zur Stadt Graz' and is dated January 1957. It is the only document in which Améry looks back at the first years of his life. The memoir breaks off in January 1925, when Améry was not yet 13 years old.
3. In: Améry, Jean, *Der Grenzgänger*. Conversation with Ingo Hermann (September 1978) in the series, 'Zeugen des Jahrhunderts', ed. Ingo Hermann, Lamuv Verlag, Göttingen December 1992, p. 21.
4. Municipal archives of Hohenems.
5. Jean Améry's letter to Franz Bertel in Bludenz (30 April 1973). DLA: 'While there were still certificates of citizenship, I had one for the municipality of Hohenems in the name of Hans Mayer.'
6. Cf. also the interview with Leo Haffner recorded in this connection, in which he describes himself officially as coming from Vorarlberg and says that his great-grandfather was an innkeeper and butcher in Hohenems, having 'come over the border' from St Gallen in Switzerland.
7. Extract from the 1617 document granting rights to Jews, to which Johannes Inama of the Jewish Museum of Hohenems kindly gave me access. Cf. also Aron Tänzer, *Die Geschichte der Juden in Hohenems*, Verlagsbuchhandlung H. Lingenhöle & Co., Bregenz 1982 (unrevised reprint).
8. Anton Legerer, 'Geisterstadt unter Denkmalschutz' in: *Jüdische Rundschau Maccabi*, 12 May 1999. 'Jewish life in Hohenems was lively and varied. Until the coming of anti-Semitic persecution around the turn of the century, manufacturers (particularly

of textiles), businessmen, street traders and craftsmen lived in the main on friendly terms with the Christian majority.'

9. Jewish Museum of Hohenems, tel. 004 3557673989, homepage: http://www.vol.at/jmh

10. My thanks to the Jewish Museum of Hohenems, which enabled me to research the genealogical table of Jean Améry's family.

11. 'Gasthof zur Stadt Graz', p. 18.

12. The original of the death certificate is in the DLA, Marbach; it comes from the 'Military Chaplaincy of the Imperial and Royal Garrison Hospital No. 10 in Innsbruck, No. 754', together with another original document; the findings of the post-mortem, in which Paul Mayer is described as a 'military driver' and by profession a businessman, resident in Feldkirch/Vorarlberg. The cause of death is given as 'impacted inguinal hernia, the illness being brought on by the stress of war' [sic], and it is signed by the doctor who performed the post-mortem on 1 August 1917.

13. Paul Mayer's grave is precisely located in his death certificate. 'Group 76B, Side I, Section 17, regimental grave.' The document is in the DLA.

14. Lore Wald, née Goldschmidt (16 October 1917), daughter of Herta Goldschmidt, the sister of Améry's mother Valerie, is Jean Améry's cousin. She spent the first 18 years of her life very close to Jean Améry, particularly during her early childhood in Vienna and Bad Ischl, where the sisters Valerie and Herta lived and worked together. She has lived in London since 1935. I owe her thanks for much information about the family, supplied during telephone conversations and on a visit of some length to her in London on 21 October 2000.

15. Cf. the 'Notification of Heads of Households' of the Residents' Registration Office of Vienna from May 1912 to December 1938, the year of Hans Mayer's emigration.

16. Picture printed in the *Marbacher Magazin*, 24 (1982), Améry. *On the Way to Oudenaarde* (hereafter referred to as *MM*, revised by Friedrich Pfäfflin, in: 'Jean Améry. Daten zu einer Biographie', p. 16.

17. 'Gasthof zur Stadt Graz', p. 10.

18. Ibid., p. 2.

19. Ibid.

20. Ibid.

21. Copy of a letter from Jean Améry to Ernst Mayer of 24 October 1964, DLA. This is the only source we have for the data of Jean Améry's education. The Phorus School in Vienna District 4 no longer has any records from this period; they were all destroyed in the war.

22. Ernst Mayer and his life's companion Erni were to enter into a suicide pact in 1980. He died; she survived.

23. 'Gasthof zur Stadt Graz', p. 1.

24. Ibid., p. 1.

25. Ibid. p. 11.

26. Jean Améry to Günter Kunert, 11 May 1975.

27. *Der Grenzgänger*, p. 106.

28. The establishment is still run under the same name, although there has been much rebuilding. A picture of Jean Améry taken in 1956 shows him in front of his mother's former inn. This was at the same time when he began writing his *Memoir*. Notice the slight change to the name of the inn in the unpublished manuscript 'Gasthof zur Stadt *Graz*'. On p. 4 of this fragment the name is first written,

undisguised, as 'Gasthof zur Stadt Prag', then 'Prag' is crossed out and corrected by hand to 'Graz'.

29. Ibid. p. 5.

30. 'When things went wrong there – in fact everything went wrong for us, as bourgeois who had come down in the world in Austria – we went to Vienna (...).' *Der Grenzgänger*, p. 21.

31. 'Gasthof zur Stadt Graz', p. 4.

32. Ibid, p. 9.

33. Ibid, p. 10.

34. Ibid.

35. Mila Theren, Améry's aunt and Valerie's sister, is also mentioned in the second supplement to No. 35 of the 'Ischler Wochenblatt' of 2 September 1906, on p. 7: 'On Thursday, Mila Theren Buchbinder gave us a guest performance of Raimann's farce (...). Frau Theren, a brilliant actress, can count the part of Josefine among her very best, and played it that evening to general admiration and applause.'

36. 'Gasthof zur Stadt Graz', p. 5.

37. At this point the memoir breaks off. Research into any further account of Améry's school education has produced no results. On page 19 of the 'Gasthof zur Stadt Graz', he says of his schooling that it 'partook of the disorder that was the fate of his entire youth'.

Chapter 2 Zirkusgasse (1924–1935)

1. Karl M. May, born in Vienna, 9 August 1893; died in Madrid, 19 April 1943.

2. One of his last works is a defence of Marlene Dietrich, whose emigration was publicly condemned in Germany as a political issue: 'Die Künstlerin Dietrich und die Öffentliche Sache' (1977). It can be found reprinted in *Jean Améry. Arbeiten zum Film*, ed. and with an afterword by Joachim Kalka, Klett-Cotta, Stuttgart 1994, pp. 28–45.

3. Conversation with Lore Wald (née Goldschmidt), London, July 2000.

4. Cf. article by Carl Junker, Vienna, November 1927: 'Festgabe. Zum fünfzigjährigen Bestande des Hauses Buchhandlung und Zeitungsbureau Hermann Goldschmid, Gesellschaft m.b.H. "Zur Geschichte des Hauses".' Kindly made available to the author by Dr Murray G. Hall.

5. Previously he had worked in the famous literary bookshop of Martin Flinker in Vienna. I have Joachim Oxenius to thank for this information.

6. Vertrauliche Akte M. section 9 – 176/59, 9 April 1959: eulogy by the Head Librarian of the city, Dr A. Mitringer, on the award of the Prize of the City of Vienna to Prof. Dr Leopold Langhammer.

7. Cf. Ernst Mayer, 'Zum Tode eines Volksbildners', unpublished MS in the DLA.

8. Langhammer's testimonial to Hans Mayer is in the files of the estate of Jean Améry in the DLA.

9. Ibid.

10. Karl Heinrich Waggerl, Austrian writer of stories (1897–1973).

11. Jean Améry, 'Ein Blick zurück', in *Weisheit der Heiterkeit,* for Ernst Schönwiese, ed. Roman Rocek, Franz Richter, Joseph Strelka, Vienna and Hamburg 1978, pp. 41–2. Cf also Dagmar Lorenz, *Scheitern als Ereignis. Der Autor Jean Améry im Kontext europäischer Kulturkritik*, Frankfurt 1991, p. 23 ff.

12. In *Die Pestsäule*, August/September 1973, pp. 704–10.

13. Many of these authors left their mark on the future writer, and Hans Mayer regarded some of them as examples to him. In the posthumously published

volume *Wiederlesen – Bücher aus der Jugend unseres Jahrhunderts*, preface by Gisela Lindemann, in: Jean Améry, *Werke*, Vol. 5, *Aufsätze zur Literatur und zum Film*, ed. Hans Höller, Klett-Cotta, Stuttgart 2003, pp. 243–503, Jean Améry could be said to describe the course of his literary socialization, like the earlier *Unmeisterliche Wanderjahre* tracing the journey from darkness into light.

14. Cf. Johann Dvorʾak, 'Die Emigration österreichischer wissenschaftlicher Intelligenz und die Wiener Volksbildung 1918 bis 1938', in ed. Friedrich Stadler, *Vertriebene Vernunft*, Vienna and Munich 1987, pp. 343–58.

15. Ibid., pp. 343–4.

16. Ibid., p. 344.

17. Ibid.

18. Ibid., p. 345.

19. Friedrich Albert Moritz Schlick, born 1882, who succeeded to Mach's professorial chair, 'was murdered by a former student for private and ideological political reasons. The murderer was released before the end of his sentence by the National Socialists, and after 1945 lived at liberty in Austria. This event marked the final destruction of the Vienna Circle.' Author of the 'Allgemeine Erkenntnislehre', 1918. Cf. Friedrich Stadler, *Studien zum Wiener Kreis. Ursprung, Entwicklung und Wirkung des logischen Empirismus im Kontext*, Frankfurt 1997, p. 775 ff.

20. Rudolf Carnap (1891–1979), a protégé of Schlick. *Der logische Aufbau der Welt*, 1938. Cf. Stadler, p. 667 ff.

21. Cf. the interview of 1978 in Hohenems, Vorarlberg, with Leo Haffner (ORF).

22. Ernst Mach (1838–1916), was a physicist, psychologist and historian of science and ideas. 'The polyhistorian Ernst Mach was of importance both as a central figure in Vienna at the turn of the century and as a reformer in the field of the natural sciences. His attempt to create a historically social and evolutionary basis of science – in close connection with his political practice – was very much in the spirit of the French and British Enlightenment.' Fritz Mauthner (1849–1923), linguistic philosopher and journalist, main work *Beiträge zu einer Kritik der Sprache* (1901), in which an anti-metaphysical and nominalistic critique of language is presented, conducted a lively correspondence with Ernst Mach; cf. Friedrich Stadler, *Studien zum Wiener Kreis*, p. 65 ff. (Mach) and p. 153 ff. (Mauthner).

23. Very enlightening in this connection is Gerhard Scheit's afterword in: Jean Améry, *Werke*, Vol. 6, *Aufsätze zur Philosophie*, Klett-Cotta, Stuttgart 2004, in particular the chapter 'Preconditons: Positivism in Vienna, Existentialism in France', pp. 612–25.

24. In: *Der Wiener Bote*, from the *Marbacher Magazin* 24 (1982), p. 16. The journal is no longer to be found.

25. *Die Brücke*, critical essays, ed. H. and E. Mayer, Vienna III, 11 Kolonitzgasse. Cover by Carl Pecina. Series 1. February 1934, 16 pp. From this issue, Hanns and Ernst Mayer, 'Foreword', pp. 1–2; Hanns Mayer, 'The present situation in German literature', p. 3 ff. The journal consists of four issues, which can be seen in the DLA.

26. Letter from Jean Améry to Ernst Mayer, 12 December 1964, DLA. The letter purports to be written in memory of the February Uprising.

27. Cf. Ernst Hanisch: 'This was the fourth trauma of the First Republic – the civil war of 12–15 February 1934, with hundreds of dead, the crushing of social democracy, over 10,000 arrests, and nine death sentences carried out. (...) The Dolfuss government was victorious. The way was open to dictatorship disguised as the corporative state.' In: *Österreichische Geschichte 1890–1990*, ed. Herwig Wolfram, Vienna 194, p. 306.

28. From *Örtlichkeiten* [Localities] in: Jean Améry, *Werke*, Vol. 2, *Jenseits von Schuld und Sühne, Unmeisterliche Wanderjahre, Örtlichkeiten*, ed. Gerhard Scheit, Klett-Cotta, Stuttgart 2002, pp. 369–70.
29. Ibid, p. 374.
30. Ibid.

Chapter 3 *Die Schiffbrüchigen*
[The Shipwrecked] (1935–1945)

1. Cf. Dagmar Lorenz, *Scheitern als Ereignis. Der Autor Jean Améry im Kontext Europäischer Kulturkritik*, p. 42.
2. Cf. Jean Améry, 'Bergwanderung. Noch ein Wort zu Thomas Mann', in: Jean Améry *Werke*, Vol. 5, ed. Hans Höller, *Aufsätze zur Literatur und zum Film*, Klett-Cotta, Stuttgart 2003, pp. 24–51, p. 25; see also Hans Höller, afterword, 'Gebrochene Kontinuität: Thomas Mann', pp. 590–3.
3. In: *Die Schiffbrüchigen*, p. 377, MS in the literary estate of Jean Améry in the DLA: published for the first time by Klett-Cotta in 2007, with an afterword by Irène Heidelberger-Leonard: 'This Philistine Eugen Althager was a man of medium height, rather slightly built. A man with ridiculously slender wrists, his right wrist encircled by a small gold chain.'
4. 'Die Tortur', in *Jenseits von Schuld und Sühne*, Jean Améry, *Werke*, Vol. 2, p. 69. English version, *At the Mind's Limits*, tr. Sidney Rosenfeld and Stella P. Rosenfeld, p. 30.
5. Letter to Maria Leitner, later Maria Améry, of 13 May 1949.
6. Letter to Maria Leitner of 28 November 1949.
7. Letter to Ernst Schönwiese of 9 October 1950.
8. Ibid.
9. It was also published, together with *Lefeu oder Der Abbruch*, as Volume 1 in Jean Améry, *Werke*, in the spring of 2008.
10. *Der Grenzgänger*, p. 74.
11. Ibid., p. 75.
12. Hermann Hakel (1911–87), poet, editor and critic, emigrated to Italy in 1939, where he was interned in various camps in the south of the country, emigrated to Palestine in 1945 and returned to Vienna by way of Rome in 1947. In 1935 he was editor of the *Jahrbuch 1935*. Poetry and short prose pieces by young authors and Austrian authors, from *Lexikon der österreichischen Exilliteratur*, ed. Siglinde Bolbecher, Konstantin Kaiser, pp. 275–7. Hermann Hakel remembers Jean Améry in a bitterly resentful short piece, a mixture of invention and fact. 'Wie aus Hans Mayer Jean Améry geworden ist' [How Hans Mayer became Jean Améry], in Hermann Hakel, *Dürre Äste, welkes Gras. Begegnungen mit Literaten. Bemerkungen zur Literatur*, ed. Gerhard Ammanshauser, E. Kovic, Richard Kovacevic. With a foreword by Hans Raimund, Vienna: Lynkeus 1991, pp. 121–9. The publication of *Die Entwurzelten*, mentioned above, is indirectly confirmed here: 'Hans, then 22 years old, had trained as a bookseller and – as he said frankly at the time – was an uncircumcised half-Jew, son of an anonymous father and a housekeeper or cook. (...) One of the friends of Mayer's youth was the present Hofrat Meier [*sic*] of the Ministry of Education, with whom he edited at the time one or two issues of a hectographed journal. Both were brothers of the mists, "moved by nature", wavering between Knut Hamsun, Hermann Hesse and Thomas Mann. In Hans's view at the time, the finest of poems

was Hans Leifhelm's "Mit dem Sichelmond, mit dem Abendstern (...)" [With crescent moon and evening star].' He adds that 'he also loved to philosophize, to throw terms out for discussion and strike you with them (...) If it had not been for his birth, which disqualified him, and his love for his very pretty Jewish girlfriend, Mayer would probably have become a Nazi intellectual. His darkly aggressive nature, his inclination to make doctrinaire statements, and his hidden love for nature and romantic forest wanderings would have fitted him for that role very well.' (pp. 121–3.) On the philosophical and poetic differences between Jean Améry and Hermann Hakel, cf. Dagmar Lorenz in: *Ein besonderer Mensch. Erinnerungen an Hermann Hakel*, Vienna 1988, pp. 170–5.

13. Letter to Friedrich Pfäfflin of 13 September 1982.
14. The summary of the novel is printed in the *Marbacher Magazin* 24/1982, pp. 41–4.
15. Cf. Stefan Braese, 'I can hardly grasp what happened.' In *Jean Améry. Der Schriftsteller*, ed. Irene Heidelberger-Leonard, Hans Höller, Verlag Hans-Dieter Heinz. Akademischer Verlag, Stuttgart 2000, pp. 37–50.
16. Cf. André Combes, 'Jean Amérys Thomas Mann-Lektüre', pp. 67–91, and Hans Höller, 'Der Schriftsteller als Leser', pp. 51–63, in *Jean Améry. Der Schriftsteller*.
17. Althager's duel is also associated with Naphta's duel from Thomas Mann's *Zauberberg*. 'Mentioning the tragic and pointless death of the Jesuit Naphta only in passing, Heinrich Hessl had spoken of Eugen's duel.' *Die Schiffbrüchigen*, p. 346.
18. A certain Odette, based on Marcel Proust's Odette, is thought to have been the model for the girlfriend. The model for Hessl – with some adaptation – will have been his school friend and co-editor Ernst Mayer, who is subjected to strong criticism in the novel and is sometimes described with great resentment.
19. In: *Die Brücke*, October 1934, p. 5.
20. Cf. Jean Améry, 'Positivismus', four-page unpublished manuscript, DLA.
21. Undated handwritten letter to Ernst Mayer, incomplete, DLA.
22. From 'Mit finsterer Entschlossenheit', 'Nachmittagspost', transcribed version p. 49.
23. Ibid. p. 75.
24. Five handwritten fragments belong to the papers with *Die Schiffbrüchigen*, access number 81.49: first, prose fragment 76 sheets; second, 16 sheets; third, 42 sheets with the titles 'A Journey around Death in 80 Hours' and 'The Fortress of Derloven'; fourth, four sheets with the title 'The Way It Was'; fifth, 'A Letter Sent Into the Unknown'.
25. First prose fragment, transcribed version, p. 54.
26. In: 'Beate', transcribed version, p. 15.
27. The manuscript is in the DLA. This text, which must be regarded as an early study for 'Torture', is 54 pages long in transcription.
28. Cf. Jean-Michel Chaumont, *Die Konkurrenz der Opfer. Genozid, Identität und Anerkennung*, Klampen, Lüneburg 2001.
29. Ibid. p. 49.
30. According to a letter from the Israelite community of Vienna to Friedrich Pfäfflin (6 September 1982), Hans/Chaim Mayer left the Jewish community on 5 December 1933 and rejoined on 15 November 1937. His parents – Paul Maier and Valerie Maier, born Goldschmidt – were married at the Israelite Community on 5 July 1908. The marriage of Hans Maier and Regine Berger or Baumgarten took place at the Israelite Community of Vienna on 12 December 1937.
31. *Örtlichkeiten*, Vol. 2, p. 374.
32. Ibid, p. 376.

33. From: Jean Améry, 'Verfemt und verbannt' [Taboo and exiled]. 30 years ago – memories of emigration. Manuscript for Deutschlandfunk, broadcast 17 February 1969, in: Jean Améry, *Werke*, Vol. 2, pp. 790–814, p. 814.

Chapter 4   Years of Wandering (1938–1945)

1. 'Wieviel Heimat braucht der Mensch?' in Jean Améry, *Werke*, Vol. 2, pp. 86–117, p. 90; AML p. 44.
2. From: Jean Améry, 'Verfemt und verbannt' [Taboo and exiled], 30 years ago – memories of emigration. Manuscript for Deutschlandfunk, broadcast 17 February 1969, in: Jean Améry *Werke*, Vol. 2, pp. 790–814, p. 790. The editor Manfred Franke remembers Jean Améry's 'obvious scepticism' on being asked 'to tell the tale' of his emigration. 'The 1938 flight from Vienna by way of Cologne and Kalterherberg to Antwerp' was regarded by Jean Améry, he says, as '"an anti-success-story" by comparison with the emigration of the great and famous'.
3. Ibid., p. 791.
4. Ibid., p. 792.
5. Cf. *Enzyklopädie des Holocaust. Die Verfolgung und Ermordung der europäischen Juden* Vol. 2, ed. E. Jäckel, P. Longerich, J.H. Schoeps, Argon, p. 1074 ff. Cf. also Ernst Hanisch, *Österreichische Geschichte 1890–1990. Der lange Schatten des Staates,* Vienna 1994, pp. 38–42, pp. 337–94.
6. *Enzyklopädie des Holocaust*, Vol. 2, p. 1075.
7. Ibid.
8. 'Verfemt und verbannt', p. 795.
9. Ibid., p. 795.
10. In the original version of 'Verfemt und verbannt' (a manuscript for radio) it is described as 'his unpublished (...) novel', in Jean Améry *Werke*, Vol. 2, the passage is wrongly printed as 'his published (...) novel.' Cf. 'Verfemt und verbannt', p. 797.
11. Cf. Gerhard Scheit's afterword in Jean Améry, *Werke*, Vol. 2, particularly Scheit's documentation and his commentary on *Örtlichkeiten*, where Améry himself reflects on his flight from Vienna to Antwerp and internment in Gurs. Cf. *Örtlichkeiten*, Vol. 2, pp. 355–422, and 'Verfemt und verbannt', pp. 789–853.
12. Ibid., p. 801.
13. On the Jewish population of Antwerp and the work of the Jewish Aid Committee, see Lieven Saerens, *Vreemdelingen in een Wereldstad. Een geschiedenis van Antwerpen en zijn joodse bevolking (1880–1944),* Uitgeverij Lannoonv, Tielt 2000. See also M. Steinberg, *Le dossier Bruxelles-Auschwitz. La police SS et l'extermination des Juifs de Belgique,* Brussels 1980; idem, *L'étoile et le fusil* (3 vols), Brussels 1984; idem, *Un pays occupé et ses juifs. Belgique entre France et Pays Bas,* Brussels 1998.
14. 'Verfemt und verbannt', p. 803.
15. Ibid., p. 807.
16. Further information on Erich Schmid may be found in Hans Mayer's article for the *St. Gallener Tagblatt* 5 April 1959, 'Die neuen Mönche. Bildnisse (un)berühmter Zeitgenossen. Unbekannter Maler E.S.', published in the *MM*, p. 44.
17. *Örtlichkeiten*, Vol. 2, pp. 395–6.
18. Particularly useful in this connection is the collection of documents entitled *Österreicher im Exil, Belgien 1938–1945,* ed. the Documentation Archive of the Austrian Resistance, selected and adapted by Dr Ulrich Weinzierl, introduction Gundl Herrnstadt-Steinmetz, Vienna 1987.

19. The newspaper article was in the private archive of Maria Améry, now in the DLA, Marbach.
20. The author thanks Dr Heinz Pollak for telephone conversations and the informative interview in Vienna on 6 December 2000.
21. *Örtlichkeiten*, Vol. 2, pp. 402–3.
22. Ibid., p. 402.
23. Ibid., p. 401.
24. Ibid., p. 406.
25. *Unmeisterliche Wanderjahre*, Vol. 2, pp. 183–349, p. 239.
26. 'Verfemt und verbannt', p. 812.
27. *Enzyklopädie des Holocaust 1*, p. 585.
28. 'Verfemt und verbannt', p. 812.
29. My thanks to Jacques Sonnenschein (d. 2002) for his valuable information and the conversations I was able to have with him in June 2000 and November 2001.
30. *Örtlichkeiten*, Vol. 2, p. 409.
31. I owe this information to Ilya Prigogine, winner of the Nobel Prize for Chemistry, professor at the Université libre de Bruxelles, who was a friend of Hans Mayer/Jean Améry until the latter's suicide in 1978.
32. The headmaster of the school, Ch. Cymring, made out a written confirmation of his activity as a teacher on 19 June 1942, which can be seen in the DLA.
33. Gundl Herrnstadt-Steinmetz, 'Jean Améry, Widerstandskämpfer und Schriftsteller' in:*Österreichische Exilliteratur in den Niederlanden 1934–1940*, ed. Hans Würzner, *Amsterdamer Publikationen zur Sprache und Literatur*, 70th Vol., Amsterdam 1986, pp. 97–105.
34. A certificate of 2 May 1945 confirms his membership of the Front National Autrichien, signed by General Secretary Dori Meisemann. Another certificate is made out for him by the Front de l'Indépendance, Secrétariat National, with which the Austrian Freedom Front was associated. Finally, there is a third document in the form of a letter (26.12.69) to George Wellers, chairman of the Comité International des Camps, in which he gives the following information about his activities in the Resistance: 'I was active in Brussels in the Front National Autrichien movement (affiliated to the Front de l'Indépendance). I was arrested in July 1943 and deported successively to Breendonck, Malines (Belgium), Auschwitz-Monowitz, Dora, Bergen-Belsen (647 days of internment in all). I am recognized as a political prisoner by the Commission de l'Etat (order number E.15.058) and I was awarded the Croix du Prisonnier Politique.' All these documents may be seen in the DLA.
35. Thanks here to the Resistance workers Harry Zimmermann (Vienna) and in particular Regine Krochmal (Brussels), a close friend of Marianne Brandt, for the information they kindly supplied.
36. Marianne Brandt did not survive deportation.
37. *Jenseits von Schuld und Sühne*, Vol. 2, pp. 59–60; AML p. 24.
38. *Österreicher im Exil*, p. 49.
39. *Jenseits von Schuld und Sühne*, Vol. 2, p. 56; AML p. 22.
40. 'Reise um den Tod: Die Festung Derloven', page numbers from a typewritten transcript, p. 8.
41. 'Reise um den Tod: Die Festung Derloven', pp. 11–12.
42. Ibid., p. 12.
43. Ibid., p. 13.
44. Ibid., p. 14.

45. Ibid., p. 15.
46. Ibid., p. 16.
47. Ibid., p. 18.
48. Ibid., p. 22.
49. Ibid., p. 30.
50. *Jenseits von Schuld und Sühne*, Vol. 2, pp. 69–70; AML p. 25.
51. See Jan Philipp Reemtsma, '172364. Gedanken über den Gebrauch der ersten Person Singular bei Jean Améry', Jean Améry (Hans Maier), ed. Stephan Steiner, pp. 63–86, here p. 63.
52. I am thinking here in particular of the two essays in *Jenseits von Schuld und Sühne*: 'Ressentiments' and 'Über Zwang und Unmöglichkeit, Jude zu sein'. [Eng. 'Resentments' and 'On the Necessity and Impossibility of Being a Jew'.]
53. *Jenseits von Schuld und Sühne*, Vol. 2, p. 61; AML p. 30.
54. Ibid., p. 71; AML p. 31.
55. Ibid., p. 75; AML p. 34.
56. Ibid., p. 79; AML p. 36.
57. Cf. M. Steinberg, 'Malines', in: *Regards*: 128 (1979), pp. 6–13; idem, 'Le dossier Bruxelles Auschwitz', Brussels 1980.
58. Grateful thanks here to Ilya Prigogine (25 January 1917–28 May 2003) for several telephonic conversations in October 2001. After Hans Mayer's liberation Prigogine and his wife, who incidentally 'collected' him on his arrival in Brussels, supported him financially and took an active part in his reintegration. The relationship was at times a very intense one: Prigogine respected the uncompromising writer and thinker, Améry had a high regard for the brilliant natural scientist. In 1971 they even collaborated on a joint publication and broadcast on 'Die tragische Philosophie Jacques Monods'. Cf. *Merkur*, 25/1971/283, pp. 1108–15.
59. Letter, 29.12.43. Source, *Marbacher Magazin*, Améry, ed. Friedrich Pfäfflin, p. 22.
60. Ibid.
61. Two manuscripts have been preserved, both of them fascinating anticipations of the later essays 'At the Mind's Limits' and 'Resentments' in *Jenseits von Schuld und Sühne* [At the Mind's Limits]. These works seem to have been conceived together and are collected under the title 'Zur Psychologie des deutschen Volkes', with a first sub-title 'Weder Schuld noch Sühne'. The beginning of the second part, 'Arbeit macht unfrei', seems to have been partly conceived in Monowitz. The signature at the end of both essays runs: 'Brussels, June 1945'. In: Jean Améry, *Werke*, Vol. 2, pp. 500–34.
62. On the initiative of the Fritz Bauer Institute, a quotation from Améry can now be seen on the commemorative plaque of the former IG Farben building. I owe this information to Werner Renz (letter of 4.9.2003).
63. 'Zur Psychologie des deutschen Volkes', Vol. 2, pp. 513–14.
64. Ibid., p. 516.
65. *Örtlichkeiten*, Vol. 2, p. 439.
66. 'Brief ins Ungewisse', transcript, p. 1, the last sentence, 'mich für sie zu interessieren', is crossed out, and an obviously incomplete replacement 'sie ziemlich (?) zu nehmen' written in beside it.
67. 'Die Festung Derloven', p. 26.
68. Cf. Ruth Klüger, *weiter leben. Eine Jugend*, Göttingen 1992 [English version: *Still Alive*, New York 2001]. It concerns her relationship with Christoph, who asks Auschwitz survivors no questions: 'I too wanted life to go on, I didn't want to be

like Lot's wife, turned to stone in looking back at the city of the dead. I wanted to get away from those who had been through the same experiences as me. Christoph's company made it easier not to talk about the incomprehensible injustice of my origin, but at the same time I felt the urge to talk about it after all, to include it in the new beginning. It was a question of [wanting to talk about it and not wanting to talk about it].' p. 213.

69. 'Die Festung Derloven', p. 26.

70. 'Nach fünftausend Zeitungsartikeln', in: *Wie ich anfing*, ed. Hans Daiber, Claasen, Düsseldorf 1979, p. 221.

71. Hety Schmitt-Maas to Jean Améry, 10.9.67.

72. Hermann Langbein (1912–1995), member of the Committee of the International Resistance Organization in Auschwitz. Secretary of the 'Comité International des camps'. Publications: *Der Auschwitz-Prozess. Eine Dokumentation* (2 vols), Europa Verlag, Vienna 1965. *Menschen in Auschwitz*, 1972.

73. Letter to Hety Schmitt-Maas of 28.9.67.

74. Letter to Dr Ferdinand Meyer of 16.10.67.

75. In: Gabriella Poli and Giorgio Calcagno, *Echi di nua voce perduta. Incontri, interviste e conversazioni con Primo Levi*, Milan 1992, p. 336.

76. Primo Levi, 'The Intellectual in Auschwitz', in: *The Drowned and the Saved*, tr. from the Italian by Raymond Rosenthal, pp. 104–5.

77. Ibid. p. 102.

78. W.G. Sebald, 'Jean Améry und Primo Levi', in: *Über Jean Améry*, ed. Irene Heidelberger-Leonard, Heidelberg 1990, pp. 115–23.

79. Ibid., p. 116.

80. Primo Levi, 'The Intellectual in Auschwitz', p. 105.

81. 'An den Grenzen des Geistes', in: *Jenseits von Schuld und Sühne*, Vol. 2, p. 29; AML p. 5.

82. Ibid., 2, p. 32; AML p. 7.

83. Ibid., 2, p. 83; AML p. 9.

84. Primo Levi, *If This Is a Man*, tr. Stuart Woolf, p. 135.

85. 'An den Grenzen des Geistes', in: *Jenseits von Schuld und Sühne*, p. 52; AML pp. 19/20.

86. Primo Levi, 'The Intellectual in Auschwitz', p. 114.

87. 'An den Grenzen des Geistes', in: *Jenseits von Schuld und Sühne*, Vol. 2, p. 25; AML p. 2.

88. Cf. Stephan Steiner: 'In extremis: Gewalt und Gegengewalt im Werk von Jean Améry', pp. 99–110.

89. W.G. Sebald, 'Jean Améry und Primo Levi', p. 119.

90. Myriam Anissimov, 'The autopsy of the Institute of Forensic Medicine confirms the suicide, although Rita Levi Montalcini and David Mendel still do not believe it.' In: *Primo Levi. Die Tragödie eines Optimisten*, Berlin 1999, p. 562.

91. Cf. Primo Levi, 'The Intellectual in Auschwitz', in *The Drowned and the Saved,* pp. 102–120. The Italian original, *I sommersi e I salvati*, Turin 1986, appeared a year before the death of Primo Levi (1919–1987).

92. 'Torture', in: *Jenseits von Schuld und Sühne*, Vol.2, p. 83; AML, p. 39.

93. 'How Much Home Does a Person Need?' in: *Jenseits von Schuld und Sühne*, Vol. 2, p. 80; AML, p. 43.

94. The only document that helps us to track the facts of Regine's death is a tiny card (in Maria Améry's private archive, now in the DLA) dated 5 April 1950 – five years after

Hans Mayer's return from the camp, with the sender's name given as the convent of 'Les Filles de la Charité de Saint Vincent de Paul'. Obviously this is a reply to a letter from Hans Mayer, thanking the nuns for nursing his wife until her death. It has been rumoured that while her husband was in the camps Regine Mayer converted to Catholicism, and indeed the nuns' reply suggests as much: 'Monsieur, thank you for your kind letter. What I did for Madame Mayer was done from my heart. She was so pleasant, and always so thoughtful and grateful, and above all only too courageous. She is happy now on high, and prays for you, for she loved you very much. I ask nothing from you, Monsieur, but if you should happen to think of our good works, done for charity, or almost entirely so, I would be very grateful.' It is signed by Soeur Madeleine. Only on 24 July 1950 was Hans Mayer able to apply to the city of Brussels for a death certificate for his wife (d. 1944), 'Regine Baumgarten, known as Berger.' A copy of the certificate is dated 19 July 1950. Regine Mayer died on 24 April at 2 a.m., 'tous autres renseignements nous manquent' [we have no further information], and it is signed by Ludovicus Claes. These documents are in the private archive of Maria Améry, now in the DLA.

95. *Die Dornenkrone der Liebe* [Love's Crown of Thorns], (1945) – the title *Distelkrone der Liebe* [Love's Crown of Thistles] was also contemplated – is the provisional title for the planned revision of the novel *Die Schiffbrüchigen* (1935).

Chapter 5　　Living On – but How and Where? (1945–1955)

1. Hanns Mayer, *Erzählung eines ländliches Lebens*, in his literary estate in the DLS, handwritten manuscript of 18 sheets.
2. *Heinrich Greyt*, 'Schauspiel in drei Akten', 1946. Typescript, 65 pages, in his literary estate in the DLA.
3. In his literary estate, DLA, typescript of 36 sheets.
4. Printed in the *Marbacher Magazin*, pp. 73–79, here p. 73.
5. *Die Selbstmörder*, in his literary estate, DLA, typescript of 93 sheets.
6. In his literary estate, DLA. Typescript of nine pages, with the comment *Kleist-Novelle*; he mentions working on this novella in a letter to Maria Leitner of 16 November 1949: 'I would like to write a novella about Kleist – bringing his suicide pact with Henriette Vogel into our own time.'
7. Ibid, p. 2.
8. Ibid., p. 5.
9. Ibid., p. 9.
10. In his literary estate in the DLA, 106 sheets.
11. Hanns Mayer. 'Der Existentialismus in Frankreich. Revolution des Geistes? Mode? Oder Dämmerung des "Esprit français"?' (1945), in his literary estate in the DLA, five sheets dated Brussels, December 1945 and signed 'Dr H. Mayer'. The 'Dr' is struck out on p. 5.
12. In German, the roots of Améry's later volume of essays *Jenseits von Schuld und Sühne* [*At the Mind's Limits*] are evident here, more than 20 years earlier, in the subtitle of *Weder Schuld noch Sühne* for this work of 1945.
13. 'Zur Psychologie des deutschen Volkes', Jean Améry, *Werke*, Vol. 2, Klett-Cotta, Stuttgart 2002, pp. 507–8. The quotation is from Friedrich Nietzsche's *Antichrist*, Vol. 2, works in three volumes ed. Karl Schlechta, Munich 1966, p. 1165. In context, it runs: 'What is good? – All that heightens the sense of power, the will as power, power itself in humanity. / What is bad? – All that stems from weakness. /

What is happiness? – the feeling that power is *growing* – that resistance has been overcome. / Not contentment but more power, *not* peace anyway but war, *not* virtue but efficiency (which is virtue as understood in the Renaissance, *virtù,* virtue free of self-righteousness). / The weak and failures should be done away with: that is the first principle of *our* love of mankind. And let us help them further. / What is more harmful than vice of any kind? – Compassion for what is done, with all its failures and weaknesses – Christianity.' Améry's attitude to Nietzsche becomes much less clear in later years. The author of *Hand an sich legen* [*On Suicide*] will cite Nietzsche and his remarks on suicide in support of his own frame of mind. Cf. also his empathetic essay 'Nietzsche – der Zeitgenosse' [Nietzsche – our contemporary]. In 'Schopenhauer als Erzieher' [Schopenhauer as teacher], *Merkur,* 29 / 1975/331, pp. 1141–49, Améry expressly revises his verdict of 1945, which was, in fact, not unusual at this time. '(I) see in Nietzsche, then, not the ancestor of Nazi barbarity, but a subjectively anarchistic revolt against the masses', p. 1147.

14. On 7 May 1945 Hamsun, in old age, published an obituary of Hitler in the Norwegian newspaper *Afterposten.* 'I am not worthy to speak out on Adolf Hitler. (...) He was a (...) warrior for humanity, carrying the gospel of justice to all nations. He was a reforming figure of the highest standing (...). We, his faithful supporters, now bow our heads at the news of his death.' Quoted from Eberhard Rathgeb, 'Kokon aus Weisheit und Wahrheit. Genug gesät: Knut Hamsun's erzählerischer Prozess gegen sich selbst.' *FAZ* 21.10.2002.

15. Letter of farewell to Knut Hamsun, written 1945, in his literary estate, DLA.

16. Ibid.

17. Cf. Jean Améry, 'Die Feinde der Zivilisation. Hamsun und die Seinen', in *Bücher aus der Jugend unseres Jahrhunderts*, Jean Améry *Werke,* Vol. 5, ed. Hans Höller, pp. 245–50.

18. Ibid., p. 247.

19. In her letter to Hans Mayer of 17.12.49, Maria Leitner quotes a passage from a letter he wrote her in 1946.

20. Maria Eschenauer (b. Vienna 20 March 1911), was a Catholic, professionally a 'business worker', the daughter of the 'local government official Franz Georg Eschenauer and his wife Maria, née Appel'. In addition, the following information can be gleaned from her Viennese marriage certificate: she married Dr Rudolf Leitner (her first husband) on 3 August 1936. Rudolf Leitner, 'of the Mosaic confession', is described as a 'sales representative'. He too was born in Vienna and was 16 years older than Maria.

21. The original of the legal divorce, made out by the district court for ZRS in Vienna on 21 March 1955, legally in force from 25 January 1955 and headed 'In the Name of the Republic', is in the private archive of Maria Améry.

22. Letter from Maria Leitner to Hans Mayer from New York, 8.11.49.

23. Kurt Peter Schindel or Pierre C. Schindel (1911–2001), described on his visiting card as 'docteur en Sciences chimique A.C. Br.' He was Jean Améry's literary executor until his death.

24. Cf. letter from Hans Mayer to Maria Leitner, 16.11.49.

25. As phrased in a letter to Ernst Mayer of 21.9.71.

26. Title of the posthumous volume published by Klett-Cotta, with an afterword by Manfred Franke, Stuttgart 1980, now in the new edition of Jean Améry, *Werke,* Vol. 2, with documentation and commentary by Gerhard Scheit, pp. 351–489.

27. This letter is undated and incomplete.

28. Ernst Mayer to Hans Mayer, Vienna, 5 February 1846. In the literary estate, DLA.
29. Ibid.
30. Cf. Jean Améry, 'Aspekte des Österreichischen', in: *Im Brennpunkt: Ein Österreich*, ed. Manfred Wagner, Vienna 1976, pp. 9–18.
31. Ibid., p. 18.
32. In: Jean Améry, 'Verfemt und verbannt'. Vor dreissig Jahren – Erinnerungen an die Emigration. Manuscript for German Radio. 1968/1969, printed in the documentation of Jean Améry, *Werke*, Vol. 2, pp. 790–814.
33. Heinz Kühn, born like Hans Mayer in 1912, in Cologne, returned to that city in 1946. He was foreign editor and then editor-in-chief of the *Rheinische Zeitung*, Cologne (1946–50), chairman of the parliamentary SPD party in the Düsseldorf Landtag from 1962, prime minister of North Rhine-Westphalia from 1966. His successor in the post was Johannes Rau. In 1983 he was chairman of the Friedrich-Ebert-Stiftung. He wrote his memoirs in *Widerstand und Emigration. Die Jahre 1928 bis 1945* (1980) and *Aufbau und Bewährung. Die Jahre 1945–1980* (1981). He died of complications following a stroke in 1992. Eulogies at his funeral were delivered by Johannes Rau and Willy Brandt. I owe the information about Heinz Kühn and Willi Eichler to the kind assistance of Christoph Stamm, archivist of the Friedrich-Ebert-Stiftung, letter of 28.6.2002. Cf. Dieter Düding, *Heinz Kühn*. Eine politische Biographie. Klartext Verlag, Essen 2002.
34. Willi Eichler (1886–1971), influential theoretician of Democratic Socialism 1945 onwards. Became chairman of the International Socialist Combat League in 1947 and was editor-in-chief of its journal *Der Funke*. Emigrated to Paris in 1933 and then to Great Britain by way of Luxembourg. Returned to Germany after the war, led the merging of the International Socialist Combat League with the SPD. Editor of the monthly magazine *Geist und Tat* 1946–1971. Chairman of the programming committee for a new SPD party programme, the 'Godesberger Programm' of 1959.
35. Letter from Heinz Kühn to Willi Eichler, Brussels, November 1945. Printed by permission of the Friedrich Ebert Stiftung.
36. In a letter from Willi Eichler to Heinz Kühn of 2.6.45, an unnamed manuscript by 'Hans Meier' is mentioned as being sent to him by the author for publication. Judging by the timing and the subject, this can only have been 'On the Psychology of the German People'.
37. *Örtlichkeiten*, Vol. 2, p. 443.
38. In the outline of *Örtlichkeiten*, Vol. 2, pp. 826–7.
39. Hans Mayer to Maria Leitner 1.6.49.
40. *Örtlichkeiten*, Vol. 2, p. 465.
41. Other newspapers and journals to be mentioned are the *Basler Nachrichten*, the *Berner Bund*, the *Burgdorfer Tagblatt*, the *Luzerner Neueste(n) Nachrichten*, the *National Zeitung Basel*, the *Neuer Berner Zeitung*, the *Tagesanzeiger Zürich* and the *Thurgauer Zeitung*. The source for these data is the *Marbacher Magazin*, ed. Friedrich Pfäfflin, p. 60.
42. Source: http://wwwrundschau.ch/showart.asp?ID=632 kindly communicated to me by Ruth Aeberli of the Dukas Press Agency in a letter of 2.3.2002.
43. Frank Dukas to Friedrich Pfäfflin, letter of 16.8.82 from Zürich.
44. Ibid.
45. 'Aspekte des Österreichischen', p. 10. Cf. on this subject Jean Améry, 'Flämischer Löwe und Gallischer Hahn', in *Merkur* no. 227, 1967, pp. 196–8.

46. Hans Mayer to Maria Leitner, letter undated except for 'Thursday', but judging by the context and the address, '56 rue Veydt', it was probably written in January.
47. Hans Mayer to Maria Leitner from Adelboden, dated 2.2.49. There is a lively correspondence between Hans Mayer and Maria Leitner between 1948 and 1952, especially during the time he spent in Adelboden.
48. Ibid.
49. Letter from Hans Mayer to Maria Leitner, Adelboden, 12.3.49.
50. Letter from Hans Mayer to Maria Leitner, Brussels, 57 rue Veydt, 2.5.49.
51. Letter from Hans Mayer to Maria Leitner 2.6.49.
52. Ibid.
53. Letter from Hans Mayer to Maria Leitner, Adelboden, 23.3.49.
54. Rue Veydt, his second address in Brussels (Ixelles), where he rented a room.
55. Letter from Hans Mayer to Maria Leitner 11.11.49.

Chapter 6   Jean Améry the Journalist (1955–1965)

1. Hans Mayer was considering the name as early as 1949, in his correspondence with Maria Leitner but 'saved' it for later. He legally adopted it before a solicitor in 1966, the document being witnessed by his two Brussels friends Pierre Schindel and Jacques Sonnenschein.
2. Letter to Ernst Mayer 10.3.58, DLA.
3. Letter to Ernst Mayer 3.11.57, DLA.
4. Jean Améry, 'Nach fünftausend Zeitungsartikeln' (After 5000 newspaper articles), in *Wie ich anfing...*, ed. Hans Daiber, Claasen, Düsseldorf 1979, pp. 215–26.
5. Letter to Ernst Mayer 10.3.58, DLA. He hated his life as a journalist from the first. In a later letter, also to Ernst Mayer (21.9.65), he writes: 'This wretched career [i.e. journalism; author's note] entails severe mental stress. The part of my character that must appear to outsiders – even you, and I can well understand it! – as anxious neuroticism is, I am sure, only the reflection of my objective situation. I find confirmation in myself of my favourite remark by Marx, to the effect that "our existence in society determines the consciousness", and I am sure that in a firmly established economic position, something that I shall probably never achieve again, I would appear a very well-balanced and equable man (...).'
6. Jean Améry, 'Nach fünftausend Zeitungsartikeln', p. 217.
7. Jean Améry, *Karrieren und Köpfe. Bildnisse Berühmter Zeitgenossen*, Thomas Verlag, Zürich 1955, in: 'Ein Wort zuvor'.
8. Richard Coudenhove-Kalergi interests Améry as a champion of the pan-European ideal, but above all as a philosopher who was able to consider aesthetics and ethics together. 'Aesthetics and ethics are two forms of a single doctrine,' Améry quotes Coudenhove-Kalergi. 'Aesthetics teaches us about the beauty around us – ethics about the beauty within us.' In: *Karrieren und Köpfe*, p. 141. Ilja Ehrenburg remains a riddle to Améry because, highly talented avant-garde writer and revolutionary genius as he was, he allowed Stalin to make a 'Soviet loyalist' of him in the 1930s.
9. Jean Améry, *Im Banne des Jazz. Bildnisse grosser Jazz-Musiker*. With 20 portraits on fine-art plates. Albert Müller Verlag, Rüschlikon-Zürich, Stuttgart and Vienna 1961. 128 pages.
10. Ibid., p. 7.
11. Jean Améry, *Teenager Stars. Idole unserer Zeit*, Rüschlikon-Zürich, Stuttgart and Vienna, Albert Müller Verlag, p. 24.

12. Ibid., p. 24.

13. Ibid.

14. Grandma Moses, as she is popularly known (real name Anna Mary Robertson Moses, an old farmer's wife born in 1860), was discovered in 1940 by the Viennese art dealer Otto Kallir, then living in the USA, and marketed very successfully as an exponent of American Primitivism. 'The secret of the effect of her works is an unusually colourful brightness, which she achieves by purely technical means in covering the cardboard on which she paints with a white ground three times, always allowing each layer to dry out carefully. Her pictures radiate a fervent joy in sun, snow, simple folk and the simple life. The freshness of her rustic scenes has been compared with Breughel's masterpieces of peasant life (...)', in: *Karrieren und Köpfe*, p. 225.

15. 'Picasso. Abenteuer eines halben Jahrhunderts. Zu seinem 80. Geburtstag am 25. Oktober 1961' was the proposal, but the article as it appeared was entitled 'Pablo Picasso – Abenteuer des Lebens und der Kunst. Ein biographischer Bericht.' This series of articles is written under the pseudonym Claude Maurain. The manuscripts are in the DLA.

16. Jean Améry, *Teenager Stars. Idole unserer Zeit*, Albert Müller Verlag, Rüschlikon-Zürich, Stuttgart and Vienna, 1960.

17. Ibid., p. 56.

18. Ibid., pp. 97–8.

19. Ibid., p. 102.

20. Jean Améry, *Cinéma. Arbeiten zum Film*, ed. and with an afterword by Joachim Kalka, Cotta's Bibliothek der Moderne, Stuttgart 1994. Cf. also Jean Améry, *Werke*, Vol. 5, ed. Hand Höller, pp. 507–67 and 617–20.

21. On Heidegger, in: *Karrieren und Köpfe*, p. 44 ff., on Jünger ibid., p. 87.

22. Ibid., p. 54.

23. Cf. Gerhard Scheit in his complex afterword to Vol. 5, Jean Améry, *Werke*, Klett-Cotta 2004, especially the chapter 'Kritik des deutschen Denkens; zwischen Ontologie und Dialektik', p. 625–35.

24. We know that Jean Améry was upset to know that he had the same publisher as Ernst Jünger. There is a correspondence about this problem with the writer his friend Alfred Andersch, who although a left-wing intellectual admired Ernst Jünger all his life.

25. Quotation from the jacket text.

26. *Gerhart Hauptmann. Der ewige Deutsche*, Mühlacker: Stieglitz-Verlag E. Händle, 1963, p. 127.

27. Ibid., p. 148.

28. Ibid.

29. Jean Améry, *Geburt der Gegenwart. Gestalten und Gestaltungen der westlichen Zivilisation seit Kriegsende*, Olten / Freibuurg im Breslau: Walter Verlag, 1961. This book also appeared in Dutch: Jean Améry, *Het moderne Westen.Culturelle outwikkeling na 1945*, Utrecht and Antwerp, 1963, and in English: Jean Améry, *Preface to the Future. Culture in a Consumer Society*, London and New York 1964. The English edition has been updated. Cf. reviews of this book by Ernst Mayer, 'Bilanz der Zukunft', in: *Die Zukunft*, No. 1, January 1962, p. 14, and Elisabeth Freundlich, 'Eine Diagnose unserer Zeit', in: *Die Kultur*, Munich, 1962/2, p. 11. The chapter on France, 'Gegenstand-Widerstand. Frankreich in den ersten Nachkriegsjahren' (abbreviated) pp. 724–32, and the chapter on Germany, 'Im Schatten des dritten Reiches. Deutsches Dichten und Denken in den Fünfziger Jahren' are reprinted in: Jean Améry, *Werke*, Vol. 2, ed. Gerhard Scheit, pp. 535–99, Stuttgart 2002.

30. Letter to Ernst Mayer of 15 May 1960. In the same letter Améry expresses his annoyance about the delay in publication. 'My good publishers, Walter-Verlag, who are bringing out the great book, informed me yesterday, when I had just written the final pages and brought myself happily to the verge of physical and mental exhaustion, that with such a late delivery of the book it could not, unfortunately, come out in the autumn of 1960.' Améry was hoping to find a home for another book with Walter, *Über die Unwahrheit*, a kind of continuation of *Preface to the Future*. However, that never materialized when the sample chapter was turned down for political reasons. Cf. letters to Ernst Mayer of 15.9.62 and 31.5.64.

31. Letter to Ernst Mayer of 20.5.62: 'My book is a disappointment of the first order so far as sales are concerned, the outcome being below the expectations even of my pessimistic moments. The many and almost uniformly favourable reviews did not lead to even respectable sales figures (...) It seems that my fate is to be sold cheap, with all that that entails (...).'

32. Elisabeth Freundlich. 'Eine Diagnose unserer Zeit. Zu dem Bericht *Geburt der Gegenwart* von Jean Améry, in: *Die Kultur*, Munich, 1962/2, p. 11.

33. In a letter of the same time to Ernst Mayer, 25 May 1960, he sets out his attitude to the Soviet Union: 'My book is devoted to "coexistence", and in fact rests on the assumption that Stalinism is now a closed chapter in the Soviet Union. Was I wrong? I still do not think so. No, war, the great "shooting war", the war of atomic and nuclear bombs, will probably not come as long as China is not in a position to start one. The danger is not the Soviet Union – nor was it in 1948 at the height of the Cold War – but the huge Eastern empire with its 700 million people and its terrible revolutionary and nowadays industrial vigour. I, who never believed in war, see a real threat in China. It is to be hoped that Mr K[ennedy] sees that too!'

34. In: Jean Améry, 'Der enttäuschte Rebell'. On the first volume of Arthur Koestler's memoirs *Frühe Empörung*. (*Spanish Testament*) Vienna 1970, p. 10. radio manuscript in Améry's literary estate, DLA.

35. Cf. letter to Ernst Mayer of 22.7.61. 'We cannot really formulate the cultural problems today as they could in the time of Lessing, Klages or Spengler, let alone answer them in the same way. I am as certain now, a neo-Marxist of 1961, as I was in 1932–1940 that today it is pointless to speak of the mind as the adversary of the soul, or ascribe the downfall of the world to the mind, or even to wonder whether history is really just the effort of the pointless to find a point. And as for literature! You are right, the cultural world of the sensitive upper middle class of 1900–1910 has almost nothing to do with us, the contemporaries of Bourguiba and Nkrumah. Only Th(omas) M(ann) has understood how to connect to his time and yet reach far beyond it and the middle-class world into the realm of historical dialectics and great literary vision. But all the others you enumerate, such as Stehr, Ponten, Scholz – oh heavens, how antiquated and inessential it all is, indeed our master Hesse too. (Let me make a reservation: the literary value of books from the Knulp period is as high as ever, and the same is true of the works of Mörike and Storm...)'.

36. Améry's more tolerant attitude towards the consumer society, the culture industry and 'mass civilisation' may perhaps be attributed to the fact that Adorno witnessed these phenomena at the time of his emigration to America, although Améry was not to visit the United States for the first time until 1970.

37. Particularly revealing in this connection is his essay on Lévi-Strauss, 'Fremdling in dieser Zeit. Zu Werk und Gestalt des Strukturalisten Claude Lévi-Strauss.' MS in Marbach. Rias. 23.5.75. After an empathetic analysis of Lévi-Strauss's method of

thinking, he concludes his discussion with the following critical remark: 'It is history, so little esteemed by Lévi-Strauss, that ultimately has the last word.' (p. 21)

38. *Preface to the Future* [*Geburt der Gegenwart*], p. 25.
39. Ibid., p. 21.
40. Bernard-Henry Lévy, *Sartre. Der Philosoph des 20. Jahrhunderts*, tr. Petra Willim, Carl Hanser Verlag, Munich 2002.
41. Ibid., p. 243.
42. Annie Cohen-Solal, *Sartre*, Gallimard, Paris 1985, p. 160.
43. Letter to Ernst Mayer of 30.11.63. Améry's assessment of Sartre's *Les Mots*: 'philosophical metapsychological memoirs, alarmingly clever, truly brilliant! No, one cannot over-estimate the man!'
44. Cf. Bernard-Henry Lévy, *Sartre. Der Philosoph des 20. Jahrhunderts*, in: 'Anmerkung zum Problem Vichy: Sartre im Widerstand', pp. 343–73. Cf. also *Preface to the Future*.
45. Cf. Annie Cohen-Solal, pp. 432–8, and Bernard-Henry Lévy, pp. 408–24. In *Preface to the Future*, p. 31.
46. Cf. Bernard-Henry Lévy, in 'Die Affäre Camus', pp. 391–7.
47. Jean Améry to Ernst Mayer, 4.9.64: 'If we no longer believe in it (the future, author's note) so much, statistically and emotionally, now that the train is so close to the tunnel, then we approach that dimension with a sense of loss and chase around it like our own shadows.'
48. The identity of the addressee is not known, as the letter begins with the salutation, 'My very dear madam'. It was written on 26 March 1967.
49. Sartre, who did his military service in Tours in 1929 in the meteorological department, was called up in 1939 (into the 70th Division) and again worked in the meteorological department. In 1940 he was a prisoner of war in Trier (Stalag XII D) and was released in 1941. We can speak of his political awakening only after his return to Paris, and even then he joined the Resistance only indirectly, that is to say in his writings. Cf. Francis Jeanson, *Sartre dans sa vie*, Editions du Seuil, Paris 1974, pp. 88–124.
50. Annie Cohen-Solal, especially the chapter 'Une métamorphose dans la guerre', pp. 189–275.
51. Ibid., 3 December 1940.
52. Ibid., Jean-Paul Sartre, *Carnets de la drôle de guerre*, 15 January 1940, pp. 202–3.
53. He was to revise his position thoroughly in *Hand an sich legen. Diskurs über den Freitod* [On Suicide], Klett-Cotta, Stuttgart 1976.
54. Améry points out that Hemingway had withdrawn two of his early short stories, in which he supported the Spanish Republicans. As for Dos Passos, he would have signed a manifesto issued by 'ultra-conservative circles'.
55. Jean Améry, *Winston Churchill. Ein Jahrhundert Zeitgeschichte*. With 422 illustrations, Lucerne and Frankfurt am Main, C.J. Bücher, 1965. Cf. letter to Ernst Mayer of 12.2.65: 'I see Churchill already like the Grand Old Man.' He complains of 'pressure of work amounting to slave labour', for this lavishly illustrated book, which nonetheless did have 100 pages of text and had to be put together in four weeks. It is a brilliant and not an uncritical study full of surprising insights. 'Churchill was an artist and a bohemian in the forms his life took, in the direction his thinking followed, in his delight in improvisation, above all in his fascination with himself, his egocentricity', p. 43. The chapter headings provide information on Améry's method of proceeding: 'Statesman of stormy days in history'; 'For King and Country'; 'Giving

Warning'; 'Blood, Tears and Sweat'; 'A Very Cold Peace'. It is also noticeable in this study that Améry never brings in himself as a Jew, or if so it is at most in the remark that Churchill is reported to have made to the effect that in the form of Hitler 'the wrong swine' had been slaughtered . This is all the more striking because at this very time he was working intensively on his essays in *At the Mind's Limits*.

56. Ibid., p. 209. Cf. also Alexander and Margarete Mitscherlich, *Die Unfähigkeit zu trauern. Grundlagen kollektiven Verhaltens*, Munich 1967: 'The restoration of the economy was our favourite child', p. 19.

57. Ibid. He gives his opinion on Heidegger one last time in his obituary, 'Die Gefahr der Verklärung' (The danger of glorification). *Die Zeit*, 4.6.76. Here he speaks of a man who 'succumbed to the calamity of thinking deeply', who could not get away from his 'metaphysical Messkirch' (the town of Heidegger's birth), from a 'sombre compliance with his roots', and 'ideological provincialism'. He indicates Adorno's *Jargon der Eigentlichkeit*, and Robert Minder's essay 'Die Sprache von Messkirch'. Finally, he calls him a 'transcendental philosopher in the conventional mould'. 'In Heidegger's day vehemence against civilisation, against science, against technology was a weapon in the hands of reaction. Heidegger had devoted himself to it; death does not cancel that.' Améry touches on Heidegger's *liaison dangereuse* with the Nazis, the fact that he withdrew his dedication to Husserl, and comes to this conclusion: 'No, Martin Heidegger was no common Nazi, or in the worst case was so for a ridiculously short span of time (...). But he was a phenomenon who, as an intellectual leader, looked backward in every respect, one of the ideological arch-patriarchs of the "conservative revolution" that finally, in its Nazi apotheosis, brought the terrible evidence that it was not conservative or revolutionary, but merely alienated the Germans more and more from themselves and the rest of the world (...). Heidegger should not be reviled and must not be glorified.' Cf. also: Jean Améry, *Werke*, Vol. 6, *Aufsätze zur Philosophie*, ed. Gerhard Scheit, Klett-Cotta, Stuttgart 2004.

58. Alfred Andersch: 'Deutsche Literatur in der Entscheidung. Ein Beitrag zur Analyse der literarischen Situation' (1947), reprinted in: *Das Alfred Andersch Lesebuch*, Zürich 1979, pp. 111–34. Cf. also Irene Heidelberger-Leonard, 'Zur Dramaturgie einer Abwesenheit – Alfred Andersch und die Gruppe 47', in: *Bestandsaufnahme – Studien zur Gruppe 47*, ed. Stephan Braese, Berlin 1999. pp. 87–103.

59. Ibid, p. 188. Frank Trommler's essay is informative on 'the missing dialogue between authors and readers', in which that part of *Preface to the Future* is described as 'one of the most enlightening essays' on the 1950s. In: Stephan Braese, ed., *Bestandsaufnahme – Studien zur Gruppe 47*, pp. 277–84.

Chapter 7   Drama of the Mind in Three Acts

For documentation and extensive information on the circumstances for the writing of the essays, their creation and their reception, I would strongly recommend Gerhard Scheit's afterword in: Jean Améry, *Werke*, Vol. 2, *Jenseits von Schuld und Sühne, Unmeisterliche Wanderjahre, Örtlichkeiten*, ed. Gerhard Scheit, Klett-Cotta, Stuttgart 2002, pp. 492–853.

1. The title of Doron Rabinovici's collection of essays *Credo und Kredit*, edition suhrkamp, Frankfurt 2001, for which he was awarded the Jean Améry Essay Prize 2002.

2. In: *Örtlichkeiten*, Vol. 2, p. 469.

3. Ibid.

4. Letter from Karl Schwedhelm to the director of programmes Dr Kehm, 21.1.64.

5. In: *Örtlichkeiten*, Vol. 2, p. 471.

6. In: *Grenzgänger*, ed. Ingo Hermann, p. 78.

7. Quoted from the essay on 'Resentments' in *Jenseits von Schuld und Sühne*, Vol. 2, pp. 129–142; English translation by Sidney Rosenfeld and Stella P. Rosenfeld, *At the Mind's Limits*, pp. 62–81.

8. Primo Levi, *I sommersi e i salvati*, 1986; English translation by Raymond Rosenthal, *The Drowned and the Saved*, 1988, p. 138.

9. Hannah Arendt, *Eichmann in Jerusalem: A Report on the Banality of Evil*, 1963. A particularly sharp attack by Améry on Arendt's criticism of the collaboration of Jews appears only later in his article 'Im Warteraum des Todes' in *Widersprüche*', Stuttgart 1971, pp. 213–32. '(...) hence the peculiar dialectic of Jewish solidarity, realized in *suffering* – whatever Frau Hannah Arendt may have said in her book on Eichmann, which shows remarkably little understanding and does not even contain the relevant facts! (...) In spite of everything, the Jewish Kapos suffered with their victims (...) They beat their fellow Jews and in so doing struck themselves. (...)' The quotation is from p. 217. A little further on, p. 227: 'Only a lack of understanding, brazen arrogance and total ignorance of the subject will condemn "Jews who collaborated" as if they were quislings in occupied Europe!'

10. Bernd Naumann, *Auschwitz, Bericht über die Strafsache gegen Mulka und andere vor dem Schwurgericht Frankfurt*, Athenäum Verlag, Frankfurt am Main and Bonn, pp. 7–8.

11. Hermann Langbein, *Der Auschwitz-Prozess*. Eine Dokumentation in 2 Bänden, Europa Verlag, Vienna, Frankfurt and Zürich 1965.

12. In: *Das Parlament*, 16.4.99, p. 5.

13. Norbert Frei, 'Der Frankfurter Auschwitz-Prozes und die deutsche Zeitgeschichtsforschung', in: ed. Fritz Bauer Institut, *Auschwitz. Geschichte, Rezeption und Wirkung*. Jahrbuch 1996 zur Geschichte und Wirkung des Holocaust, Frankfurt am Main, 1996, pp. 123–38, p. 124. Cf. also Irmtrud Wojak, 'Die Mauer des Schweigens durchbrochen. Der erste Frankfurter Auschwitz-Prozess 1963–1965', in: ed. Fritz Bauer Institut, '*Gerichtstag halten über uns selbst... Geschichte und Wirkung des ersten Frankfurter Auschwitz-Prozesses*', Jahrbuch 2001 zur Geschichte und Wirkung des Holocaust, pp. 21–42.

14. Marc von Miquel, '"Wir müssen mit den Mördern zusammenleben!" NS-Prozesse und politische Öffentlichkeit in den sechziger Jahren', in: *Gerichtstag halten über uns selbst* Jahrbuch 2001, pp. 97–116.

15. Dr Jörg Hucklenbroich of the Historical Archive of SWR has kindly listed all of South German Radio's broadcasts by and with Jean Améry. From this it can be seen that Améry was already contributing short pieces to Programmes 1 and 2 (including the cultural programmes of Europa magazine) from 27 June 1960, broadcasting from Brussels. Dr Hucklenbroich has made copies of the entire correspondence between Jean Améry and Heissenbüttel available to me, and I would like to thank him again warmly here.

16. Letter from Jean Améry to Kurt Schwedhelm of 18.1.64, in his estate in the DLA.

17. *Die Weltwoche*, 5.6.64, Number B. After the broadcast it also appeared in *Christ und Welt* 1.11.64, in the 'Informationsdienst des Clubs Republikanischer Publizisten' 1964, and in the 'Club Voltaire Jahrbuch für kritische Aufklärung II', ed. Gerhard Szczesny, Munich 1965, pp. 360–77.

18. Alfred Andersch, 'Anzeige einer Rückkehr des Geistes als Person', in: *Die Blindheit des Kunstwerkes*, pp. 125–41, Zürich 1979, first published in *Merkur*, 1971.

19. Letter from Suhrkamp Verlag to Jean Améry, 10.8.65, quoted by Jean Améry in a letter to Hans Paeschke of 6.10.65.

20. Jean Améry, 'Auschwitz – An der Grenze des Geistes', in: *Spiegelungen unserer Zeit*, Krausskopf-Verlag, Mainz 1965, pp. 154–69.

21. Jean Améry, 'Les intellectuels à Auschwitz', in: *documents*, 20e année, May–June, pp. 12–33.

22. Ibid. He divides the essay into four units of ideas, entitled, 'L'esprit dissocié des structures sociales', pp. 16–19; 'La culture entre les mains de l'ennemi', pp. 19–21; 'La logique des autres', pp. 21–7; 'L'esprit impuissant en face de la mort', pp. 27–33.

23. Titles now available in French are: *Du viellissment*, Edition Payot, 1991, tr. Annick Yaiche; *Charles Bovary, médecin de campagne* (1991), *Par-delà le crime et le châtiment* (1995), *Lefeu ou la démolition* (1996), and *Porter la main sur soi* (1996), Actes Sud; all four volumes translated by Françoise Wuilmart.

24. Jean Améry, preface to *An-klagen. Schriften für amnesty international*, ed. Urs M. Fiechtner and Claus Magiera, Neuer Verlag Bernhard Bruscha, Tübingen 1971, pp. 7–9.

25. The *Merkur* version is reprinted in: Jean Améry, *Werke*, Vol. 2, pp. 599–624. On the cuts, see Gerhard Scheit in his afterword, pp. 650–651.

26. Theodor W. Adorno, *Metaphysik. Begriff und Probleme* (1965), ed. Rolf Tiedemann. Nachgelassene Schriften Abt. 1V, Vorlesungen Vol. 14, Frankfurt am Main 1998, p. 166. Quoted in Gerhard Scheit, 'Nathan der Gefolterte. Jean Améry und die Dialektik der Aufklärung', in: *Jean Améry. Der Schriftsteller*, ed. Irene Heidelberger-Leonard and Hans Höller, pp. 93–105, p. 101. Cf. also Gerhard Scheit, afterword to *Jenseits von Schuld und Sühne*, in: Jean Améry, *Werke*, Vol. 2, pp. 673–7.

27. Cf. Jean Améry, 'Jargon der Dialektik', first published at the time in *Merkur* 236, Nov. 1967, later printed in *Widersprüche*, Ernst Klett Verlag, Stuttgart 1971, pp. 53–78.

28. The student movement, which had praised him for years as its most competent critic of society, turned away from him in 1969, accusing him of hostility in practice. At this time there were demonstrations, and meetings were broken up. Adorno wrote, shortly before his death: 'The break in practice does not cure minds of resignation, as long as it is paid for by the secret knowledge that it will not work anyway.' A few weeks after the turbulent incident at Frankfurt University, Adorno died.

29. Ingeborg Bachmann, 'Drei Wege zum See', in: Ingeborg Bachmann, *Gesamtausgabe*, ed. Christine Koschel, Inge von Weidenbaum and Clemens Münster, Vol. 2, p. 431.

30. Bachmann refers back to the character of Trotta in Joseph Roth's *Die Kapuzinergruft*.

31. See Jean Améry's obituary of Ingeborg Bachmann, 'Am Grabe einer ungekannten Freundin', in: Jean Améry, *Werke* Vol. 5, ed. Hans Höller, Stuttgart 2003. For further connections between Jean Améry and Ingeborg Bachmann, cf. Irène Heidelberger-Leonard, 'Ingeborg Bachmann und Jean Améry. Zur Differenz zwischen der Ästhetisierung des Leidens und der Authentizität traumatischer Erfahrung' and 'Versuchte Nähe Ingeborg Bachmann und Jean Améry' in: Irène Heidelberger-Leonard, *Jean Améry im Dialog mit der zeitgenössischen Literatur, Essays*, ed. Hans Höller, Akademischer Verlag, Stuttgart 2002, pp. 103–116 and 17–128.

32. Title of a posthumous essay in: *Autoren im Exil*, ed. Karl Corino, Fischer Taschenbuch, 1981, pp. 254–64. On the same subject, see also Jean Améry, 'Die ewig Unerwünschten. Vorurteile gegenüber Emigranten', in: *Vorurteile in der Gegenwart*, ed. Axel Silenius. Tribüne Bücher, Frankfurt 1966, pp. 71–80.

33. This reference to Ernst Bloch is in Améry's essay 'Jargon der Dialektik' (his confrontation with the Frankfurt School) in: *Widersprüche*. 1971, p. 99, where he also quotes Bloch's definition of philosophy as 'inquiring amazement', to which his own phraseology obviously owes something.

34. Complementary is the later radio talk 'Verfemt und verbannt' for Deutschlandfunk, ed. Dr Manfred Franke, broadcast 16.2.69. It is published with a commentary by Gerhard Scheit in: Jean Améry, *Werke*, Vol. 2, pp. 790–813.

35. Highly recommended as an alternative to the current way of reading is the following commentary on the 'Resentments' essay: Horst Meier, 'Hitler zurücknehmen. Zum antinazistischen Imperativ bei Jean Améry', in: Jean Améry, *Ressentiments*, Europäische Verlagsanstalt Reden, Vol. 18, Hamburg 1995, pp. 47–87.

36. Hans Egon Holthusen, 'Freiwillig zur SS', Part 1, *Merkur* 223, October 1966, pp. 921–31 and Part 2, *Merkur* 224, November 1966, pp. 1037–49.

37. Jean Améry, 'Fragen an Hans Egon Holthusen – und seine Antwort', *Merkur* 1967/4, pp. 393–5.

38. Not uninteresting in this context is Primo Levi's uncomprehending remark on the formulation of the title 'On the Necessity and Impossibility of Being a Jew', in a letter to Hety Schmitt-Maas: 'What's supposed to be so difficult about it? I am a Jew – it's perfectly simple (...)' (Hety Schmitt-Maas to Jean Améry, 25.10.67).

39. Jean-Paul Sartre, *Betrachtungen zur Judenfrage* [original French *Réflexions sur la question juive*; published in English as 'Anti-Semite and Jew'], subtitle 'Psychoanalysis of anti-Semitism', three essays written in 1946, German edition with an afterword by Walter Schmiele, Ullstein, Berlin 1965, pp. 108–90, quoted here p. 184.

40. Ibid., p. 113.

41. Bernard-Henry Lévy, *Le Siècle de Sartre*, 2000, English version, *Sartre. The Philosopher of the Twentieth Century*, 2003. German version *Sartre. Der Philosoph des 20. Jahrhunderts*, Hanser Verlag, Munich and Vienna 2002, p. 386.

42. Jean Améry, *Mein Judentum*, ed. Hans Jürgen Schultz, Kreuz Verlag, Stuttgart 1978, pp. 80–9, here p. 80.

43. Jean-François Steiner, *Treblinka*, Fayard, Paris 1966, with a preface by Simone de Beauvoir.

44. Jean Améry, 'Erlösung in der Revolte', in: *Literatur im Spiegel*, ed. Rolf Becker, Rowohlt, Reinbek bei Hamburg 1969, pp. 178–83.

45. Gerhard Scheit's afterword (Vol. 2, pp. 669–92) provides information about the reception of this work and how, for all the understanding it received, elementary failures of comprehension crept in.

46. For precise documentation of the circumstances in which *Über das Altern. Revolte und Resignation* [On Aging] was written, and a presentation of its structure, the works on which it was modelled, and its reception, I refer readers to Jean Améry, *Werke*, Vol. 3, ed. Monique Boussart, which appeared in autumn 2004, published by Klett-Cotta. At this point I would like to offer warm thanks to Monique Boussart, who generously placed her still unpublished manuscript at my disposal.

The working title for the radio broadcasts, which Heissenbüttel resumed from July 1967, was 'An incurable illness'. It was only for the book, and after discussion with his new editor at Ernst Klett Verlag, that Améry adopted the title *Über das Altern. Revolte und Resignation* [On Aging], Ernst Klett Verlag, Stuttgart 1968. Rowohlt were originally to publish the book, but Klett offered to bring it out at once.

47. Jean Améry, 'Nach fünftausend Zeitungsartikeln', in: *Wie ich anfing...* (1979), p. 220.

48. Jean Améry to Paeschke: 'The whole book is set out so that, as you so rightly say, I am playing chess with myself (...). There are as good as no references in the book. It makes no claim to objectivity' (19.11.67).

49. Among the many literary influences, one might have expected to find Paul Nizan, on whom Améry wrote a wonderful essay, 'Menschlichkeit triumphiert über Ideologie' [Humanity triumphs over ideology], saying among other things, of the *Leben des Antoine Bloyé*, that he is crushing himself 'simply by aging'. A central theme of this novel is the 'fate of the body'. The essay is in: Jean Améry, *Werke*, Vol. 5, *Aufsätze zur Literatur und zum Film*, ed. Hans Höller, pp. 191–206.

50. A first letter from H. Arbogast to Jean Améry was dated 20 May 1968: 'Herr Heissenbüttel had sent us a part and Herr Paeschke the whole of your typescript, and both gentlemen recommend it strongly. That would not have been necessary, for the subject of your essays will leave no one who has passed the age of 30 or 40 indifferent. The fact that you then succeed in giving cogent expression to your own dismay and the dismay of all makes reading the essays – I almost said a pleasure, but I mean the word in the same sense as Schiller when he spoke of the pleasure to be found in tragedy.' I owe to Dr Arbogast the information that Améry had, in fact, received an acceptance from Rowohlt Verlag but preferred the offer from Klett Verlag because Klett were prepared to bring the book out six months earlier (Conversation with H.A. on 4.1.2003, cf. also letter from Jean Améry to Ernst Mayer, 3.4.68.)

51. In: Werner Höfer, *Was ich noch fragen wollte. Themen und Thesen des Internationalen Frühschoppens 1969–1970*, transcript of the broadcast of 14.12.69, Ullstein, Frankfurt, Berlin and Vienna, 1970, p. 42.

52. In: Herbert Plügge, *Der Mensch und sein Leib*, pp. 86 ff.

53. Here again Sartre is the presiding spirit. Améry writes to Ernst Mayer on 12.4.68, 'I am against all resignation (see my essays on aging). The "reality principle" is to be recognized only in part. In Sartre it is otherwise; a human being understands the world as anti-physis (and thus as transcending the "reality" that after all is conditioned by us just as it conditions us). "Only death is no part of my possibilities now" [J-P. Sartre].'

54. Very subtle too is the review by the philosopher Heinz Robert Schlette in *Publik*, 7.2.69, recommending the book to Christians in particular 'so that they may become more realistic and humane, and learn to revolt against aging, dying and death, for the Bible teaches that these things are not allowed.' p. 21.

55. Handwritten document in the private archive of Maria Améry, now in the DLA.

56. Typewritten document in the private archive of Maria Améry, now in the DLA, captioned, 'Miscellaneous reminiscences, private, literary, etc.', written on 20.8.84. She surveys her memories of 1969–1973 here.

57. Handwritten letter from Jean Améry to Dr Burger of 18.1.71: 'Here at last is the preface to my *Wanderjahre*. After much thought, I have finally kept it as short as possible. As the whole work is very personal, the preface ought not to be of a confessional character.'

58. On 5 November 1969 he writes to Ernst Mayer: 'For the rest, I am working on the first essay in the series, which will make up another book (an intellectual biography of our period).'

59. Gerhard Scheit in Jean Améry, *Werke*, Vol. 2, pp. 712–87.

60. The connections between 1968 and the *Unmeisterliche Wanderjahre* are worked out with particular clarity by Gerhard Scheit in his afterword to Jean Améry's *Werke*, see Vol. 2, pp. 712–87.

61. *Unmeisterliche Wanderjahre* appeared in the spring of 1971 (Klett), and in the autumn of 1971 he published a collection of disconnected cultural, critical and political essays of the same period (1967–71) under the title of *Widersprüche* [Contradictions]. The chapter headings dividing up the latter work provide information about the subjects, on some of which he had already reflected in the *Unmeisterliche Wanderjahre*: 'From God to Sartre', 'Left, where there is no home', and 'Jewish unrest'. Reviews of the *Unmeisterliche Wanderjahre* were 'for the most part excellent', cf. Hartung's review in *Die Zeit*, but sales were slow and disappointing. 'It remains only for me to bear my lack of success with some composure.' (J.A. to E.M. 27.6.71)

Chapter 8   Jean Améry as a Writer of Fiction

1. In: Alfred Andersch, *Norden Süden rechts und links*, Diogenes Verlag, Zürich 1972, reprinted in: *Über Jean Améry. Zum 65. Geburtstag von Jean Améry*, Ernest Klett, Stuttgart 1977, pp. 19–38.
2. Ibid.
3. Jean Améry in the exhibition catalogue of the Galerie Kriegel, 36 avenue Matignon, Paris VIII, 1972, reprinted in the Viennese catalogue, see Note 13.
4. In: 'Mens sana in corpore sano – ein Missverständnis und seine Folgen', unpublished manuscript dated 18.9.72, in Améry's literary estate, DLA.
5. Hanjo Kesting, 'Der Tod des Geistes als Person. Leben und Werk des Jean Améry', in: *Dichter ohne Vaterland*. Gespräche und Aufsätze zur Literatur, J.H.W. Dietz Verlag, 1982, pp. 171–87, p. 174.
6. Portraits, in Stephan Steiner, *Jean Améry (Hans Maier)*, with a biographical pictorial essay and a bibliography. Stroemfeld, Basel and Frankfurt am Main, 1996, pp. 123–52.
7. Helmut Heissenbüttel in his afterword to the posthumously published collection of essays *Der Integrale Humanismus*, Klett-Cotta, Stuttgart 1985, p. 275.
8. In: *Leporello fällt aus der Rolle. Zeitgenössische Autoren erzählen das Leben von Figuren der Weltliteratur weiter*, ed. Peter Härtling, Fischer Taschenbuch Verlag, Frankfurt 1971, pp. 185–97.
9. The title given by Jean Améry to his review of Michel Tournier's novel *Der Erlkönig* in: *Merkur*, Vol. 27, 1973, pp. 75–8,
10. Jean Améry, 'Leben ohne Dürer' in: *Am Beispiel Dürers*, Bruckmann, Munich 1972, pp. 69–81, here p. 77.
11. Cf. the summary that he sends to the organizer of the Dürer Symposium Ulf von Dewitz (17.4.71), in the DLA: 'He [Améry, author's note] cannot form a "successful relationship" with the master because he thinks that, in this work, he discerns objective human indifference to evil and tragedy.'
12. Jean Améry, *Lefeu oder Der Abbruch* (Améry is inconsistent in his versions of this title, sometimes writing the article with a capital D, as *Lefeu oder Der Abbruch*, sometimes with a lower-case initial, as *Lefeu oder der Abbruch*). Ernst Klett Verlag, Stuttgart 1974.
13. Two books with reproductions of his paintings can be recommended: *Erich Schmid*. 1981, Associations Les Amis d'Erich Schmid, in particular the very well devised catalogue for the Vienna exhibition of 2002, which emphasizes the Schmid–Améry–Lefeu connection by connecting Schmid's pictures with the relevant passages in Améry's text: *Erich Schmid*, Vienna 1908–Paris 1984, ed. Claudia Widder and Roland Widder: Bibliothek der Provinz, Weitra, 2002.

14. 'Die neuen Mönche. Bildnisse (un)berühmter Zeitgenossen: Unbekannter Maler E.S.', reprinted in the *Marbacher Magazin*, pp. 44–8, here p. 46.

15. Erich Schmid to Maria Améry, undated letter in the DLA, like all Erich Schmid's letters.

16. Vienna exhibition catalogue, p. 17. I have also taken the biographical information about Erich Schmid from this catalogue.

17. In the private archive of Maria Améry, now in the DLA, four pages headed 'Lefeu reading (Mainz)', undated.

18. Alfred Andersch, 'Kritik zur Buchmesse', in: *Frankfurter Rundschau*, 25/26 10. 1975.

19. Eduard Mörike, 'Der Feuerreiter', reprinted in the *Marbacher Magazin* 24/82, pp. 58–89.

20. From: 'Mit den Büchern von gestern', broadcast on Bavarian Radio on 26.9.73.

21. 'Heinrich Mann, ein unbekannter Autor', Jean Améry, *Werke*, Vol. 5, ed. Hans Höller, pp. 52–85.

22. Helmut Heissenbüttel, *Über Literatur*, Klett-Cotta, Stuttgart 1995 (first edition 1966). *D'Alembert's Ende*, Luchterhand, Neuwied and Berlin 1979.

23. Ernst Klett, 'Antianthologie'. Gedichte in deutscher Sprache nach der Zahl ihrer Wörter geordnet von Franz Mon und Helmut Heissenbüttel, *Merkur* no. 313, June 1974, pp. 593–5.

24. Letter from Jean Améry to Hans Paeschke 7.7.74. 'Herr Klett's discussion of the anti-anthology was excellent, better than a review by a professional critic!'

25. In a letter from Jean Améry to Wolf Seidl, 16.4.75.

26. Marcel Reich-Ranicki, 'Schrecklich ist die Verführung zum Roman', *Frankfurter Allgemeine Zeitung* 1.6.74, and Wolfram Schütte, 'Tabula rasa oder am Ende doch eine Illusion?' *Frankfurter Rundschau* 6.7.74.

27. In the private archive of Maria Améry, now in the DLA.

28. Jean Améry, *Hand an sich legen. Diskurs über den Freitod*, Edition Alpha, Ernst Klett Verlag, Stuttgart 1976 [translated into English as *On Suicide. A discourse on voluntary death,* tr. John Barlow, Indiana University Press, Bloomington and Indianapolis, 1999].

29. In: *Frankfurter Rundschau* 27.11.71.

30. Cf. Gerhard Scheit in his afterword to *Örtlichkeiten.* Jean Améry, *Werke*, Vol. 2, pp. 828–48.

31. Cf. closing discussion at the A 4/78 seminar, 'Hitler – eine Erweckungsbewegung?', held on 6–8 January 1978 at the Theodor-Heuss-Akademie, Gummersbach. Manuscript in Améry's literary estate, DLA, also printed in *liberal*, Vol. 20 (1978), No. 6, pp. 447–70.

32. Cf. Hety Schmitt-Maas, 'Er leistete "Trauerarbeit" für andere. Jean Amérys gedenkend', in: *Die Neue Gesellschaft* 12 (1978), p. 1001.

33. Jean Améry, *Charles Bovary. Landarzt. Porträt eines einfachen Mannes*, Ernst Klett, Stuttgart 1978.

34. 'Jean-Paul Sartres Engagement', in: *Macht und Ohnmacht der Intellektuellen*, ed. K. Hoffman, Hamburg 1968, pp. 76–90.

35. *Les Mots*, Paris 1964, p. 211.

36. Ibid.

37. *Macht und Ohnmacht der Intellektuellen*, p. 90.

38. The accusation is finally withdrawn.

39. 'Die Wörter Gustave Flaubert', in: *Der integrale Humanismus*, ed. Helmut Heissenbüttel, Stuttgart 1985, p. 169.

40. In: *Weiterleben – aber wie?*, ed. G. Lindemann, Stuttgart 1982, pp. 126–50. The essay first appeared in: *Merkur* 12 (1974).

41. Ibid., pp. 126–7.

42. Ibid., p. 148.

43. On 4 December 1974, after encountering many difficulties, Sartre received permission to visit Andreas Baader in Stammheim prison. Their conversation was not a success, says Annie Cohen Solal in her biography *Sartre*, Paris 1985, p. 643 ff.

44. Améry's speculation is correct: Sartre's support of the Stammheim prisoners in their demand for more humane conditions was merely registered by the press as 'tactless'. Baader himself, it seems, was extremely abusive to Sartre.

45. Cf. *Sartre: Grösse und Scheitern*, p. 149.

46. Ibid.

47. Helmut Heissenbüttel, 'Ich ziehe meine Klage zurück', comments on Jean Améry, in: *Text + Kritik*, 99, p. 7.

48. Most extensively in *Entretien avec J.-P. Sartre*, in: *Sartre. Politique et Autobiographie*, Situations X (1976), and in *Notes sur Madame Bovary*, in: *L'Arc 79, Flaubert*, pp. 33–43.

49. Cf. *Entretien sur moi-même. Sur 'L'Idiot de la Famille'*, in: Situations X, pp. 91–115.

50. *L'Idiot de la Famille*, Paris 1971, p. 333.

51. Ibid., p. 1115.

52. Ibid., p. 1202.

53. Ibid., p. 1358.

54. Cf. *Entretien sur moi-même*, p. 134 ff.

55. 'Die Stunde des Romans. Zum 150. Geburtstag des "Meisters der Bovary"' (1971), in *Über Flaubert*, Zürich 1980, pp. 324–31.

56. Ibid., p. 322.

57. Ibid., p. 323.

58. Ibid., pp. 328–9.

59. Cf. *Lenz*, in: *Georg Büchner: Werke und Briefe*, Munich 1965, p. 72.

60. Letter to his family, February 1834, ibid. p. 165.

61. Cf. *Hermannstrasse 14*, special edition on Jean Améry, ed. H. Heissenbüttel, pp. 22–31.

62. Ibid., p. 23.

63. *Hermannstrasse 14*, p. 24.

64. Ibid., p. 24 ff.

65. *Aufklärung als Philosophia perennis*. Speech of thanks given at the award of the 1977 Lessing Prize of the Free and Hanseatic City of Hamburg, reprinted in: *Über Jean Améry*, Stuttgart 1977.

66. See Hanjo Kesting: 'Der Tod des Geistes als Person', in: *Dichter ohne Vaterland*, Bonn 1982, pp. 171–87. Cf. also Hanjo Kesting's interpretation of Améry's last novel, in: *'Charles Bovary. Landarzt*, oder das Totenreich der Kunst. Anmerkungen zu Flaubert, Sartre, Jean Améry', in: *Über Jean Améry*, ed. Irene Heidelberger-Leonard, Winter Verlag, Heidelberg 1990, pp. 91–113.

67. Jean Améry, 'Imaginäre Rezension. Statt eines Vorworts', undated typescript in the DLA.

68. This radio discussion with Martin Walser, chaired by Hanjo Kesting, the last in which Améry took part, must have been painful for all involved. On 3 October 1978 he thanks Kesting for the invitation: 'The occasion was what it was. You know that better than anyone, and were visibly suffering.'

69. Cf. Hans-Martin Gauger's review, 'Gustave Flaubert und Charles Bovary' in: *Neue Rundschau*, Dec. 78, pp. 120–7.

70. Other associations, although Améry does not mention them, play a part here, for instance, André Delvaux's film of magical realism *Rendez-vous à Bray* (1971), screenplay from the novella by Julien Gracq, or Delvaux's film *Belle* (1973), also in the genre of magical realism, in which there is an amorous encounter between dream and reality in Les Fagnes (near Spa).

71. Revealing in this connection is Jean Améry, *Werke*, Vol. 5, essays on literature and cinema, ed. Hans Höller, Klett-Cotta, Stuttgart 2003. See also Hans Höller's afterword, which is devoted to the entire spectrum of Améry's 'biography in reading and writing', pp. 570–640.

72. In: Helmut Heissenbüttel, Afterword, p. 277, to Jean Améry: *Der integrale Humanismus. Aufsätze und Kritiken eines Lesers 1966–1978*, Klett-Cotta, Stuttgart 1985, pp. 274–8.

73. I owe this information to Hubert Arbogast, in a conversation of 23.5.03.

74. The projected novella *Rendezvous in Oudenaarde* can also be read as meta-fiction connected with Thomas Mann's *Zauberberg*, particularly with Castorp's experience in the snow, cf. André Combes, 'Jean Amérys Thomas Mann-Lektüre', in: *Jean Améry: Der Schriftsteller*, ed. I. Heidelberger-Leonard and H. Höller, Akademischer Verlag, Stuttgart 2000, pp. 65–91.

75. The chapter heading for the planned fourth chapter of *Oudenarde* was 'Flight by way of Bruges. A little phenomenology of fear. All whom V. meets are afraid and frighten him. Persecution mania and genuine persecution.'

    The other chapter headings are as follows: I. *In search of lost time*. From the dreams to departure. II. *Mist over the High Ardennes*. The long way round to Spa. Meetings there. III. *Northward by the compass*. Travelling along byways. The lovers Effi and Werther; and V. *The Dangerous Land*. Final chapter. From Bruges to the way into Oudenaarde, and the shot in the mist. Mention should be made of the illustrated de luxe edition of *Rendezvous in Oudenaarde*. Project for a novella, with an afterword by Franz J. van der Grinten. With five signed original engravings by Rudolf Schoofs. Limited edition: 100 copies.

Chapter 9   Last Things

1. In this connection, Christian Schultz-Gerstein's *Der Doppelkopf* is significant. This work was 'from a conversation with Jean Améry in July 1976', just after the publication of *Hand an sich legen* [On Suicide]. März at Zweitausendeins, 1979.

2. Michael Krüger recollects the correspondence thus: 'I still remember his letters justifying the suicide book clearly (...). I was extremely anxious to tell him that he must not, for heaven's sake, kill himself, a matter he had discussed with me several times. And I still remember my last communication from him (...): a card (...) about his visit to Munich (...). The comment, logically following that information, "We must talk, it's important," was heavily underlined.' Letter from Michael Krüger to the author, 6.6.2003.

3. Cf. Jean Améry, 'Heinrich Mann über die Bürgerzeit'. Jean Améry *Werke*, essays on literature and the cinema. Vol. 5, ed. Hans Höller, p. 435.

4. Eight-page unpublished manuscript in Améry's literary estate, DLA, posthumously published and modified in *Universitas*, April 1991, no. 538, pp. 323–7.

5. Cf. Lothar Baier, 'Echec und Dignität. Jean Amérys Nachdenken über den Freitod', in: *Jean Améry. Der Schriftsteller*: ed. Irene Heidelberger-Leonard and Hans Höller, Verlag Hans-Dieter Heinz, Akademischer Verlag, Stuttgart 2000, pp. 107–20.

6. 'Alleinsein vor dem Tod', Hessian Radio, 10.1.77. 13-page unpublished typescript in the DLA.

7. Cf. Helmut Heissenbüttel, 'Zum Lesen empfohlen. Hand an sich legen.' North German Radio 3, 17.10.76.

8. Helmut Heissenbüttel: 'Améry has tried to show that hope and Utopia are only of a verbal character, and that Utopia shrinks to an act of the rejection of the world, to suicide. He is concerned (....) not with Seneca's renaissance or the apologia of the flight movement, he is concerned with thinking out a historical situation which no longer has a solution to its end.' In: *Nachruf Jean Améry*, from Klett-Cotta, *Das erste Jahrzehnt* 1977–1987. An Almanach, ed. Thomas Weck, Stuttgart 1987, p. 336.

9. In the private archive of Maria Améry, DLA.

10. Ibid.

11. This quotation from Wilhelm Busch is in a letter to Ernst Mayer of 17.6.65.

12. In conversation with Schultz-Gerstein, *Der Doppelkopf*, p. 62, and in the following letter: 'Recently a young man asked me: *si vous plaidez pour le suicide , pourquoi vous ne vous êtes-pas suicidé?* I replied, rather embarrassed and ashamed: *un peu de patience, s.v.p.*' (J.A. to Inge Werner 21.12.75).

13. 'Revision in Permanenz. Selbstanzeige als Zweifel', in: *Über Jean Améry* (Zum 65. Geburtstag von J.A. Am 32, October 1977), Klett-Cotta, Stuttgart, pp. 14–18.

14. In: *Wie sie sich selber sehen*. Antrittsreden der Mitglieder vor dem Kollegium der Deutschen Akademie. With an essay by Martin Gauger, ed. Michael Assmann, Wallstein Verlag, Göttingen 1999, pp. 184–6. Horst Krüger read the speech on 25 October; Jean Améry had taken his own life on 17 October.

15. Typescript by Maria Améry, dated 1.6.79, in Maria Améry's private archive, now in the DLA.

16. Jean Améry, 'In den Wind gesprochen' (IdWg), in: *Die zornigen alten Männer*. Thoughts on Germany since 1945, ed. Axel Eggebrecht, Rowohlt, Reinbek 1979, pp. 258–79.

17. Julien Benda, *Der Verrat der Intellektuellen*, with a foreword by Jean Améry. Hanser Verlag, Munich, 1978.

18. Cf. Gerhard Scheit's afterword in Jean Améry, *Werke*, Vol. 6, *Aufsätze zur Philosophie*, Klett-Cotta, Stuittgart 2004, pp. 607–642.

19. In: Morbus Austriacus. Bemerkungen zu Thomas Bernhards *Die Ursache* und *Korrektur*. Jean Améry, *Werke*, Vol. 5, ed. Hans Höller, p. 135.

20. Although Jean Améry seldom speaks of this dangerous illness in his correspondence, Mary Cox-Kitaj told her children that Améry had killed himself because he was suffering from Lupus, according to her son Paul in a conversation with me.

21. The books are *Wohlbefinden und Missbefinden* and *Der Mensch und sein Leib*, Max Niemeyer Verlag, Tübingen 1969.

22. On a sheet from a note pad. In the DLA.

23. Jean Améry, 'DieWelt des leidenden Menschen. Hinweis auf zwei Bücher von Herbert Plügge', *Merkur*, 1969/251, pp. 297–299.

24. R.B. Kitaj (1932–2007), American painter, studied, painted and taught in England from 1958. Was associated with the London Group, a group of post-war painters including Frank Auerbach, Michael Andrews, Francis Bacon, Lucian Freud and Leon Kossoff. Here I would like to thank R.B. Kitaj, who turns out to be an enthusiastic reader of Améry, for his kind reply to my question. Particularly helpful to me in my research was Karma Kitaj (Boston, USA), Mary's niece, who invited me to visit her in Boston. I would also like to express heartfelt thanks to Paul Kitaj, Mary's son,

for telling me so much about this painful chapter in his life. I owe many insights to him.

25. Conversation with Paul Kitaj in Gilbert, Arizona, January 2003. Paul provided me with information about the events concerned from his point of view. He and his sister, as teenagers, suffered very much from this relationship. Améry, they felt, took their mother away from them and in the end 'let her down'. After Améry's suicide, Mary went first to Pocatello, where she worked as a secretary. In 1980 she moved to Tacoma, Washington. Her life was wrecked; she lived only in the past and never got over Améry. Mary had to go into a nursing home suffering from muscular atrophy, and died there of a heart attack in 1997 at the age of 73.

26. My thanks to Dita Ruland of Marburg for this helpful information in a telephone conversation of 22 June 2003.

27. The essay on Stefan Zweig – like *On Suicide* – was written in 1975.

28. Hubert Arbogast thinks that Mary Cox-Kitaj accompanied Jean Améry to the Austrian border, and Améry then went on to Salzburg while she returned to Germany.

29. Copies of these letters are in the DLA.

30. Hubert Arbogast gave me a copy of the letter for publication before his death on 24 May 2003.

31. There is a copy of Jean Améry's letter to Maria Améry in the DLA.

32. Horst Krüger gives the memorial address at the German Academy of Language and Literature in Darmstadt: 'Your life was only an attempt at living,' he writes in his obituary in *Die Zeit* (27.10.78). The literary critic Hans Mayer gives the memorial address at the Academy in Berlin. Klett-Cotta devotes a special memorial volume to Améry with *Hermannstrasse 14* (1978). For the far-reaching reception of Jean Améry to the present day, see Volume 9 of Jean Améry, *Werke*, Stuttgart, Klett-Cotta (2008). On the reception of the author of *Jenseits von Schuld und Sühne, Unmeisterliche Wanderjahre,* and *Örtlichkeiten*, see Vol. 2, edited by Gerhard Scheit (2002). For *Zur Literatur und zum Film*, see Vol. 5, edited by Hans Höller (2003), and for *Philosophie* see Vol. 6, edited by Gerhard Scheit (2004).

33. He is buried in Vienna's Central Cemetery, in a Grave of Honour Group 40 (gate 2). His gravestone, which is now overgrown with ivy, bears the name of Jean Améry, his dates of life and death, and his Auschwitz number, 172364.

Picture Credits

Index of Works

(List of the works of Jean Améry mentioned in the book)

291

Index of Names